Domestic Negotiations

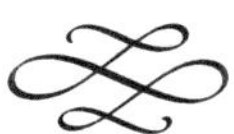

LATINIDAD

Transnational Cultures in the United States

This series publishes books that deepen and expand our knowledge and understanding of the various Latina/o populations in the United States in the context of their transnational relationships with cultures of the broader Americas. The focus is on the history and analysis of Latino cultural systems and practices in national and transnational spheres of influence from the nineteenth century to the present. The series is open to scholarship in political science, economics, anthropology, linguistics, history, cinema and television, literary and cultural studies, and popular culture and encourages interdisciplinary approaches, methods, and theories. The series grew out of discussions with faculty at the School of Transborder Studies at Arizona State University, where an interdisciplinary emphasis is being placed on transborder and transnational dynamics.

Carlos Velez-Ibañez, Series Editor, School of Transborder Studies

Rodolfo F. Acuña, *In the Trenches of Academe: The Making of Chicana/o Studies*

Adriana Cruz-Manjarrez, *Zapotecs on the Move: Cultural, Social, and Political Processes in Transnational Perspective*

Marivel T. Danielson, *Homecoming Queers: Desire and Difference in Chicana Latina Cultural Production*

Rudy P. Guevarra Jr., *Becoming Mexipino: Multiethnic Identities and Communities in San Diego*

Lisa Jarvinen, *The Rise of Spanish-Language Filmmaking: Out from Hollywood's Shadow, 1929–1939*

Regina M. Marchi, *Day of the Dead in the USA: The Migration and Transformation of a Cultural Phenomenon*

Marci R. McMahon, *Domestic Negotiations: Gender, Nation, and Self-Fashioning in US Mexicana and Chicana Literature and Art*

A. Gabriel Meléndez, *Hidden Chicano Cinema: Film Dramas in the Borderlands*

Priscilla Peña Ovalle, *Dance and the Hollywood Latina: Race, Sex, and Stardom*

Luis F. B. Plascencia, *Disenchanting Citizenship: Mexican Migrants and the Boundaries of Belonging*

Maya Socolovsky, *Troubling Nationhood in U.S. Latina Literature: Explorations of Place and Belonging*

Domestic Negotiations

*Gender, Nation, and Self-Fashioning
in US Mexicana and
Chicana Literature and Art*

M ARCI R. M C M AHON

RUTGERS UNIVERSITY PRESS
NEW BRUNSWICK, NEW JERSEY, AND LONDON

Library of Congress Cataloging-in-Publication Data

McMahon, Marci R., 1975–

Domestic negotiations : gender, nation, and self-fashioning in US Mexicana and Chicana literature and art / Marci R. McMahon.

p. cm. — (Latindad: Transnational Cultures in the United States)

Includes bibliographical references and index.

ISBN 978–0–8135–6095–3 (hardcover : alk. paper) — ISBN 978–0–8135–6094–6 (pbk. : alk. paper) — ISBN 978–0–8135–6096–0 (e-book)

1. American literature—Mexican American authors—History and criticism. 2. Identity (Psychology) in literature. 3. Mexican Americans in literature. 4. Mexican American arts. 5. Mexican American artists. 6. Nationalism and literature—United States—History. I. Title.

PS153.M4M46 2013

810.9'86872—dc23   2012033358

A British Cataloging-in-Publication record for this book is available from the British Library.

Visit our website: http://rutgerspress.rutgers.edu

Manufactured in the United States of America

Contents

Illustrations

Acknowledgments

I owe an enormous debt to the many mentors who have encouraged, supported, and shaped this project and my academic career. The underlying goals of this book—the analysis of Chicana history through literature and visual art—has its roots in San Antonio, Texas, where as a high school student at Incarnate Word, I became active in social justice and literary arts movements in the city. At Incarnate Word, I was fortunate to be among a community of teachers that nurtured arts and activism, and I am particularly thankful to my high school English teacher, the late Mrs. Carol Mengden, who encouraged and nourished my writing skills and aspirations that made this book possible. I owe special gratitude to the faculty and graduate students in the English Department at the University of Texas at Austin, including Ann Cvetkovich, Barbara Harlow, Lisa Sánchez González, and Sheila Contreras, for introducing me to Chicana literature as an undergraduate. Like many, due to the Anglocentric histories and literatures of Texas's educational systems, it was not until college that I read Chicana feminist authors, specifically the writings of Gloria Anzaldúa and Chela Sandoval. As a result of these UT faculty members, I became a feminist through Chicana feminism; border theory and third world feminism gave me the words to challenge socioeconomic and gendered divisions and to critically understand my white privilege. I extend my thanks to Zilla Goodman and Cvetkovich, who guided the completion of my undergraduate thesis, teaching me research skills and literary analysis, therefore enabling me to see myself as a scholar. I also offer my gratitude to Amalia Malagamba for introducing me to Chicana visual art; my interview with San Antonio artist Kathy Vargas at the Guadalupe Cultural Arts Center for her class was a critical point in my intellectual development; I thank Kathy Vargas for generously devoting her time and slides to that project.

My personal and academic interests in Chicana/o and Latina/o culture were deepened and expanded as a graduate student at the University of Southern

California by Teresa McKenna, an incredible scholar and mentor. In McKenna's classes, I was trained in Chicana/o literary and cultural studies and first studied the performance group Asco and the art of Patssi Valdez. Many other faculty members at USC guided this project, and I owe enormous thanks to Alice Gambrell and Laura Pulido for providing words of encouragement and asking critical questions. I offer a special note of gratitude to John Carlos Rowe, an incredible mentor, scholar, and role model, who continues to offer advice on the profession, providing guidance and encouragement. I am deeply grateful to George Sánchez for supporting my work and providing a space for doctoral students doing work on race and ethnicity at USC; the seeds of this book were first nurtured in the Summer Dissertation Workshop led by Sánchez in the Department of American Studies, Race, and Ethnicity, which was funded by the Irvine Foundation. Special appreciation is also due to the many faculty members at USC for supporting this project and my academic trajectory, specifically David Román, Viet Nguyen, Heather James, Rebecca Lemon, Karen Tongson, David Lloyd, Bruce Smith, Tony Kemp, and the late Anne Friedberg, among others. I extend a note of thanks to Jack Blum and John Holland for nurturing the development of my teaching and pedagogy, which I continue to implement in my classrooms today.

Special and enormous gratitude is owed to my mentor and now friend and colleague Tiffany Ana López, who from the beginning provided incredible guidance of this project through numerous meetings, phone calls, and conference chats, and who continues to offer generous championing of my scholarship. I am indebted to López for teaching me how to be a mentor and pushing me to articulate my stakes and position within this profession. She introduced me to the work of Diane Rodríguez and Migdalia Cruz, providing me with a necessary pathway to conduct interviews with Rodríguez. My frequent conversations with López about this book and the academy—including conversations about race, gender, and tenure in the academy—have pushed me toward thinking critically about the impact I can have in academia and in the classroom. There are not enough words to thank Tiffany for her incredible and supportive mentorship.

Several institutions, foundations, and family have supported the completion of this project. With a Greenleaf Library Visiting Researcher Travel Grant from the Latin American and Iberian Studies Institute at the University of New Mexico and a Faculty Research Grant from the College Council at the University of Texas, Pan American, I conducted archival research on Fabiola Cabeza de Baca Gilbert, specifically at the Center for Southwest Research at the University of New Mexico, Rio Grande Historical Collections at New Mexico State University, Hobson-Huntsinger University Archives in Las Cruces, and the Santa Fe Public Library. I am enormously grateful to Ala Qubbaj, vice provost for faculty affairs at the University of Texas, Pan American, for providing necessary funding for the images included in this book. At USC, this project benefited from the support of a Merit Dissertation Fellowship from the Department of English; a Diane Meehan Research Fellowship in Feminism and Communication from the Center for Feminist Research; a Marta Feuchtwanger Research Fellowship from the College of Letters, Arts, and Sciences; a Final Summer Dissertation Fellowship from the Department of English; and an Academic Professionalization Project Grant from the College of Letters, Arts, and Sciences. Special thanks to the staff at the Center for Southwest Research at the University of New Mexico, as well as to Tom Shelton at the Institute of Texan Cultures for sharing his extensive knowledge on the chili queens and San Antonio history, and for introducing me to the library's acquisition of the Atlee B. Ayres's papers documenting Ayres's fiesta events. I also thank Pamela Anderson-Mejías and Dean Dahlia Guerra at the University of Texas, Pan American, for supporting my attendance at conferences and time spent in archives necessary to complete this project. I would be remiss if I did not acknowledge and thank the various McMahon family research grants for enabling the completion of this project through many visits to art exhibits in Los Angeles and stays at my parents' home while conducting archival research on the chili queens at the University of Texas at San Antonio's Library special collections.

I am fortunate to have met many scholars along the way who have helped shape and guide this project. I am grateful to Raúl Villa, Elizabeth Maddock Dillon, Mary Pat Brady, Nancy Armstrong, Margaret D. Jacobs, and Victoria Haskins for providing feedback on early stages of this book and their overall support of my work in the fields of Chicana/o studies and American studies. Special thanks to Norma Cantú for enabling me to present my research on Diane Rodríguez for Women's History Month at UT–San Antonio, as well as to Tanya González and Eliza Rodríguez y Gibson for organizing Latina/o Literature and Culture Society Panels at the American Literature Association, in which I have presented many portions of this book. I also thank Erica Stevens Abbitt for organizing the Women and Theatre Debut Panel at the Association for Theater in Higher Education conference, where I received feedback on my scholarship on Migdalia Cruz. Special thanks is also owed to Karen Mary Davalos for her extensive comments on my work on Alma López's visual art and her incredible mentorship in Chicana/Latina studies; to Josie Méndez-Negrete and the Mujeres Activas en Letras y Cambio Social community, including Sandra Garza, for their encouragement and support of my scholarship; to Chon Noriega for his enthusiasm and support of my work on Asco and Patssi Valdez; and to Sarah Spurgeon for her feedback and encouragement of my criticism on Alma López's visual art. I also extend my sincere thanks to the San Antonio Society for Psychoanalytical Studies, particularly Shelley Probber, Richard Reed, Wayne Ehrisman, Cynthia Diaz De Leon, Lisa Chatillon, Deborah Morrow, and Margot Zeulzer, for their invitation and their support, encouragement, and insights into my chili queens of San Antonio chapter as I gave the Eighth Frank C. Paredes Lecture. I also thank academic collaborators Roxanne Schroeder-Arce, Patricia Trujillo, and Patricia Herrera for their feedback on my work and support over the last few years in the form of conference panels.

Many folks have formed necessary writing communities and support for this project. I am especially thankful to Priscilla Ovalle, William "Memo" Arce, Karen Bowdre, and Joshua Smith (members of the fABD-5) who helped shape the ideas that are the foundation of this book. I thank my dear friends and colleagues in the English department at USC, including James Penner, Samuel Park, Amy Braden, Sun Hee Teresa Lee, Jeffrey Solomon, Christina Wilson, Yetta Howard, Tanya Heflin, Ruth Blandon, Tom O'Leary, Michael Cucher, Nora Gilbert, Erika Wright, Michael Robinson, Annemarie Pérez, Dave Tomkins, and Jennifer Malia for their intellectual and personal kinship. A special note of gratitude to Jeffrey Solomon, who read and provided extensive feedback on many portions of this book. Special thanks to the American Studies and Critical Studies students at USC who provided feedback on this project and continue to provide networks of support, including Hilary Jenks, Lalo Glicon, James Thing, Ilda Jiménez y West, Shakira Holt, Lorena Muñoz, Perla Guerrero, Belinda Lum, Araceli Esparza, Laura Sachiko Fugikawa, Reina Prado, Ana Rosas, Karen Beavers, and Jenny Clark. I am especially grateful to Laura Barraclough and Jennifer Stoever-Ackerman, who continue to provide mentorship, guidance, emotional support, and necessary collaborations.

At the University of Texas, Pan American, I am thankful to be among a community of scholars and friends who have supported my scholarship and career. An enormous amount of gratitude is owed to Rebecca Mitchell, who read and provided feedback on every chapter in this book; I am immensely grateful to Rebecca for our writing sessions and her guidance in the profession. I also thank the strong *mujeres* of the Mexican American studies program, without whom I would not have completed this project, including Stephanie Alvarez, Sonia Hernández, Emmy Pérez, Edna Ochoa, and Petra Guerra. I am deeply appreciative of the support and mentorship of colleagues Danika Brown, Melynda Nuss, Jose Skinner, Linda Belau, Ed Cameron, Jessica Lavariega-Monforti, Miguel Díaz-Barriga, Margaret Dorsey, Jean Braithwaite, Debbie Cole, Marianita Escamilla, Virginia Gause, Leila Hernández, Amy Cummins, Shawn Thompson, Kamala Platt, Eric Wiley, Amy Hay, and Cynthia Brown. I am fortunate to have taught incredible undergraduate and graduate students in the English and Mexican American studies programs at UTPA; from these students I have learned a great deal and they continue to inspire. These scholars, writers, and intellectual pathbreakers include Marlene Galvan, Orquidea Morales, Monica Montelongo, Edna Camacho, Stephanie Brock, Lauren Espinoza, Christian Ramírez, José Torres Flóres, Anna Muñoz, Roberto Reyna, Teresa Hernández, Amanda Jasso, Haydee Villareal, Nicki González Moreno, Robert Moreira, Mary Ruth Chen, Veronica Sandoval (Lady Mariposa), Isaac Chavarria, Rodney Gomez, Minerva Vasquez, Cathy Lopez, and others. A special note of thanks and deep gratitude goes to Stephanie Brock, without whose co-teaching support, intellectual prowess, and general kindness and enthusiasm, I would not have completed this book. I also thank those in the Rio Grande Valley community who continue to provide inspiration, including Elva Michal and Pedro García.

For their arts and activism and thus enabling me to write this book, I wish to thank Harry Gamboa Jr., Patssi Valdez, Alma López, and Christina Fernandez for granting me permission to reproduce their images. I owe special thanks to Leslie Mitchner, my editor at Rutgers University Press, for taking on this project, her encouragement, and seeing it through its completion, as well as to the Latinidad: Transnational Cultures in the United States series editors for their support of this book. I also thank Lisa Boyajian, editorial assistant, and Rick Delaney, for their keen revisions and expert guidance. Finally, special thanks to Ellie D. Hernández, for her incredible support through generous feedback and enthusiasm for this project.

I thank my families and friends, including my parents, Sharon and Lance, who nurtured my activism by driving me to numerous protests, demonstrations, and arts events, opening up our home in San Antonio for activist meetings in high school and college, and supporting these endeavors, often financially. I wish to thank my twin sister, Melanie, for providing me with necessary escapes from academia through our visits with one another. I also thank my immediate and extended families, Lance and Brenda McMahon, Mary and Hank Jung, Cindy and George Jung, Willma and Kirby Whitehead, and Kerry Whitehead for their love, support, and humor. I also thank longtime friend Pamela Rooney-Barnes for her friendship throughout the years, as well as Kristina Avila and Leah McMahon for cheering me on as I completed this book. Special thanks and gratitude to my dear friend Carol Brochin-Ceballos for helping me to develop my political consciousness as I witnessed her burgeoning Chicana activism in high school and college; I am deeply grateful for our continued friendship, support, and conversations, and I am awed by her academic career. Last but not least, I am blessed to have met my husband, Daniel Flutur, musician and intellectual co-conspirator while in graduate school. It's a testament to his love, kindness, and patience that we began and nurtured our relationship during those difficult graduate school years. Dan, you have been amazingly supportive, and I am deeply thankful that we are in each other's lives.

An early version of chapter 2 appeared as "Politicizing Spanish-Mexican Domesticity, Redefining Fronteras: Jovita González's *Caballero* and Cleofas Jaramillo's *Romance of a Little Village Girl*," in *Frontiers: A Journal of Women's Studies*, Special Double Issue on "Domestic Frontiers: The Home and Colonization" 28.1–2 (2007): 232–259.

A portion of chapter 5 appeared as "Self-Fashioning through Glamour and Punk in East Los Angeles: Patssi Valdez in Asco's *Instant Mural* and *A La Mode*," in *Aztlán: A Journal of Chicano Studies* 36.2 (fall 2011): 21–50. A section of the Epilogue appeared as "Alma López's *California Fashions Slaves:* Denaturalizing Domesticity, Labor, and Motherhood," in *Chicana/Latina Studies: The Journal of MALCS* 11.1 (fall 2011): 158–193.

A Note on Terminology

Given the historical breadth and variety of local contexts in this study, I use distinct terms throughout this book to refer to women of Mexican descent living and working prior to, during, and after the Chicano/a Movement of the 1960s and 1970s in various regions of the US Southwest. In the chapters where I discuss authors and artists of the early and mid-twentieth century, that is, prior to the Chicano/a movement, I use the terms *Mexican American, Mexicano,* and *Mexicana.* "Mexican American" connotes a person of Mexican descent born in the United States; I also use the label to denote a bicultural sensibility in cultural production. I use the terms *Mexicano* and *Mexicana* to refer to a broader community of people of Mexican descent and women living in the United States, even though the label designates officially those born in Mexico and who are immigrants to the United States. I do so to signal a shared experience of racialization with US-born Mexican Americans in this nation, regardless of immigration status. As Rosa Linda Fregoso argues, "Current debates over nomenclature are based on legal distinctions between 'Mexicanas' as immigrants to the US and 'Chicanas' as native. While such distinctions may serve policy interests or demographic aims, in the realm of cultural representation, the difference between 'Mexicana' and 'Chicana' is often obscured and erased" (2003, xiv).

In my early chapters on Jovita González, Cleofas Jaramillo, and Fabiola Cabeza de Baca, I use the terms *Mexican American,* as well as *Spanish Mexican* to refer to those men and women who trace their identities to Spanish-speaking communities in the Southwest border region and who lived under the Mexican flag after 1821. The latter term is appropriate when referring to these authors, as they each claimed Spanish identity and ancestry to stake claims within the literal and figurative borders of the United States. Yet as I point out in these chapters, their claims of Spanish ancestry create fictive claims to a pure identity, and thereby reinforce racial, class, and economic divisions. Deena González importantly notes, "even though these communities referred to themselves as 'españoles' or 'Spaniards,' the majority were not Spanish but mestizos, persons of mixed ancestry, specifically a person of Native indigenous and Spanish heritage" (1999, xix).

In my chapters on contemporary female authors and artists working during and after the Chicano/a Movement of the 1960s and 1970s, I use the terms *Mexicana* and *Chicana* to refer to cultural production that affirms a woman's rightful ownership of a borderlands and *mestiza* cultural identity. The terms *Chicano* and *Chicana* have links with contemporary political movements, including the Chicano/a Movement and Chicana feminism. The label *Chicana* is appropriate when referring to cultural productions by Patssi Valdez, Carmen Lomas Garza, Sandra Cisneros, Diane Rodríguez, and Alma López, many of whom either developed their artistic work during the Chicano/a Movement or as Chicana feminist responses. In my final chapter, I explore Diane Rodríguez's collaboration with Puerto Rican playwright Migdalia Cruz. This chapter seeks to make important connections and distinctions between Chicana and Latina experiences of domestic ideologies and racial formations. I therefore use the term *Latina/o* to refer to the broader population of those with Latin American ancestry living in the United States. Yet I am careful to remind readers that Latina, similar to the encompassing terms *Mexican American women* or *Chicana,* refers to a culturally and ethnically diverse group of women. Ultimately, I aim to show that terms of identity are not fixed and shift in particular contexts (Habell-Pallán 2005).

Domestic Negotiations

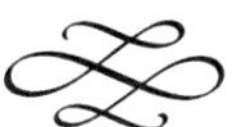

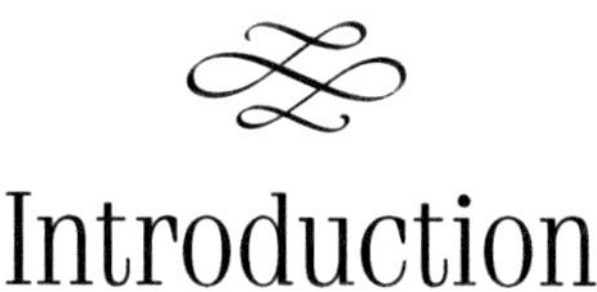

Introduction

In her six-photo series *María's Great Expedition* (1995–1996), the artist Christina Fernandez recounts the personal history of her great-grandmother María's migrations between the United States and Mexico by posing as her great-grandmother. In each of the sepia-toned photos and in the final chromogenic photo, the artist depicts the distant and recurring circumstances of her great-grandmother's life, centering on gender roles and domestic space. The first photo, "1910, Leaving Morelia, Michoacán, Mexico," shows Fernandez as María wearing her hair in braids and wrapped in a rebozo, contemplating her departure. The accompanying text explains that after three years in Juárez, Mexico, María left for the United States both pregnant and without her husband, which led to great controversy. The second photo, "1919, Portland, Colorado" (fig.1), depicts Fernandez as María standing in front of a clothesline that holds three shirts, representing her three children and new life in the United States. Fernandez's dress, the clothes on the clothesline, and other items—including a tin washtub, a wooden and metal "El Rey" washboard, a cardboard box of "Iris All Purpose Laundry Detergent," two plastic gloves, and a plastic "Iris Bleach" container—are rendered in stark white against the sepia-colored background. With the tin, wood, and cardboard objects alongside the modern plastic gloves and jug, the photo links the past and present. These items of Anglo American and Mexicana domesticity reference the great-grandmother's lived experience as a woman of Mexican descent in the United States; they also depict the role of consumerism in the process of Americanization. The only nonwhite image in the photo is the black fanny pack, which Fernandez holds in front of her body. The fanny pack, an object of the present, suggests a contemporary fast-paced lifestyle, referencing impermanence or the journey of the immigrant who travels "lightly."

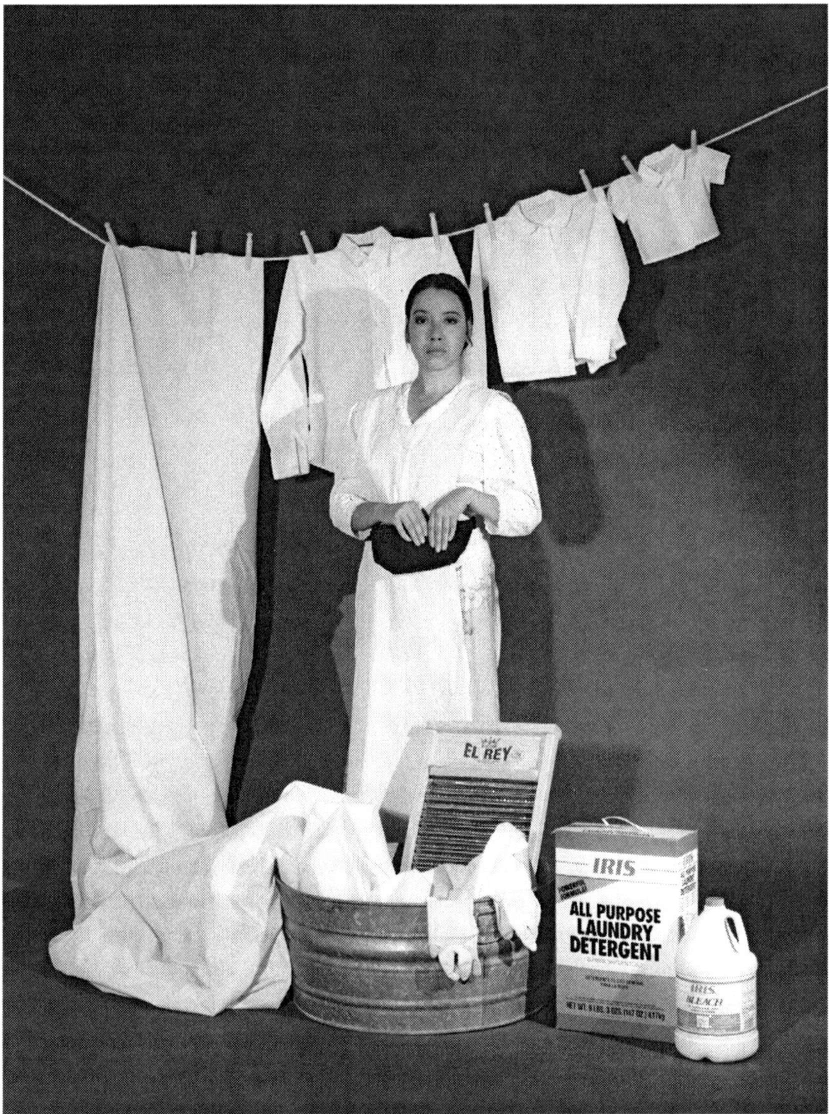

Figure 1. Christina Fernandez, "María's Great Expedition: 1919, Portland, Colorado,"
1995. Gelatin silver print, sepia-tone image, 16 × 12 inches. Permanent Collection of the
Smithsonian American Art Museum. Courtesy of the artist.

The third photo in the series, "1927, Going Back to Morelia," features Fernandez as María waiting anxiously beside railroad tracks, sitting atop one large
black chest (the historic version of traveling "lightly"), holding sewing needles
in her right hand and papers in her left hand, possibly letters from family members or notes that she penned. Wearing late-1920s attire and makeup, and with
a coiffed flapper hairstyle of the period, her fashion and dress departs from the

first photo. In the fourth photo, "1930, Transporting Produce, Outskirts of Phoenix, Arizona," Fernandez as María stands beside crates of produce, signifying the labor she performs as a fruit picker, while the fifth photo, "1945, Aliso Village, Boyle Heights, California," shows Fernandez as María standing in front of a clothesline, but this time outside the residence of a family she works for as a maid. She poses confidently in front of the camera and wears a simple maid's uniform and apron. The final photo, "1950, San Diego," depicts Fernandez as her great-grandmother standing in front of her stove; she holds a "99-Cent" store circular, signaling the recurring acts of survival in the present.

Even as the settings, contexts, fashions, and postures change in each photo, the series consistently shows Fernandez, as María, in domestic and laboring roles (González 1995, 20). Each photo highlights María's relationships to various spheres: from her defiance of traditional gender roles by leaving her husband while pregnant, to her physical labor in the agricultural fields, to domestic labor in her household and those of others, to the implied "space of her own" in the final photo, which through the "99-Cent" store circular centers the process of making the most "from the least" through the site of domesticity, or what Mesa-Bains terms "rasquache domesticana" (2003). Notably, the act of Fernandez posing as her great-grandmother María in each photo powerfully creates an "overlapping of identification between generations," with a narrative that links the past with the present (González 1995, 20). Yet as Mario Ontiveros explains, Fernandez "does not collapse the distance between her life and her great-grandmother's, but instead makes visible the act of tending to one's history as a process that occurs in the present. It is a process that ultimately resists letting the past become too distant from the self" (2008, 152). In short, even as the photos document Fernandez's great-grandmother's recurrent experiences of domestic labor, gender, and race in the present, *María's Great Expedition* suggests the younger generation's break from the past in the act of documenting and self-authoring history.

Like Fernandez's series, *Domestic Negotiations* presents a collective history of Mexicanas' and Chicanas' experiences of gendered roles and domestic space across national and regional borders, from the early twentieth century to today. Similar to the photos, I show the recurrence of the past in the present by analyzing the continued appearance of domestic roles and national narratives that have shaped Mexicanas' and Chicanas' relationships to the domestic sphere throughout distinct historical moments. Yet like the active negotiations and self-fashioning of Fernandez as María in the series, women of Mexican descent in various decades have actively contested and negotiated domestic roles by recreating and authoring their own histories.

I argue that in different historical periods and regions, Mexicana and Chicana authors and artists enact *domestic negotiations* that both challenge and reinforce geographical, racial, gendered, and national borders. I show how these authors and artists use the space of the domestic to negotiate the domestic/foreign, white/nonwhite, and legal/illegal binaries that have sought to exclude their communities from belonging in the US nation. I use the term *domestic* throughout this book, as Amy Kaplan does, to refer to the double meaning of the domestic as both household and nation (2002, 183). The term references both the gendered and racialized ideologies that have sought to circumscribe women of Mexican descent to both household and national labor space in different historical moments (Fregoso 2003, 92; Romero 2008; Ruiz 1998; Sánchez 1993). With the concept of negotiation, I refer to domestic representations that may not refuse gendered or racialized hierarchies, yet that instead use dominant ideologies as a route to resistance. Such negotiations are necessitated by the prevalence or persistence of views that have associated women of Mexican descent to the domestic. I show how, across different historical moments, Mexicana and Chicana authors and artists—from the site of domesticity—represent, restage, counter, yet sometimes uphold the specific gendered and racial ideologies of their time. Whether through critique or negotiation, they assert their agency to author their own narratives and histories. In contrast to popular discourse that views domesticity as relegated to the private sphere, this book underscores the domestic as connected to the many political and recurring debates about domestic space, race, gender, and immigration affecting the lives of Mexicanas and Chicanas in the early, mid-, and late twentieth century and early twenty-first century.

The Mexicana and Chicana authors and artists in this volume engage with the domestic through a process of *self-fashioning*. The term signals how authors and artists actively construct their identities and histories in response to dominant, political, cultural, and popular representations of Mexicana/Chicana subjectivity. When referring to performance and the visual arts, the concept highlights the intersections of dress with bodily performance and the possibility of these sites in the negotiation of gendered and racialized ideologies. My use of the term in this context comes from Jennifer Craik, who employs the concept to refer to the process of clothing the body as "an active process or technical means for constructing and presenting a bodily self" (1994, 1). That is, dress constructs an identity rather than disguising a natural body or real identity (5). In this sense, codes of dress communicate the relationship between a particular body, its lived experience, and the space it occupies (4–5). Laura E. Pérez, in her analysis of Chicana visual artists of the 1980s and 1990s, underscores that dress in Chicana arts "call[s] attention to both the body as social and to the social body that constitutes it as such, specifically through gendered and racialized histories" (2007, 51). While I relate self-fashioning to the visual arts and performance, I also apply the concept to a variety of other media, including street vending, autobiography, romance novels, cookbooks, novels, children's literature, among other popular forms. With various representational practices, Mexicanas and Chicanas fashion their identities to negotiate multiple national, regional, and cultural contexts. (Quintana 1991, 76).

To analyze self-fashioning in relationship to the domestic, the book applies Amalia Mesa-Bains's concept of "domesticana," a neologism coined to signal how

Chicana visual artists utilize the materials of domestic space in order to reconfigure gender relations and power within and outside the private realm (Mesa-Bains 2003, 302–303). Mesa-Bains conceives domesticana as a concept for Chicana visual arts, yet its focus on a sensibility of the domestic, rather than on a specific medium or form, makes it applicable to other cultural productions by Mexicanas and Chicanas, including everyday culture, literature, fashion, and performance (González 2003, 321). Domesticana is concerned with the "conflictual and contradictory nature of the domestic and familial world" for Mexicanas and Chicanas who, as a result of their marginalization in the domestic sphere due to patriarchy and cultural nationalisms, aim to reconfigure the domestic as a space of power for women (Mesa-Bains 2003, 304). In short, domesticana is the "affirmation of cultural values but from women's restriction within the culture" (2003, 302). Since Chicanas' imbued power in the domestic sphere is the result of uneven gender relations, Mesa-Bains explains that a tension emerges in Chicana cultural and artistic renderings of domestic space—that is, between "spiritual affirmation and cultural reclamation" of women's recuperative power in the domestic sphere and "feminist interrogation" of patriarchal structures (2003, 302). Domesticana conveys this tension through a "survivalist irreverence" that includes narratives of paradox, irony, subversion, bricollage, irreverence, and a bicultural aesthetic (González 2003, 321; Mesa-Bains 2003). Ultimately, domesticana is the process of reclaiming women's power in the domestic sphere through the act of consistently negotiating the power relations that marginalize women to the domestic.

With its focus on a woman's location within the domestic sphere due to patriarchal marginalization and cultural restrictions, domesticana shares characteristics with the notion of "domestic power" that circulated in the early twentieth century—the idea that Anglo American women used the gendered association of their identities in the domestic sphere as a way to assert space in the nation. "Domesticana," unlike the concept of "domestic power," however, provides an analytical method by which to explore the intersections of gender, race, and class in Mexicanas' and Chicanas' material and lived realities of domestic space. Racialized and gendered discourses have shaped women of Mexican descent's relationship to the domestic sphere throughout the twentieth and early twenty-first centuries. "Domesticana" enables me to engage critically with the works of Mexicanas and Chicanas who assert power from the domestic sphere to contest and negotiate dominant ideologies.

Anglo American women's uses of domestic space in various cultural forms to assert power in society—including literature, women's clubs, and home economics, for example—have been studied extensively (Armstrong 1987; Baym 1978; Douglas 1977; Gere 1997; Tompkins 1985; Welter 1966). The marginalization of women of Mexican descent as a result of Anglo American women's domestic programs in the early and mid-twentieth century, including Americanization and home economics, has also been studied in depth (Romero 2008; Ruiz 1998;

Sánchez 1993). Yet Mexican American women from privileged class positions in the early twentieth century who asserted domestic power as a way to stake claims in the national sphere have yet to be studied in detail, with a few notable exceptions, including scholarship by María Cotera (2008) and Maureen Reed (2005). Many Mexican American women in the early and mid-twentieth century utilized the concept of domestic power in a variety of fields, from home economics to literature. In the latter half of the twentieth century and early twenty-first century, women of Mexican descent continue to assert their voices and critiques of nation at the site of the domestic. Even as middle- and upper-class professionals, Chicanas still confront the association of their identities to the domestic sphere in the dominant culture, regardless of class and immigration status. And, working-class Mexicanas and Chicanas continue to be situated in the familial space as mothers/wives (reproducers) and in the national labor space as workers (producers) (Fregoso 2003, 92; Romero 2008; Ruiz 1999; Sánchez 1993). By using the domestic in their critiques, contemporary Chicana authors and artists respond to and critique the continued cultural, political, and nationalist discourses that locate their identities in the domestic household and labor space.

In order to show the circulation of domesticity across time and space, this book follows a pattern that travels between different time periods and regions. The book begins in San Antonio, Texas, and explores the "chili queens" who, through street vending and fashion, disrupted dominant ideologies linking Mexican American women with cooking and service that flourished in the San Antonio fiestas, and challenged xenophobic views of Mexican American domestic spaces prevalent during the Great Depression and Americanization movements of the 1930s. I then travel to South Texas and northern New Mexico to closely read the self-authored histories of Jovita González and Cleofas Jaramillo, who, from the space of the domestic, both counter and cater to nativist and anti-immigrant policies prevalent from the 1930s to 1950s. Staying in northern New Mexico, I then analyze the home economics work of Fabiola Cabeza de Baca, whose writings begin during the Progressive Era and Americanization movements of the early twentieth century and end in Patzcauro, Mexico, during the Cold War of the 1950s; in each of these spaces, Cabeza de Baca both dismantles and reifies borders.

In the second half of the book, I return to the US Southwest to show how the nativist and xenophobic rhetoric that the "chili queens," González, Jaramillo, and Cabeza de Baca negotiated and contested continues from the 1960s to today. In this section, I return to San Antonio, Texas, to begin with the "purple house" controversy—the debate over author Sandra Cisneros's choice to paint her house purple in the 1990s, which for many exposed the historic exclusion of Mexicano homes and communities from the city's historic record. I then figuratively travel north to Chicago to closely read Cisneros's writings about Chicanas' desires for "a house of one's own," followed by a trip back south to Kingsville, Texas, to analyze Carmen Lomas Garza's paintings and children's books of domestic space, which she created during the Chicano/a Movement. As a result of these travels, I put Garza's work in dialogue with Cisneros's writings of domestic space. In the final chapters, I head to Los Angeles to analyze Patssi Valdez's self-fashioning and performance during the Chicano/a Movement and her contemporary domestic interiors. I also explore Diane Rodríguez's performances and direction of domesticity; both Valdez and Rodríguez developed as artists during and after the Chicano/a Movement and amid contemporary Chicana feminism of the 1980s and 1990s. The closing of this book presents another moment of figurative travel across time and space, focusing on artist Alma López's depictions of anti-immigrant rhetoric of the 1980s and 1990s in Los Angeles, which she traces to early twentieth-century anti-immigrant discourse in the US Southwest.

Domestic Power

The literary and artistic project of using domestic space to seek inclusion in the US nation has a fraught and complicated history. Late-nineteenth- and early-twentieth-century American authors, such as Catharine Maria Sedgwick, Harriet Beecher Stowe, and Catherine Beecher, and British authors, such as Jane Austen and Virginia Woolf, among many others, utilized the association of women with domestic space to wage political critiques of gender and nation (Armstrong 1987; Baym 1978; Douglas 1977; Tompkins 1985; Welter 1966). Their works show how women, from the space of the private sphere, authored female histories and engaged in political debates of the time (Armstrong 1987). Yet many of these early Anglo American and Anglo British authors, as Amy Kaplan argues, in their use of women's "domestic power," ultimately created binaries of domestic/foreign and civilized/uncivilized. While they argued for women's emancipation, they ultimately excluded the many "others" of their time in their liberating rhetoric. In this sense, the domestic, as Amy Kaplan explains, makes most sense when read "in intimate opposition to the foreign":

> This deconstruction of separate spheres, however, leaves another structural opposition intact: the domestic in intimate opposition to the foreign. In this context *domestic* has a double meaning that not only links the familial household to the nation but also imagines both in opposition to everything outside the geographic and conceptual border of the home. The earliest meaning of *foreign*, according to the *Oxford English Dictionary*, is "out of doors" or "at a distance from home." Contemporary English speakers refer to national concerns as domestic in explicit or implicit contrast with the foreign. The notion of domestic policy makes sense only in opposition to foreign policy, and uncoupled from the foreign, national issues are never labeled domestic. The

> idea of foreign policy depends on the sense of the nation as a domestic space imbued with a sense of at-homeness, in contrast to an external world perceived as alien and threatening. Reciprocally, a sense of the foreign is necessary to erect the boundaries that enclose the nation as home. (2002, 183)

As many historical events have demonstrated, while middle- and upper-class Anglo American men and women may have generally inhabited different gendered spheres in the late nineteenth and early twentieth century, they were ultimately allies against several racialized "others."

As a result of the societal configuration of gendered spheres, many Anglo American women used their presumed natural, social, and biological relationship to the home to assert their power in the national sphere. The field of home economics, for instance, which emerged during and after the Progressive Era, reflects the dominant view that women's domestic leadership in the public sphere was a logical extension of domestic duties in the private sphere (Rich 2009). Yet on a national scale, home economics reflected the goals of a racialized Americanization, which, as Anne Ruggles Gere explains, took a "racist, exclusionary, and elitist perspective on citizenship, putting white Protestant Anglo-Saxon males at the top of the national hierarchy, and insisting that immigrants emulate that model" (1997, 58). For many racial and ethnic minorities, the early twentieth-century Progressive Era up to the 1950s was defined by nativist and racial fears and increased immigration restrictions and racial segregation (Rich 2009; Ruiz 1998; Sánchez 1993). Americanization proponents of the 1930s generally viewed many Eastern European, Mexican, and Asian immigrants, as well as native-born US citizens of Mexican descent, as social problems who had the ability to become "Americans" if only they were to change their domestic practices (Romero 2008; Sánchez 1993). Home economics, as a profession, reflected these values, and the field often focused on the assimilability of nonwhite immigrants into monolithic definitions of US identity (Romero 2008; Sánchez 1993). Examples include targeting the domestic spaces of racialized minorities and immigrants by offering women classes in hygiene, cooking, language, civics, and vocational training, including sewing, as well as promoting the preparation of food by "American" standards, emphasizing women's abilities to serve food properly (Ruiz 1998, 34; Sánchez 1993, 104). Such beliefs carried over into the public sphere as Americanization programs trained Mexican women, for instance, to be housemaids, laundresses, seamstresses, and service workers in response to a shortage of such workers during the Depression (Romero 2008, 1366; Sánchez 1995, 100).

Many white communities also defended their domestic spaces against racialized groups who they considered "foreign" or who did not conform to American nationalist ideals of race and patriotism. During the Second World War, domestic power became the idea of defending the United States against many foreign "others." Nativist fears of the "other" led to drastic material consequences for several racialized groups, particularly a questioning of their patriotism and citizenship. The racialized distinctions between those who belonged in the nation and those who did not were evident in the displacement and relocation of many racialized "others" from their homes and communities. Eduardo Obregón-Pagán writes, "Although the war may have seemed 'good' for some, it was not for all. The nation celebrated a kind of patriotism that was layered with troubling assumptions about power, race, and culture. Indeed, those who looked foreign or failed to conform to the celebrated 'American' ideal often paid the price" (2003, 7). The Japanese Internment in 1942, for instance, forcibly removed over 100,000 Japanese Americans and Japanese from their homes to "War Relocation Camps" because they were considered potential "enemy aliens." It was also the year of the Sleepy Lagoon trial in Los Angeles, which wrongly accused and racially vilified Mexican youth in the press for the murder of Jose Diaz. The Zoot Suit Riots, a reaction to the trial, was a conflict over space and race in Los Angeles during a time when people of Mexican descent were deemed undeserving of rights and belonging in the United States. The year 1942 was also the first year of the Bracero Program, a temporary guest worker program, which shifted the racial and ethnic demographics in the US Southwest, leading to xenophobic responses to a new group of Mexican immigrants, characterized by a larger discourse that sought to exclude all people of Mexican descent from inclusion in the US home.

During the 1950s, the household and national spheres were also powerfully linked, with the period experiencing a revival of domesticity. This resurgence of women's domestic power occurred in a decade characterized by Cold War–era rampant anticommunism as exemplified by the McCarthy investigations, in which many US citizens, based on race, political affiliations, and ideological positions, were considered suspect. During this era, many conservative house-wives used the notion of "domestic power" to become central leaders in an activ-ist movement that was anticommunist and antiforeigner, such as the American Public Relations Forum, a conservative anticommunist women's organization established in 1952 (Nickerson 2003). Michelle Nickerson explains, "Groups of predominantly white, middle-, and upper-class wives and mothers took advan-tage of their privileged social circumstances to become militant anticommunist crusaders" (2003, 2). "Domestic containment," a term popularized by Secretary of State John Foster Dulles in the 1950s, also has strong connotations of exclu-sion: it was the ideology of containing and suppressing communist and subver-sive activity, including deviant gender and sexuality (May 1990). After the war, as Elaine Tyler May argues, the household became the site where "potentially dan-gerous social forces of the new age might be tamed, where they could contribute to the secure and fulfilling life to which postwar women and men aspired" (1990, 14). The idea of "domestic containment" also applies to those minority com-munities within the nation who were considered suspect and whose citizenship was questioned. For example, "Operation Wetback," implemented in 1954, was a government-sponsored program to deport citizens and noncitizens of Mexican descent. This mass deportation was a product of racial discrimination against a new wave of undocumented Mexican immigrants that came to the United States through the Bracero Program, many of whom were blamed for the nation's economic problems (García 1980, 169–182).

The above varied examples indicate the numerous ways domestic/foreign, white/nonwhite, and legal/illegal binaries were used to exclude people of Mexican descent, primarily women, from belonging in the US nation throughout the early and mid-twentieth century. Early and mid-twentieth-century Mexican American authors, such as Jovita González, Cleofas Jaramillo, and Fabiola Cabeza de Baca—while marginalized by Anglo discourses of domesticity due to their race—asserted "domestic power" to seek inclusion in the nation. All three writers utilized the Progressive Era and postwar view of "domestic power" as a way to assert the need for social change in seemingly nonthreatening ways. González and Jaramillo, for example, inserted the histories of their Spanish Mexican communities in Texas and New Mexico, respectively, by using representations and critiques of domesticity in their many folklore writings and folklore activities, as well as in their fiction and memoirs. Yet both women claimed Spanishness or whiteness in order to distance themselves from the racialized "others" of their time, including Mexican immigrants, mestizos, and natives, while also narrating links between domesticity and whiteness in order to assert their belonging in the nation. By doing the latter, both González and Jaramillo marginalized, even enacted racial violence against, working-class Mexican and Native American women in their rhetoric (Guidotti-Hernández 2011). Cabeza de Baca, an agricultural extension worker and home economist, also utilized the notion of "domestic power" in her writings and work. In both New Mexico and Mexico, Cabeza de Baca engaged in larger national and transnational debates about racial and ethnic identity from the 1920s to 1950s, decades defined by nativist fears of the ethnic and immigrant "other" and increased immigrant restrictions along the US southwest frontier. Cabeza de Baca's writings both catered to and challenged nativist and dominant fears of the marginalized ethnic "other" prevalent in the contexts and periods in which she worked.

Domesticana

The domestic/foreign and illegal/legal binaries that circulated in the first half of the twentieth century reappeared with intensity in the latter half due to the demographic shifts in the United States, particularly the growth of Latina/o and Asian immigration post-1965. The contemporary Chicana authors and artists in this book—Cisneros, Garza, Valdez, Rodríguez, and López—use domestic space to engage with dominant narratives in their respective works, particularly the ascription of domesticity on the Chicana body in a framework of domestic/foreign and legal/illegal. One example includes the ways in which white communities sought to protect their domestic spaces from an allegedly menacing foreign "other" during the debate over Proposition 187, on the ballot in California in 1994, which sought to deny undocumented immigrants healthcare and education.[1] Supporters of the proposition depicted Mexicans as invading the nation through their fertility and domestic spaces (Chávez 2007, 2001; Gutiérrez 2008). Mexicanas and Latinas represented long-term settlement and signified the "dramatic growth of a 'minority group'" (Chávez 2007, 68; De Genova 2006; Gutiérrez 2008; Romero 2008). Several national television programs situated Latina/o immigrants as perpetrating crimes against a white California citizenry through the bodies of Latinas and Latina/o domestic spheres. "Born in the USA," a *60 Minutes* segment, for instance, opened with a narrative suggesting how droves of pregnant Mexican women were crossing the border into the United States. This notion was followed by interview clips claiming that Mexican immigrants were coming to the United States to soak up social services for themselves and their children (Chang 2000, 6–7). Bette Hammond, an activist proponent of Proposition 187, echoed this notion of invasion on another television program, suggesting: "They come here, they have their babies, and after that they become citizens and all those children use social services" (qtd. in Chávez 2007, 68). Such rhetoric reappeared the during the 2010 midterm elections when conservative pundits and politicians referred to the children of undocumented Latina immigrants as "anchor babies."

The claim that Latina immigrants invade the United States with their fertility resurfaced in Arizona in 2006 with the women's anti-immigration activist group Mothers against Illegal Aliens (MAIA), which cast Latina mothers as threatening the cultural cohesion of the US nation with unfit mothering (Romero 2008). MAIA relied on a discourse that constructed Anglo American families as possessing normative family values and praising white domesticity (Romero 2008). State mandates in Arizona, such as SB 1070 or the Support Our Law Enforcement and Safe Neighborhoods Act in 2010 and similar calls to enforce such legislation nationally, also targeted domestic spaces of Latina/o communities by focusing on the Latina body. While SB 1070 outwardly focused on the public sphere through affirming the requirement that immigrants register with the US federal government (making it a state misdemeanor to not have registration documents in one's possession at all times), the political rhetoric supporting the bill recycled earlier views of Latinas' naturalization to motherhood and domesticity. C. Alejandra Elenes explains, "Laws such as SB 1070 not only create a hostile environment for Latinas/os in Arizona but are part of a national narrative of race and gender in the U.S. resulting from demographic changes and fears about the 'browning' of America. In this climate, the female brown body is particularly targeted and objectified."[2]

Although a much different nationalism in its aims to critique Anglo domination, the Chicano/a Movement of the 1960s and 1970s also naturalized women of Mexican descent to the domestic sphere in verbal and visual rhetoric. Nationalisms generally have excluded women's voices, and many postcolonial scholars have explored the "close connections between the structure of the family and the structure of the nation" (Enloe 1989; Fanon 1963, 360; McClintock 1997). Anne McClintock suggests, "Nations are frequently figured through the iconography of familial and domestic space" (1997, 90). In the 1960s and 1970s Chicano/a Movement activists linked family and nation in political and cultural terms. Nationalist documents emphasized the importance of the family and domestic spaces in the fight against racial injustice and Anglo American racism (Rodríguez 2009). *El Plan Espiritual de Aztlán*, for instance, states, "Cultural values of our people strengthen our identity and the moral backbone of the movement. Our culture unites and educates the family of *La Raza* towards liberation with one heart and one mind. . . . *Our cultural values of life, family, and home will serve as a powerful weapon to defeat the gringo dollar value system and encourage the process of love and brotherhood*" (Chicano Liberation Youth Conference 1972, 405, emphasis added). Explaining the link between *La Raza* and family, Maylei Blackwell explains, "*La familia* functioned as an allegory of *La Raza* and as a structuring metaphor for the Chicano Movement as a whole" (2011, 98).

These Chicano/a Movement writing and images, which produced and reified normative family structures, naturalized women to the domestic sphere by valorizing male authority in the household and rendering women as biological and cultural nurturers and reproducers of the family and nation. For example, sociologist Alfredo Mirandé configured Chicanas as the conduits of cultural reproduction in service of nationhood: "At the center of the family and the mainstay of the culture and its traditions, the Chicana has helped to counter the encroachment of colonialism. She perpetuates the language and values of Chicanos" (1977, 775). Mirandé continues, "In an environment where Chicano institutions have been rendered subordinate and dependent, the family has been the only institution to escape colonial intrusion" (1977, 775). Mirande's view on family promotes "political familism," or the "phenomenon in which the continuity of family groups and the adherence to family ideology provide[s] the basis for struggle" (Baca Zinn 1975, 16). Mirande's "political familism," and other texts of the Chicana/o Movement, idealized constructions of Chicanas as mothers of the nation, configuring women as reproducers of conservative and normative constructions of culture, family, and tradition (Blackwell 2011, 98). Other examples of women configured according to nationalist and patriarchal views include the treatment of women in the Brown Berets who were often relegated to tasks in the private sphere, either through secretarial work or domestic tasks (Espinoza 2001, 33). These domestic tasks were emphasized in Chicano/a Movement murals, which frequently depicted women as passive wives and mothers, Indian princesses, and betrayers such as La Malinche (Latorre 2008).

Many entrenched cultural representations have also sought to naturalize women of Mexican descent to the domestic sphere, yet within a binary that has configured women as either domesticated (virgins, mothers, and nurturers) or sexualized (whores and traitors) (Alarcón 1989; Anzaldúa 1987). The virgin/whore binary circumscribes women's relationships to the domestic through the cultural icons of La Virgen de Guadalupe and La Malinche. As many Chicana feminist studies scholars have argued, Guadalupe is the site by which Chicanas are constrained by motherhood and reproduction because she signifies maternal femininity and ideal motherhood. As both virgin and mother, Guadalupe embodies chasteness and ideal femininity; she is constructed as the unselfish and suffering mother. While Guadalupe prescribes idealized motherhood and maternal femininity, cultural figures such as La Llorona and La Malinche serve to define negative femininity, and all three figures serve to reinforce idealized womanhood (Anzaldúa 1987; Hondagneu-Sotelo and Avila 2008, 391).

With "domesticana" strategies, contemporary Chicana authors and artists challenge such discourses that seek to naturalize women's identities to the domestic sphere. Both Cisneros and Garza use domestic space to include Chicana/os in the nation, yet they do so by deconstructing and using the association of Chicanas with home as part of their claims to national space. Valdez self-fashions her identity through dress in the public sphere to counter cultural and gendered ideologies that have cast Chicanas as demure and submissive. Her paintings of domestic interiors interrogate the sites of domesticity that have shaped cultural constructions of beauty and gender, including the dresser, kitchen, and bedroom. Rodríguez, with performance and direction, negotiates dominant scripts that have sought to ascribe domesticity to the Chicana/Latina body. López denaturalizes the association of Chicanas and Latinas with domestic labor by showing the domestic and motherhood as constructed concepts, and by providing a visual representation of Chicanas outside of xenophobic frameworks of domestic/foreign and legal/illegal.

Domestication in "Spanish Fantasies"

Throughout this book, I also show how, along with public policy, political rhetoric, and nationalist movements, popular narratives—including the Spanish Fantasy Heritage and Spanish Revival throughout the US Southwest—have sought to render women of Mexican descent as having a passive relationship to the domestic sphere. The many Mexicana and Chicana writers and artists that I explore in this book challenge and negotiate such narratives that seek to domesticate their identities to the private sphere in their works. First explored by Carey McWilliams, the concept of the Spanish Fantasy Past refers to the several nostalgic representations of Mexican descent peoples in the US Southwest that promoted a "romanticized vision of a leisurely Spanish colonial society devoted to little more than fiestas and fandangos" (Hernández-Ehrisman 2008, 10). Such imagery emphasized the Spanish and European ancestry of people of Mexican descent and circulated in a wide variety of media, including festivals, popular literature, women's magazines, and native markets. In an article in the 1914 issue of the popular journal *Harper's Weekly*, for example, the author praises the pure "Spanish" stock of upper class Mexican/os in New Mexico: "Spanish people in New Mexico . . . are not of the mixed breed one finds south of the Rio Grande, or even in Arizona, where there is a small remnant of Spanish blood. Indeed, it is probable that there is no purer Spanish stock than in Old Spain itself" (qtd. in Padilla 1993, 216). This emphasis on a Spanish past, tradition, and culture, as many have argued, obscures the hybrid, mestizaje, and lived experiences of people of Mexican descent in the region and nation; by focusing on a Spanish past, the Spanish Fantasy heritage elided a Mexican present (Habell-Pallán 2005). In this way, Spanish Fantasy Heritage discourse configured Mexicans and Mexican Americans as premodern, while positioning the culture and identity of people of Mexican descent outside of the borders of the US nation, thereby reinforcing the domestic/foreign binaries prevalent in political rhetoric and policy.

Anglo American women club members and philanthropists were leaders of the Spanish Fantasy Heritage and Spanish Revival in their respective locations. The Spanish Past became a site for them to assert agency and a public voice (Kropp 2006, 56). Yet they asserted their voice in a larger Spanish Fantasy narrative that configured Mexicanas and native women in domesticated, passive roles such as cooks, dressmakers, folk dancers, and weavers; such images excluded and silenced the voices and histories of people of Mexican descent, particularly women (Montgomery 2002, 154). Furthermore, many women's clubs, comprised mostly of upper-class Anglo American women, sought to preserve a built environment that upheld "Spanish" culture, thereby excluding the homes and lives of working-class Mexicanos in their respective locales. The San Antonio Conservation Society (SACS)—an organization founded mostly by Anglo American women in San Antonio in the 1920s to restore Spanish missions throughout the city—also excluded the homes of Mexicanos from their historical records. Additionally, many Mexicanos labored in the homes of the elite club members (Hernandez-Ehrisman 2008, 78). In Southern California many women's clubs, comprised mostly of elite Anglo American women, built clubhouses in the Spanish colonial style, while also excluding women of Mexican descent from participating in and having a voice in their organizations (Kropp 2006, 58).

The Spanish Fantasy Past and Spanish Revivals led to the simultaneous appropriation and exclusion of Mexicana/os, particularly women. For example, in New Mexico, a handicraft revival led by Anglo philanthropist Mary Austin and artist Frank Applegate—who both founded the Spanish Colonial Arts Society in 1925—inspired Santa Fe philanthropists in the 1930s to establish the "Native Market" to provide a space for Mexican and native artisans to sell their wares (Nestor

1978, 6). Even the women's fashion magazine *Vogue* featured the Native Market in its pages (Jensen 1986b, 38–39). The Native Market mostly favored handicrafts that conformed to "authentic" representations of native peoples that were consistent with the Spanish Revival's emphasis on native peoples as part of a folk culture locked in the primitive past (Macaulay 2000). Disparities between Anglo American club women who accessed agency in the Spanish past and the domestication of Mexicanas and native women are also evident in the many events held by SACS in San Antonio from the 1920s to the 1940s, including society clubwomen dressing up and playing as "Mexicans" and "natives" in their many society events and fiestas, a topic I explore in chapter 1.

The Mexicana and Chicana authors and artists that I analyze in this volume both challenge and negotiate the Anglo-controlled discourses of Spanish Fantasies by authoring accounts of their own histories, contesting images that have sought to domesticate and render their identities as passive, and fighting to preserve the homes of Mexicana/os and Chicana/os in the historical record. For example, the "chili queens" of San Antonio actively negotiated the dominant rhetoric that sought to domesticate and consume their identities in the public plazas and fiestas by donning fashion that challenged stereotypical imagery of Mexicanas as cooks and folk dancers, and by continuing to assert their right to vend in the plazas as many nativist projects sought to exclude them. González, Jaramillo, and Fabiola Cabeza de Baca either actively participated in Anglo-dominated folklore and home economics clubs or founded their own folklore and women's clubs to preserve the culture and history of Mexicana/os in the US Southwest, once again negotiating the Anglo-dominated discourse of the Spanish Past by emphasizing "Spanish" culture in their preservations, while at the same time seeking to include their communities in the historical record. Contemporary author Sandra Cisneros also actively fought to include the homes of Mexicana/os in San Antonio's historical record in response to the debate over her purple-painted house in the King William District, in which, after researching the preservation of the homes of Mexicana/os in San Antonio, she discovered that the homes of Mexicana/os did not exist in SACS's preservation efforts. Her book *The House on Mango Street* addresses the historic exclusion of Latina/os in Chicago by narrating a young Chicana's desire for space in the city and nation, signaled through the site of the domestic. Rodríguez confronts the legacy of the Spanish Fantasy Heritage in the present in her participation in a Home and Garden Television (HGTV) special, where her home décor is rendered as stereotypically "Spanish" in a discourse that constructs the lived experiences of Chicana/os in Los Angeles as outside the nation and located south of the border, thereby eliding Chicana/o experiences and hybrid and postmodern cultural forms in the United States.

DOMESTIC NEGOTIATIONS: BEYOND A BINARY
OF RESISTANCE/ACCOMMODATION

Due to the persistence of domestic and nationalist ideologies, along with the circulation of domesticated imagery in popular culture, Mexicana and Chicana artists who seek to critique the domestic have often been deemed "traitors" for crossing and mediating between several homes, communities, nations, and institutions. During the Chicano/a Movement, for instance, women who critiqued patriarchal and nationalist structures were labeled *malinchistas* or *vendidas.* Both Mexican and Chicano nationalist discourses have configured La Malinche as both whore and traitor for "selling out" her people to the Spaniards (Paz 1961). Chicana feminists, however, have reconfigured La Malinche as a powerful icon of female agency who skillfully negotiated patriarchal and nationalist structures (Alarcón 1989; Anzaldúa 1987; Cisneros 1991b). In this sense, she was a skillful negotiator between the nations of Spain and Mexico, between the Spaniards and indigenous people, and within her own domestic sphere as laborer and mistress to Hernan Cortés. Rather than view her as a passive victim of the conquest, a view which has dominated the historical record, many Chicana feminists have argued that La Malinche strategically used language, intuition, and knowledge to survive the conquest during her lifetime (Alarcón 1989; Anzaldúa 1987; Cisneros 1991b). With negotiation, she was able to survive the fate offered to her by historical circumstances.

The negotiating practices of female authors and artists in general have been under-theorized due to binary frameworks of power. Scholar Elaine Neil Orr explains how "[t]he patriarchal bias in literary criticism led feminist critics of the 1970s and 1980s to prefer an oppositional poetics. For many, the possibility of women's voice seemed to reside in textual subversions and cultural separations" (1997, 4). Such "oppositional poetics" were central to Chicano/a nationalist rhetoric in the 1960s and 1970s and the field of Chicana/o studies in the late twentieth century, where an emphasis on resistance led early scholars to overlook those writers and cultural producers whose works did not fall into a binary of accommodation/resistance. As a result, early Chicana/o studies scholars praised writers who, while they challenged dominant racial formations, also upheld hegemonic nationalisms, patriarchy, and other forms of racial violence (Guidotti-Hernández 2011). Tey Diana Rebolledo was the first to critique scholars for analyzing early female authors of Mexican descent within a rigid binary of accommodation/resistance. She argued that analysis of these early female authors with frameworks of opposition overlooked the difficult positions of female authors of Mexican descent as they lived and wrote within rigid racial and gendered hierarchies in the US Southwest. In short, Rebolledo and others, including María Cotera, emphasized the importance of placing early Mexican American female writers in their historical contexts and analyzing their writings according to the racial-class hierarchies of their time, as well as their gendered constraints (1997, 2008).

Many contemporary Chicana authors and artists, like these early writers, confronted the critique or neglect of their work according to a binary of resistance/accommodation. Despite the now acclaimed and canonical status of Cisneros's *The House on Mango Street* in both Chicana/o and US literature, some Chicano studies scholars first criticized Cisneros for reifying the myth of the American Dream and supporting an assimilationist mythology that valued conformity to US society and dominant culture (Morales 1993; Rodríguez 1984). Works by Chicana artists Valdez and Garza were first deemed apolitical by art reviewers and scholars, with Valdez's self-fashioning with the art group Asco critiqued for upholding patriarchal gendered representations. The "deceptively simple" (Noriega 2010) imagery of Garza's depictions of US-Mexico border family practices have led many to overlook the political context and stated goals of her work, which is to garner social equality, inclusion, and respect for Latina/o communities in the United States. In contrast to earlier neglect and criticisms, Cisneros, Valdez, and Garza are now considered crucial voices of contemporary Chicana literature and arts due to the pathbreaking writings by many Chicana literary scholars and art historians (Cortez 2011; Mesa-Bains 1991, 1999, and 2003; Pérez 2007; Quintana 1996; Romo 1999).

In order to analyze artistic representations of domestic space as complex negotiations of gender ideologies and racial formations, I turn to "third space" feminism, foundationally theorized by Emma Pérez, Chela Sandoval, and Gloria Anzaldúa. Third space feminism emphasizes the lived experiences of Chicanas outside of either/or frameworks of power. Anzaldúa's "mestiza consciousness" underscores the negotiated strategies of Chicanas who claim power by mediating several, competing identities. Pérez's "decolonial imaginary" centers the voices of marginalized women who have been overlooked in dominant male genealogies and histories (1999). Her theory of decolonial imaginary suggests how "silences, when heard, become the negotiating spaces for the decolonizing subject" (1999, 5). Since Mexicanas and Chicanas have been marginalized in nationalist rhetoric and imagery, their representations maneuver within the "gaps, interstices, silences, and crevices" of dominant power to reconfigure nationalist constructions of gender (Blackwell 2011, 109; Pérez 1999). Chela Sandoval's concept of "differential consciousness," grounded in Michel Foucault's theories of power, suggests how women of color—who are multiply situated in various communities—confront the tension between being viewed as empowering one community at the expense of betraying another; as a result, they must negotiate power depending on political needs (2000). The act of analyzing negotiation therefore draws inspiration from third space feminism and border theory's views of identity as a mediation of several, competing identities.

I turn to cultural studies and performance studies to analyze the negotiated strategies of Mexicana and Chicana authors and artists who wage their critiques within male-dominated and Anglo-controlled discourses and contexts. I take to heart Angela McRobbie's assertion that studies of subcultures have viewed them as inherently male, thereby ignoring the sphere of family, domestic life, and the sexual division of labor in women's relationships to subcultural movements (McRobbie 1991, 29). By focusing on the spheres of family and domestic life, McRobbie's scholarship opens up a space for exploring women's roles in subcultural movements outside of masculinized frameworks of power. Michelle Habell-Pallán's scholarship on Chicana punk centers the intersectionality of race, gender, and class in subcultural movements, while also foregrounding how Chicana punks asserted agency in an otherwise male-dominated movement. Habell-Pallán explains how East LA punk in the late 1970s and early 1980s functioned as a "visual and sonic language" that enabled working-class Chicanas to respond to marginalization and abuse in their homes, as well as to defy cultural constraints (2005, 156). Punk's ability to subvert dominant culture, Habell-Pallán explains, appealed to working-class Chicanas who experienced racial and economic marginalization; with punk, Chicanas could see themselves as empowered subjects. The methodologies deployed by Habell-Pallán and McRobbie, although they focus on subcultural movements, help me to illuminate the negotiated practices of Mexicanas and Chicanas in other forms of cultural production, including folklore, autobiography, romance novels, fashion, glamour, theater direction, among other genres and mediums.

For many authors and artists who work in fields dominated by hegemonic racial and gendered representations, negotiation is an act of survival. To understand the choices and strategies of Chicanas and Latinas who work in Hollywood, the museum, and the publishing industry, I explore their acts as employing a process of "disidentification," a term coined by Jose Muñoz to describe how racial outsiders negotiate the majority culture not by aligning themselves with the dominant narrative but by transforming it for their own cultural purposes (1999). As Muñoz states, "[D]isidentification is about cultural, material, and psychic survival. It is a response to state and global power apparatuses that employ systems of racial, sexual, and national subjugation. . . . Disidentification is about managing and negotiating historical trauma and systemic violence" (1999, 161). With disidentification, many Chicana authors and artists have been able to get their "work out there" within Anglo-controlled academic disciplines, hostile political racial climates, a publishing industry invested in publishing mostly Chicana young adult and children's literature, and a Hollywood industry that frequently casts Latina actors in domestic roles, to name a few examples of hegemonic institutions explored in this book.

Finally, the concept of negotiation also applies to my own mediations and navigations of my position as a white female academic. The seeds of this book developed from my lived experiences as an insider/outsider in Chicana/o culture. Having grown up in San Antonio, Texas, I am all too familiar with the domesticated rhetoric of Mexicanas as part of San Antonio's fiestas, which I explore in chapter 1. As an outsider with specialized knowledge of Mexican American culture and Chicana feminisms, trained in the fields of Chicana/o literature and cultural studies, as well as my own personal history growing up in South Texas and my coming into feminism through Chicana feminism as an undergraduate student in the 1990s, I am constantly reminded of the importance of navigating the inside/outside and public/private spaces that shape knowledge production. With my intimate close readings of primary texts, along with extra-textual information from the authors and artists' biographies, unpublished and published interviews, including my own personal interviews, my goal has been to supplement the academy's otherwise theoretical focus and to nurture a personal engagement with the authors and artists I study.

Organization of the Book

My discussion of domestic negotiations begins in the 1930s with "The Chili Queens of San Antonio," the title given to the many Mexican American and Mexican immigrant female street vendors who sold chili con carne and other working-class Mexican foods in the plazas of San Antonio from 1880 to 1943, when their stands were shut down due to health regulations. I explore how the independent female chili vendors in the 1930s and 1940s specifically negotiated the prevalence of xenophobic rhetoric that sought to both remove them from the plazas and appropriate them in the fiestas, acts that sought to overshadow their agency as businesswomen outside of the home. Much of San Antonio's tourist rhetoric romanticized the chili queens, eclipsing their arduous work as female street vendors, as well as eliding their double burden of working in both the domestic space of the household and the public plazas. I argue that through dress and the act of street vending, the independent chili queen vendors actively responded to the textual and visual rhetoric of "domestication" and "consumption" that sought to render their vending and physical presence in the plazas as passive. Rather than read the independent female chili vendors as passive victims of San Antonio tourism and fiestas, I recognize their strategies of negotiation, particularly how they benefited from narratives of "domestication" and "consumption" as part of the city's constructions of Mexicanness to make a living, but also how they challenged these same narratives by continuing to assert their rights to vend in the plazas on their own terms. By challenging the domestication of their identities and asserting their rights to vend in the public plazas, the chili queens accessed voice and identity in the 1930s and 1940s.

In the three chapters that follow, I explore how Jovita González, Cleofas Jaramillo, and Fabiola Cabeza de Baca—from distinct regional and class positions—use the notion of "domestic power" to both cater to and challenge racial discourses about Mexican communities throughout the 1930s to the 1950s. In doing so, they gained entry into academia, the publishing industry, and the home economics profession, using these public spaces to enact a more pointed critique of dominant ideologies in their respective periods.

In chapter 2, I explore Tejana author Jovita González and New Mexican writer Cleofas Jaramillo, whose representations of domestic spaces in literature, autobiography, and folklore societies negotiate racialized nationalisms and gendered ideologies. If we consider the social contexts in which González and Jaramillo lived and wrote as women of Mexican descent specifically, their valorizations of Spanish Mexican identity at the expense of reifying racial hierarchies speaks to their complex positions as Spanish Mexican women in their respective locales of Texas and New Mexico. With signifiers of Spanishness, they enacted "whiteness demonstrations," a term coined by María Carla Sánchez to refer to "a range of individual traits that perpetuate social and sometimes economic dominance," and which also served as a "symbolic shorthand for genealogical connection to imperial Spain and its colonizing projects (2001, 65). With their representations of Spanish identity and culture, González and Jaramillo gained entry into academia and the publishing industry, which subsequently enabled them to publicly contest stereotypes of their communities, specifically patriarchal views of women's roles within the domestic; yet as I explain, their proto-feminist critiques ultimately upheld racial-class hierarchies. González's historical romance novel *Caballero* (1930s/1940s), coauthored with Eve Raleigh, enacts a proto-feminist critique of the confinement of upper-class Spanish Mexican women to the private sphere that was deemed necessary in the colonial project of maintaining "Spanish" honor, manhood, social status, and wealth; in doing so, the novel disavows mestizaje and excludes mestizas from the text's feminist framework. Jaramillo's autobiography *Romance of a Little Village Girl* (1955) uses a discourse of nostalgia in order to assert the prominence of upper-class Spanish Mexican women's culture in dominant US historical narratives. Even with her assertions of an upper-class status, Jaramillo's text reveals profound tensions between her romanticized assertions of Spanishness as a way to claim elite status and her actual racial and economic disenfranchisement.

Chapter 3 focuses on New Mexican autobiographer, cookbook writer, and Americanization agent Fabiola Cabeza de Baca, a contemporary of Cleofas Jaramillo, who asserted "domestic power" from her position as a home economics and agricultural extension agent in both New Mexico and Mexico from the 1920s to the 1950s. As an Agricultural and Home Extension Service agent in rural northern New Mexico, Cabeza de Baca assisted Mexican American and indigenous women with the task of improving their homes to meet the needs of food production in a devastated New Mexican rural economy. She also worked for the United Nations Education, Scientific, and Cultural Organization (UNESCO) in Patzcuaro, Mexico, in the 1950s as part of a UN effort to train Central and South American students to set up agricultural extension programs in their home countries with the aim to eliminate illiteracy in Latin America. Through close readings of Cabeza be Baca's unpublished journal entries, published writings, newspaper articles, and cookbooks about these experiences, I argue that the domestic sphere became the site upon which she both upheld and challenged class, racial, and geographical borders on both sides of the US-Mexico border. In both New Mexico and Mexico, Cabeza de Baca's home economics work engaged in larger national and transnational debates about racial and ethnic identity from the early to mid-twentieth century, a period defined by nativist fears of the ethnic and immigrant "other" and increased immigrant restrictions along the US Southwest frontier. Her writings about home economics in both the United States and Latin America powerfully illustrate the double meaning of the domestic as both household and nation because, as a home economist, she was often expected to improve the homes and lives of marginalized communities according to racialized definitions of regional and national identity. While home economics was frequently linked to projects related to the assimilation of nonwhite women or third world peoples into racialized nationalisms, Cabeza de Baca sought to affirm the value of Mexican and indigenous women's lives and cultures. In New Mexico, she challenged monolithic definitions of identity by representing culture as a process of exchange of customs, traditions, and values between various subcultures. In Mexico, she promoted cultural tolerance for the communities she assisted and emphasized the social and cultural factors that lead to their poverty—a focus on structural factors that was often missing in the accounts by many other home economists in this period.

In part two, I explore how contemporary authors and artists Sandra Cisneros, Carmen Lomas Garza, Patssi Valdez, and Diane Rodríguez—despite socioeconomic mobility outside of confined domesticity in their work as professional writers and artists, and even with a publishing industry now invested in publishing narratives about Chicana experiences—found themselves consistently positioned in the domestic as a result of Chicano/a cultural nationalism, celebratory multiculturalism, and popular cultural representations, including Hollywood film and television. As with González's, Jaramillo's, and Cabeza de Baca's texts, these authors and artists use the site of domesticity—through depictions of women's experiences and roles in domestic spaces, family rituals, and celebrations, as well as through fashion and glamour—to wage their gendered and racialized critiques.

Chapter 4 closely reads Cisneros's *The House on Mango Street* and Garza's *Cuadros de Familia* and *En Mi Familia* as critical texts that use home and domesticity to assert Chicana/o representation and inclusion in the US national sphere. While both authors use domestic space to include Mexicanos in the nation, they deconstruct and negotiate the association of Chicanas to home as part of their claims to national space. Their texts do so by critiquing patriarchal and nationalist constructions of gender. I argue that while their works share both a negotiated and a counter-hegemonic approach to the domestic sphere, mainstream reception of their texts has frequently elided their critical and feminist critiques of gender and race, and both authors have been situated (while positioning themselves) in a domesticated role as teachers and nurturers of Chicano/a culture. I also explore how Cisneros's and Garza's distinct relationships with Chicano/a cultural nationalism lead them to approach domestic space and family in different ways. Garza frequently cites Chicano/a nationalism as a direct influence on her art work, and her children's books emphasize the Chicano/a nationalist perspective of valuing the domestic realm as a bastion against Anglo domination and racism. Yet her works depict egalitarian gendered relations within the domestic, deconstructing the association of women to the domestic sphere and as reproducers of the nation. In this sense, Garza depicts the domestic realm from a "domesticana" vantage point. Cisneros's *The House on Mango Street*, in contrast, presents a Chicana feminist critique of home, depicting domestic space from a postnationalist perspective that critiques patriarchal and heteronormative ideologies of family and gender. Despite their differences, both authors share a counter-hegemonic approach to the domestic sphere with the aim to create public space for Chicana/os in the United States.

Chapter 5 continues the book's discussion of Chicana artistic representations of the domestic by specifically focusing on performance and the visual arts, two mediums that emerged in Chicana feminist discourse in the 1960s and 1970s. The chapter examines visual artist Patssi Valdez, one of the most influential, yet understudied female artists of the Chicano/a Movement. While many critics have either placed Valdez in a passive role in Asco or deemed her solo works of domestic interiors as "apolitical," I argue that Valdez's work with the conceptual art group Asco and her solo art demonstrates a politics of negotiation that responds to the gendered ideologies and the racialized public/private sphere she confronted as a Chicana in East Los Angeles and as an artist in the museum. I begin the chapter by closely reading Valdez's work as one of the original and long-term female members in Asco, suggesting that Valdez's use of punk aesthetics and glamour counter stereotypical and romanticized images of women as passive wives and mothers, goddesses, and virgins that were prevalent in the Chicano/a Movement. This section challenges the prevailing view that Valdez's significant artistic contributions did not occur until her solo work in the late 1980s and her critical recognition as a painter in the early 1990s.

In the second part of the chapter, I analyze Valdez's solo work, specifically her paintings and set designs of domestic spaces. This body of work extends the concerns with self-fashioning that were central to her work in Asco. Shifting from a focus on self-fashioning itself, her solo art concentrates on the sites that have structured Chicana femininity and beauty, including the domestic sphere and dressing. These paintings extend her earlier focus on glamour and beauty to the sites of the costume, dress, and masquerade. This section also challenges the initial prevailing view of Valdez's solo work as "apolitical" and as a significant departure from her multimedia and site-specific work with Asco. I conclude the chapter with an analysis of Valdez's set designs for Gregory Nava's *Mi Familia*, demonstrating how she extends her focus on self-fashioning and performance with Asco in her work with the film. I explore the set designs as alternative representations to patriarchy and nationalism within the cinematic space of the film.

In my final chapter, I turn to actor and director Diane Rodríguez, a pivotal figure of Latina/o theater and performing arts whose body of work has yet to be fully theorized and explored in Latina/o theater and cultural studies. Like Valdez's, Rodríguez's artistic expressions of Chicana domesticity cannot be easily read within a framework of resistance/affirmation. In the chapter, I closely read Rodríguez's career trajectory, from her performances in the activist theater troupe El Teatro Campesino, to her roles as a character actor in Hollywood cinema and television, to her direction of Latina/o theater. I argue that her acting and directorial work function as a process-related, ephemeral, and enacted negotiation of various hegemonic scripts that have sought to ascribe domesticity to the Latina body. These negotiations, on the one hand, support and further the stereotype of Latina domesticity, but on the other hand, challenge them. As she has consistently confronted dominant narratives in her career, Rodríguez has used performance and direction to negotiate those narratives, whether it is through her performance of lines or direction of a play. Regardless of the hegemonic script, Rodríguez's approach has been to destabilize the dominant discourse of Latina domesticity. Rodríguez's artistic career is therefore an example of what an artist can do when she is working within structures that are not of her own making, but who seeks to be part of the construction of that script. In the chapter, I explore how Rodríguez takes an existing narrative and intervenes in it with either performance or direction. I read her performances and direction of Latina domesticity as acts of "disidentification," and I utilize Charles Ramírez Berg's theorizations of acting as an embodied performance that has the potential to transgress stereotypes on screen (2002). In the second part of the chapter, I explore Rodríguez's direction of Puerto Rican playwright Migdalia Cruz's *The Have-Little* in 2002 to suggest that Rodríguez's directorial choices function as a "redirection" of the confinement of Latinas to domesticity that she experienced as an actor early in her career. The term "redirection" highlights the choices a director makes to shift the tone and focus of the play script. I suggest that with redirection in Latina/o theater, Rodríguez negotiates narratives about Latinas and domesticity she encountered in mainstream media, as well as creates a space for complex and diverse images of Latinas in visual representations.

My epilogue turns to visual artist Alma López's digital print *California Fashions Slaves* (1997), which presents a critique of several binaries—legal/illegal, white/nonwhite, domestic/foreign—that frame the dominant narrative of Mexicana and Chicana domesticity that I discuss throughout the book. Even though the artist produced the print in 1997, I read her print as a powerful commentary on the current political climate linking Mexican immigrants and all people of Mexican descent as threatening the cohesion of the nation, particularly by racializing and gendering the bodies of Chicanas and Latinas. *California Fashions Slaves* provides a visual representation of Chicanas outside of the colonial binary of virgin/whore and xenophobic frameworks of domestic/foreign and legal/illegal, and centers Mexicanas' and Chicanas' powerful strength, creative adaptation, and agency in response to such forces.

Jennifer A. González suggests that a public conversation and public staging of the domestic is necessary to transform and reconfigure hegemonic frameworks. González's perspective on "domesticana" is that it is the "method by which the private spaces of the home—particularly spaces traditionally associated with women—are brought into the public spaces of exhibition, not merely to reflect but to actively construct new sites of identification for members of the audience who are invited to discover fragments of their own histories and memories in the signs presented" (J. González 1999, 201). Ultimately, by placing the domestic experiences of Mexicana and Chicanas into the public eye, *Domestic Negotiations* invites readers to engage with their own gendered and racialized histories and those of others in the aim to dismantle dominant frameworks of power.

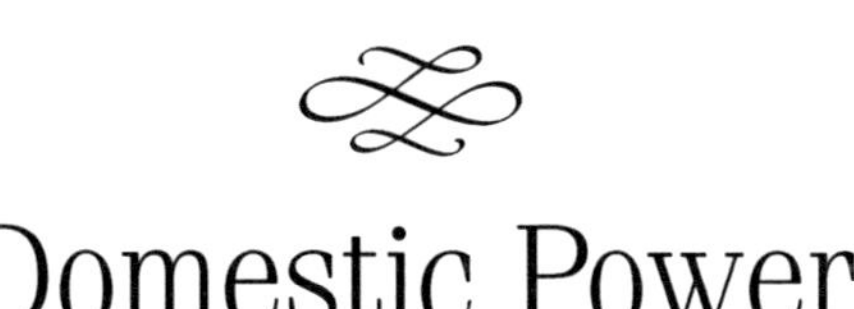

Domestic Power

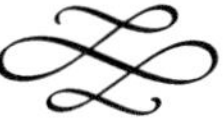

CHAPTER 1

The Chili Queens of San Antonio

CHALLENGING DOMESTICATION THROUGH STREET VENDING AND FASHION

In April 1938, Atlee B. Ayres, an architect known for commercial and residential projects in San Antonio and throughout Texas, held Fiesta Mexicano, a night of music and performance sponsored by the Fiesta San Jacinto Association at the Municipal Auditorium in San Antonio.[1] As an active director of the Fiesta Association, Ayres staged La Noche de Fiesta events annually from 1936 to 1943. Ayres's synopsis for the 1938 event details the elaborate spectacle:

> Participants will all dress in native Mexican costumes which will consist of mounted *rurales* [rural police], bull-fighters, various types of Mexican vendors, such as those seen in the rural section of Mexico carrying crates of chickens, eggs, pottery, etc, on their backs, also other typical effects. There will be four floats with groups of costumed girls and boys on them. . . . A large papier-mâché bull might be provided and have large red luminous eyes. Burros and herds of goats would also be used in the parade. Different bands will take part in the parade, all of which would be in Mexican costume. . . . *The space in front of the auditorium would be roped off by boy scouts forming a semi-circle, and in the enclosed space would be placed possibly half a dozen booths and chili stands.*[2]

Other elements included "a typical Mexican string orchestra," "fancy roping, acrobats, cock fighting, bull fight dance, Marimba players . . . folk-dancing, accordion duets, trained dogs," and "tightrope or slack wire balancing acts."[3] With these events, Ayres constructed Mexicanness, or a dominant mythology of Mexican culture and identity (Bost 2003, 494; Habell-Pallán 2005, 15–16). The event description, like those for Ayres's many other fiestas throughout the years, stipulated that cast members and entertainers must not only wear Mexican costume but that they must also be "native Mexican" or "Latin-American," terms frequently used by Ayres and other Anglo Americans to regulate an authentic and proper Mexicano identity, one located south of the US-Mexico border and outside of the literal and figurative borders of the United States.[4] In another fiesta event description, Ayres declares his events' abilities to show off "good" and "colorful" Mexicanos to the public, echoing nativist rhetoric that rendered Mexicanos within binaries of good/bad and civilized/uncivilized during this period: "San Antonio has among its Mexican people some of the most talented dancers and musicians to be found anywhere" and they "have never appeared in better form than in this colorful spectacle."[5]

Included among the list of "colorful" performers at Ayres's annual fiestas are the "chili queens"—a late-nineteenth-century moniker given to working-class women of mostly Mexican descent who cooked pots of chili con carne, as well as other Mexican foods, at home and then brought them to the various plazas in San Antonio to sell at makeshift stands.[6] Women (and some men) operated chili stands in San Antonio from approximately 1879, two years after the arrival of the first passenger train to the city, until 1943, when city officials shut them down due to health regulations.[7] The chili queens were savvy business entrepreneurs who vended in various public plazas in close proximity to what is now downtown San Antonio, including in Military Plaza from 1879 to 1892, Alamo and Milam Plazas from 1892 to 1909, and Haymarket Plaza from 1909 to 1943. They were widely and nationally known throughout these various decades, serving as popular tourist attractions in the city.[8] Despite their popularity, the Mexicana chili vendors were frequently displaced from the public plazas due to city revitalization projects and nativist sentiments (Pilcher 2008). In 1936, the city enacted the strictest ordinance against the chili queens when officials ordered hundreds of Mexicana female chili vendors to leave Haymarket Plaza due to sanitation fears, citing tuberculosis death rates as the underlying cause. Three years later, in 1939, Mayor Maury Maverick continued the ban, explaining in exaggerated rhetoric: "We will not have a thousand chili queens rushing in and violating the sanitation laws."[9] Echoing dominant and prevalent discourses about Mexicanos during this period as threatening the cohesion of the nation, Maverick's words depict people of Mexican descent as invading the city in large numbers. City officials' calls to remove the chili queens from Haymarket Plaza due to sanitation concerns also mirror dominant discourses that linked Mexicanos and immigrants during this period, particularly their domestic spaces and cooking practices, with germs and disease (Hernández-Ehrisman 2008, 59; Ott 1996, 67; Slocum 2011, 6). The Boy Scouts who "rope off" the area occupied by the chili vendors in Ayres's Fiesta Mexicano description therefore figuratively reference American identity, patriotism, and the borders of the US nation seeking to define and exclude Mexican identity and culture during this period.

In this chapter, I explore the many Mexican American and Mexican immigrant female chili vendors in the 1930s and 1940s who continued to vend in San Antonio's public plazas despite city health ordinances, xenophobic rhetoric, and nativist sentiments about the domestic spheres and lives of Mexicanos in the city and nation. These independent female chili vendors consistently negotiated the prevalence of xenophobic rhetoric that sought to both remove them from the plazas and appropriate them in the fiestas, acts which sought to overshadow their agency as businesswomen outside of the home. Much of San Antonio's tourist rhetoric romanticized the chili queens, eclipsing their arduous work as female street vendors, as well as eliding their double burden of working in both the domestic space of the household and national space of the plazas. I argue that with dress and the act of street vending, the independent chili queen vendors countered the textual and visual rhetoric of "domestication" and "consumption" that sought to frame their vending and physical presence in the plazas as passive. With the terms *domestication* and *consumption*, I refer to the dual images of Mexican American female identity as either domesticated (as virgins, mothers, and nurturers) or sexualized (as beautiful señoritas) in dominant cultural and societal representations (Alarcón 1989; Anzaldúa 1987; Fregoso 1993; Hernández 2009; Sandoval-Sánchez 1999, 28–29).

Rather than read the independent female chili vendors as passive victims of San Antonio tourism and fiesta, this chapter recognizes their strategies of negotiation, particularly how they benefited from narratives of "domestication" and "consumption" as part of the city's constructions of Mexicanness to make a living, but also how many challenged these narratives by continuing to assert their rights to vend in the plazas on their own terms. Rather than wear the expected and stereotyped "colorful Mexican" costume, as exemplified by the Ayres's fiestas and other city events, the independent chili vendors in the plazas opted for everyday fashions that reflected their identities as young woman in San Antonio. Similar to pachucas, who in the 1940s donned highly stylized clothes to signal their claim to public space in Los Angeles, the chili queens donned the latest fashions, signifying with dress that they were part of the city and nation (Ramírez 2009). Additionally, the chili queens were active agents and savvy business woman who used calculated cultural performance to make profits. While the female chili vendors ranged in age, the younger women for instance handled the visible operations at the front of the stand, passing out chili to customers, while older women either cooked chili at home or behind the scenes at the stand; such acts suggest the vendors' intended use of gendered constructions that value youth and beauty to sustain their businesses.

SPANISH FANTASY HERITAGE: DOMESTICATION AND CONSUMPTION

The many Mexican American female chili vendors in the 1930s confronted various domesticated and sexualized images of Mexican American women as part of the "Spanish Fantasy Heritage" in San Antonio's fiestas and plazas. First explored by Carey McWilliams, the concept of the Spanish Fantasy Past refers to the several nostalgic representations of Mexican-descent peoples in the US Southwest, which promoted a "romanticized vision of a leisurely Spanish colonial society devoted to little more than fiestas and fandangos" (Hernández-Ehrisman 2008, 10). As many have documented, this emphasis on a Spanish past, tradition, and culture has obscured the hybrid, mestizaje, and lived experiences of people of Mexican descent in the region and nation; by focusing on a Spanish past, the Spanish Fantasy Heritage elided a Mexican present (Habell-Pallán 2005). The Spanish Fantasy Past has largely represented Mexican women as locked in the past, as objects of desire, and, in many respects, as "beautiful señoritas," a concept termed by Alberto Sandoval-Sánchez to describe the "idealization and mythification of US Latina women as objects of beauty, exoticism, passion, and desire of/ for otherness" (1999, 150).

Two photos from the Ayres's La Noche de Fiestas and other fiesta-related events in the city from 1936 to 1942 indicate the colorful chili queen and Mexican costumes to which the Ayres and Maverick events refer (figs. 2 and 3). There are no photos available of chili queens at the Ayres fiestas, as well as at other events that sought to regulate the look of the chili queens, including Maverick's "model chili stands" in 1939, which stipulated that the chili vendors must "wear Spanish costume" and "those engaged in the trade be either Latin-Americans or wear typical dress of Mexico."[10] Yet the two photos from the fiesta events capture the expected dress of the chili queens and the dual imagery of Mexican women, the "beautiful señorita" and "domesticated" woman, both in service to Anglo viewers, prevalent in San Antonio fiesta textual and visual rhetoric. A 1940s photo shows women in the china poblana fashion, with Mexican-style peasant blouses

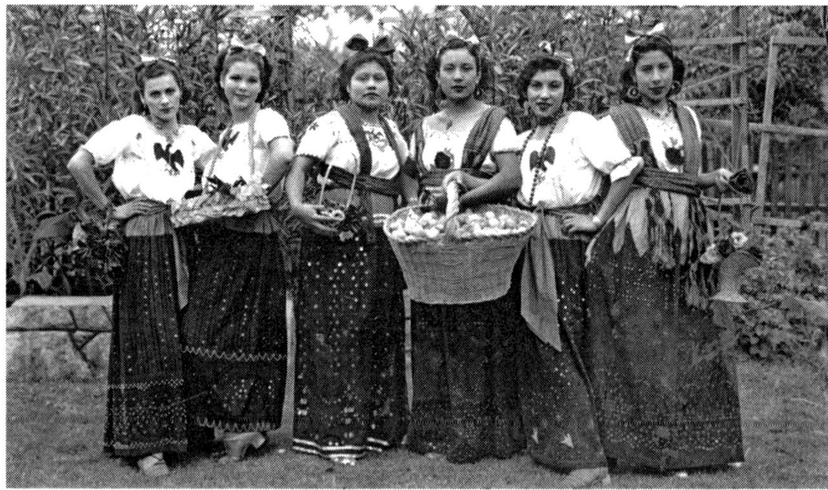

Figure 2. Women in Mexican costumes pose with baskets of cascarones and paper flowers, San Antonio, Texas, 1940s. Photo: General Photograph Collection, University of Texas at San Antonio Libraries Special Collections, No.083–0630.

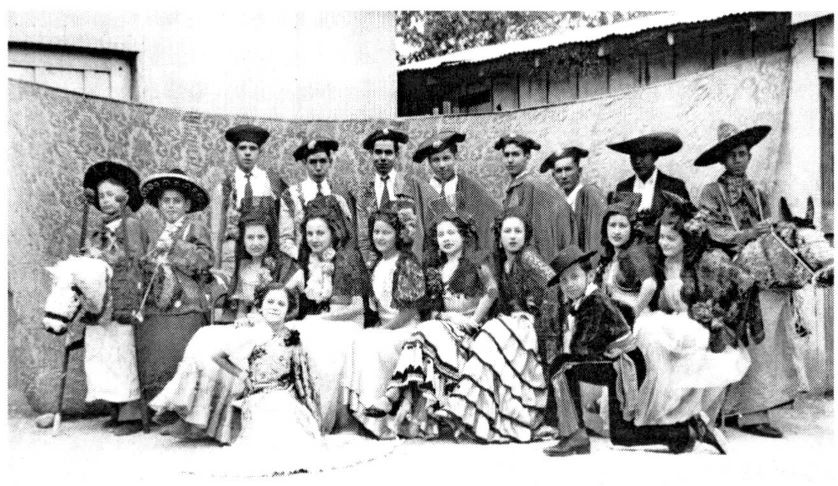

Figure 3. Performers in Mexican costumes, Atlee B. Ayres's "Night in Old Mexico," San Antonio, Texas, 1936. Photo: General Photograph Collection, University of Texas at San Antonio Libraries Special Collections, No.083–0619.

and adornment posing with baskets of *cascarones* and paper flowers (fig. 2); it depicts an image of Mexican female identity catering to the gaze of the viewer, linking Mexicanas with food and service.[11] A 1936 photo from Ayres's Night in Old Mexico reveals women in Spanish flamenco costumes and wearing black Spanish lace mantillas, suggesting a more exoticized, "Spanish" image (fig. 3). These constructions of San Antonio Mexicanas as both domesticated (serving and cooking) and sexualized (beautiful señoritas) pervade the many tourist and fiesta depictions of the chili queen vendors throughout their time in various San Antonio plazas. Yet even while constrained by dominant images of Mexicannness, the young women who wear the china poblana costumes create their own look, wearing bows instead of traditional colorful braided ribbons in their hair (fig. 2). In both photos, the young women (and young men in the second photo) appear to enjoy posing for the camera, with assertive stances suggesting they are proud to don costumes that signify Mexican culture and identity, as well as to strike poses demonstrating they are trained professional dancers. Therefore, similar to the chili queens, the performers in San Antonio's fiestas also negotiated constructions of Mexicanness in San Antonio's tourist imagery by using fashion to assert their presence in the city.

To many communities in San Antonio and the nation, the chili queens represented a constructed, domesticated Mexican American female identity in San Antonio, one that linked Mexicanas simultaneously with exoticization, food, and service. From the beginning, tourist brochures and newspaper articles from the 1890s lauded the chili queens as "dark-eyed Mexican"[12] girls and "dusky beautiful señoritas," suggesting how advertisements were not only selling the chili, but an exoticized Mexican American female body. Additionally, many newspaper accounts of the chili queens in Military Plaza indicate how Anglo American tourists linked the chili queens with sex and service. There is no documented evidence that the chili queens were prostitutes, yet the connection of the chili queens to sexual pleasure, as Pilcher suggests, "exemplifie[s] the Mexican American woman's role providing the conjugal duties of food and sex to Anglo men" (2008, 194–195). The association of the chili queens to sex also arises due to the city's increasing links with vaudeville and prostitution in the nineteenth century and the close proximity of the chili stands to San Antonio's "Reservation," an area of tolerance for prostitution (Blackwelder 1984, 17; Pilcher 2008, 184).[13] Other accounts of chili queens in the plazas describe them as feeding and serving the alimentary needs of soldiers, tourists, and various publics, including both Anglos and Mexicanos, throughout various decades.[14] The chili queen vendors no doubt served a fundamental and alimentary need in the plazas. Yet domesticated images of Mexican women in San Antonio tourism, and the visibility and images of Mexicanas serving chili in the public plazas, conform to and reinforce societal and cultural constructions of Mexicanas as mothers, nurturers, and connected to the domestic sphere. This domesticated imagery has worked to overshadow the context of labor, street vending, and agency enacted by the chili queen vendors in the plazas.

With the consumption of food, along with domesticated and feminized images of Mexican Americans in San Antonio's fiestas from the 1920s to the 1940s, Anglo Americans were able to both appropriate comfortable aspects of Mexican American culture and exclude Mexican Americans themselves from American culture and national identity. The city's health ordinances against the chili queen vendors in the plazas in the 1930s took place during the Great Depression, which impacted an already economically and racially marginalized Mexicano population in the city. The period of the 1930s and 1940s was also marked by repatriation drives, "voluntary" programs that uprooted hundreds of thousands of Mexicans in the United States, under the belief that they were a danger to the social, political, and economic stability of the country.[15] Despite a small upper class of Mexican exiles that had fled the Mexican Revolution decades earlier, the majority of Mexicanos in San Antonio during this period were part of a segregated laboring class. The lack of opportunities for educational achievement, due to this racialized, economic segregation and labor employment, led to Mexican American women's lower-class status. The vast majority of Mexican American women worked in the labor force during the Depression, engaged in "women's work" as seamstresses, in the garment industry, although many also sought work in the food processing, pecan shelling, and tobacco industries, forms of labor that relegated many working-class Mexican immigrant and Mexican American women to low wages and exploitive working conditions (Blackwelder 1984, 77; Ruiz 1998). The 1930s was also the height of the Americanization movement, a series of efforts that worked to domesticate and construct a passive Mexican American female labor force suitable for the factory and garment industries (Sánchez 1993, 104).

METHODOLOGY AND NEGOTIATION

It is difficult to analyze the chili queens' various acts of negotiation, because there are little to no self-authored accounts or oral histories documenting their point of view; newspaper accounts of the many meetings about the city's health ordinances against the queens do not record the vendors' viewpoints. The many historical and contemporary descriptions of the chili queens—found in newspaper articles, reenactment festivals, online blogs about chili, and tourist websites—are infused with appropriation, nostalgia, and tourist rhetoric. As a whole, they reenact the domestication and sexualization of the chili queens prevalent in Spanish Fantasy Heritage rhetoric. Although accounts from the perspective of the chili queens are minimal, they include a few sentences from chili queen vendor Consuela Vasquez in a 1941 *San Antonio Light* article; a brief 2005 interview with Isabel Sánchez, granddaughter of a chili queen, with assistance from Isabel's daughter Graciela Sánchez; as well as quotes from former chili queens in newspaper articles from the 1980s (Nelson and Silva 2005). The 2005 oral history with Isabel and Graciela Sánchez can be attributed to the airing of a segment on the National Public Radio *Hidden Kitchens* special in 2004 by the Hidden Kitchen Sisters Davia Nelson and Nikki Silva, which spotlighted the chili queens as inventors of chili con carne and detailed their role in various communities in the San Antonio plazas. The radio program included interviews with historians and scholars, namely Jeffrey Pilcher, who has published the only two scholarly articles devoted to the chili queens. The *Hidden Kitchens* radio segment was followed by a section on the chili queen vendors in Nelson and Silva's book of the same name (2005).[16]

The *Hidden Kitchens* NPR special led to the overwhelming interest in the chili queens presently found in online blogs, websites, and newspaper articles; the chili queens are now included as one of the originators of chili con carne in the Wikipedia entry on "chili."[17] The abundance of popular online material about the chili queens follows a romanticization and national interest in memorializing the queens that has long been alive in San Antonio proper. The Return of the Chili Queens Festival, begun by the El Mercado Association in 1985 and which continues today—intended as a "recreation of the chili queens' era" (Jennings 1996, 46)—is a testament to the popularity and role of the chili queens in San Antonio and their enduring legacy in tourism. Taking place during Memorial Day weekend in Market Square, the El Mercado Chili Queens festival is part nostalgic celebration and part community festival, intertwining various publics who have a stake in memorializing the queens.[18] Many websites cite the Return of the Chili Queens festival as an important city event and tourist attraction, suggesting how the queens are still used to generate economic profit for the city of

San Antonio.[19] A Chili Queen Cook-Off at the Bonham Exchange, a well-known and popular gay bar in San Antonio, located behind the Alamo and begun in 2006, is also held the first Sunday in April, the beginning of all Fiesta events in San Antonio; the event is centered in parody and queering the chili queen image and other images of Fiesta.[20] The performance of sexuality and self-fashioning at the Bonham Chili Queens Cook-Off suggests how gay communities, within San Antonio's larger Fiesta, have both asserted claims to public space by challenging heteronormative imagery as part of San Antonio's fiestas, and exposed the romanticized rhetoric that has dominated accounts of the chili queens.

Chili Queens in the Plazas: Removal, Sanitation, and Appropriation

Before the Ayres fiestas, Mayor Maverick's "model chili stands," and other appropriations of the chili queens in the 1930s and 1940s, many groups in San Antonio advocated revitalization projects, which resulted in the removal of the chili vendors from Military, Alamo, Milam, and Haymarket Plazas. The various relocations and removals of the chili queens reflect the city's approach to memorialization and tourism. In these periods, the chili queens were either removed to facilitate the construction of new buildings or incorporated in the plazas to serve tourists. In either case, these revitalization projects augmented racial and economic segregation in the city, making it difficult for Mexicanos to use the plazas as public sites of gathering. The first removal of the chili queens from the plazas took place from approximately 1886 to 1901, when city reconstruction projects disrupted the use of Military and Alamo Plazas as public spaces in the aim to construct a more "cosmopolitan" and European architectural facade in the downtown plazas. Under the direction of Mayor Bryan Callaghan, these Progressive Era projects, including the construction of a new city hall in 1892 and a new courthouse in 1896, diminished the use of Military Plaza as a public and open-space market, social center, and general gathering place (Arreola 2002, 135; Pilcher 2008, 181). Even though Military Plaza remained an important social space for both Anglos and Mexicanos, the new city hall occupied most of the plaza and therefore made it difficult for many of the Mexican produce and food vendors to use the plaza as a place of business.[21]

These city reconstruction projects effectively removed the chili vendors from Military Plaza, and the vendors soon relocated to the Alamo Plaza, a space that, in the 1890s, experienced a developing tourist industry due to the enshrinement of the Alamo, a site that, to many, symbolizes centuries of oppression and betrayal of Mexicanos in Texas (Flores 2002). The chili vendors also moved to the Municipal Market House (later named Milam Plaza), in the barrio west of the San Pedro Creek, another new site of tourist activity, yet that primarily functioned as a public plaza for the Mexicano community on the West Side, indicating the chili vendors' function to not only tourists, but to a growing Mexican and US-born

Mexican population. The chili queens were effectively shut out of Alamo Plaza as Mayor Callaghan spearheaded new projects of "urban hygiene" at Alamo Plaza in the late 1890s, including transforming the plazas into a manicured landscape parkway, with new trees, shrubberies, and a gazebo in the center of the plaza; this landscaping followed other city reconstruction projects he implemented years earlier, in 1886, including a grand opera house at Alamo Plaza. These many city revitalization projects at the Alamo made it very difficult for all street merchants to set up shop, including the chili vendors.

The chili queens' presence in Alamo Plaza was supported, however, by a group of city residents who petitioned the city council in 1896 to allow the vendors to work in the area, the first signs that many in the city regarded the chili queens as central to tourism and the "fame of the Alamo City 'chili stands'" that had spread throughout the nation (Pilcher 2008, 184). In 1899, in preparation of new construction, the city ordered all of the primarily Mexican street vendors out of the plaza, yet many of them remained and continued to vend (Pilcher 2008, 181). In 1901, recognizing their importance to tourism and the "picturesque-ness of the city," other city officials introduced a resolution to grant the chili queens the ability to set up their stands in certain sections of Alamo Plaza. Even though the city council ultimately rejected both requests, citing sanitation concerns, the chili queens continued to set up their places of business (Pilcher 2008, 184). During the ban on the street vendors in Alamo Plaza, many chili queens relocated to Milam Plaza, across San Pedro Creek. Yet the construction of a new Municipal Market House on Milam Plaza led the chili queen vendors to relocate to the adjacent Haymarket Plaza, their location for forty years until they were ultimately shut down due to the city's sanitation regulations in 1943 (Bechtol 1987). Despite the official ban on chili queens in 1943, many continued to vend independently and make appearances in specialized events throughout San Antonio.[22]

While the displacement of the chili queens from Military and Alamo Plazas up until the 1900s was mainly the result of city revitalization projects, which effectively shut out Mexicanos from the plazas and augmented racial and economic segregation, the displacement of the chili queens from Haymarket Plaza throughout the early twentieth century was primarily due to exaggerated public sanitation and health concerns. While there were some instances of vendors who cooked their chili con carne in unsanitary housing, such conditions were the result of poor living environments confronted by many Mexicanos on the Westside, which were caused by structural factors, including poverty. Concerns over sanitation, however, expressed racist and xenophobic rhetoric that linked Mexicanos and immigrants themselves, particularly their domestic spaces and cooking practices, with germs (Hernández-Ehrisman 2008, 59; Ott 1996, 67; Slocum 2011, 6).

In 1936 on the eve of the centennial celebrations of Texas independence, the West Side Improvement and Taxpayers Association, for instance, argued that the chili stands threatened the health of the neighborhood and called for their removal.[23] While they cited the tuberculosis death rates as cause for concern, their arguments did not consider how the Mexicano community in San Antonio experienced high tuberculosis rates in the 1930s due to poor living conditions, the inability of many migrants to access affordable health care, and most likely their fear of accessing health services due to fears of deportation (Blackwelder 1998, 112, 178). As with other efforts targeting racialized groups and immigrants for unsanitary conditions during this decade, the opponents of the chili queen vendors conflated the Mexican immigrants, not their conditions, with germs and disease (Hernández-Ehrisman 2008, 59; Ott 1996, 67; Slocum 2011, 6).

Many booster, political, and civic groups, including the San Antonio Centennial Association (SACA); the San Antonio chapter of the League of Latin American Citizens (LULAC), consisting of a rising middle class and Mexican American elites; the San Antonio Conservation Society (SACS); Mayor C. K. Quinn in 1936, and Mayor Maverick in 1939 sought to keep the chili queens in Haymarket Plaza throughout 1936–1939, revealing their own negotiations and enforcement of the city's use of the chili queens in the Spanish Past, tourist promotions, and for profit. With pressure from LULAC on one side to come up with a solution to keep the chili vendors in the plazas and pressure from the West Side Improvement and Taxpayers Association on the other to remove the vendors, Mayor Quinn came up with a resolution to the issue, which went into effect on March 1, 1936. The chili vendors would be allowed to remain in Haymarket Plaza, but only in screened enclosures. The San Antonio Centennial Association soon after, led by co-chairman of the organization Oscar Miller, protested the decision on grounds that the screened enclosures would "ruin one of the city's most picturesque points of interest" and requested that the chili queens be exempted from the ordinance.[24] As an organization primarily invested in promoting San Antonio tourism, SACA was most likely concerned that the screening of the chili vendors would diminish tourist activity in the plaza, particularly as the industry relied on the image of Mexican women serving and cooking food. SACA was soon joined by LULAC in protesting the screening of the chili vendors, since this civic organization received pressure from the Mexicano community to support the chili vendors' ability to remain in the plazas. Dr. S. L. Boccelato, of the West Side Improvement and Taxpayers Association, objected to both SACA and LULAC, saying health conditions on the West Side "had been deplorable," and adding, "The life of one citizen is worth more than the whole Centennial celebration."[25] Both SACA and LULAC ultimately succumbed to the arguments to keep the chili vendors enclosed in sanitation screens by the West Side Improvement and Taxpayers Association at a March 4, 1936, meeting, yet only with the agreement that the old city market, where the chili queens vended, be razed and replaced with a New Deal Works Progress Administration (WPA) building that would include new sanitary sheds and sinks for the chili vendors.[26] The representatives also agreed that the chili queens be allowed to vend at a later date in Washington Square, south of

Milam Plaza, as plans were in the works to create a "typical Mexican atmosphere project of chili stands, arts and crafts shops, and a flower mart."[27]

Acts of Appropriation and Decontextualization: Promoting the Chili Queens through Anglo American Domesticity and Tourism

While many cited health and sanitation as causes of concern and as a way to defend the screened enclosures, the rhetoric about the Mexicano community in these meetings reveals a condemnation of the living conditions of Mexicanos on the West Side generally, and an assertion of Anglo American domesticity as superior to Mexicana domesticity.[28] This assertion of the purity of white homes is most evident in the approach taken by members of the San Antonio Conservation Society (SACS), many of whom were part of the Centennial Association Committee, who wanted to ensure the visibility of the chili queens in the San Antonio plazas.[29] Decrying the use of screening enclosures, SACS members announced their solution at the March 4, 1936, meeting: they would cook the chili at the homes of the SACS members, the majority of whom were white middle-class women.[30] The idea included chili queens' preparation of their chili in the presumably sanitary homes of the SACS members and then keeping it warm for vending in the public plazas; it is unclear whether or not the SACS members assisted the chili queens with getting the chili from their homes to the plazas.[31] SACS members' relationships to the chili queens goes back to 1928, when Rena Maverick Green (Mayor Maverick's cousin) wanted to reconstruct the atmosphere of Haymarket Plaza, including the implementation of electric lanterns to recreate a typical Mexican atmosphere. Throughout 1928, many announcements in the society pages of the *San Antonio Express* and *San Antonio Light* also cite festive and colorful chili queens serving Mexican food at the homes of the Anglo elite, including SACS members' homes.[32]

SACS's method of offering up their upper-middle-class homes to the chili queens to ensure the vendors' presence in the plazas enforced a binary of domestic/foreign very much prevalent in Americanization rhetoric in the 1920s and 1930s. Many Americanization programs in the 1920s and 1930s targeted the domestic spaces of racialized minorities and immigrants by offering women classes in hygiene, cooking, language, civics, and vocational training, including sewing (Ruiz 1998, 34). They also promoted the preparation of food by "American" standards, emphasizing women's abilities to serve food properly (Sánchez 1993, 104). During the sanitation campaign to remove the chili queens from the San Antonio plazas in 1936, the local Red Cross also worked with the health department to offer special hygiene classes in Spanish, illustrating their incorporating of this Americanization mindset (Pilcher 2008, 191).

The constructed binary between the sanitary conditions of white homes and the nation, and the unsanitary state of Mexican homes and culture was also pronounced in Gebhardt chili advertisements throughout the 1920s and 1930s.

Gebhardt, the first company to can chili con carne in 1911, promoted their many canned Mexican foods, including chili con carne, tamales, and enchiladas in a 1923 recipe booklet, *Mexican Cookery for American Homes*. This booklet incorporated the language of both appropriation and Americanization, emphasizing distinctions between Mexican homes and American homes: "few but the native born even learned the art of properly preparing and blending various spices that make the real Mexican tang. . . . It was only when Gebhardt succeeded in preparing and blending these spaces into piquant perfection . . . that Mexican dishes really became practical so far as American homes were concerned."[33] Other areas of the recipe booklet emphasize the company's sanitation processes: "The Gebhardt kitchens are among the finest in America from a standpoint of cleanliness, sanitation, fresh air and efficiency. . . . All foods are . . . packed by white clad daughters of Mexico under rigid supervision of a US Government inspector."[34] The image of Mexican women wearing white uniforms packing Gebhardt's chili parallels the SACS proposal to have the chili queens cook chili and other Mexican foods under white supervision at their homes. SACS, like Gebhardt, sought to remove the chili queens from the context of their homes and place them in the context of white domesticity; both acts function to decontextualize the chili queens and the chili itself from Mexican American culture and identity, and thereby, similar to Americanization, enact cultural sanitation.

After a year of screened enclosures and an intensive sanitary campaign, the chili vendors were ultimately driven out of Haymarket Plaza in 1937 and did not reappear until 1939 with Mayor Maverick's "model chili stands," aimed at enforcing new sanitation procedures to increase tourism to the plaza.[35] Maverick's "model chili stands," like Ayres's fiestas, were more concerned with regulating the look of the Mexican American woman vending at the stands and of the stands themselves, thereby underscoring a larger desire to display an authentic and proper Mexican American female identity in the public spheres of San Antonio. Maverick and others regulated this "look" by holding many chili queen beauty contests. Ayres, for instance, held a contest for the "most attractive chili queen" at his inaugural 1936 fiesta, awarded to then fifteen-year-old chili vendor Consuela Vasquez. He also hosted a "Mexican dinner served by the exotic chili queens" at the final 1943 affair.[36] In 1939, Haymarket Plaza officials also held a "Queen of the Chili Queens contest," where the woman voted most attractive chili queen would be sent to New York or San Francisco to promote San Antonio tourism.[37] At many of the fiestas and private events then, the youthful chili queens were hailed for their beauty, yet a beauty linked with cooking and service, as well as whiteness, as the winners were often hailed for their Spanishness and labeled as Latin American; both terms emphasize European ancestry. By constructing the winners of the chili queen beauty contest as Spanish and Latin American, Ayres, as he did with his fiestas, catered to distinctions of "good" and "bad" Mexicans prevalent in this period.

The look of the chili stands was also regulated, expected to display a nostalgic and authentic Mexican atmosphere in the open-air plazas. Mayor Maverick's "model" chili queen stands, for instance, had to include lanterns, and he brought in three lanterns to be copied as "necessary equipment."[38] One of the lanterns was from a nineteenth-century Alamo plaza chili stand, while two others were from Mexico, made explicitly for the mayor. A decade earlier, in 1928, Rena Maverick Green, Maury Maverick's cousin and the president of the San Antonio Conservation Society (SACS)—in an attempt to "recreate the authentic flavor of a Mexican Market" in Haymarket Plaza for the 1928 National Federation of Women's Clubs convention—held a design contest for an electric lantern that best resembled the original candle-lit tin lanterns of the nineteenth-century chili stands. The event also included prizes for the "most attractive and cleanest of the chili stands on market square" and described "beautiful Mexican girls, dressed in native costume . . . to make [a] scene of brilliant color and gaiety."[39] Even at the Ayres fiestas, the chili stands were expected to signify an "authentic" Mexican identity, with event descriptions instructing that the stands be both decorated in bright oilcloth tablecloths and illuminated with electric versions of traditional colorful Mexican lanterns, reminiscent of the candle-lit lanterns at the late-nineteenth-century chili queen stands in Military and Alamo Plazas.[40]

Furthermore, during the same time that the chili queens are not allowed to vend and make a living in the plazas from 1937 to 1938, their image becomes a caricature and a performance of stereotypical Mexican identity and culture at the many Anglo-controlled festivals, clubs, and society events in San Antonio. In these private events, many Anglo American women dress up and play parts as "Mexicans," including "chili queens." In November 1937, for instance, SACS hosts their first "Harvest Festival" at the San Jose Mission, which includes "staging fascinating productions of ancient scenes," including "old Mexican and Indian customs." A picture from the event shows SACS members posing in Spanish costume, including mantillas and fans, a man wearing a mariachi costume, and a woman seated on the floor wearing a rebozo.[41] The event included a group of twenty-three "young matrons," all presumably Anglo as evidenced by their surnames, serving as "chill queens" under the direction of Mrs. Laurie Huck, chairman, and Mrs. Edward Darvin, co-chairman.[42] The Harvest Festival was not the first event by SACS members or the elite of San Antonio to include members performing as "chili queens." In 1928, a "Mexican Supper" at the San Antonio Country Club included members of the Junior League wearing "Chino Poblano" (a misspelling of "China Poblana") costumes and other "native dresses of Mexico," serving as "chili queens" at the tables, "which will reproduce as nearly as possible those used on the Market plaza."[43] In 1933, the History Club of San Antonio sponsors a history day program, which includes a variety of historical enactments, including a cowboy impersonator and a "negro mammy impersonation," followed by an afternoon tea with the president and charter members of the club "wearing the colorful costumes of Mexican chili queens."[44] Several years later, in 1941, *San Antonio Light* reporter Molly Heilman writes a spunky and lighthearted news piece about being a chili queen titled "She's Chili Queen for a Night," where she concludes, "I think the life of a chili queen is great. When I master those rolling r's, I am going to change my costume for a spangled one, buy myself a charcoal stove, and give Gladys [one of the chili queens she helps that night] a little competition."[45] The act of playing and being a "chili queen" for an event or for the day by the many society women of San Antonio and SACS club members function as sites of appropriation, where, in this instance, the chili vendors are not only removed from the context of Mexicana domesticity and placed in white homes, but are also literally removed from their bodies and identities.[46] Regarding similar appropriations within the context of Southern California, Phoebe S. Kropp explains how such performances reinforced racial and class divisions, stating, "Anglo women profited from the Spanish past while Mexican women appeared to live within it" (2006, 11).[47]

Removed from the plazas and from actual sites of labor, the "chili queens" become sites of appropriation and signify nostalgic and stereotyped images of Mexican domesticity, images used by many to support tourism to San Antonio.[48] Perhaps no better example of the appropriation of the chili queens for tourism and profit are the various ways Mayor Maverick used the chili queens in 1939 to promote tourism to the city. After his "model chili stands" in summer 1939 proved somewhat successful, Maverick must have felt confident about the "picturesqueness" of the stands, as he frequently cited the chili queens as must-see tourist events to many dignitaries visiting San Antonio that year. In a letter to the League of Texas Municipalities, an organization of 200 Texas mayors who visited the area in fall 1939, he writes, "See La Villita, river beautification all in one spot, to the tune of beautiful bands and food of the chili queens" and signed the letter "Alcalde of the Ancient and Modern City of San Antonio."[49] Agreeing to visit, the mayors are feted with a Mexican dinner at La Villita at the close of their convention with chili queens serving the meal; each mayor also receives a pamphlet on the "La Villita Project," a proposal to turn La Villita into a lively Mexican market and tourist spot.[50] A month later, in December, the mayor has "chili queens on hand to furnish typical Mexican food" at a celebration to announce the funding of the "La Villita Project" by the Carnegie Foundation.[51] With such successful appropriations of the chili queens for his various tourist projects, Maverick went on record as saying, "Bringing the chili queens back was the most popular thing my administration has done. It is even more popular than the balancing of the budget."[52] The mayor's "model chili stands" and the incorporation of chili queens as cooks and servers at his various booster events, most likely in "Mexican" or "Spanish" costume as cited by the regulations for his model stands, reveal that the sanitation regulations were less about health concerns and more about aims to organize the street vendors into an appealing tourist experience, one that relied on an image of proper domesticated Mexican identity in the public plazas and tourism events. Yet a photo of two chili queen vendors just a few weeks after the mayor's "model stands" on July 9, 1939, reveals what the caption refers to as two "modern" chili queens.[53] These women are wearing modest and everyday clothes reminiscent of late 1930s silhouettes. They are not wearing "colorful" "Mexican" or "Spanish" attire as they vend in the plazas.

WHERE ARE THE "COLORFUL" CHILI QUEENS? CHILI VENDOR FASHION AND STREET VENDING AS DOMESTIC DOUBLE BURDEN

Many photos of chili queen vendors not affiliated with the Ayres fiestas and Maverick chili stands in the 1930s depict women wearing the latest fashion of the times, indicating an important distinction between the constructed chili queens of the staged fiestas and the independent chili queen vendors in the open air markets. In a 1933 photo of a chili stand at Haymarket Plaza, for instance, taken three years before the city's screened enclosure ordinance to ensure sanitation, three young women in the center and one woman in the far right all wear clothing typical of 1930s silhouettes, along with silver and pearl necklaces and earrings, 1930s footwear, and hairstyles contemporary of the period (fig. 4).[54] Those frequenting the chili stand in the photo include a diverse group of mostly men, some of

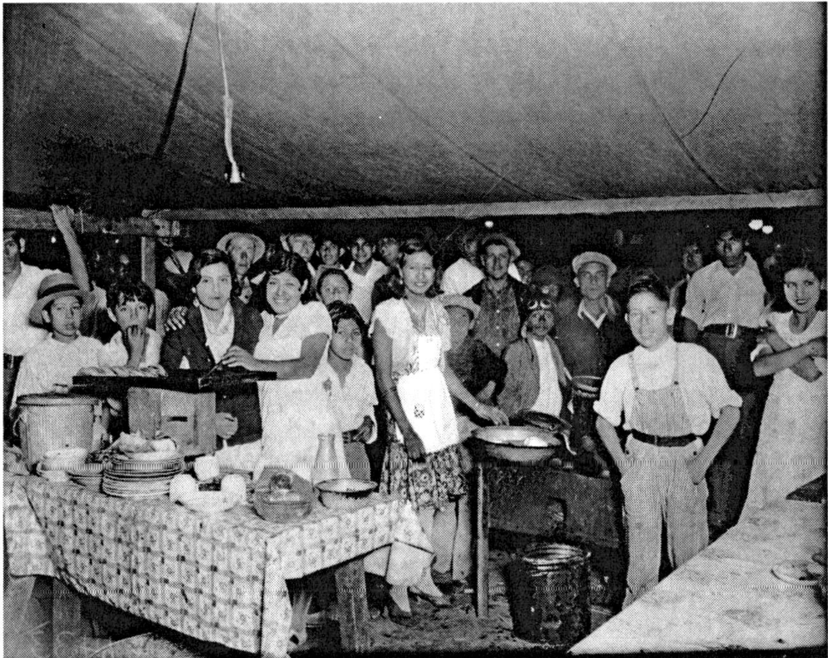

Figure 4. Chili stand, Haymarket Plaza, 1933. Photo: San Antonio Light Photograph Collection, University of Texas at San Antonio Libraries Special Collections, No. L-1433-F. Courtesy of the Hearst Corporation.

whom, as indicated by other photos of the same night, are guitarists providing entertainment for profit in the plazas.[55] No one in the 1933 chili stand photo is wearing "Mexican" or "Spanish" costume, and there are no Mexican lanterns, as they were no longer practical with the implementation of electric lighting in the plazas in 1928. A 1941 photo of chili queen Dolores García shows her donning a dark-colored, long-sleeved blouse and an apron, while Molly Heilman, the Anglo American reporter who played a chili queen for a night, wears a colorful Mexican costume; Heilman's attire is similar to photos of SACS members dressed up as chili queens in the 1940s.[56] A 1941 photo of Consuela Vasquez, voted the most attractive chili queen in 1936, working at her chili stand, shows her pictured (and described by the reporter) as wearing a yellow dress and small gold crucifix. These photos, like all the other photos of chili queens at their stands in Haymarket Plaza from 1930 to 1940, show women wearing fashionable, yet modest contemporary silhouettes of the period.[57] The independent female chili vendors therefore counter and challenge, and even pose a threat, to the romanticized, exoticized, and domesticated imagery of Mexican female identity and culture central to San Antonio's fiestas and tourism. These women are active agents and entrepreneurs, seeking a livelihood both within and outside the context of San Antonio's fiesta tourism.

If the expected and constructed image of the chili queen in the tourist industry was a woman wearing a colorful "Mexican" costume, why didn't the independent chili queen vendors wear this attire, especially if donning this look would presumably help them make a profit? First, "Mexican" or "Spanish" attire did not reflect their lived experiences as Mexican American women seeking to make a livelihood and create space for themselves in the United States. The chili vendors opted for everyday clothing that reflected their identities as young women of Mexican descent in San Antonio. Mexicanas in the early twentieth century, as Ruiz explains, "negotiate[d] across specific cultural contexts" blending diverse elements in their fashion and style (1998, 54). Similar to pachucas, who in the 1940s donned highly stylized and modern clothes to signal their claim to public space in Los Angeles, the chili queens signaled with American-inspired fashion that they were part of the city and nation (Ramírez 2009). Furthermore, Mexican attire was not necessary because the chili vendors did not make an income only from tourists but from many groups who frequented Haymarket Plaza, including the Mexicano community, as well as diverse constituents of the city brought to the plaza because of its nightlife.

The romanticized and appropriated accounts of the chili queens by Ayres, Maverick, and SACS have obscured their roles in the public plazas as street vending laborers and entrepreneurs, as well as active agents. One of the key examples of this is the term *chili queen* itself, which came into use by newspaper reporters in late-nineteenth-century accounts to describe the most beautiful female chili vendor in the plazas, yet which then gets applied to all chili vendors in the twentieth century. Yet according to reporter Heilman, who interviewed Gladys Vasquez, the owner of a chili stand on Haymarket Plaza in the 1930s and 1940s, the term "chili queen" among the vendors refers to the woman who sells the most chili at the stand for that night.[58] The chili queens therefore appropriate the term to refer to the vendor who makes the most money, shifting the concept of the "chili queen" from a marker of beauty to an emphasis on business and the marketplace. While the "queen" might make the most money because of her beauty, the vendors' reasoning places more emphasis on profit. Many vendors did use established gender constructions to sell the chili, particularly using beauty and youth to sustain their businesses. While the chili queens ranged in age, many younger women served the chili to customers and took the money from the customers, while older women either cooked the chili at home or passed the spooned bowls of chili to the young woman at the stand.[59]

The chili queens were active agents and savvy businesswomen who also used calculated cultural performance to make profits. For instance, many chili vendors shouted with exaggerated Spanish pronunciation the names of their foods, "chili," "enchiladas" and "tamales," as well as bantered with male customers to get customers to their stands. There are numerous romanticized accounts of the chili queens' Spanish pronunciations and their playful bantering with customers, with many male reporters describing the sensuousness of the chili queens' language and their repartee as a form of flirtation and sexual enticement. For example, one writer describes the chili queens as "coquettish señoritas"[60] and another explains how "your chili queen would answer you with speech peppery as her wares."[61] Another writer explains, "They all used the Spanish dialect when they had special customers, despite the fact that other tongues came easier to some of them by nature."[62] The chili queens' playful use of Spanish and their flirtations therefore functioned as strategic acts of performance to sell their foods and make a profit; in these instances, the chili vendors make productive use of various cultural performances, or what Walter Little terms "tourism as performance" (2003, 528) to attract customers' attentions to their stands.

Much of San Antonio's tourist rhetoric has romanticized the chili queens, overshadowing the arduous work performed by the female street vendors, as well as the double burden of working at both home and in the plazas. Many women of Mexican descent in the 1930s and 1940s took up street vending because it allowed them to generate an income to support their families, an income that in many instances supplemented domestic and factory employment. Workers who participate in the informal economy are typically led to work in this sector because it augments inadequate and unsatisfactory working conditions (Muñoz 2006, 75). As self-employed entrepreneurs in the informal economy, many of the chili vendors received immediate cash for goods as opposed to relying on wages from their employers. Mary Vasquez and her eighteen-year-old sister-in-law Gladys Vasquez (both related to Consuela Vasquez), for instance, both owned and operated a chili stand in Haymarket Plaza throughout the 1930s and 1940s and used their income to support nine people.[63] The vending hours of the chili queens typically began about 6 P.M.—at dusk and after the produce vendors had cleared out their stands—and ended about 1:30 A.M. These late-night hours were suitable to either working other jobs or performing domestic tasks at home during the day; many vendors also prepared and cooked the food for the plazas during the day at home prior to the 1940s. While the late-night hours of the chili vendors in the public plazas have led to lots of romanticized accounts of their work, including linking the chili queens to prostitution, for many vendors, the light-night hours were simply practical. Many chili vendors brought their children to their stands; many photos show chili queens accompanied by children, most likely their own, at their booths. At Mary and Gladys Vasquez's stand in 1941, the three-year-old son of one of their employees slept in an automobile behind the stand, as both his grandmother and mother worked in the chili stand.[64] The operating of chili stands at night therefore enabled many women to work two jobs while also to take care of their children. In this regard, however, street vending functions as a double burden for many Mexicanas, as domestic chores and the chores (cooking the chili and preparing the stand) performed in order to obtain paid work operate in a never-ending cycle, one domestic task following the next one (Nuñez 1993, 79). So while the female chili vendors transgressed gendered ideologies that ascribed them to the domestic sphere and reproductive roles by working outside the home and owning their businesses, this paid work often led to a double burden at both home and work (Nuñez 1993, 74).

While the chili queens were able to generate a living vending in the plazas, new guidelines and regulations in the 1930s and 1940s due to sanitation concerns made it more cumbersome to make a profit. For instance, each chili stand was required to pay fifty cents to the market master, the individual in charge of all market activity, and this money went to support the central cooking and cleaning stations at the market house, where all the dishes were cleaned in steaming water.[65] On many nights, the chili vendors just broke even after they factored in the cost of food and supplies, as they charged from ten to fifteen cents for their items, including a bowl of menudo, enchiladas, hamburger stew, and three tacos, each worth ten cents; tamales and chili garnered fifteen cents, and anything with extra chili on top cost an extra nickel. On very active nights, yet "very special nights," a chili stand could make as much as twenty or twenty-five dollars.[66] Other sanitation measures enforced in the 1940s, including obtaining a business health card from the city and other regulations, many of which entailed a cost, made it, as Concepción Chávez explains, "too troublesome to make the tiny profit from their arduous work seem worthwhile."[67] The increased regulations led the chili queens to turn to the increasing jobs in the expanding garment industry in the wartime economy (Pilcher 2008, 194). Many other chili vendors made the choice to relocate indoors and begin their own restaurants or work for others (Nelson and Silva 2005, 44; Pilcher 2008).[68] When the chili stands were officially closed in Haymarket Plaza in 1943, Trinidad García, for instance, began to work for the Jorge Cortez family as a waitress at San Antonio's Mi Tierra restaurant in Market Square (Nelson and Silva 2005, 33).

Much of the rhetoric about the chili queens has viewed them as passive, particularly the approach by many during the sanitation campaigns of the 1930s and 1940s. There are no records of chili vendors' perspectives on these regulations, and instead, various players, including SACS and LULAC, take the role of representing the vendors at these meetings. Yet an interview with Consuela Vasquez at her chili stand in 1941 reveals her pointed criticism of the bans with humor. A *San Antonio Light* newspaper reporter indicates, "Consuela laughed at the suggestion her chili, tacos, menudos, and tamales were a menace to public health," with Vasquez stating, "Nobody has been poison[ed] here yet," and then she explained her sanitation procedures: "We use them [paper plates and cups] once. Then throw them away. The knives, forks, and spoons, we wash them with strong soap, and then we boil them over the charcoal fire. . . . Limpia? Of course, [it] is clean. We cook at home, and [our] home is clean."[69] The various organizations that sought to represent the chili vendors in the sanitation campaigns viewed the women as passive not only because of their marginalized status as working-class Mexicanas, but also because of their status as laborers in the informal sector, an arena considered by many to be dominated by uneducated and unskilled workers who lack formal training. Regardless of the education, work skills, and English-language proficiency of the chili vendors, these sanitation debates imply that the perspectives of the chili vendors were not valued (Nuñez 1993, 68). The chili vendors' responses to the sanitation regulations reveal that they were not passive, ignorant, or incapable of making choices, but rather that they made strategic choices in response to the sanitation measures. Despite city ordinances and harassment, the chili queens continued to vend in the plazas, suggesting how they asserted agency and challenged the appropriation of their stands by many in San Antonio's tourist industry. By continuing to vend throughout various decades, Mexican American female chili vendors consistently asserted their "rights to the city" (Lefebvre 1996). Even as they were officially banned from the plazas in 1943, they made strategic choices to start their own business or work for others.

Cultural Citizenship and Rights to the City

The many acts of appropriation of the chili queens have also failed to recognize the vendors' roles in a broader movement by Mexicanos to establish cultural citizenship in the San Antonio public plazas. Cultural citizenship, as William Flores and Rina Benmayor argue, includes a "range of social practices which, taken together, claim and establish a distinct social space for Latinos in this country" (1997, 1). Historian Felix Almaraz describes the plazas as public spaces of congregation: "The plaza was buzzing with life, with people yelling greetings to each other. The chili queens would bring their pots and their fires and set up shop for the night. . . . For a dime, you could get chili con carne, tamales, beans, coffee" (Nelson and Silva 2005, 47). Graciela Sánchez, the great-granddaughter of chili queen Teresa Cantu Rocha and the director of the Esperanza Peace and Justice Center in San Antonio, depicts the plazas of the 1920s as sites of public literacy and political dialogue for both the Mexican and US-born Mexicano population in San Antonio:

> the *mexicano* community in San Antonio used to congregate, [it was] a true farmer's market. And in the afternoon people would come to listen to the newspaper being read aloud. You had a lot of people who couldn't read. They'd post the newspaper, and one or two people would read the paper to the community. There were people in San Antonio who were fleeing the Mexican Revolution—both pro-revolution and anti-revolution—so there was a lot of the political dialogue occurring right there in the plaza. As it got dark, the chili queens would arrive, and the walking troubadours, musicians like Lydia Mendoza and her family, would begin to set up and play. They were all trying to make some money to survive. (Qtd. in Nelson and Silva 2005, 42)

Joseph Aguilar, the owner of West Commerce Mercado, also describes the plazas as sites of cultural citizenship for working-class Mexicanos in San Antonio. He explains, "My grandfather had a produce stall right here at Haymarket Plaza, where the chili queens would gather and make tacos and tamales. In the 1920s and 1930s everyone congregated there. One o-clock in the morning, it was booming—thousands of people. There were trucks and trucks and trucks of produce. People would go from stall to stall, and they would buy. I got to see it before we lost it, before they started tearing down old buildings" (qtd in Nelson and Silva 2005, 53). Aguilar describes the plazas as crucial places where Mexicanos and others claimed rights to public space in an otherwise segregated city, made an income through produce and street vending in difficult economic times during the Depression, and asserted biculturalism through food and music.

Musician Lydia Mendoza also includes the chili queens as part of the claiming of public space in San Antonio through music and biculturalism. When she was a teen playing Tejano music in the public plazas in the 1930s, she describes the scene: "Down at the Plaza del Zacate [Haymarket Plaza], there used to be chili queens—they sold spicy menudo soup and chili. . . . And at night, whole bunches of people would be down there, going from table to table. So we would bring our old chairs and sit right there and start singing too. . . . Everybody was chasing after the centavos in those days. And near the chili was the place to get them" (qtd. in Nelson and Silva 2005, 48). Mendoza's music, like the Mexican and American food of the chili vendors, represents the biculturalism of the Mexican American community in San Antonio and South Texas, functioning as an "embodiment of U.S.-Mexican culture . . . as well as a participant in raza people's protracted struggles for survival" (Broyles-González 2001, xiii).

The chili queens also served their chili and other Mexican foods to pecan shellers, which comprised a large segment of San Antonio's working-class Mexicano population in the 1930s and 1940s. In 1939, as the mayor implemented his "model chili stands" in Haymarket Plaza, many chili queen vendors, rather than return to the Haymarket Plaza, continued to vend at pecan-shelling plants, discovering that they could make a decent income vending to the pecan shellers at lunchtime. The chili queens continued to work outside the pecan-shelling plants, until they were given the ultimatum to "clean-up or close-up" in December 1943.[70] Many Mexicanas who worked in the pecan shelling industry in San Antonio in the 1930s and 1940s faced poor labor and health conditions, including the demands of production speed-ups, substandard pay, sexual harassment, and many other hazardous conditions (Ruiz 1998, 148).[71] Similar to the chili queens, these women lacked representation and a voice, yet they asserted their voice and rights through labor organizing, particularly under the leadership of Emma Tenayuca and other labor organizers.[72] While chili queens did not claim public space through labor activism, as did many other Mexican American women who worked in the pecan-shelling and garment industries in San Antonio in the 1930s and 1940s, like these women, they did redefine space, gender, and race by asserting their rights to vend in the plazas.[73]

CONCLUDING REMARKS

Within the segregated spaces of San Antonio, the presence of the chili queens in the plazas and various public sites in the city represents a claiming of public space for working-class Mexicanos in the 1930s and 1940s against the backdrop of appropriation, sanitation campaigns, racial-economic disenfranchisement, and questioning of citizenship within repatriation programs. Given the various discourses of domestication, racialization, and appropriation of the chili queens, their acts of selling chili in the public sphere should be read as powerful negotiations of dominant narratives of race and class in San Antonio's public plazas and fiestas. The chili queens claimed a public presence and cultural citizenship during a time when dominant racialized discourses sought to ensure their literal invisibility in the plazas and hyper-visibility through exoticized rhetoric. The chili queens' refusal to leave the plazas indicates how they claimed cultural citizenship by declaring the plazas entitled public spaces for San Antonio's working-class Mexican American community, particularly women.

The chili queens' various negotiations of domestic space, including their challenge to the domestication of their identities by asserting their rights to vend in the public plazas, reveal the particular way they accessed voice and identity in the 1930s and 1940s. Through fashion that departed from stereotypical imagery of

Mexicanas as either "domesticated" or "consumed," and with street vending, the Mexicana chili vendors asserted rights and agency in the nation. In the chapters that follow, I explore how three authors, Jovita González, Cleofas Jaramillo, and Fabiola Cabeza de Baca—from distinct regional and class positions—negotiated constructions of race, gender, and nation through their claims to "Spanishness" in the self-authored accounts of their experiences. These three authors use the space of the domestic to both cater to and challenge racial discourses about Mexican communities throughout the 1930s to the 1950s. In doing so, they gained entry into academia, the publishing industry, and the profession of home economics, using these public spaces to enact a more pointed critique of dominant ideologies in this period.

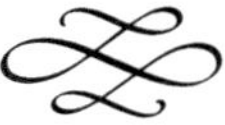

CHAPTER 2

Claiming Domestic Space in the US-Mexico Borderlands

JOVITA GONZÁLEZ AND EVE RALEIGH'S *CABALLERO* AND CLEOFAS JARAMILLO'S *ROMANCE OF A LITTLE VILLAGE GIRL*

In an important scene of the historical romance novel *Caballero* (1930s–1940s),[1] mid-twentieth-century Tejana author and folklorist Jovita González and coauthor, Anglo American writer Eve Raleigh, depict Padre Pierre, a French priest who lives in a Spanish Mexican land-owning community in nineteenth-century rural South Texas, advising the families to gain Anglo American sympathy and approval of Mexican presence in Texas by displaying their "Spanish" colonial homes:[2]

> You have your beautiful homes filled with many treasures, ordered households where courtesy reigns; food of the best, served graciously. . . . I say this: Seek the *Americano* officials who have influence and invite them to your homes and entertainments. Show them that we have much to give them in culture, that we are not the ignorant people they take us to be, that to remain as we are will neither harm nor be a disgrace to their union of states. They are far too well acquainted with the lowest of the Mexicans and not at all with the best. (González and Raleigh 1996, 54)

According to the priest, the elite Spanish Mexican families should use the space of the domestic to demonstrate the esteemed and civilized qualities of their culture and heritage, so as to distinguish themselves from the "lowest of the Mexicans." Padre Pierre's statement occurs precisely at the moment when racial tensions are escalating between this Spanish Mexican land-owning community and the Anglo American settlers during the United States–Mexico war, tensions that continued to intensify after the signing of the Treaty of Guadalupe Hidalgo in 1848, when legal interpretation of the treaty by the American courts denied Mexican inhabitants their legal and political entitlements as US citizens. This urging of the upper-class Spanish Mexicans to publicly display their Spanish-colonial homes as a strategy for resisting the categorization of their communities as nonwhite, primitive, and foreign speaks to the shifting racial constructions of Spanish and Mexican peoples in the US Southwest at the time. Before the arrival of white settlers to the region, existing Anglo inhabitants often viewed Spanish land-owning families and Mexicans who worked the land as belonging to distinct racial and social categories. Yet, after the treaty, as historian David Montejano explains, "[T]here were no longer any significant differences between the displaced 'Spanish' elite and the landless 'Mexicans.' Now a Mexican was simply a Mexican" (1987, 115). Montejano cites the words of an Anglo old-timer of Nueces County who was shocked by the new white settlers' inability to make such distinctions: "a newcomer here did not distinguish between an old Spanish family and other Mexicans; it was embarrassing to them and to me" (1987, 115). Such new categorizations of Spanish elite communities as "Mexican" and inferior led many Spanish land-owning families to assert their whiteness through Spanishness as a way to reclaim entitlement to land and citizenship within the region. Of course, even though these communities referred to themselves as españoles or Spaniards, the majority were not Spanish but mestizos, persons of mixed ancestry, specifically of both Native indigenous and Spanish heritage. Ultimately, the priest's appeal to the land-owning Spanish Mexicans to deploy Spanish colonial domesticity suggests the powerful role of the domestic in negotiating prevailing nineteenth-century racial discourses of Mexican-descent peoples within a white/nonwhite racialized binary and a civilized/savage dichotomy.

González's and Raleigh's positioning of Mexicana/o homes and communities as Spanish bears a striking resemblance to the folkloric activities and narratives of domesticity by a mid-twentieth-century Spanish Mexican author, New Mexican folklorist Cleofas Jaramillo. In similar ways to the narrative of *Caballero*, Jaramillo's autobiography, *Romance of a Little Village Girl* (1955), depicts the domestic sphere within a discourse of racial purity amid the social and cultural life of nineteenth-century Spanish Mexican communities of the Southwest, specifically in the lives of Hispano women in New Mexico. If we look at the year Jaramillo's autobiography was published, just one year after "Operation Wetback"—the United States' mass effort to deport so-called illegal aliens to Mexico—Jaramillo's nostalgia for a Spanish ancestry reads as a response to mid-twentieth-century Anglo racial discourses of Mexicans as foreign and illegal. Racial projects such as Operation Wetback served to strengthen already established binaries of Mexicans as nonwhite, primitive, and foreign that operated a decade earlier, during the time González and Raleigh wrote *Caballero*.

González and Raleigh produced *Caballero* in the 1930s and 1940s, the decades prior to "Operation Wetback," as anti-Mexican hysteria and racial discourses about legal and illegal immigration flourished when several interest groups believed that a new influx of Mexican immigrants that came to the United States under the "Bracero Program"—a contract labor program intended to bring

Mexican laborers to the United States temporarily—were a danger to the social, political, and economic stability of the country.[3] The goal of the Bracero Program was to incorporate Mexican workers as temporary migrants who would not adversely affect the wages and working conditions of domestic farm workers. Yet rather than bring Mexican laborers to the United States legally and temporarily, the program led to an influx of thousands of undocumented Mexican migrants who began to work and live in the United States; many Mexican migrants entered the United States without documentation because only one out of ten applicants ever received a contract under the Bracero Program. Racial discrimination toward this new wave of Mexican immigrants led to "Operation Wetback," which operated as a series of Border Patrol operations that swept across the agricultural regions of the Southwest. These threats of mass deportation were intended to pressure undocumented Mexican immigrants to leave the United States voluntarily, yet led to the direct deportation of Mexican immigrants and US citizens of Mexican descent (García 1980, 169–182). The signifiers of whiteness in both *Caballero* and *Romance of a Little Village Girl* suggest how both texts engaged with prevailing racial discourses about Mexican communities against the backdrop of the Bracero Program and "Operation Wetback."

In this chapter, I argue that representations of domesticity and domestic space function in *Caballero* and *Romance of a Little Village Girl* as places from which to negotiate racialized nationalisms and gendered ideologies. If we consider the social contexts in which González and Jaramillo wrote as women of Mexican descent specifically, their valorizations of Spanish Mexican identity at the expense of reifying racial hierarchies speaks to their complex positions as Spanish Mexican women in their respective locales of Texas and New Mexico. While *Caballero* represents a critical collaboration between "two historical perspectives, one Anglo and one Mexican American" (Cotera 2008, 199), I explore *Caballero* from the perspective of González's positionality as a woman of Mexican descent, considering how the text mirrors her own racial positioning as part of an elite Spanish Mexican class in the US Southwest.[4] Both González and Jaramillo confronted configurations of public and private spheres set up by the dominant discourses about people of Mexican descent, specifically women, and views of womanhood set up by their own cultures and communities. In this way, both González's and Jaramillo's writings employed several domestic negotiations with dominant discourses in order to subsequently subvert them. Their valorizations of whiteness reveal the Anglo-dominated discourses in which they worked and their difficult navigation of Anglo racial binaries that circulated during their lifetime. With signifiers of Spanishness, they enacted "whiteness demonstrations," a term coined by María Carla Sánchez to refer to "a range of individual traits that perpetuate social and sometimes economic dominance," and which also served as a "symbolic shorthand for genealogical connection to imperial Spain and its colonizing projects" (2001, 65). As Sánchez argues, even though whiteness demonstrations may signify a variety of traits that seeks to claim privilege, along with social and economic dominance, they do not necessarily translate into social and economic power (2001, 65–66). With such whiteness demonstrations, González and Jaramillo disavowed their mestizo Mexican cultural heritage, thereby creating racial distinctions among people of Mexican descent. While their portrayals of home and domesticity respond to the Anglo conquest and colonization of Texas and New Mexico, their literary interventions also ironically served to crystallize racial and class hierarchies. González's and Jaramillo's literary representations of the domestic therefore both buttressed and undermined colonial regimes of racial power.

Considering mid-twentieth-century racial attitudes toward people of Mexican descent and the Eurocentric context of the societies they lived in, their commitment to representing their respective cultural heritages is significant. With assertions of Spanish identity and culture, they gained entry into academia and the publishing industry, and then later challenged stereotypes of their communities, specifically patriarchal views of women's roles within the domestic. González and Raleigh's *Caballero*, penned sometime between 1936 and 1939, after González gained entry into academia, suggests how González's later writings contested her earlier depictions of Spanish Mexican patriarchy in her folklore writings produced for the university prior to 1935. In *Caballero*, González and Raleigh portray critical depictions of women's precarious roles as objects of Spanish culture and tradition, a proto-feminist critique not evident in González's early texts. In Jaramillo's case, her aim to document Spanish cultural traditions suggests a radical move to control public representation of Spanish Mexican cultural practices and domesticity within the Anglo-controlled discourse of the Spanish Revival. Jaramillo's autobiography, *Romance of a Little Village Girl*, ultimately upends the image of Spanish Mexican women as passive recipients of the feminization and domestication of their communities. Like her folkloric activities, her autobiography illustrates the importance of the domestic sphere in negotiating dominant Anglo racial discourses circulating during her lifetime.

Tey Diana Rebolledo was the first to argue that Chicana/o studies scholars should critically assess the complex position of female authors of Mexican descent as they lived and wrote within rigid racial and gendered hierarchies in the US Southwest. Her argument arose in response to Raymund Paredes's controversial essay "The Evolution of Chicano Literature," in which he argued that early New Mexican female authors, such as Cleofas Jaramillo, had a "hacienda mentality" for romanticizing Mexican culture and catering to Anglo racial hierarchies. Rebolledo contended that such scholars needed to shift their perspective of these early writers to account for the difficult circumstances of racial and gendered marginalization that these female authors confronted. In short, Rebolledo foregrounded women's status within racial-class hierarchies, as well as their gendered constraints (1997, 1995, 1994). Elizabeth Jacobs joins Rebolledo in suggesting that "we should reframe our understanding of the 'hacienda mentality' when considering the works of these writers. Not only did they face strong stereotyping tendencies from the Anglo American community, but were also constrained by Hispano society and codes of conduct, all of which militated against women's independence, educational opportunities and literary expression" (2000, 44). Genaro M. Padilla also cautions against reading this early work as assimilationist, arguing that these women did not directly criticize Anglo encroachment, for otherwise they would have difficulty getting their work published (1993). Rebolledo, Jacobs, and Padilla powerfully remind critics that given these early women writer's gendered constraints, it is a wonder that they wrote at all. Similar to Rebolledo, Jacobs, and Padilla, I caution against reading early female authors of Mexican descent within a rigid binary of accommodation/resistance. This chapter challenges frameworks of resistance by closely reading González's and Jaramillo's life and writings through the lenses of negotiation and situational agency.[5]

Even though González and Jaramillo lived and wrote in their distinct regional contexts of Texas and New Mexico, both shared similarities as female writers of Mexican descent in the US borderlands in the early twentieth century. Both were also instrumental in using domesticity to preserve Spanishness in their respective locations. They were each involved in folkloric activities, were befriended by Anglo Americans who encouraged them to archive their Spanish culture, and negotiated institutionalized spaces in the university and gala events that used official narratives to preserve Spanish Mexican culture while it was being systematically dismantled. Their representations of the domestic sphere, through organizing folkloric events, publishing, and writing manuscripts, are central to the way they claimed Spanishness and whiteness, as well as to the way they engaged with prevailing racial discourses.[6]

In what follows, I examine how González's and Jaramillo's claims to Spanishness in their texts respond to gendered ideologies that position Spanish Mexican women as objects of Spanish culture and identity. Both *Caballero* and *Romance of a Little Village Girl* foreground the precarious relationship of Spanish Mexican women to the domestic sphere as they simultaneously find themselves desiring to affirm their culture, signified by the domestic realm, while also desiring escape from patriarchal confinement in the private domain. In *Caballero*, González and Raleigh enact a proto-feminist critique of the confinement of upper-class Spanish Mexican women to the private sphere that was deemed necessary in the colonial project of maintaining Spanish honor, manhood, social status, and wealth. Yet in doing so, they disavow mestizaje and exclude mestizas from their feminist framework. As a result, they enact racial violence, marginalizing working-class Mexican and Native American women in their rhetoric (Guidotti-Hernández 2011). Their elisions of mestizas and indigenous women in their accounts are predicated on a nostalgic view of the US Southwest as the domain of Spanish colonial settlers and enact an "imperialist nostalgia" for a "past when conquistadores of aristocratic means ruled the land, an attitude which sets up a desire to maintain a kind of racial and class structure that originated with early impe-rial practices in New Spain" (Guidotti-Hernández 2011, 138). Their performances of imperialist nostalgia are reactions to the racial marginalization of Mexican-descent communities in the US Southwest. Jaramillo's *Romance of a Little Village Girl*, for instance, uses imperialist nostalgia in order to assert the presence of her Spanish Mexican community's culture in dominant New Mexican histori-cal narratives. As Padilla explains, "nostalgia is a realization that there are future stakes involved in the reconstruction(s) of the past. To remember is not only the act of not forgetting, but an act of not being forgotten" (1993, 325). Ultimately, Jaramillo's autobiography reveals profound tensions between her romanticized and nostalgic assertions of Spanishness as a way to claim elite status and white-ness, and her actual racial and economic disenfranchisement. *Romance of a Little Village Girl* powerfully exposes Spanish-colonial domesticity as a public site: for while it enabled Spanish Mexicans to resist the erasure of Spanish culture in the public sphere, institutionalized displays of Spanishness ultimately masked the decline of Spanish Mexican women's social status and material wealth in the mid-twentieth century.

The Domestic as Home and Nation: Spanish Colonization and the Treaty of Guadalupe Hidalgo

The link between women of Mexican descent and the domestic stems from inter-cultural ideologies derived from Spanish colonialism and patriarchal Catholi-cism. Such associations of Mexican women with the domestic realm intensified with intranational projects, such as the Treaty of Guadalupe Hidalgo in 1848 and its aftermath in various national projects, such as Americanization programs of the 1920s and 1930s. Throughout these various historical moments, women of Mexican descent have been associated with the domestic in the service of colo-nization and nation. The alignment of Spanish Mexican women to the domestic to buttress colonialism began in Spanish colonial societies of the "New World." After the Spanish conquest, the Spanish Mexican woman was perceived as the highest-valued commodity because, biologically speaking, she carried the purity of the Spanish bloodline. In order to maintain the supposed purity of Spanish bloodlines, women were confined to the private sphere due to patriarchal views of women as objects of property. A women's sexual chastity was thus deemed necessary to continue a patriarchal Mexican code of honor. As Ramón Gutiér-rez explains, Spanish Mexican men's honor was upheld by enforcing female purity: "Male authority enforced through seclusion was one way to guarantee female virtue and maintenance of family's honor" (1991, 213). Conversely, it was perceived that men could not be secluded, because conquest and domination were considered intrinsic qualities of masculinity necessary in protecting family honor (Gutiérrez 1991, 214).

Jean Franco's study of women's struggle for power in relationship to Catholicism and to the nation in Mexico explores the ways Spanish Mexican women of the Southwest were constricted by Catholic hegemony and Spanish cultural beliefs that emerged prior to Cortés. Even though Franco discusses the role that this dual legacy plays for women in Mexico, her work is useful for examining how Spain's long legacy of protecting Spanish bloodlines by Spanish colonizers in the Western hemisphere impacted women in the US Southwest. Franco states, "[T]he virtual confinement of married women to the home had not only been required by the Church but was also intended to insure the purity of blood that Spanish society imposed after the war against the Moors" (1988, 507).

In the US Southwest specifically, those land-owning families who claimed Spanish ancestry confined women to the private sphere to prevent so-called contamination from Indian and later African blood. John M. Nieto-Phillips explains how the objectified Indians and Africans in the Americas were perceived as opposites to the spiritual, racial, and cultural purity of Spanish colonizers and that "individuals who were not born to Catholic, white, and Spanish parents were deemed inferior and were therefore subject to conversion, enslavement, or some other form of exploitation" (2004, 23). This view of indigenous and African peoples of the region as threats to the purity of Spanish bloodlines speaks to the racialized, gendered, and economic hierarchy of the Southwest. Spanish colonization was based on male-patriarchal authority over Mexican servants and Indian *peones*, as well as women within a gendered and racial hierarchy. As historian Tomás Almaguer explains, the *rancho* system consisted of the "Spanish" upper class on the top, an intermediate stratum comprised of small landholding ranchers and farmers and skilled rancho laborers and foremen, and an Indian and small mestizo population on the bottom (1992). Within this hierarchy, Indian and mestizo women were the most marginalized, and their confinement to the domestic sphere was mostly born out of the paternalism of the elite families, as well as due to a racial-class hierarchy that confined them to labor in the domestic (Almaguer 1992, 62–63).

With Anglo colonization of the US Southwest and subsequent racial projects, the nation's configuration of public and private spheres according to both racial and gendered divisions had profound consequences for Mexican-descent communities, especially women. If we consider US policies that configured the domestic within racialized binaries of domestic/foreign and white/nonwhite, such as those stipulated in the Treaty of Guadalupe Hidalgo in 1848, then the domestic becomes a site, as Amy Kaplan explains, "in intimate opposition to the foreign": "This deconstruction of separate spheres, however, leaves another structural opposition intact: the domestic in intimate opposition to the foreign. In this context *domestic* has a double meaning that not only links the familial household to the nation but also imagines both in opposition to everything outside the geographic and conceptual border of the home" (2002, 183). The double meaning of the domestic as both household and nation entails a reconsideration of the domestic sphere as an isolated private space of femininity. This dual meaning of the domestic complicates the traditional feminist view that middle-class nineteenth-century and early-twentieth-century social life was organized by two separate spheres: a dominant public male realm of production (the city) and a subordinate private female realm of reproduction (the home).[7]

Kaplan's double meaning of the domestic makes evident how middle-class Anglo American men and women—even though they may have inhabited different gendered spheres in the late nineteenth and early twentieth centuries—were ultimately allies against a racialized other. Yet she does not explain how women of Mexican descent, such as González and Jaramillo, often found themselves marginalized by Anglo discourses of domesticity, while also using racial categories for their own gains. In this way, Kaplan's theory of "manifest domesticity" does not consider how female authors of Mexican descent, like González and Jaramillo, engaged with representations of domesticity to assert whiteness through Spanishness on the one hand and to resist their marginalized status as racialized Mexicans on the other. Both women asserted their whiteness in order to distance themselves from racialized others, the new Mexican immigrants of their time period, while also narrating links between domesticity and whiteness in order to assert their place within the nation. By doing the latter, both González and Jaramillo enacted racial violence, marginalizing working-class Mexican and Native American women in their rhetoric (Guidotti-Hernández 2011).

Links between citizenship and whiteness were established with the Anglo conquest of the US Southwest, where Mexican homes and communities became viewed as threats to white hegemony. This view of Mexican culture as outside the literal and figurative borders of the nation was institutionalized with the Treaty of Guadalupe Hidalgo in 1848. While the treaty ended the US-Mexico war and sought to provide American citizenship to Mexicans living in the border region, it can be better understood as the first major document that led to the construction of illegality in regards to Mexican communities (De Genova 2006; Gómez 2008). Additionally, the treaty stipulated that Mexico cede more than half its territory to the United States (Gómez 2008, 4). The treaty specified the land rights of Mexicans living inside the newly annexed territory of the Southwest border region and the citizenship privileges of Mexican inhabitants within the Union of the United States. Nevertheless, as Martha Menchaca explains, "[t]ragically, within a year of the treaty's ratification, the United States government violated these citizenship equality statements and began a process of racialization that categorized most Mexicans as inferiors in all domains of life" (2001, 215). Interpretation of the treaty by the US courts established a racial order in which Mexicans who were considered white were provided full legal rights as US citizens, while mestiza/os, Mexicans of African descent, and other indigenous groups were disenfranchised and afforded inferior legal rights (Menchaca 2001,

217). Native Americans were not protected by the treaty and therefore confronted extreme forms of racial discrimination (215, 274).

The Treaty of Guadalupe Hidalgo promised Mexicans full equality with other inhabitants of the United States if they adopted American cultural values. Given the social and cultural conquest of the US Southwest, and the racialization implemented by the treaty, American identity in this context should be understood as in conflict with the culture and language of Mexican and indigenous communities. Article IX of the Treaty of Guadalupe Hidalgo states that Mexicans are to become US citizens and be treated equally to Americans as long as they renounce their Mexican citizenship and adopt American cultural values: "The Mexicans who, in the territories aforesaid, *shall not preserve the character of citizens of the Mexican Republic* . . . shall be incorporated into the Union of the United States, and admitted as soon as possible, according to the principles of the Federal Constitution, to the enjoyment of all the rights of citizens of the United States. . . . With respect to political rights, their condition shall be on equality with that of the inhabitants of the other territories of the United States."[8] While the language of the treaty sought to give these communities rights as US citizens, legal interpretation of the treaty by the American courts often denied these Mexican inhabitants their legal and political entitlements as US citizens. Such associations between US citizenship and whiteness, along with the role of the domestic in either carrying out or eliminating Mexican cultural practices, illustrates how, for people of Mexican descent, the domestic has been a contested space. In González's and Jaramillo's cases, they viewed the domestic sphere as necessary to resist the construction of their communities as foreign in response to dominant discourses about citizenship and land entitlement.

The treaty intensified and institutionalized Mexican women's existing marginalization to domestic ideologies. Anglo colonization of the US Southwest served to solidify the literal and figurative confinement of women of Mexican descent to the domestic due to the project of maintaining Mexican honor, manhood, social status, and wealth. Ruiz cites how nineteenth-century Spanish-language newspapers reveal the double standards applied to women: "Women were to be cloistered and protected to the extent that some residents of New Mexico and Arizona protested the establishment of coeducational public schools" (1998, 5). Women's confinement was also a way for male members of the community to solidify their masculinity as they experienced emasculinization by the Anglo colonizers. Anglo colonization of the region emasculated men of Mexican descent and positioned them in a disempowered space in contrast to the configured masculine space of the colonizer.[9] There was also a real economic fear of land passing into the hands of Anglo American men through marriage. Indians and mestizas were doubly marginalized because they were confined to the domestic out of the paternalism of both the elite Spanish Mexicans and their low status in the racial-class hierarchy (Menchaca 2001). *Caballero* reveals how Spanish Mexican women from the land-owning class found themselves in precarious positions if they challenged the prescribed gender roles set up by Spanish colonialism and patriarchy.

DOMESTIC NEGOTIATIONS AND PROTO-FEMINIST
CHALLENGES TO PATRIARCHY IN *CABALLERO*

González's *Caballero*, a historical romance novel coauthored with Anglo American author Eve Raleigh (pseudonym for Margaret Eimer), is based on the ethnographic research González conducted as a graduate student at the University of Texas at Austin under the direction of her advisor, J. Frank Dobie, as well as informed by González's experiences growing up as a woman of Mexican descent in South Texas. Scholars agree that the racial and political climate of the 1930s and 1940s most likely led González to ask Raleigh to coauthor *Caballero*, yet scholars have distinct views on the nature of the collaboration itself.[10] According to José Limón, González must have asked Raleigh to coauthor the manuscript because, as a public school teacher in Corpus Christi, Texas, González was most likely concerned about the public's reception of the novel's critique of Anglo American domination.

The production of *Caballero* therefore represents a negotiation between two authors positioned distinctly in the US-Mexico borderlands. María Cotera has provided the most extensive research on the nature of the collaboration between González and Raleigh (2007, 2008). Cotera explains that both González and Raleigh began to write the novel in the late 1930s in Del Rio, Texas, and continued to work on the novel together after they each relocated to different cities— González to Corpus Christi and Raleigh to Joplin, Missouri (2008, 199). While the exact nature of the collaboration is still not entirely clear, Cotera explains that the two women exchanged letters spanning three decades from the late 1930s to the mid-1960s, which addressed issues of plot, character development, and editorial changes. Cotera describes how Raleigh even apologizes to González in one letter for putting her name first on the manuscript title page; with Raleigh's name listed first, some publishers mistakenly thought Raleigh to be the main author and overlooked Raleigh's and González's roles as coauthors (Cotera 255– 256, n.3). For Cotera, "the dual voices of the *Caballero* manuscript are not small critical matters because they constitute a material reminder that the text itself was forged in the borderlands between at least two historical perspectives, one Anglo and one Mexican American" (2008, 201). Within the space of this chapter, I consider how the novel represents González's assertions of a privileged racial and class status in 1930s and 1940s South Texas. In this way, I attribute the text's problematic racial representations and romanticizations of white patriarchy to both González and Raleigh.

González's representations of people of Mexican descent in her folklore and in *Caballero* are framed by the historical moment in which she lived and her position as a Spanish Mexican woman within the public institutions in which she wrote. While González was a master's student at the University of Texas at Austin, Dobie encouraged her to write about Mexican culture.[11] She explains, "Heretofore the legend and stories of the border were interesting, so I thought, just to me. However, he [Dobie] made me see their importance and encouraged me to write them" (qtd. in Garza-Falcón 1998, 75). The subject of González's master's thesis, "Social Life in Webb, Starr, and Zapata Counties," explores the social history of Spanish Mexicans in South Texas and suggests González's project to write about her culture within academia (Garza-Falcón 1998, 75). After receiving her master's degree, González returned to San Antonio to teach high-school Spanish; in 1934, she received a one-year fellowship from the Rockefeller Foundation. This fellowship, as Limón speculates, gave González the time and resources to collect the ethnographic data that would form the foundation of *Caballero* (Cotera 2008, 6; González and Raleigh 1996). González's contributions to *Caballero*—particularly representations of the social and cultural history of people of Mexican descent in nineteenth-century South Texas—therefore reflect the academic institutions, particularly folklore studies, in which she was trained.

Most likely influenced by the discourse of "Southwestern regionalism" in the scholarship by Dobie, González's folklore writings draw upon the distanced and romanticized perspective about South Texas Mexicans, generating distinctions between the Spanish land-owning families and "common Mexicans." The writings of J. Frank Dobie, considered to be influential in Southwestern regionalism, exemplify this movement. According to Montgomery, "[S]outhwestern regionalists remained largely uninterested in the problems of racial and material inequality, or even in the relationship, so central to the life of the folk, between oral tradition and economic production" (2002, 202). Rather, Southwestern regionalism projected a fantasized image of a pure Spanish past where Spanish elites, mestizos, and Indians lived a utopic life. In her scholarly folklore narratives, González refers to her family as aristocrats in a highly stratified caste system, although her memoir about her family history indicates otherwise (Garza-Falcón 1998, 80). She states, "My father, Jacobo González Rodríguez, a native of Cadereyta, Nuevo Leon, Mexico, came from a family of educators and artisans. His father, Pablo González, taught poor boys the trade of hat making" (qtd. in Garza-Falcón 1998, 74). As Garza-Falcón explains, "This image of a wealthy Spanish landowner's daughter created for or by her is certainly one that made her presence more acceptable in academic circles, where imagined or desired perceptions of her identity could flow more freely if they were far removed from stereotyped images of working-class Mexicans" (1998, 76). Such images of a wealthy Spanish past are evident in González's folklore writings. In these texts, she describes mid-eighteenth-century settlers of the Rio Grande Valley as Spaniards with divine rights to land, indicating that the Spanish settlements were predestined to flourish because of the "desirable character of its citizens" (qtd. in

Garza-Falcón 1998, 80–81). González's history of the aristocratic Spanish *don* in these texts evokes the image of a respectable white European character that functions as a response to racial discourses prevalent during her lifetime: she used such distinctions to construct a Spanish identity and elite status against the new working-class Mexican immigrants.

González's representations of domesticity in her folklore activities valorized Spanish identity and culture. As an influential member of the Texas Folklore Society in the 1940s, particularly as vice president and president (for two terms), González directed *pastorelas*, pageants, and Christmastime *posadas*, with local Mexican children playing the parts of pilgrims for a mostly Anglo audience (Cotera 2008, 5; Garza-Falcón 1998, 98). While these events importantly brought to the public eye the richness of Mexican culture that was previously confined to private spaces, such representations, like her writings, privileged a pure Spanish elite class and ignored racial and class differences. Such depictions served to provide only "local, nonpoliticized, color" for the Texas Folklore Society, a largely Anglo and mostly male academic organization, interested in viewing nonthreatening images of the Mexican and indigenous population (Cotera 2008, 5; Garza-Falcón 1998, 98). Just as she did in her folklore scholarship, González's direction of these events in the Texas Folklore Society worked to esteem an elite pure Spanish ancestry.

Her belief in a hierarchy of land-owning Spanish Mexicans and working-class mestizos speaks to the anti-Mexican hysteria that circulated throughout the 1930s and 1940s. As González wrote *Caballero* with Raleigh during the Depression, prejudice against Mexican Americans flourished, as several interest groups blamed Mexican immigrants for the nation's financial problems. Evidence of this racialized nativism can be found in statistics from this period: from 1930 to 1939, approximately 2 million people of Mexican ancestry—including approximately 1.2 million who were US citizens and legal residents—were deported from the United States to Mexico (Balderrama and Rodríguez 1995, 50–53).[12] Such statistics make clear how the deportation and repatriation of Mexicans during the 1930s put people of Mexican descent in a tenuous status as they saw their citizenship status questioned.

González's negotiation of South Texas's racialized binaries of legal/illegal and white/nonwhite is evident in *Caballero*'s representations of Spanishness. *Caballero* focuses on the fictionalized Spanish Mexican land-owning family of Don Santiago de Mendoza y Soría and on the family's conflict with the newly arrived Anglo American settlers in what is now Southwest Texas. The novel illustrates the tensions between various colonial systems in Southwest Texas: the Spanish colonization of the Southwest in the sixteenth century and the nineteenth-century US imperial project of redefining Mexican provinces in this same region. The text also depicts the precarious position of Spanish Mexican women of the land-owning classes who became objects of Spanish identity and culture, focusing on Spanish Mexican women who rebel against the prescribed gender roles of

Spanish colonialism and patriarchy. Ultimately, González and Raleigh's text presents a powerful critique of the very Spanish colonial system that González often upheld in her folkloric writings and activities, even as she reifies domestic/foreign binaries. By focusing on women of the land-owning families who claimed Spanishness, *Caballero*'s proto-feminist critiques of patriarchy exclude mestizas, eliding the racial-class hierarchies that impacted women's confinement to the domestic sphere and economic labor.

Caballero begins with descriptions of an uncontaminated Spanish lineage and unsettled sixteenth-century landscape. In doing so, the text emphasizes land-owning Spanish Mexicans' entitlement to land and the community's lineage within the current borders of the United States. The story begins with a description of the Mendoza y Soría family as descendants of noble Spaniards and depicts the settlement of land by Don José Ramón de Mendoza y Robles, the first Mendoza y Soría ancestor to arrive in the Southwest with a land grant provided by the Spanish government. González and Raleigh's narrator describes the patriarch as having a divine right to colonize this land, a landscape depicted as pure and unsettled:

> Here was the place for his home. In the months of travel as surveyor for the Crown, with the exploratory expedition sent by the viceroy of New Spain, he had ridden over much land that lay fair, camped at many a spring and river, yet nowhere had a place beckoned and smiled. None of it had whispered, so softly that only he could hear, "I have been waiting for you." . . . In its middle the magic of the mind saw a palm tree. La Palma de Cristo, he mused. . . . A glorious triumphant name—Rancho La Palma de Cristo! Hadn't he first seen his dream home on this Palm Sunday? La Palma, for short, and it would be known all over the countryside. . . . Not a little home, but a great *hacienda* worthy of his name. (González and Raleigh 1996, xxxvi)

This opening scene of *Caballero* overlooks the social history of the Southwest by ignoring the profound Native American influences on the Southwest border, as well as the reality of Spanish intermarriage with many "savage Indians." In contrast to the novel's depiction, this land was not pure and unsettled—thousands of Indian people inhabited the region. Alonzo describes how Spanish colonizers of the Lower Rio Grande Valley region in the sixteen and seventeenth centuries attempted to conquer the natives through Catholic conversion. He explains, "The Spanish *pobladores* who occupied this new province also had to contend with the presence of thousands of unsettled Indians" (Alonzo 1998, 23). Furthermore, by esteeming a pure Spanish heritage and origins in South Texas, *Caballero* ignores the racial-caste system that subsequently grew out of Spanish colonization.

González and Raleigh's depictions of South Texas social history in *Caballero* also evoke nineteenth-century Anglo views of Mexicans within a comprehensive racial binary. Evidence of *Caballero*'s reification of such binaries can be found in the narrative's distinctions between the Spanish families and mestizo workers. In contrast to the description of the Mendoza y Sorías as regal, divine, and in a heavenly class, the novel describes the servants as closer to earth, dirty, and primitive. As the narrative describes the present-day patriarch of the Mendoza y Soría family, Don Santiago, commanding his household, it states, "Servants came out of the rooms opposite, their flat *huaraches* making flapping sounds on the portico floor. Peons came on silent bare feet through the small gate from their quarters outside the wall; dozens of them, from naked infants suckling noisily at bare young breasts down to bent, old people" (González and Raleigh 1996, 4). In contrast, the text depicts Don Santiago's patriarchal authority and regality: "Don Santiago de Mendoza y Soría strode through the wide gateway when three clangs of the bell that hung in the arch above the well in the center of the patio had shattered into a chorus of notes against the house walls calling to each other. . . . The household had orders to wait . . . [s]uch was Don Santiago, lord of land many miles beyond what his eye could compass, master of this *hacienda* and all those that would soon gather before him" (González and Raleigh 1996, 3). González and Raleigh's distinctions of Spanish Mexicans as members of a higher and more civilized class than that of the servants, who are mostly "Mexican" and Indian and seen as poor and primitive, speaks to the racialized, gendered, and economic hierarchy of the Southwest. Spanish colonization was based on male-patriarchal authority over Mexican servants and Indian peones, as well as women within a gendered and racial hierarchy. *Caballero*'s distinction between regal Spanish communities and primitive Mexican workers also serves to position an elite Spanish South Texan class against the newly arrived Mexican immigrant laborers of the 1930s and 1940s. That is, representations of Spanish patriarchy in *Caballero* not only reflect González's keen eye in representing gendered hierarchies within Spanish colonial communities. They function to remind her readers of an elite Mexican class allied with Spanishness or whiteness. With such distinctions, González and Raleigh contrast a legal and land-owning Spanish Mexican class with an undocumented Mexican laboring class in the United States during the era in which they wrote *Caballero.*

Caballero demonstrates how the Spanish Mexican code of honor that configures upper-class women as objects of Spanish property led men to use the female body as a site of resistance to Anglo American settlers. As the narrative of *Caballero* unfolds and the conflict emerges between the Anglo American soldiers, the "blue-eyed strangers," and the Spanish Mexican community, Don Santiago, as the male head of the household, seeks to protect Spanishness and honor through safeguarding objects of colonial domesticity, as well as the highest commodity of Spanish identity—the elite Spanish Mexican woman. While this desire to sequester women in the private sphere arises from the dual legacy of Catholicism and the Spanish conquest, González shows how this need intensifies with the aim to protect Spanish Mexican entitlement to land after the treaty. With the treaty's advent, patriarchal authority through ownership of land was called into question, and Spanish Mexican land-owning men feared losing their political and legal entitlement to their homes. In response, Don Santiago sequesters Spanish Mexican women in the home out of fear that the women of his household will destroy the purity of Spanish bloodlines by intermingling with Anglo American men.

Don Santiago's use of Spanish Mexican women to resist the Anglo American colonizers is rooted in Spanish colonialism and patriarchal views of women as objects of property who carry Spanish wealth, family, and honor. As the conflict ensues between the Spanish Mexican community and the Anglo American Rangers, Don Santiago first appraises Spanish cultural objects of the home. He views his culture as purely Spanish and free of mestizaje, thereby evoking the text's project to position an elite Mexican class as white. In the following passage, Spanish colonial items are described as under threat by the Anglo American invaders: "Don Santiago slowly circled the *sala*, then stood at its center. How long, he wondered would this great living room with its family background and tradition remain as it was? The fireplace was a black maw against half of the north wall. Against the white wall above it hung a large black and silver crucifix flanked by massive silver candelabra resting on the wide mantel. . . . Would the *Americanos* dare to take these symbols of his faith and change them to silver dollars?" (González and Raleigh 1996, 13). As the passage continues, the narrator depicts the cultural objects Don Santiago prizes. These are mostly objects of the Spanish colonial past, including religious symbols ("the black and silver crucifix"), weapons used by his ancestors ("rapiers, lances, knives, long-barreled *pistolas*, an *escopeta* with a brass bell-opening at the muzzle, bits of old armor"), furniture of a "former splendor in Spain" ("mahogany chairs and tables finely carved and a great harp of gilt"), and products of the ranch land ("chairs, stool, benches, and a couch of stave and rawhide") (González and Raleigh 1996, 13). For Don Santiago, these various domestic and ranching objects signify Mexican political and legal entitlement to land derived from the descendants of Spanish conquistadores in Southwest Texas. In keeping with his need to protect fictive Spanish bloodlines, Don Santiago's assessment of his home space does not include symbols of indigenous and native Mexican people, many of whom work his land.

The role of Spanish women as objects and signifiers of Spanish identity and honor creates a nefarious relationship for the female and male characters in *Caballero* who do not follow Spanish colonialism's prescribed gender roles. Don Santiago's various family members—his wife, Doña María Petronilla; widowed sister, Doña Dolores; beautiful and rebellious daughter, Susanita; intelligent daughter, María de Los Angeles; and artistic and foppish son, Luis Gonzaga— defy his authority and patriarchal views of the female body deemed necessary to uphold Spanish Mexican honor. Only Don Santiago's brave and hyper-masculine son, Alvaro, follows Don Santiago's prescribed rules on resisting Anglo American presence in their community, specifically by claiming Spanish manhood.

With the character Luis Gonzaga, González and Raleigh reveal how constructions of Spanish identity and manhood occur through the propertied female body. The artistic son, Luis Gonzaga, challenges conventions of Spanish patriarchy and masculinity set by his culture through resisting fighting in battle and the military bravado of his father and brother. His implied queer identity also defies Spanish codes of manhood. Throughout the text, the narrative depicts how Luis's choices go against Don Santiago's Spanish colonial tenets of masculinity. According to Don Santiago, Luis is not a "man" because he fails to desire a future as a soldier who fights gallantly against the Anglo Americans. The narrator describes Don Santiago's perspective: "Luis Gonzaga, the *marica*! Eighteen and without an affair, never even kissing the servant girls he sketched. He sighed. Perhaps Luis might still be a man, given time."[13] Here, Don Santiago defines manliness through the female body; Luis is unmanly because he has not yet had a relationship with a woman. As a result of such critiques of his manhood by his father, Luis feels that he does not belong in his Spanish Mexican community. Luis Gonzaga upsets Don Santiago by going north to pursue his artistic talents with an Anglo American painter. When Luis befriends an Anglo American artist, Luis begins to feel that he belongs: "For a moment—a happy, expanding moment—he had a feeling that he belonged. That he would not have been considered peculiar and effeminate, as his family and those his age saw him to be, he felt certain" (González and Raleigh 1996, 104). Yet such movements reveal how González and Raleigh's depictions of egalitarian Anglo American cultural values and patriarchy also valorize white masculinity in ways that render Anglo American gender roles and oppression as invisible.

Caballero illustrates how Spanish colonialism relegates and confines women's bodies to the private realm by positioning women as objects and property. The text shows that Spanish Mexican women who enter the public sphere threaten to destroy the Spanish lineage and their associated role as Spanish property. For instance, when Don Santiago's daughter Susanita rides from Rancho La Palma to Matamoros on horseback to warn her brother Alvaro of his fate to be killed by the Rangers, she defies both Spanish and US colonial patriarchal views of a woman's proper place in the home. Furthermore, because Susanita is accompanied by a male servant, presumably a dark mestizo or Indian, she exposes her Spanishness to possible contamination by a Mexican. In response to Susanita's defiance of the codes of Spanish patriarchy, both Alvaro and Don Santiago react with outrage: "Ironically, the Mexican *caballero* gave stern codes of honor to his women—waiting but the chance to dishonor them. . . . No woman exposed herself alone in public, that was the law, and when she did expose herself she announced to the world that she belonged to men. . . . Honor! It was a fetishism. It was a weapon in the hand of the master, to keep his women enslaved, and his fingers had twisted upon it so tightly he could not let go" (González and Raleigh 1996, 280). Here, the narrative depicts how a Spanish Mexican patriarchal and colonial code of honor enables both Alvaro and Don Santiago to react to Susanita's action with shame.

The novel also demonstrates the role of Spanish Mexican women as conduits of whiteness in their intermarriage with Anglo American men. Such intermarriages were often based on the view that elite Spanish Mexicans were white and therefore intermarriage with Anglo Americans was a natural extension of a shared racial identity. Such intermarriages between elite Spanish Mexican women and Anglo men were typical among elite Tejano, New Mexican, and Californio families. They were also commonly depicted among late-nineteenth- and early-twentieth-century women writers of Mexican descent, especially in the novels by María Amparo Ruiz de Burton, including *The Squatter and the Don* (1885) and *Who Would Have Thought It* (1872). *Caballero* depicts how such intermarriages often upset the patriarchal use of Spanish Mexican women of land-owning families as objects of Spanishness necessary to protect manhood and honor. As Don Santiago intensifies his confinement of his daughters to the private sphere in response to the Anglo American invasion, his daughters Susanita and María de Los Angeles go against their father's prescribed views by leaving the confines of the private sphere and subsequently falling in love with Texas Rangers. The narrative shows how Susanita's and María de Los Angeles's desire to marry the male occupiers disrupts Don Santiago's attempts at challenging Anglo American hegemony through his attempts at protecting the supposed purity of his Spanish bloodlines. For the female characters Susanita and María de Los Angeles, their desires to wed the Texas Rangers is one method for them to secure a place for themselves in the new social and racial order of South Texas.

The text depicts how Susanita's and María de Los Angeles's love of the Texas Rangers is driven by their view of the Anglo American settlers as offering domestic freedoms and better homes in contrast to the patriarchal confinement represented by the patriarch Don Santiago. In doing so, the novel suggests that the liberation of both men and women is ultimately circumscribed by their respective associations and intermarriages with Anglo American men who will presumably end their oppression under the Spanish Mexican patriarch. As a result, the text proposes that Anglo American culture is egalitarian while Spanish Mexican culture marginalizes and oppresses both men and women. Garza-Falcón comments on González and Raleigh's treatment of the Texas Rangers and praising of Anglo American patriarchy in the text, "The Americanos, on the other hand, will supposedly not be their master/owner, will not abuse their daughters, will not whip them into subservience, but instead offer them wages, an opportunity to vote, and mastery over their own destiny" (1998, 123). Of course, Anglo American marginalization of people of Mexican descent, Native Americans, and African Americans, among many other groups, indicates that such egalitarian treatment has not been the case, thereby suggesting a romanticized view of white patriarchy offered by González and Raleigh in *Caballero*.

To a certain extent, González's valorizations of whiteness reveal the Anglo-dominated field in which she worked and her difficult navigation of Anglo racial binaries that circulated during her lifetime. Considering the social context in which González wrote as a woman of Mexican descent, her valorization of Anglo American masculinity speaks to her complex position as a Mexican American woman in the academy: her novel illustrates how she negotiated both the Eurocentric and male world of the university and gendered ideologies of her culture and society. González's commitment to representing her culture within academia and the larger public is significant. Her representations of women's resistance to the view of their identities as objects of culture and tradition in *Caballero* indicates how she used her folkloric work to critique gendered ideologies during a time when both the social and cultural history of Mexicanos in the US Southwest and women's histories were marginalized in the academy and publishing industry.

PUBLIC DISPLAYS OF DOMESTICITY AND NOSTALGIA IN *ROMANCE OF A LITTLE VILLAGE GIRL*

Cleofas Jaramillo also esteemed Spanish Mexican heritage and culture from the space of the domestic during a time of increased stigmatization of people of Mexican descent in the mid-twentieth century. The historical context in which she wrote, and her experiences growing up as a *Nuevo Mexicano* woman in the northern New Mexican village of Arroyo Hondo, shape her public discourse of Spanish elitism. Jaramillo's early experiences positioned her among the elite *Nuevo Mexicanos.* Her father's success in livestock, mining, and merchandising, along with her husband Venceslao Jaramillo's prominence in politics and business, led to Jaramillo's comfortable lifestyle in the upper-class New Mexico political scene. Jaramillo's representations of Spanishness are therefore influenced by her class and social status.

Jaramillo's claims to elite status are influenced by the dominant Anglo racial discourses circulating in academia and gala events about people of Mexican descent. Such discourses emerged and developed within a tourist culture that was at the heart of the Spanish Revival in New Mexico, spanning 1880 to 1930 (D. González 1999; Montgomery 2002; Nieto-Phillips 2004). In New Mexico, racialized discourses of Spanish identity and culture were institutionalized on a statewide level, for they played a central role in the annexation of New Mexico as a US territory. In the push for statehood, Anglo American and Spanish Mexican politicians positioned the majority Mexican population as descendants of a pure Spanish, or white, ancestry. Such associations were intended to render communities of Mexican descent in New Mexico as deserving of self-government and American civic rights and responsibilities (Nieto-Phillips 2004, 82). In the process of advocating statehood, Anglo American politicians vigorously constructed a tourist industry using racial binaries that portrayed Mexicans as descendants of Spanish conquistadores and Indians as docile, sedentary, and semi-civilized; such discourses were deemed necessary to assert the "civility" of New Mexico's Indian and Mexican inhabitants against nineteenth- and twentieth-century constructions of Indians as "savages" and Mexicans as "greasers" (Nieto-Phillips 2004, 119).

Jaramillo played a central role in the Spanish Revival, and, through this role, she catered to Anglo discourses of Spanishness with her founding of the La Sociedad Folklórica in New Mexico in the 1930s. La Sociedad Folklórica was a social network of women whose membership was only open to those women who claimed a Spanish ancestry. Jaramillo began the organization intent on educating Anglo American newcomers who did not understand and appreciate Spanish cultural traditions. Her aim to document Spanish cultural traditions suggests her radical move to control public representation of Spanish Mexican cultural practices within the Anglo-controlled discourse of the Spanish Revival. Her decision to found La Sociedad Folklórica was generated by a newspaper article on the public display of Anglo American heirlooms in antebellum mansions of the Deep South. Jaramillo decided that if Southern Anglo American women could assert their domestic traditions within institutionalized and public spaces, then Spanish Mexican women should also have the power to do so. Jaramillo writes, "This sounds so much like our Santa Fe Fiesta ought to be, I thought. Our mansions have crumbled back to the earth from which they sprung. Nevertheless, if we were to ransack our mothers' old trunks, I believe we would find some old-fashioned silk gowns and jewels. So far we have been seeing mostly what Americans have arranged" (Jaramillo 2000, 174).

Despite Jaramillo's aim to document Spanish Mexican women's experiences and homes from the perspective of women of Mexican descent (in response to what she saw as an exclusion of their perspectives in the historical record), La Sociedad Folklórica was not inclusive. The organization excluded mestizas from membership in the society, since Spanish ancestry and heritage was a criterion for inclusion in the group. Such prerequisites indicate how Jaramillo aligned herself as Spanish and white, excluding mestizas and Native American women as part of the historical record of the US Southwest. According to Jaramillo, "[T]he society should be composed of only thirty members, all of whom must be of Spanish descent, and that the meetings must be conducted in the Spanish language, with the aim of preserving our language, customs, and traditions" (Jaramillo 2000, 176). The women whom Jaramillo invited to the first La Sociedad Folklórica event, "twenty [women] from the elite of the Spanish families of the city," demonstrate that proof of one's Spanishness was ultimately tied to class (Jaramillo 2000, 174). And, like Spanish colonialism's preservation of pure Spanish bloodlines, Jaramillo's society sought to maintain the "nobility" of the organization through establishing claims to whiteness. Ultimately, Jaramillo's La Sociedad Folklórica valorized and upheld a supposed Spanish Mexican culture that was white and upper class, and not mestizo and working class, to Anglo American audiences.

The discourses of Hispanophilia and Southwestern regionalism that grew out of the Spanish Revival were influential in shaping Jaramillo's public articulation of a supposed pure Spanish heritage. The Anglo-controlled discourse of Hispanophilia constructed people of Mexican descent and Native Americans as embodying noble virtues, such as idealism, piety, gentility, generosity, manliness, and benevolence. Hispanophiles argued that these so-called Spanish traits were disintegrating with the rise of Anglo American materialism and individualism (Nieto-Phillips 2004, 147). Thus, the Hispanophilia Movement argued that noble Anglo Americans must preserve and protect the Spanish identity of New Mexico in order to return to a utopic and "simpler" way of life for people living in New Mexico. Several texts by Anglo American writers about the Southwest, such as Dobie's *Coronado's Children* (1930) and Charles F. Lummis's *The Land of Poco Tiempo* (1893), depict the Southwest as a "picturesque social utopia" where Mexicans lived out of time and isolated from social and cultural events (Padilla 1993, 208–213). Popular authors of Hispanophilia painted charming scenes of New Mexico's colonial past to attract Anglo American tourists to the region and to help new Anglo residents make sense of the state's racial demographics (Nieto-Phillips 2004, 147). Several popular magazines also participated in the discourse of Hispanophilia. As early as 1914, an article titled "Our Spanish-American Fellow Citizens" in *Harper's Weekly* states that "Spanish people in New Mexico . . . are not of the mixed breed one finds south of the Rio Grande, or even in Arizona, where there is a small remnant of Spanish blood. Indeed, it is probable that there is no purer Spanish stock than in Old Spain itself" (qtd. in Padilla 1993, 216).

Given the prominence of Anglo American racial discourses in New Mexico's assertions of Spanishness, Jaramillo's role in the Spanish Revival is significant. Her establishment of La Sociedad Folklórica illustrates the important role of Spanish Mexican women who sought to control and self-author Anglo public discourses about their communities; in contrast to Hispanophilia, Jaramillo employed *Hispanidad*, which entailed claiming ownership of her history, language, values, and belief systems (Nieto-Phillips 2004, 170–171). As Padilla explains, "Romanticizing memorials about the past [is an attempt] to exercise some control over the discourse in which native peoples were represented" (1993, 222). Yet Jaramillo's involvement also illustrates the Spanish Revival's problematic incorporation of women's voices, because a more feminized discourse was perceived to be more palatable to Anglo American outsiders. As Montgomery explains, just as Anglos were more comfortable with people of Mexican descent who were so-called Spanish rather than mestizo and Mexican, they were also at ease with a feminized representation of this Spanish culture. Montgomery explains, "As weavers, dressmakers, cooks, and folk dancers, women symbolized a domesticated people, a people who built stable households in picturesque villages" (2002, 154).

Jaramillo's autobiography, *Romance of a Little Village Girl,* ultimately upends the image of women of Mexican descent as passive recipients of the feminization and domestication of their communities. Like her folkloric activities, her autobiography illustrates the important role of the domestic sphere in negotiating dominant Anglo racial discourses circulating during her lifetime.[14] During the 1950s, when Jaramillo wrote *Romance of a Little Village Girl,* anti-Mexican hysteria and racial discourses about legal and illegal immigration that began in the 1930s reintensified when several interest groups claimed that undocumented Mexican immigrants were once again a menace to the white working-class American community in the United States. These groups believed that a new influx of Mexican immigrants that came to the United States in the 1940s under the Bracero Program were a danger to the social, political, and economic stability of the country. Racial discrimination toward this new wave of undocumented Mexican immigrants led to "Operation Wetback," which, as Juan Ramón García notes, deemed the citizenship and legal status of all people of Mexican descent as suspect. Even though the campaign was aimed at "illegals," Operation Wetback targeted one racial group, placing the burden of proving citizenship on anyone who claimed or appeared to have Mexican ancestry (1980, 230–231). Jaramillo's valorization of a pure Spanish ancestry in *Romance of a Little Village Girl* therefore illustrates a desire to position her Spanish culture as elite and white against the Anglo American conception, commonly accepted during the 1950s, of all Mexicans as laborers, racialized as nonwhite, and illegal.

Like González's novel, Jaramillo's autobiography represents her Spanish Mexican community in a nostalgic discourse that ultimately constructs a fantasized view of the past that overlooks the social history of the Southwest. For Jaramillo, this nostalgia is a strategy of ensuring that New Mexican histories do not exclude her community. Such moments of nostalgia disregard the Native American influences on the Southwest border region and the complex racial-caste system that grew out of Spanish colonization and intermarriage. In the following passage, Jaramillo configures her home and community as an isolated paradise that elides such social histories. In Jaramillo's social utopia, people of Mexican descent freely practice their traditions and customs, uncontaminated by the outside world: "In this little valley of the Arroyo Hondo River, situated in the northern part of the state of New Mexico, hemmed in by high mountains and hills, sheltered from the contamination of the outside world, the inhabitants lived peacefully, preserving the customs and traditions of their ancestors. Here in this verdant little nook the authoress was born and reared . . ." (Jaramillo 2000, ix).

Jaramillo's perspective of her community as "sheltered from the contamination of the outside world" functions to project the image of a pure Spanish bloodline she traces back to the conquest of the region. As Nieto-Phillips explains,

"The initial 'contaminant' of Spanish blood in America was 'Indian' blood; however, with the spread of African slavery, so-called negros (blacks) also became an additional referent against which Spanish identity would be cast" (2004, 23). Her romanticization and construction of an isolated Spanish past and assertions of her community as pure and white is one more example of how Jaramillo used her writings to claim whiteness.

Despite such attempts to cater to existing racial categories, Jaramillo's autobiography reveals profound tensions between assertions of Spanish elitism and the actual social strife and decline of material wealth experienced by her family. Jaramillo used Spanish-colonial domesticity in her folkloric activities and in *Romance of a Little Village Girl* to resist the elision of Hispano culture and society in dominant New Mexican histories. Yet she also used representations of domestic spaces to mask the decline of her social and economic status, enabling her to retain her dignity in a hostile racial climate. According to Montgomery, public displays of Spanish heritage operated on a symbolic level and were purposefully fashioned for public experience. He explains, "On the upper Rio Grande, the modern Spanish heritage was not only expressed and dramatized in public but was constructed as a public realm, a figurative place in which all New Mexicans— Hispano and Anglo, rich and poor—might reside" (Montgomery 2002, 14). If we consider public displays of Spanishness, specifically domestic spaces, as symbolic sites, then Jaramillo's assertions of Spanish domesticity functioned as powerful rhetorical tools: they enable her to resist, while simultaneously mask, the widespread racial disenfranchisement and socioeconomic marginalization of her Spanish Mexican community in New Mexico.

Furthermore, Jaramillo's autobiography reveals that Anglo Americans rarely viewed people of Mexican descent as their equals. Such discrepancies are made evident by the economic deterioration of her birthplace. In the following passage, Jaramillo narrates the visible economic and social shifts occurring in Arroyo Seco—a town close to the neighborhood of Arroyo Hondo. She describes the noticeable shifts that have taken place in this nearby community, as the formerly esteemed "idyllic paradise" has been destroyed in the early twentieth century. Jaramillo is brought to tears as she recounts her visit to Arroyo Seco in the 1920s, when she finds the homes deteriorating: "After lunch, I thought of the Valdez home at Placita. The round *torrion* always had marked this nice home for me; but now I could not find it; and we rode on to Arroyo Seco to see the fine Gonzales home. We were standing right before it, but I did not recognize it. 'Where is Juanita Gonzales' home?' I asked a man in the yard. 'This is the house,' he answered. The whitewashed porch with blue railing posts was gone, and the whole house was in ruins" (Jaramillo 2000, 119). Jaramillo's discovery that several homes of this neighboring community are in ruins devastates her: "It was hard to believe my eyes that what I was seeing were the melting remains of these once big, fine lively homes. A sob choked in my throat" (Jaramillo 2000, 119). The material decline of Jaramillo's community exposes public displays of an elite Spanishness articulated by both Anglo Americans and Spanish Mexicans in New Mexico as facades. As Deena González reminds us, Spanish Mexican women "who survived the conquest . . . emerged financially poorer than when it began, and their descendants remain there today. In that sense, their accommodation to Euro-American ways can be depicted as a linear descent into poverty" (1999, 5).

Jaramillo's autobiography reveals how Anglo American articulations and calls to preserve Spanishness in New Mexico mostly took place on a symbolic level. During the time she writes her autobiography, the social landscape of her community shifted both demographically and architecturally from a Spanish-identified, Mexican, and Native American population to one that was increasingly Anglo and European. Jaramillo notes how the architecture of the region reflects these demographic shifts. Jaramillo challenges Hispanophilia when she argues that Anglo racial projects of whiteness led to the decline of Spanish Mexican culture in the region. As Jaramillo recounts her visit to Arroyo Hondo in the 1940s, she explains how Anglo American domination of the area has shifted the Spanish Mexican cultural and social landscape into a homogenized white identity. By calling attention to the colonial structures of power that threaten her Spanish Mexican heritage, Jaramillo challenges the tenets of colonial discourse: "What a different aspect it now presented! High pitched roofs, a new, modern-looking schoolhouse—with nothing left but memories of our once lively, happy home, now in melting ruins. Only the foundation was left of the *capilla*, or chapel, of the Holy Family which my father had so devotedly cared for and repaired as long as his health permitted him to go there. With a sigh, I turned away from this sad sight" (Jaramillo 2000, 187). Jaramillo's description of her community makes clear how a Spanish colonial past built on Catholicism has been literally destroyed, a decline that began with US imperialism via the US-Mexico War in 1846 and subsequently the Treaty of Guadalupe Hidalgo in 1848. Jaramillo's reference to "high pitched roofs" indicates how traditional Spanish architecture that previously defined the region has been supplanted by English and German elements. That the Spanish schools have been replaced by "modern" ones alludes to the Americanization of the educational systems at that time. That her father, who had maintained the surviving chapel, is no longer alive, indicates the passing of the Spanish Mexican male lineage of the community. The phrase "melting ruins," which Jaramillo uses repeatedly throughout the text to describe her destroyed community, subverts the "melting pot" ideology of American identity. With the term, Jaramillo emphasizes how such projects sought to eliminate "Spanish" culture through assimilation. The expression "melting pot" has been used historically to define the acceptance of "multiculturalism" in the national sphere, premised on "foreign" cultures assimilating or "melting" into a white homogenized identity. That the homes of Jaramillo's community are in "melting ruins" suggests that the dominant culture views Spanish Mexican culture as needing to assimilate into a white American identity.

Jaramillo's actual social and economic status in the 1930s and 1940s as a "financially troubled widow living in a small apartment off the main plaza in Santa Fe" also calls attention to the symbolic nature of "Spanish" Fantasy Heritage discourse (Padilla 1993, 220). Jaramillo's financial position stands in stark contrast to her construction of herself as an elite Spanish doña with her folkloric activities. Deena González explains that the material and economic decline of Spanish Mexican women in New Mexico began soon after the Anglo American conquest of land in 1846. She states, "[C]olonialism on the former Mexican northern frontier affected all classes and both sexes. Even the upper-crust Spanish Mexicans suffered as they watched their wealth decline" (1999, 11). The decline of Jaramillo's wealth and social status occurred, like that of many other widowed upper-class Spanish Mexican women, when Jaramillo's husband, Venceslao, died in 1920; as a result, she was forced to sell their ranch. By the mid-1920s, Jaramillo responded to the losses of the *rico* Spanish Mexican families by positioning herself as a descendent of Spanish conquistadores (Montgomery 2002, 22).

In response to the decline of upper-class Spanish Mexican women's wealth, Jaramillo's autobiography illustrates how visible representations of Spanish Mexican homes functioned as strategies of survival. As Jaramillo reflects back on the modest Santa Fe apartment where she has lived for several years, she explains the central role of her home in the preservation of her Spanish culture. Despite various offers, presumably by Anglos, to purchase Jaramillo's new home as Santa Fe becomes a popular tourist attraction (money that Jaramillo could no doubt use as a widow of modest financial means), she refuses to sell her apartment. She explains, "For more than ten years people have been coming, trying to buy my house. 'I like the location,' they tell me. And when they see the nearly three-foot thick inside walls, they add, 'And these substantial walls.' I like them, too. I have become too attached to their warmth, and the deep window sills which furnish me space on which to keep my only living companions, my flowering plants. This house is a symbol of the past which I love" (Jaramillo 2000, 192). Jaramillo's refusal to sell her apartment illustrates how she viewed the home as a symbol of Spanish culture and identity necessary in the project to resist the colonization of her community.

Jaramillo also demonstrates how public displays of Spanish Mexican homes ultimately enabled upper-class women to resist certain aspects of their colonization. Toward the end of her autobiography, she portrays the effect of the tourist culture at the heart of the New Mexican Spanish Revival on women's sense of themselves and their culture. In these moments, Jaramillo conveys traces of resistance to Anglo racial discourses: she begins to articulate how commodification of Spanish Mexican culture within New Mexico's Spanish Revival is responsible for the decline of her wealth and prestige. After Jaramillo discovers the ruined Gonzales home, she and her Anglo American friend Ruth Laughlin Barker go inside and visit with Juanita Gonzales. Barker was an influential member of the Spanish Revival in Santa Fe. Her book *Caballeros*, interestingly close in title to Jovita González's novel, is a romantic account of Santa Fe that connects ordinary Mexicans of New Mexico to a Spanish legacy to assert their whiteness and validity as New Mexican residents (Jaramillo 2000, 198). Barker initiates the visit to Arroyo Seco with Jaramillo because she is writing a book on Spanish-style houses. Jaramillo explains the transaction that occurs:

> Juanita, whom her mother always had kept so well dressed at school, came to the door with torn hose and shabby shoes. She asked us to come in. I asked her if she had some of her mother's fine jewelry and table-silver. She brought out a silver set with an exquisite design and silver grape bunches on the lids. My friend [Barker] became interested right away to buy it. Juanita asked $35.00. I am sure it was worth more, but my friend continued to bargain until she finally said, "I will give you a $15.00 check." I shook my hand at the side "no," but Juanita only smiled at me . . . and answered, "Alright." This is how our rich Spanish families have been stripped of their most precious belongings. "Why did you do it?" I whispered as I was going out the door. "I need the money to fix the house," she said. (Jaramillo 2000, 119)

The economic transaction that occurs between Ruth and Juanita indicates that Ruth views Spanish culture as a product for consumption and appropriation. Yet what is most interesting is Jaramillo's and Juanita's response to Ruth's problematic co-optation of Spanish Mexican culture. Jaramillo's reaction to Juanita's choice to sell her silver—her gesture "no" and subsequent question "why did you do it?"—reveals Jaramillo's mournful response to the effect of Anglo colonization and appropriation of Spanish culture on upper-class Spanish Mexican women's social status. Juanita's reluctant choice to sell her Spanish colonial objects of domesticity so that she may presumably fix the outside of her home suggests that public visibility and appearance of her Spanish Mexican home has become more important than clinging to the culture within it. Yet while it might appear that Juanita is complicit in Anglo American consumption of Spanish culture because she sells her silver, it is important to remember the two choices that confront her: she must either sell the objects within her home to fix it or continue to live in a visibly disintegrating home. One perspective of this transaction would suggest that by selling traditional cultural objects, Juanita is surrendering to a commodity culture and giving up her Spanish Mexican identity. Yet the tranquility with which Juanita gives up her silver pieces suggests that a second economy influences her decision, one which often goes by the term "potlatch" economy or "economy of the gift." According to the logic of this economy, increased value does not depend on selling objects for profit. Rather, increased value depends on how much one can give away, or, in Juanita's case, sell at a loss, without losing the one thing, which Annette B. Weiner terms the "inalienable possession," that maintains the identity of the group (1992).[15] In this light, Juanita's choice to sell her silver suggests that Spanish New Mexican women were perhaps able to maintain their cultural identity by preserving something, whose value others cannot see, even while selling everything else.

Concluding Remarks

As Jaramillo's autobiography reveals, rhetorical assertions of Spanish domesticity could not slow the material decline of her community or close the socioeconomic gap between Mexican and Anglo American communities. As Nieto-Phillips explains, "By the 1940s both 'American' and 'Mexican American' observers regarded [the Spanish revival] as little more than a Spanish façade masking widespread poverty and profound tensions among Anglos and *Nuevo Mexicanos*, and among Mexican-origin peoples in the Southwest more broadly" (2004, 8). Yet while it might appear that González and Jaramillo accommodated Anglo American racial discourses, they managed to resist aspects of their colonization and refute colonialism's basic tenet of domination by authoring their histories. The role of the domestic in their representations must not be understated. Both authors reveal the important role of the domestic as a site of negotiation for women of Mexican descent living amid the legacy of colonialism and mid-twentieth-century immigration projects that utilized discourses of white/nonwhite and legal/illegal. Their texts illustrate that the home, while it can function in the safety of the private sphere, can also be used as a space to respond to gendered inequalities, as well as ethnic and racial injustice. The chapter that follows illustrates how the domestic sphere became the site by which New Mexican home economist and author Fabiola Cabeza de Baca both upheld and challenged class, racial, and geographical borders on both sides of the US-Mexico border. Similar to González and Jaramillo, Cabeza de Baca's home economics work and writings about the domestic sphere respond to nativist fears of the ethnic and immigrant "other" and increased immigrant restrictions along the US Southwest frontier. Her narratives also engaged with national and transnational debates about racial and ethnic identity, particularly from the late 1920s, the end of the Progressive Era, to the 1950s, the postwar and cold war period.

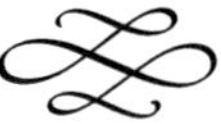

CHAPTER 3

Domestic Power across Borders

FABIOLA CABEZA DE BACA'S HOME ECONOMICS WORK IN NEW MEXICO AND MEXICO

In her essay "New Mexican Diets" in the *Journal of Home Economics*, Fabiola Cabeza de Baca recounts her visit to northern rural New Mexico in 1929 and her surprise at being served fried potatoes with canned corn beef and white bread by a family of Mexican descent who invited her to dinner (1942).[1] Cabeza de Baca was visiting the family as part of her home extension service work for the New Mexico Agricultural Extension Service (NMAES), a New Deal government agency, to assist families with the task of improving their domestic economies in both their households and farms in order to meet the needs of food production in a devastated New Mexican rural economy. Northern New Mexican farms were greatly affected by the spread of the Great Depression from urban to rural areas, heightened by one of the worst droughts in the history of the US Southwest, which left thousands of farm families economically distressed (Jensen 1986b, 29). In her article, Cabeza de Baca explains that while the family served her this separate meal, they ate beans, chili, whole-wheat tortillas, cheese, and other milk dishes—dishes that were more native to the region. When she asked them why they did not serve her the same food they ate, they inquired: "We thought you didn't like the kind of food we poor people ate?" (1942, 668).

Whether the family served Cabeza de Baca Americanized food to be good hosts, or whether the family was unable to afford such food to feed everyone at the dinner table, their response indicates a knowledge of the dominant view of their diet as inferior and lower to "American" food. In the *Journal of Home Economics* article, Cabeza de Baca attributes this view of native foods as inferior to the newcomers—many of them Anglo and of non-Mexican descent—to the region in the nineteenth century: "With the coming of the railroad, a varied population, many of them adventurers, began to come into New Mexico. They found the Indian and Spaniard hard to understand and criticized and ridiculed

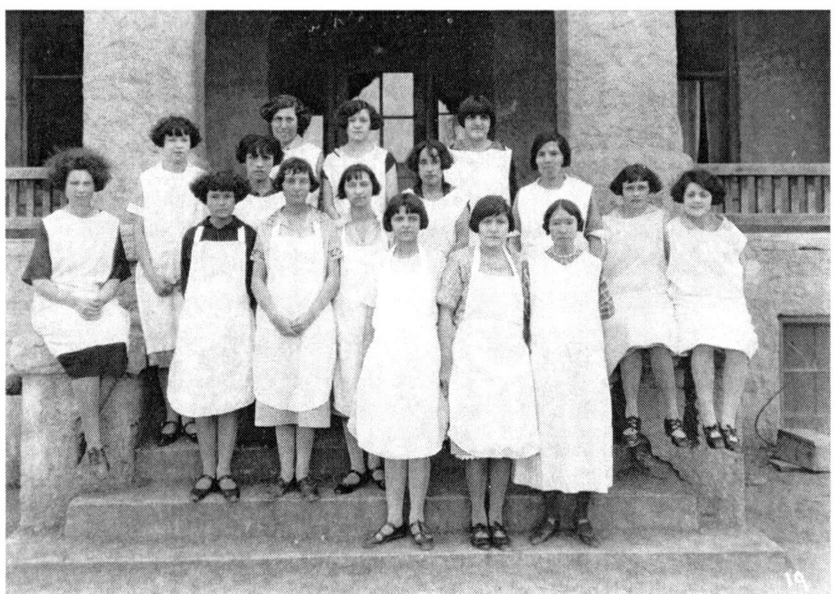

Figure 5. Fabiola Cabeza de Baca Gilbert with home economics students at El Rito
Normal School, c. 1928. Fabiola Cabeza de Baca Gilbert Photograph Collection (PICT
000–6030), Center for Southwest Research, University Libraries, University of New
Mexico.

their social customs, religion and food habits" (1942, 668). Since Cabeza de Baca
was an agent of the NMAES and was of a higher social and class position than
many of the women with whom she worked, they must have viewed her as a
descendant of one of these outsiders. If they were self-conscious or embarrassed
about their food, they might have eaten the potatoes, corn beef, and white bread
right along with her. Yet the family's performance of serving Cabeza de Baca one
thing, and eating something distinctly different in front of her, serves to highlight
a consciousness of these racial and class differences.

Cabeza de Baca's visit and exchange with the northern New Mexican family captures a fundamental aspect of her work in her over thirty-year career
as a home economist: as a Spanish-speaking woman of Mexican descent, she
valued and comprehended the cultural and culinary traditions of the families
she assisted. She therefore often functioned as a cultural mediator between the
dominant paradigms of the agencies she worked for and the native and indigenous cultural beliefs of the women she frequently promoted in her writings.
Similar to the women she assisted, Cabeza de Baca was of Mexican descent and
had extensive knowledge of native foods in New Mexico, shared some of their
cultural traditions, and spoke the same language. Yet distinct from these women,
she was born into a distinguished ranching and land-owning family in northern

New Mexico and was therefore of a higher class status; like many women of her social class, she also attended high school and received a college education. As one of the few Spanish-speaking home extension agents in the area, she also frequently prepared and published recipes and bulletins in Spanish to encourage the women in the northern New Mexican villages to gain knowledge on "modern" food preparation, such as using pressure cookers and canning (fig. 5). Yet because she was an agent of the NMAES and was of a higher social and class position, many of these families viewed her as an outsider. She therefore had to work hard to convince the northern New Mexican families that she was "one of them" because she shared their tastes and valued their foods.

Due to her expertise in home economics, her Spanish-language fluency, and her previous work with rural communities in New Mexico, Cabeza de Baca was asked by the United Nations to assist efforts to train Central and South American students to set up agricultural extension programs in their home countries among indigenous communities. She therefore extended her role as a cultural mediator in New Mexico to her work with rural and indigenous women across the US-Mexico border in Mexico. In 1951, she served as a home demonstration agent in Patzcuaro, Mexico, through a United Nations Education, Scientific, and Cultural Organization (UNESCO) effort to address poverty in Latin America.[2] Her home demonstration work in Mexico was part of a larger UNESCO project to eliminate poverty and illiteracy in Latin America under a philosophy called "fundamental education," in which illiteracy and basic health needs are viewed in conjunction. In Patzcuaro, she trained over fifty aspiring home economists from Peru, Ecuador, Bolivia, Costa Rica, Guatemala, Honduras, Haiti, El Salvador, and Mexico; this work indicates how her home economics philosophies would ultimately extend beyond both New Mexico and Mexico into Latin America. Students who enrolled in the UNESCO program went with Cabeza de Baca to work with Tarascan Indian villages in Patzcuaro to observe the skills she had gained working with Mexican and indigenous communities in New Mexico, skills that they would later apply in their home countries. Cabeza de Baca's few published articles about her home economics work in Mexico indicates how she, as she did in New Mexico, affirmed the indigenous culture and food traditions of the Tarascan men and women she assisted.

This chapter explores the various domestic negotiations that Cabeza de Baca enacted in her career as a home economist from the late 1920s to the 1950s. I argue that the domestic sphere became the site by which she both upheld and challenged class, racial, and geographical borders on both sides of the US-Mexico border. In both New Mexico and Mexico, Cabeza de Baca's home economics work engaged in larger national and transnational debates about racial and ethnic identity from the early to mid-twentieth century, a period defined by nativist fears of the ethnic and immigrant "other" and increased immigrant restrictions along the US Southwest frontier. Her writings about home economics in both the United States and Latin America powerfully illustrate the double meaning of the domestic as both household and nation because, as a home economist, she was often expected to improve the homes and lives of marginalized communities according to racialized definitions of regional and national identity. As Kaplan describes, "the *domestic* has a double meaning that not only links the familial household to the nation but also imagines both in opposition to everything outside the geographic and conceptual border of the home" (2002, 183).

I examine both Cabeza de Baca's unpublished notes and her published writings about home economics.[3] These writings convey how she sought to affirm the cultural traditions and foods of the women she assisted to home economists, agricultural extension workers, and the general public. Depending on her audience and her particular goal of the moment, Cabeza de Baca's writings either catered to or challenged nativist and dominant fears of the marginalized ethnic "other" prevalent in the contexts and periods in which she worked.

Cabeza de Baca began her work as a home economist in 1929,[4] several years after the end of the Progressive Era, a period that many scholars argue did not live up to its optimistic rhetoric of an advancing society. For many racial and ethnic minorities, the Progressive Era was defined by nativist and racial fears and increased immigration restrictions and racial segregation (Rich 2009; Ruiz 1998; Sánchez 1993). The remarkable visibility of home economics reflected the view that women's domestic leadership in the public sphere was a logical extension of domestic duties in the private sphere (Rich 2009). On a national scale, home economics reflected the goals of a racialized Americanization, which, as Anne Ruggles Gere explains, took a "racist, exclusionary, and elitist perspective on citizenship, putting white Protestant Anglo-Saxon males at the top of the national hierarchy, and insisting that immigrants emulate that model" (1997, 58). For example, Americanization proponents viewed many Eastern European, Mexican, and Asian immigrants, as well as native-born US citizens of Mexican descent, as social problems who had the ability to become "Americans" if only they were to change their domestic practices (Romero 2008; Sánchez 1993). Home economics, as a profession, reflected these values, and the profession often focused on the assimilability of nonwhite immigrants into monolithic definitions of US identity (Romero 2008; Sánchez 1993). Yet as a worker for the NMAES, Cabeza de Baca was able to transgress certain aspects of Americanization, as the agency's success in the Northern New Mexico region depended on its ability to incorporate the culture and language of the majority Mexican and native peoples.

Cabeza de Baca's work in Mexico during the postwar era of the 1950s was also tied to a "modernization" mindset that viewed rural Mexican and indigenous peoples as in need of modern domestic technology to improve their homes and lives. Though UNESCO promoted a politics of inclusivity and mandated the eradication of racial and geopolitical borders through economic development in the third world as a response to the end of the Second World War, the organization expected Cabeza de Baca to introduce "Western" domestic technologies and philosophies to the Latin American agricultural and home extension agents she trained. Defined as an essential component of economic development in Latin America, UNESCO's literacy program in Patzcuaro sought to facilitate "the westernization of poorer countries, of fostering a social and political consciousness among their peoples along, in essence, western lines" (Jones 1988, 34).

Cabeza de Baca's work with rural and indigenous communities has profound significance. While home economics was frequently linked to projects related to the assimilation of nonwhite women or third world peoples into racialized nationalisms, Cabeza de Baca sought to affirm the value of Mexican and indigenous women's lives and cultures. In New Mexico, she challenged monolithic definitions of identity by representing culture as a process of exchange of customs, traditions, and values between various subcultures. In Mexico, she promoted cultural tolerance for the communities she assisted and emphasized the social and cultural factors that lead to their poverty—a focus on structural factors that was often missing in the accounts by many other home economists in this period.

Language was crucial to the way Cabeza de Baca both reified and challenged the tenets of Americanization and racialized nationalism. In both the United States and Mexico, her home economics training and history of success—augmented by what the NMAES and UNESCO perceived as essential Spanish-speaking skills—were perceived as great assets in those agencies' goals to modernize rural and indigenous populations. Spanish fluency combined with domesticity therefore became a source of professional status and upward mobility for Cabeza de Baca. Yet for the women she assisted, language and domesticity often became a means to not only empowerment but also marginalization. By introducing modern domestic technologies, such as canning and the pressure cooker, into these women's homes, she assisted their economic development but also facilitated the loss of native preserving traditions, such as drying.[5] As an agent of the NMAES and UNESCO, she represented institutions that emphasized government intrusion into communities that had previously been able to survive through adaptation (Deutsch 1987, 185).

Cabeza de Baca's work and writing are therefore not without their contradictions and complications. Her focus on modernizing the ethnic "other" reflected the goals of the various agencies she worked for and the larger dominant narratives about ethnic minorities in the nativist periods in which she worked. Such views also reflected her own personal narratives about race as an upper-class woman of Mexican descent living and working in a hostile racial climate in the United States. Even though she valued the culinary and cultural traditions of the women she assisted, she also frequently positioned herself as racially distinct from the Mexicano and indigenous communities in the United States and Mexico she sought to help. As we saw with Jaramillo and González in the previous chapter, Cabeza de Baca's autobiographical and professional writing also frequently claimed a Spanishness and whiteness that separated her from rural Mexicano and native communities in the United States. In this way, both her personal and professional writings often upheld the nativist rhetoric that she sought to challenge in her home economics publications.[6] Yet unlike González and Jaramillo, Cabeza de Baca used the space of the domestic to cross racial and class borders, even as she reified them.

An unpublished and undated diary entry by Cabeza de Baca exemplifies how she often signified Spanishness as a primary characteristic of her identity. She writes that she was brought up by her father, Don Graciano Cabeza de Baca, and grandmother, Estefanita Delgado Cabeza de Baca, both of whom she describes as "very Spanish."[7] This is a significant rhetorical gesture or "whiteness demonstration," a "symbolic shorthand[s] for genealogical connection to imperial Spain and its colonizing projects" (Sánchez 2001, 66). With "whiteness demonstrations," Cabeza de Baca signified the Spanishness of her family as a way to stake claims within the literal and figurative borders of the US nation. She also wrote fondly about her paternal great-grandfather, Don Luis María Cabeza de Baca, who was given a land grant title by the Mexican government in 1823 (Reed 2005, 125). She therefore felt she belonged to a family with prominent roots in New Mexico's Spanish colonial past. As discussed in the previous chapter, while Cabeza de Baca and other women of the upper classes in New Mexico may have referred to themselves as "Spaniards," the majority were not Spanish, but mestizos, persons of mixed Native/indigenous and Spanish ancestry (D. González 1999; Nieto-Phillips 2004).[8] Furthermore, the rural Mexican and indigenous women Cabeza de Baca assisted were not able to assert claims to a New Mexican identity through whiteness because markers of Spanishness were connected to social status (D. González 1999; Nieto-Phillips 2004).

Cabeza de Baca's capitulation to dominant racial binaries of her time in many of her published writings, including her most popular works, *We Fed Them Cactus* and *The Good Life*, troubled early Chicana/o studies scholars. Her reception by Chicana/o literary scholars was similar to the negative responses to New Mexican writer and folklorist Cleofas Jaramillo and Tejana novelist and folklorist Jovita González, discussed in the previous chapter. Raymund Paredes was the first Chicana/o studies scholar to dismiss Cabeza de Baca and other Mexican American female authors of this period for espousing what he termed a "hacienda mentality" or claims to Spanish identity status that cater to dominant Anglo American narratives of race (1982). It was not until Chicana feminist scholar Tey Diane Rebolledo praised and argued for the critical role of these early Mexican American women writers that authors such as Cabeza de Baca became esteemed within the Chicana/o literary canon. Chicana/o studies scholar Genaro Padilla also argued that early Mexican American female authors did not overtly critique Anglo domination and the marginalization of their communities, because otherwise they would not have gotten their work published (1993). As a result of

Rebolledo's and Padilla's path-breaking work on early women writers like Cabeza de Baca, many contemporary Chicana/o studies and American studies scholars now acknowledge the important contributions of Cabeza de Baca's writings to the ethnic studies literary canon, as well as her profound contributions as a home economist.[9]

In what follows, I carefully situate Cabeza de Baca's writings about her home economics work in both New Mexico and Mexico alongside dominant racial narratives prevalent in both spaces. I do so to suggest that, while there are elements in her texts that cater to existing binaries of domestic/foreign, citizen/noncitizen, and civilized/primitive, her emphasis on cultural diversity, tolerance, and the social structures leading to poverty, stands in stark contrast to the nativist and exclusionary narratives that circulated about the communities she assisted. Such writings illustrate the way she used home economics to speak to a broader public about the pertinent issues affecting marginalized communities in both New Mexico and Mexico, at times both challenging and supporting audience's racialized assumptions about these groups.

Domestic Power: Home Economics as a Response to Nativism

In the "New Mexican Diets" essay for the *Journal of Home Economics* discussed at the outset of this chapter, Cabeza de Baca used the example of her exchange with the rural New Mexican family to persuade home economics workers to tolerate cultural diversity. After she recounts her visit, she writes the following: "The public worker must be sympathetic with people she works with regardless of their background or extraction; she must respect their customs, their habits and beliefs; and foremost she must know that though individuals may differ, people are people in language, race, or creed" (1942, 668–669). Given the wider home economics movement focused on racialized nationalism, Cabeza de Baca's multicultural focus in this national home economics journal is significant. Her focus on tolerance and diversity counters a larger xenophobic climate, reflected in the other articles in the entire November 1942 *Journal of Home Economics* issue, as well as in the majority of the 1942 volume of the journal.

The 1940s was a pivotal decade, defined by nativist movements that had drastic material consequences for racialized groups who were considered "foreign" or who did not conform to American nationalist ideals of race and patriotism. The Japanese Internment in 1942, for example, led to the forced removal of over 100,000 Japanese Americans and Japanese from their homes to "War Relocation Camps" because they were considered potential "enemy aliens." It was also the year of the Sleepy Lagoon trial in Los Angeles, in which the press wrongly and racially vilified Mexican youth for the murder of José Diaz. The year 1942 was also the first year of the Bracero Program, a temporary guest worker program, which shifted the racial and ethnic demographics in the US Southwest, leading to xenophobic responses to a new group of Mexican immigrants, characterized by a larger discourse of "good" versus "bad" Mexicans. As Eduardo Obregón-Pagán writes, "Although the war may have seemed 'good' for some, it was not for all. The nation celebrated a kind of patriotism that was layered with troubling assumptions about power, race, and culture. Indeed, those who looked foreign or failed to conform to the celebrated 'American' ideal often paid the price" (2003, 7). During the war, nativist fears of the "other" led to drastic material consequences for several racialized groups in the United States, particularly a questioning of their patriotism, and ultimately their citizenship, which often broke up families and led to further economic disenfranchisement.

Cabeza de Baca's philosophy on respecting cultural diversity and tolerance within the pages of the national home economics journal stands in stark contrast to this larger context of wartime anxiety and fear of the "other." This xenophobia dominates the opening essay in the November 1942 *Journal of Home Economics* issue, titled "What We Must Teach" by Elmer Davis, referred to in the head note as the "now director of the Office of War Information." Davis's essay is an excerpt from a talk that he gave at the National Institute on Education and War. In it, he argues that teachers (and in the context of the journal, this would include home economists) should educate children about the particular wartime moment, specifically that "this is no ordinary war and no ordinary crisis, but probably the greatest turning point in human destiny to date" (1942, 633). As the article proceeds in dramatic fashion about the non-ordinariness of the war, Davis tells his audience: "Teach your students that the leaders of Japan and of Germany have taught their peoples that they are master races with a God-given right to rule everybody else—including us; and that an immense number of Japanese and Germans really believe it. Teach your students what it feels like to be conquered by such people—there is plenty of evidence, from Europe and Asia too. Teach your students that there is no safety, for us or anybody, till those men are beaten down" (1942, 634). Davis's remarks exemplify the larger nativist and wartime rhetoric of fearing the "other" in this period. It also stands in stark contrast to Cabeza de Baca's message of racial and cultural tolerance.

As would be expected, the majority of the articles in the 1942 volume of the *Journal of Home Economics* concern the effect of wartime realities on the home spaces of middle-class American families. For instance, in the essay "Family Saving and Spending Plans" in the same issue, the author Day Monroe focuses on the challenges of wartime spending on the American middle class. Yet the article's focus on this economic group presumes that all American families are confronting the economic impact of the war similarly. The essay's oversight of the connections between race, class, and gender becomes most apparent when compared with Cabeza de Baca's focus on the economic needs of the rural Mexican and native families in New Mexico, published in the same issue. All of the other articles in the entire 1942 volume discuss families, men, and women generally and generically, thereby indicating the role of whiteness and normative gender roles as invisible categories in the home economics journal.

When nonwhite groups are included in the 1942 volume of the *Journal of Home Economics*, they are mentioned in terms of a specific style of decoration or home décor in the advertisement section. For instance, in this and other volumes of the journal in the 1940s, advertisements frequently reference "Hispanic furniture," "Hispanic glass," "Hispanic lace," which, in this context, means "Spanish"; there are also frequent references to "Japanese embroidery." These examples only serve to illustrate the role of nonwhite culture as decoration in the pages of the volume, further adding to the journal's oversight of the home economics needs of nonwhite communities. Cabeza de Baca's focus on the specific needs of Mexican and native families in New Mexico in the 1942 issue is therefore significant— she is the only author that addresses nonwhite families or the specific cultural and ethnic needs of nonwhite communities.[10] Cabeza de Baca makes the following statement within her two-page essay: "The New Mexican housewife of Spanish extraction, like other wives, takes great pride in being a good homemaker, a good cook, and a good mother" (1942, 669). In saying this directly, she inserts the presence of the "New Mexican housewife of Spanish extraction" within the pages of the mostly Anglocentric journal.

Yet if we consider the rhetoric Cabeza de Baca uses to describe her ethnic identity and the communities in which she worked, we also see a woman catering to nativist binaries and fears of "good" and "bad" Mexicans during this period. In "New Mexican Diets," she repeatedly refers to the women and the families she sought to assist as "Spaniards" and "Indians," and repeatedly uses the phrase "of Spanish extraction." With such a phrase, she seeks to signal how she and the communities she worked for are of pure Spanish stock—and can therefore be traced back to the Spaniards—and are thus "good" Mexicans. With the term "Indian," she also conjures up popular representations of native peoples in New Mexico as noble and docile, images that were central to the Spanish Revival (Montgomery 2002). The repeated phrasing "of Spanish extraction" becomes further solidified as part of a dominant racialized rhetoric if we consider the "Editor's Note," which immediately follows the essay: "Mrs. Gilbert is herself of Spanish extraction and had part of her education in Spain" (1942, 669). This Editorial Note serves to further explain—just in case there are any questions by the reader—that Cabeza de Baca is indeed "Spanish," especially since "part" of her education took place in Spain. In reality, Cabeza de Baca only spent a year studying abroad in Spain as a primary student, with the majority of her education taking place in New Mexico. The editor's reference to Cabeza de Baca as Mrs. Gilbert, her husband's surname, also serves to obscure her Mexican heritage, even though Cabeza de Baca often used "Cabeza de Baca" as shorthand for her Spanishness. Cabeza de Baca was married to Carlos Gilbert from 1931 to 1941, so, at the time of the essay, she would no longer have been officially "Mrs. Gilbert." The editor's use of "Mrs.

Gilbert" therefore only serves to reinforce the whiteness of the journal, as well as the gendered norm of referring to a woman by her husband's surname after their separation.[11] It is also worthy to note that the other essays in the issue do not include an "Editorial Note" explaining the ethnic background of the authors, further supporting whiteness as an invisible category in the journal. Such "whiteness demonstrations" (Sánchez 2001) by both Cabeza de Baca and the editor illustrate the 1940s' larger nativist context and questioning of one's patriotism and racial identity.

The emphasis on whiteness in the 1942 issue of the *Journal of Home Economics*, with the exception of Cabeza de Baca's essay (even as it caters to whiteness definitions), reveals the strong links between domesticity, race, and nation in this period. As stated earlier, Cabeza de Baca's home economics work in northern rural New Mexico in the late 1920s through the 1940s took place amid a broader Americanization movement linked with racial nationalism. For people of Mexican descent, much of this movement targeted Mexican immigrant and Mexican American women and their families in their homes as a way to assimilate their families and communities into a white and English-language definition of US identity (Romero 2008; Ruiz 1998, Sánchez 1993). Many white, middle-class clubwomen and home economists participated in such Americanization projects, utilizing the extension of domesticity into the public sphere in their aims toward assimilating non-white communities into a racially white constructed US identity. Their goal was to "cleanse" their cities of undesirable immigrants, often associated with crime and "alien" qualities (Gere 1997, 78; Rich 2009, 24; Ruiz 1998). If we consider this larger context for Cabeza de Baca's 1942 "New Mexican Diets" essay, then her focus on rural New Mexican families—even as she positions them as "Spanish"—and her emphasis on tolerance and racial diversity reveals how she used her writings about her home economics work to intervene in dominant racial narratives affecting both the communities she assisted and herself.

DOMESTIC CONSUMPTION: CELEBRATING
THE ETHNIC "OTHER" IN NEW MEXICO

While Cabeza de Baca often used examples from her home economics work to emphasize cultural diversity to broader and national audiences, her calls for racial tolerance also catered to dominant narratives about Mexican and native communities, particularly within larger celebratory narratives about these communities in New Mexico. As discussed in the previous chapter, New Mexico has a long history of embracing its Mexican and indigenous populations within celebratory forms of multiculturalism, which has lead to romanticized portrayals of native and Mexican-descent peoples—celebratory and romantic narratives that stand in stark contrast to the material, racial, and economic disenfranchisement experienced historically by these groups in the region (D. González 1999; Montgomery 2002;

Nieto-Phillips 2004). Celebratory multiculturalism, as Lisa Lowe suggests, "levels the important differences and contradictions within and among racial and ethnic minority groups according to the discourse of pluralism" (1996, 86).

Cabeza de Baca's most praised publication, *Historic Cookery*, an English-language cookbook of "Indian, Spanish, Mexican and American" foods first printed in 1939 as a New Mexico Extension Circular and with subsequent printings, is credited by many as the first widely distributed New Mexican cookbook. This cookbook stands as a strong example of the contradictions of such celebrations of culture in New Mexico alongside structural inequalities. It also exemplifies the contradictions embedded in Cabeza de Baca's home economics work. The text was originally a twenty-page booklet, and later grew to a forty-eight-page booklet, of popular New Mexican recipes that Cabeza de Baca had compiled while working with Mexican and native communities. The cookbook was first published by the NMAES, and was basically distributed by request throughout the state's county extension offices (Reed 2005, 145).[12] The recipes were drawn from her family's culinary traditions, as well as from those of the women she assisted. She published the circular with the goal to teach the nutritional values of New Mexican food, which she described as "Indian, Spanish, Mexican and American," to other extension agents as well as the general public. According to several biographies, the cookbook received the attention of New Mexico governor Thomas Mabry in the late 1940s, which led to the book's overwhelming popularity among the general public in New Mexico, as well as beyond the borders of the state. As Reed explains, "He believed this guide to tri-cultural cooking would make an excellent public relations tool, and according to one newspaper, he sent copies to the governors of every other US state, 'along with a sack of the pinto beans so necessary for carrying out its recipes'" (2005, 123).

The strategic use of *Historic Cookery* by the state to promote a celebratory multicultural New Mexican identity corresponds with the concerted representations of New Mexico created by authors and architects of the Spanish Revival (Nieto-Phillips 2004). The New Mexican governor wanted to promote a multicultural identity with the cookbook, even as many of the state's Mexican and native residents were the most disenfranchised and economically affected by the Depression. *Historic Cookery* illustrates what Virginia Scharff argues, in another context, is a fundamental aspect of Cabeza de Baca's writings: how "she worked to venerate and preserve a more mixed and dynamic New Mexico heritage, the product of centuries of interaction between Hispanics, Indians, and Anglos" (2003, 18). Cabeza de Baca's introduction to the cookbook bolsters this multicultural image of New Mexican history and culture to the book's general readership, a view situated in a romanticized language of the past. She tells her readers: "Try the recipes. And when you do, think of New Mexico's golden days, of red chile drying in the sun, of clean-swept yards, outdoor ovens, and adobe houses on the landscape. Remember the green valleys where good things grow. And think too of families sitting happily at the tables—because good food and good cheer are natural *compadres* and because, as the Spanish proverb says, a full stomach makes a happy man. *Buen provecho*, amigos" (1970, 2).

Cabeza de Baca's implementation and acquisition of these recipes in the context of her home economics work in New Mexico in the 1930s during the Depression is not evident from her nostalgic imagery of a "cheerful" and "golden" New Mexican past. Her imagery of such a past also elides the economic hardships endured by many of the northern New Mexican families she assisted, families in economic hardship due to the lack of "green valleys" and "growth" because of the drought. Such representations, however, mirror her romanticized narratives about her family and cultural history in the opening scenes of her autobiography, *The Good Life,* idyllic images that contrast with depictions of disenfranchisement later in the text. By the end of *The Good Life*, Cabeza de Baca details the gradual loss of her family's land due to drought, plowing and fencing practices by homesteaders, and other political disenfranchisement (Rebolledo 1994, xxii). Such idyllic representations of a New Mexican past and her childhood in both *The Good Life* and *Historic Cookery*, alongside images of social and economic marginalization, are therefore responses to marginalization (Rebolledo 1994). They are narrative moments in which Cabeza de Baca seeks to establish her family's right to land, as well as the right of others of Mexican descent (presumably those of "Spanish" origin).

Historic Cookery, like her other writings, is therefore not without its contradictions. The cookbook also reveals Cabeza de Baca's commitment to critical multicultural views of identity. Critical multiculturalism, in contrast to celebratory forms of multiculturalism, "explores the fissures, tensions, and sometimes contradictory demands of multiple cultures, rather than (only) celebrating the plurality of cultures by passing through them appreciatively" (Palumbo-Liu 1995, 5). In the preface to the cookbook, she writes, "The recipes . . . are a product of the past and present—an amalgamation of Indian, Spanish, Mexican, and American. They are typically New Mexican" (1958). By articulating New Mexican food as a combination of Indian, Spanish, Mexican, and American cultures, she describes New Mexican identity as a contact zone (Pratt 1991) between distinct cultures in the region. In doing so, she challenges definitions of national identity rooted in a monolithic white racial identity. By using the term "amalgam," she suggests an overlay or overlap of cultures, rather than a mixture of cultures blending together to make a single regional identity.

With her emphasis on the recipes as products of the "past and present," she indicates Mexican and Indian cultures as existing in the present and not stuck in the "past," a view that dominated the Spanish Revival (Montgomery 2002). In the introduction, she also says, "New Mexico is a land of changes. . . . There have been changes in its people, in its customs and culture, and naturally in its food habits" (1958). Here, she furthers the idea of New Mexican culture and identity as defined by social and cultural change. With this last statement, Cabeza de Baca counters her earlier call for her readers to remember a "golden New Mexican past," unaffected by change. The difference between these two statements, one celebrating "change" and the other elevating the idea of a "golden past," indicates the various overlapping, at times contradictory, views in her writings. Such contradictions ultimately serve the same idea: New Mexico is a region defined by its Mexican and native culture and origins, and even with the "American" present, these cultures will remain present in the state's identity, particularly in its culinary traditions.

The overwhelming popularity of Cabeza de Baca's *Historic Cookery* across the nation indicates how the book was used to promote the consumption of a particular version of New Mexican identity: a celebratory multicultural version of New Mexican identity as a mixture of Indian, Spanish, Mexican, and American culture, even though these communities were in fact racially and economically segregated on a material level in this pre–civil rights period. Cabeza de Baca's and Governor Mabry's celebrations of New Mexican culture as sites of cultural and ethnic mixture in the state, which serve up nostalgic images of a "golden" New Mexican past, echo the celebratory definitions of New Mexican identity that were central to the Spanish Revival, which allowed for the mixture of the various ethnic groups in the state only at the level of food and nostalgia.

With her home economics work, Cabeza de Baca also contributed to the tourist consumption of Mexican and native peoples by encouraging them to sell native handicrafts, such as textiles and *colcha* embroidery, to supplement their farm incomes. The Spanish Revival included a handicraft revival led by Anglo philanthropist Mary Austin and artist Frank Applegate, who both founded the Spanish Colonial Arts Society in 1925 (Nestor 1978, 6). A group of Santa Fe philanthropists in the 1930s also established the "Native Market" to provide a space for Mexican and native artisans to sell their wares; the women's fashion magazine *Vogue* even featured the "Native Market" in their pages (Jensen 1986b, 38–39). The Native Market mostly favored handicrafts that conformed to "authentic" representations of native peoples and that were consistent with the Spanish Revival's emphasis on native peoples as part of a folk culture locked in the primitive past (Macaulay 2000). As Suzanne Macaulay explains of the Native Market of the 1930s, "Innovation and change were not considered . . . [*colcha* embroidery] had to remain static to remain authentic" (Macaulay 2000, 79).

It would be remiss to overlook the agency of the native and Mexican women who participated in the market. Many rural native women actively participated in the market and capitalized on the consumption of their culture in order to supplement their farm income. Families in heavily populated areas were successful in supplementing their earnings with handicrafts (Jensen 1986b). As Jensen describes, "For urban Anglos and artists, the arts revival was tinged with romantic conservatism about preserving the 'native' past. For farm families, it was a way of modernizing to survive agricultural hard times" (1986b, 38). Given this profitability, the NMAES, through federal and state government relief projects, provided funds and personnel for education in craft making and marketing in northern regions of the state (Deutsch 1987, 192–193). Some NMAES agents, however, discouraged handicrafts and creative arts for native and Mexican descent families because they viewed the tourist market as an inconsistent income, and therefore excluded crafts from extension club activities. The NMAES agents' discouragement of families who focused on crafts as a means of economic development suggests how the agency encouraged economic independence only if it did not involve the families making an income from an activity that would perpetuate their cultural presence—for farm incomes were also seasonal.

Cabeza de Baca strongly felt that the NMAES should have listed embroidery and needlework as a focus of extension clubs,[13] stating that this was a missed opportunity for the agency to "combine the creative interests of women with support for a marketable product" (Jensen 1986b, 47). She also praised handicrafts as not only having a marketable value, but also a nonmaterial one. Writing about the women who did *colcha* embroidery, Cabeza de Baca writes: "They may not have accomplished very much materially, but they have gained much spiritually" (qtd. in Jensen 1986b, 51). Cabeza de Baca's affirmation of native handicrafts speaks to how she respected the women's creative arts as having cultural value, thereby countering the Spanish Revival's framing of native crafts as solely marketable products for consumption. Even though she facilitated the loss of these women's cultural traditions as an agent of the NMAES, other instances reveal how she also emphasized the value of their culture.

Cabeza de Baca's simultaneous catering to and challenging of racialized narratives of Mexican and indigenous New Mexican communities, at times even in the same publication, demonstrates the various negotiations she made as a home demonstration agent in New Mexico. In the following section, I explore Cabeza de Baca's Spanish-language home economics publications and suggest they signal her attempt to speak directly to a New Mexican Spanish-speaking public. These writings indicate how she both upheld and challenged the tenets of Americanization and racialized nationalism.

Linguistic and Domestic Power: Reifying and Challenging Americanization

As a Spanish-speaking and bilingual woman who worked with a mostly Spanish-speaking population, Cabeza de Baca found the role of language combined with the Progressive Era view of feminine power in the public sphere to be a great asset for her career as a home economist. For the Spanish-speaking women she assisted, her incorporation of Spanish in her home economics training helped her reach northern New Mexican families, particularly in her efforts to teach modern domestic science, such as the use of canning and the pressure cooker. Similar to other agents in New Mexico, Cabeza de Baca viewed canning as an essential practice that would enable rural women both to provide a nutritional diet for their families and to save money for their households (Jensen 1982, 361). Unlike other agents, she published her canning and food preparation bulletins in Spanish. This act signals not only how she used language to reach the women she assisted but also how she ultimately used Spanish to value Anglo American domestic technology. Cabeza de Baca's use of Spanish therefore facilitated, in some respects, the loss of these women's cultural traditions, despite her critique of modernization as a process that she believed lead to the loss of cultural traditions. That is, even as she introduced modern technology, such as canning and the pressure cooker, she also emphasized the value of native foods and culture in her writings. She even mourned the loss of cultural traditions as a byproduct of modernization, stating "As a home economist I am happy to see modern kitchens and improved diets, but my artistic soul deplores the passing of beautiful customs" (1949, 4).

Her use of Spanish in her home economics work was largely supported by the NMAES. In fact, her ability to speak Spanish combined with her home economics training led the NMAES to recruit her in the first place. At the time, the NMAES did not have the resources to train their few monolingual and mostly white home extension agents to speak the language (Ponce 1995; Reed 2005). Since more than half of the rural women in New Mexico were Spanish speakers of Mexican descent, the agency actively recruited home economics workers who spoke fluent Spanish. When the NMAES was established in 1914, staff officials understood that their success in a bilingual state depended on their ability to recruit bilingual agents. A. C. Cooley, a staff official, wrote in his 1915 report, "It is almost impossible to find properly trained Mexicans capable of filling a county agent's position and it seems equally as hard to find an American who speaks Spanish and understands the Mexican people" (qtd. in Jensen 1982, 369). Cabeza de Baca was approached by NMAES director W. L. Elser, a student in one of her Spanish classes, about the possibility of working for the Extension service (Reed 2005). Cabeza de Baca also reportedly learned Tewa in order to work with families living in the Pueblos.[14]

Cabeza de Baca worked for the NMAES in the 1930s and 1940s when there was state support for bilingual education. New Mexican congresswoman Concha Ortíz y Pino de Kleven advocated bilingual education, stating that Spanish was important for children of Mexican descent so that they could maintain their New Mexican cultural identity (Jaehn 1994; Reed 2005 315). Cabeza de Baca herself greatly valued bilingual education, recounting in her autobiography *We Fed Them Cactus* how teaching material in Spanish and English to her mostly Spanish-speaking students in her first teaching job facilitated their learning process. She notes her frustrations with the bilingual readers that mostly focused on American colonial history, and not local history, which her students supplanted with their stories in the classroom (1954). Yet Cabeza de Baca's focus on bilingualism also reflects the use of language in order to reach women they were seeking to assist through a Progressive Era approach, which often pushed these communities toward Americanization, a philosophy that often led to the loss of their native and cultural traditions and language.

Cabeza de Baca also strongly felt that publishing NMAES bulletins in Spanish and her Spanish translations of English-language NMAES circulars would affirm and empower the women she assisted: both by documenting their culinary traditions to other extension agents and by making information on canning and food preparation directly available to the women. She published the first Spanish bulletins about nutrition and food preparation and preservation for the NMAES in the 1930s, including *Los Alimentos y su Preparación* (1934, repr. in 1937 and 1942) and *Boletín de Conserver* (1935, repr. in 1937 and 1941). Explaining her reasons for publishing in Spanish, she explained, "Psychologically, these people needed encouragement and orientation. . . . Most did not read English, and there was no material on canning or food preparation available in Spanish" (1942). Cabeza de Baca further explained how, "next to her prayer books, the rural Spanish-speaking woman treasures these two booklets" (1942, 668). She also translated several English-language extension circulars into Spanish.[15]

Cabeza de Baca's use of the Spanish language to reach multiple audiences, including rural women and a larger Spanish-speaking public, illustrates how she viewed language and the maintenance of cultures, specifically through food, as a connected process. She used Spanish and other native languages to negotiate Americanization and its links with racial nationalism by speaking directly to the women she assisted. She also spoke to a broader Spanish-speaking public within the pages of *The New Mexican*. Her use of language at the same time, as discussed above, facilitated the loss of Mexican and native traditions in NMAES's aim toward the modernization of the domestic spheres and farms of marginalized communities. In this way, Cabeza de Baca's incorporation of Spanish in her home economics work represented elements of the Spanish conquest that she also celebrated as part of her heritage.

Crossing Domestic Borders:
Home Economics and "Domestic Containment"

Cabeza de Baca's Spanish-language fluency and home economics successes led UNESCO to recruit her in their aims to modernize and support the economic development of indigenous populations in Latin America. The Government of Mexico and the Organization of American States joined UNESCO to send Cabeza de Baca to Patzcuaro, Mexico, in 1951 to start a home economics program to train Central and South American students to work with indigenous communities in their home countries.[16] She was part of the teaching faculty of the center, comprised of instructors with specialties in sanitation, hygiene, agriculture, handicraft industries, home economics, and literacy training (Behrman 1951). Cabeza de Baca explains matter-of-factly that she was asked to work for UNESCO because "They need[ed] a woman that would speak Spanish" (1983). According to an article about the Patzcauro center in the *UNESCO Courier*, "Since Spanish is spoken in nearly all Latin American countries, and, in many of them, educators have to face the problem of a bilingual Indian education, it is felt that the methods and materials which have proved successful among the Tarascan Indians of Patzcuaro will be valuable to educators throughout much of the Western hemisphere" (Behrman 1951, 50). The use of Spanish to address illiteracy in a bilingual Tarascan Indian community—three-fourths of whom speak both Purépecha (their native language) and Spanish—signals the colonial framework of the UNESCO illiteracy program in Mexico.[17]

Very few accounts of Cabeza de Baca's work for UNESCO in Mexico exist.[18] The published accounts include an article titled "Cabeza de Baca Gilbert Describes Her Work on UN Project in Mexico at Altrusa Dinner" by an unknown author published in the "Society-Clubs" section edited by Calla Hay from *The New Mexican* in 1951 and an essay by Cabeza de Baca titled "UNESCO's Pilot Project" published in the *New Mexico Extension News* in 1952. The two articles contain important distinctions. The unknown author of *The New Mexican* article describes Cabeza de Baca's work through a dominant US framework that views indigenous populations within a primitive/civilized binary, arguing that indigenous peoples in Latin America are inherently primitive and therefore need to be civilized through Westernization. Cabeza de Baca's article, distinct from the third-person account, stresses the social and structural factors that have resulted in the Tarascan Indians' poverty, illustrating the many ways she sought to address these social factors as an agent of UNESCO, while also using her philosophies on domestic technology drawn from her experiences in New Mexico.

Both articles illustrate the impact of 1950s cold war politics on definitions of nationhood and race, and Cabeza de Baca's essay criticizes postwar conservatism's impact on the field of home economics. During the cold war, home and nation were powerfully linked. The 1950s was a decade characterized by cold war–era rampant anti-communism, in which many US citizens, because of race, political affiliations, and ideological positions, were considered suspect. This was the decade of the McCarthy investigations, when thousands of US residents— particularly government employees, educators, union activists, and those in the entertainment industry—became the target of antagonistic investigations and inquiries accusing them of being communists or communist sympathizers by government agencies, panels, and private industries. During this cold war era, many conservative housewives become central leaders in an activist movement that was decidedly anticommunist and antiforeigner (Nickerson 2003). Michelle

Nickerson explains, "[T]he 1950s revival of domesticity had a politically radicalized effect on many women. Groups of predominantly white, middle-, and upper-class wives and mothers took advantage of their privileged social circumstances to become militant anticommunist crusaders" (2003, 2).[19] Many of these women established and became part of conservative women's groups, including the American Public Relations Forum, an anticommunist women's organization established in 1952. Florence Fowler Lyons, educator turned anticommunist activist, began an aggressive campaign against UNESCO and described the organization as a "stark, grinning, crimson clad Pied Piper called UNESCO. He's piping a tune he calls peace ... I warn you—if you do not stop his march through the streets and schoolrooms of America ... this nation will die, and you and you alone will be to blame" (qtd. in Nickerson 2003, 10). Senator Joseph McCarthy also expressed alarm during this period at UNESCO's alleged "leftist activity" at the Tarascan training center in Patzcuaro (Jones 1988).

As Elaine Tyler May argues, "domestic containment," a term popularized by Secretary of State John Foster Dulles in the 1950s, had strong connotations: it was the ideology of containing and suppressing communist and subversive activity, including deviant gender and sexuality, as exemplified by the McCarthy investigations. After World War II, as May argues, the home became the site where "potentially dangerous social forces of the new age might be tamed, where they could contribute to the secure and fulfilling life to which postwar women and men aspired" (1990, 14). The idea of "domestic containment" also applied to those minorities within the nation who were considered suspect and whose citizenship was questioned. For example, Operation Wetback, implemented in 1954, was a government-sponsored program to deport many citizens and noncitizens of Mexican descent. The repatriation project was a byproduct of racial discrimination toward a new wave of undocumented Mexican immigrants that came to the United States through the Bracero Program, many of whom were blamed for the nation's economic problems (García 1980, 169–182).

Cabeza de Baca's home economics work across the US-Mexico border for UNESCO stands in stark contrast with the larger postwar conservative domesticity movement and the domestic containment of ethnic "others" in the United States. Her work instead suggests how she crossed taboo borders by assisting the most marginalized communities in Latin America. When placed alongside this postwar conservative domesticity, her home economics work represents a humanitarian perspective that addresses the structural inequalities behind global poverty and illiteracy, an idea she also emphasized as a home economist in New Mexico. As Reed claims, "Contrary to popular wisdom that the 1950s were a time in which women's power was constrained by the ideals of tradition and domesticity, Cabeza de Baca had actually learned during her experiences in [home economics] in the 1930s and 1940s that these ideals could be powerful routes for change" (2007, 131).

The New Mexican article recounts Cabeza de Baca's speech about her home demonstration work in Patzcuaro to the Santa Fe chapter of the Altrusa club for their yearly Christmas dinner. Altrusa, a Progressive Era women's club, was started in 1917 as a social and professional group for women entering the workforce during World War I. The focus of the club was (and still is) on service, particularly literacy and health issues, and in 1935 the club became international with its first chapter in Mexico; Altrusa sent its first representative to the United Nations in 1946. The third-person account of Cabeza de Baca's speech is striking because it documents Cabeza de Baca's recounting of her UNESCO work for the mostly white home economics agents, some of whom had also been involved with international home economics projects. That is, while *The New Mexican* article reflects the writer's account of her speech, it also represents Cabeza de Baca's performance of that narrative to a mostly white female audience.

The article opens by describing the setting of the speech and formalities of the dinner:

> The Altrusa club's Christmas dinner Saturday night in the Coronado room at la Fonda was a beautifully appointed formal event highlighted by a fascinating account by a member, Mrs. Cabeza de Baca Gilbert, of her work during the past six months in Mexico for UNESCO. Mrs. Gilbert recently returned to resume her duties as the state's home demonstration agent at large.
>
> Members and guests were seated at a long T-shaped table lighted by huge red Christmas candles tied with red satin bows. Red carnations and greens were centered at the speaker's table. Placecards were marked with the Altrusa club emblem and small pine cones held tiny candles which could be lighted at one side. Candy Santa Claus figures were favors.
>
> Mrs. John Updike, club president, introduced the guests and called upon Mrs. Anna Kilene to outline plans for the club's Christmas charity in which food and clothing will be given to a needy family.
>
> Mrs. Charles O. Greenwood, district governor of Altrusa, introduced Mrs. Gilbert, speaking with pride of the local club being cited in the international program because of the large percentage of members who have served notably in foreign lands under United Nations and other governmental programs. In addition to Mrs. Gilbert, she pointed to Miss Mary Mitchell and Mrs. Ann Nolan Clark as these members. (Hay 1951)

The description of the event indicates this to be a very formal and elite occasion. The opening of the article also establishes several of the gendered and racialized binaries—including male/female, civilized/primitive and domestic/foreign—that will circulate throughout the article. The description of Cabeza de Baca's recounting of her visit confirms Gere's view that "white middle class club women, for whom race was a prominent feature of their self-identification . . . devoted considerable energy to constructing and affirming their positions of privilege and power by using exclusionary tactics, both literally and figuratively" (1997, 5). First, the detailed descriptions of the table decorations—the table lighted by "huge red Christmas candles" and "red satin bows"—indicate an Anglo Christian focus, which will contrast with the description of the native and "primitive" arts of the Tarascan Indians offered later in the essay. Second, the decorations serve to highlight the luxury of the affair, thereby indicating the social status of the club members as distinct from the villagers Cabeza de Baca assisted in Mexico. The formal listing of the women's names according to their husband's surnames in the passage also serves to indicate a high social status, and a gendered performance by these women or subscription to women's proper roles. That Cabeza de Baca is referred to as Mrs. Gilbert throughout the article contrasts with her rhetorical resistance to be referred to by her husband's last name after their divorce, as evident in her crossing out of "Mrs. Carlos Gilbert" on a Red Cross Certificate dated November 1, 1946, and replacing it with her maiden name, "Cabeza de Baca."[20]

Furthermore, the emphasis by the author on the "pride of the local club being cited in the international program because of the large percentage of members who have served notably in foreign lands under United Nations and other governmental programs" illustrates the links between home economics, citizenship, and patriotism. The phrase "served notably in foreign lands" is typically used to refer to military personnel who represent and protect the nation overseas; such words indicate the author's perspective of home economics as a service to the nation and as a patriotic duty. The visa and passport that Cabeza de Baca uses to gain entry into Mexico in 1951 to work in Patzcuaro represent this double meaning of the domestic as both household and nation. The English translation of the Spanish-language text of the visa reads, "The holder is commissioned by the food and agricultural organization of the United Nations in the function as home economics technician."[21] The visa inscribes her home economics work with nationhood and transnationalism: she will serve as a home demonstration agent as an employee of both the US government and the United Nations, serving on a global mission.

The article continues by describing how Cabeza de Baca's talk "transported the urban dwellers of the United States to a land where there are strange contrasts between the original *extremely* rural life of the Indian village dwellers and the modern innovations in housekeeping which are now offered to them" (Hay 1951, emphasis mine). Here, the unknown author makes a similar rhetorical move as Cabeza de Baca does in her unpublished diary entry when she describes her family and ancestors as "very Spanish." By using the adverb "extremely," the author exaggerates the rural lifestyle of the Tarascan Indians, described here as "Indian village dwellers" in contrast with the "urban" and "modern" dwellers in the United States. The rhetorical contrasts between urban and rural, and modern and primitive, also serve to reinforce a racialized binary of Indian peoples as primitive and backward, a binary that echoes the Spanish Revival, as well as a larger discourse about native peoples in the Americas (D. González 1999; Montgomery 2002; Nieto-Phillips 2004). Such racialized distinctions between the communities Cabeza de Baca worked with and the women at the Altrusa club Christmas dinner illustrate how club women during this period, as Gere argues, "affirmed their whiteness with discussion topics rooted in genteel high culture or benevolence projects designed to underscore the difference between white middle-class clubwomen and those they helped" (1997, 5).

The notion that Cabeza de Baca's speech will "transport urban dwellers" to a "strange" land also highlights her role as a tour guide for club members in the audience who will travel, as tourists do, to a foreign place. This tourist view of native cultures as "other" is also expressed through the article's description of the Tarascan Indians' cultures as objects to be consumed. Significantly, the audience experiences the consumption of the native culture in Patzcuaro through Cabeza de Baca's tourist consumption. The author describes that Cabeza de Baca "brought home some of their art and it was demonstrated in her costume. Her black gown and rebozo were gorgeously embroidered in cross-stitch. Her necklace and earrings were the traditional silver balls and red bead 'rosaries' worn by brides among the Indians, handed down through families" (Hay 1951). Further solidifying Cabeza de Baca's position as a tourist, even though she is on a humanitarian mission for UNESCO, is the article's description of the accommodations provided for Cabeza de Baca and her colleagues on the UNESCO mission: "The project was set up in extremely beautiful headquarters loaned by President Cardeñas of Mexico. There was his Quinta Erendira, a gorgeous storied building, an addition to Tres Reyes, a group of bungalows which had been built originally for a tourist court" (Hay 1951).[22] Such descriptions give the impression that Cabeza de Baca and her colleagues are in Patzcuaro on vacation, thereby further suggesting how her speech is intended to transport the audience, in the role of tourists, to the region.

The author of the article, through Cabeza de Baca's recounting, also indicates a fascination with the modern technology and consumer goods that can be found in Mexico, therefore constructing the view of Mexico as a primitive space. The author states: "[S]he was amazed when she found things in the Mexican hardware stores that are unseen here, the most modern of household electric aids. There is now, she says, a Mexican 'REA' [Rural Electric Administration] put through some of the villages and in one came the great contrast where she saw an electric plate used as the *fogon* [stove]" (Hay 1951). Perhaps one of the article's strongest views of the Tarascan Indians as primitive and locked within the past occurs in a caption to two photos from Cabeza de Baca's visit: "Tarascan Indians learned something of health and sanitation from the UN project on which Cabeza de Baca Gilbert worked, but in the two scenes above *the long way they have to go* is suggested. A shawled but shoeless Tarascan woman who washes her clothes on rocks in the lake and has never known hot water to cleanse dishes, is seen at the left. At the right is one of the men driving his loaded burros past a typical tile-roofed but non-window dwelling, where families sleep on straw mats, cook on stones, and use tortillas as their only eating utensils" (Hay 1951, emphasis mine).

Even though Cabeza de Baca's speech to the Altrusa Club has indicated the several areas of improvement she and her fellow home demonstration agents sought to make through their work with the Tarascan Indians, the unknown author relies on the visual imagery of the Tarascan Indians and a dominant perspective of the Tarascans as primitive to make the argument that they "have a long way to go" (Hay 1951). The photo of the "shawled but shoeless Tarascan woman" washing her clothes on rocks in the lake, becomes visual evidence to the author that the Tarascans are locked in a primitive past and therefore resistant to modernization. The imagery of the man driving a loaded burro past a house where "families sleep on straw mats, cook on stones, and use tortillas as their only eating utensils" is also used by the author as further support that the Tarascan Indians have "a long way to go," or, in other words, are locked in a primitive past. Such descriptions of the Tarascan Indians by the third-person narrator of the article, and the editor who created the captions, indicate how Cabeza de Baca did not necessarily control the larger discourse surrounding her work. This is made evident when the third-person account of Cabeza de Baca's speech is compared with Cabeza de Baca's first-person account of her experiences in Patzcuaro.

In contrast to *The New Mexican* article from 1951 and its reinforcement of several racialized binaries of primitive/civilized and modern/backward in its description of the Tarascan Indians, Cabeza de Baca's first-person account in her essay "UNESCO's Pilot Project," published a year later in the *New Mexico Extension News,* reveals her emphasis on the sociohistorical conditions confronting the Tarascan Indians she assisted in Patzcuaro.[23] Even though her language upholds a Westernized perspective of the Tarascan Indians, her narrative represents a humanitarian perspective that addresses the structural inequalities behind global poverty and illiteracy, an idea she also emphasized as a home economist in New Mexico.

Cabeza de Baca begins her 1952 article by providing insight into her critical multicultural and humanitarian view of home demonstration work in Mexico, which she connects to her work in New Mexico. She opens her essay not in Mexico but in the United States by describing her home extension work for the NMAES. Here, she asserts the importance of maintaining the "best elements" of the culture of the communities she has worked with, even as she promotes modernization: "For forty years we have had in this country an educational program for adults and young people which we have called extension service. The aim of this educational program [New Mexico Extension Service] has been to help men and women live fuller and happier lives in adjustment with the changing times and environment, to develop the best elements in their own culture, and to achieve the social and economic progress which will enable them to take their place in the modern world and to live together in peace" (Cabeza de Baca 1952, 4). While her notion of "maintaining the best elements in their own culture" comes across as Darwinian, she is asserting the notion of respecting and maintaining culture within the larger context of racialized nativism in the cold war era. With words like "change," "develop," and "progress," she signals the influence of Progressive Era values on her thinking in the 1950s; the emphasis on "peace," however, situates her perspective in the postwar era.

Cabeza de Baca also explains her rationale for working for UNESCO: "We have gone a long way since the extension program was inaugurated, but there are countries less fortunate than we are. Three-fourths of the world's population are under-housed, under-clothed, under-fed and illiterate" (1952, 4). Here, she indicates how her home economics work has now taken on an international dimension because she has accomplished many of her aims with the NMAES and because there are rural communities south of the US-Mexico border experiencing extreme poverty. With her emphasis on literacy, her article echoes the UNESCO philosophy of fundamental education and her phrasing seems to come directly from UNESCO manuals on this approach. Her approach to literacy parallels the words from a *UNESCO Courier* article, which states: "Illiteracy is part of a tragic circle of underproduction, malnutrition and endemic disease. The circle cannot be broken by an attack on only one of these elements" (Behrman 1951, 6). Cabeza de Baca's passion for addressing illiteracy is not surprising given how her home economics work in New Mexico often focused on literacy and access; her publications and translations of important NMAES bulletins in Spanish are important examples.

While the *New Mexican* article attributes the poor living conditions of the Tarascan Indians to their inherent primitive qualities, Cabeza de Baca's essay attributes their poor conditions to social and structural inequalities, not to the Indians themselves. A comparison of the same and similar photos, along with their captions, illustrates such distinct perspectives clearly. In the *New Mexican* article, the captions are most likely written by the unknown author or the editor of the column, while the captions for Cabeza de Baca's essay are taken directly from the text of her essay. In the *New Mexican* article, the caption that accompanies the photo of a Tarascan woman, as discussed earlier, states: "A shawled but shoeless Tarascan woman who washes her clothes on rocks in the lake and has never known hot water to cleanse dishes, is seen at the left" (Hay 1951). In Cabeza de Baca's article, we see presumably the same woman, now pictured washing clothes. In Cabeza de Baca's article, she is described in the collective as, "The women in the villages take their clothing to the edge of the lake or to water holes to launder. Stones are used for washboards" (1952, 5). In the text of the article, Cabeza de Baca continues, "The lack of water is one of the reasons for the lack of cleanliness" (1952, 5).

The terms used to describe the same Tarascan woman and the reasons given for the absence of clean water by Cabeza de Baca and the *New Mexican* article author contain a slight, but important distinction. The emphasis in Cabeza de Baca's article is on the shortage of water in the woman's community, which implies the environmental conditions that have led to the deficiency of water, such as inadequate infrastructure. In the *New Mexican* article, the woman's lack of cleanliness is attributed to the woman herself, who, remember, "has never known hot water," thereby emphasizing how the woman herself lacks knowledge of hot water and therefore attributing the primitive conditions to her lifestyle (Hay 1951). This view contrasts with Cabeza de Baca's caption, which assigns the shortage of water to larger structural factors, such as the lack of plumbing (1952, 5).

The two articles also contain the same photo of the same Tarascan woman smiling at the camera, and a comparison of the two captions reveals varying perspectives on the underlying causes of the Tarascan women's poverty. In the *New Mexican* article, recall, the woman is described as a "shawled but shoeless Tarascan woman" (Hay 1951). The article's emphasis on her lack of shoes only serves to emphasis a characterization of the woman and Tarascans as primitive. In the *New Mexican Extension News* article, Cabeza de Baca's caption to the same photo describes the Tarascan Indians as "a colorful people" (1952, 5). Cabeza de Baca continues, "The women wear pleated skirts about ten yards in width, a light blouse, and always their rebosos" (1952, 5). In the text of the essay, she continues, "They do not wear shoes. The men wear white cotton trousers which tie around their waists, a white shirt, straw hat, and a poncho. They wear the shoes, sandals or guaraches" (Cabeza de Baca 1952, 5). Even though Cabeza de Baca's descriptions comes across as anthropological and her use of the term "color" shares similarities with other Anglo American accounts of Mexican peoples as "colorful" as discussed in chapter 1, her narration of the women's and men's clothing provides a gendered explanation for the women's lack of shoes: the men wear shoes and the women do not. By describing in detail the particulars of the women's and men's clothing, she also conveys reverence to the women and men she assisted in Patzcauro. This respect and understanding of the Tarascan's emphasis on maintaining dignity despite their impoverished conditions is evident later in her article when she notes that, no matter how poor, these people decorate their houses and have beautiful churches, another description missing from the *New Mexican* article. Cabeza de Baca explains: "Every home, no matter how poor, has a patio filled with blooming plants. The churches are beautiful, and the altars are always provided with fresh flowers" (1952, 5).

Cabeza de Baca's emphasis on the underlying structural factors for the Tarascan Indian's poverty is most evident in the last statement of her essay: "This area has everything, but it remains to be evolved" (1952, 5). Recall the caption in the *New Mexican* article, which reads: "in the two scenes above *the long way they have to go* is suggested" (Hay 1951, emphasis added). While Cabeza de Baca's statement stresses how the area itself "remains to be evolved," the third-person caption suggests that the Tarascans themselves have a "long way to go." Significantly, Cabeza de Baca focuses on the land itself, and the structural and historical reasons for a lack of "evolvement," while the third-person account of her speech focuses on the Tarascan Indians as inherently primitive.

As an agent of UNESCO, Cabeza de Baca clearly represented an institution intent on "Westernizing" the third world "other." Yet as her *New Mexico Extension News* article suggests, she used her position as a home economist in Mexico, as she did in New Mexico, to articulate the importance of understanding and valuing the communities she assisted, in this case the Tarascan Indians of Patzcuaro. Cabeza de Baca's travel to Mexico as a home economist to assist and come in contact with the ethnic "other" stands in stark contrast with the larger context of "domestic containment" that was manifested as a fear of the ethnic "other" in both the United States and abroad.

Concluding Remarks

In an interview for the Museum of Albuquerque Bicentennial Exhibit in 1975, Cabeza de Baca expressed that she felt that she had not accomplished all that she had set out to do in Patzcuaro, specifically stating, "many of the students seemed to look down on the people they were supposed to be helping" and that she felt that they might never be able to "reach" them.[24] Such remarks convey in earnest Cabeza de Baca's respect and commitment to the communities she sought to help with home economics, a tone that is evident throughout her home economics writings. While she certainly represented institutions that sought to Westernize and Americanize the ethnic "other," and catered to nativist fears in her affirmations of her Spanish ancestry, her writings, as a whole, indicate how she both challenged and upheld those discourses in her writings.

Furthermore, as a result of the Progressive Era and postwar view of women's home economics as a logical extension of women's roles in the domestic sphere, the site of the domestic became a way for Cabeza de Baca to assert the need for social change in nonthreatening ways. In several respects, Cabeza de Baca benefited from the association of women to domesticity. In her writings, she frequently positioned herself as both an "old-fashioned Hispanic Doña" and as a "progress-minded home economist" (Reed 2005, 167). Newspaper headlines such as "A Patrona of the Old Pattern" (1968) and "New Mexico's Famous Home Economist" (1954) emphasize both the conventional and unconventional aspects of her work.[25] Cabeza de Baca engaged with both versions of these representations to build her career in domestic science and to appeal to various publics.[26]

Jovita González, Cleofas Jaramillo, and Fabiola Cabeza de Baca each resisted the feminization and domestication of their communities, particularly the view of Mexican American women's passivity, by self-authoring and giving voice to their experiences amid Anglo-controlled discourses of people of Mexican descent in the early twentieth century. They waged their critiques against racialized nationalisms and gendered marginalization, while also reifying racial-class hierarchies, from the space of the domestic. This is a result of the association of women to the domestic sphere during this period as a result of Progressive Era views of women's feminine power in the domestic sphere, and also as a result of racialized nationalisms seeking to locate Mexican American female identity in the private space of the home. In the following chapters, I explore how contemporary authors and artists Sandra Cisneros, Carmen Lomas Garza, Patssi Valdez, and Diane Rodríguez—despite socioeconomic mobility outside of confined domesticity as middle-class professionals, and even with a publishing industry now invested in publishing narratives about Chicana experiences—found themselves consistently positioned in the domestic as a result of Chicano/a cultural nationalism, celebratory multiculturalism, and popular cultural representations, including Hollywood film and television. As we saw with González's, Jaramillo's, and Cabeza de Baca's texts, these authors and artists use the site of domesticity— through depictions of women's experiences and roles in domestic spaces, family rituals, and celebrations, as well as through fashion and glamour—to wage their gendered and racialized critiques.

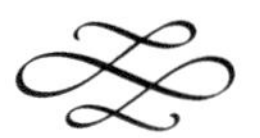

PART TWO

Domesticana

CHAPTER 4

Postnationalist and Domesticana Strategies

SANDRA CISNEROS'S *THE HOUSE ON MANGO STREET* AND CARMEN LOMAS GARZA'S *FAMILIAS*

In summer 1997, the now well-known "purple house" controversy ignited in the King William District in San Antonio, quickly spreading throughout the city and the nation. At issue was acclaimed author Sandra Cisneros's choice to have her late-Victorian cottage, built circa 1903, painted purple, or more precisely Sherwin Williams Corsican Purple, in 1997. With headlines such as the "King William 'Color Flap,'" "The Color Purple," and "Purple Politics," the story dominated the local and state press that summer, eventually obtaining national status with a story in the *New York Times*. While the city's Historic Design and Review Commission, along with the King William Association, decried the author's choice of purple as historically "inappropriate" and "incorrect" for the neighborhood, Cisneros explained that purple was a color "I consider Mexican and beautiful" (qtd. in Satz 1997). For the author and many of her supporters, the outcry against Cisneros's purple was not about the color itself but about the racial-economic segregation and exclusion of Mexicanos in San Antonio's history and built environment: "My history is made up of a community whose homes were so poor and unimportant to be considered worthy of historic preservation. No famous architect designed the houses of the Tejanos, and there are no books in the San Antonio Conservation Society (SACS) library about houses of the working-class community, no photos romanticizing their poverty, no ladies' auxiliary working toward preserving their presence. Their homes are gone; their history is invisible. The few historic homes that have survived have access cut off by freeways because city planners did not judge them important" (1997). As Cisneros's remarks elucidate, efforts at preserving and documenting the neighborhoods of San Antonio have worked to eliminate the presence of working-class Mexicanos in the city's historic records.

Two years prior to the purple house uproar in 1997, Cisneros won a MacArthur "genius" grant, having already established her reputation as an acclaimed author with her highly praised *The House on Mango Street* (1984, with subsequent reprints, and a 2009 twenty-fifth anniversary edition).[1] The text, a collection of vignettes set in Chicago's lower West Side, follows Esperanza Cordero's desire for a "house of one's own": "A house all my own. With my porch and my pillow, my pretty purple petunias" (1991a, 108). The book represents both the young protagonist Esperanza's challenge to patriarchy and the exclusion of Esperanza, a Mexicana, and the others of her Latina/o community, due to racial-economic segregation. By 1996, the book had sold over half a million copies, quickly becoming required reading in primary and secondary school curricula in the United States. Today, the text has sold over four million copies, has been translated into seventeen languages, been adapted into a play by several theater companies, and continues to be requisite school reading, although the text is still "much better known in minoritized US Latino/a literature circles than in mainline American, Latin American, and comparative literature seminars and institutions" (Saldívar 2012). The irony, of course, is that in 1997, while *The House on Mango Street*—a story about a young Chicana's desire for space in the nation, signaled through the space of the domestic and the metaphor of "purple petunias"—received critical acclaim and overwhelming praise in 1997, Cisneros herself found it difficult to create a space of her own through the visual language of Mexican culture and identity in San Antonio.[2]

The widespread celebration of *The House on Mango Street* and the local exclusion of Cisneros's purple color palette—representing Mexican presence, space, culture, and identity in the nation—illuminates a tension that has surrounded the text since its initial publication in 1984: Much of the discourse and curriculum related to the text have celebrated Esperanza's desire for a "house of one's own" with a universalizing and celebratory rhetoric that continues to exist alongside the material and structural exclusion of Latina/os and Latina/o culture in the United States. Cisneros wrote and published *The House on Mango Street* during the 1980s and 1990s, decades characterized by a resurgence of immigrant backlash through English-language-only policies; "Save Our State" initiatives; and ballot proposals such as Proposition 187 in California, which sought to deny healthcare and education to undocumented immigrants; among many other nativist policies.[3] Public praise for texts such as *The House on Mango Street* alongside the continued marginalization of Latina/os in the nation suggests that many people are willing to read about Esperanza's story and her desire for space in the United States, yet the national sphere itself has been unwilling to fully accept Latina/os in the domestic space of the nation.

Carmen Lomas Garza, the creator of many paintings and installations that are now in permanent collections in major museums, has also received critical and mainstream acclaim for her artistic representations of Chicana/o families and domestic spaces. Similar to Cisneros's *The House on Mango Street,* Garza's children's literature books, *Family Pictures/Cuadros de Familia* (1990, repr. 2005) and *In My Family/En Mi Familia* (1996), claim national space for Mexicanos, particularly by humanizing and affirming US-Mexico border families and domestic practices in South Texas.[4] Like Cisneros's work, Garza's children's literature texts have been acclaimed and embraced for their educational qualities, with *Cuadros de Familia* and *En Mi Familia* receiving awards from the *School Library Journal,* the American Library Association, and the Library of Congress; several of Garza's paintings featured in her children's books are now part of the permanent collection in the Smithsonian Museum; and an interactive traveling children's exhibit of *In My Family/En Mi Familia* is now permanently housed at the Austin Museum of Art.[5] Due to their works' focus on the domestic, home, and family, and because both Garza's and Cisneros's texts have been used in educational curricula, both artists have taken on roles as education and arts advocates to Latina/o youth. For such work, two different primary schools in Los Angeles named their institutions after Garza and Cisneros in 2007 and 2009, respectively: the Carmen Lomas Garza Primary Center, a pre-kindergarten-through-second-grade school was established in East Los Angeles and the Sandra Cisneros Learning Academy, a kindergarten-through-middle-school academy, opened in Echo Park, Los Angeles. The naming of these schools after Garza and Cisneros is historic, as it has been rare for institutions to name schools after women of color, let alone Latinas.[6] Yet in several respects, the expectation and status given to both Cisneros and Garza to educate today's youth about Chicana/o families and culture has positioned the authors in domestic roles.

This chapter closely reads Cisneros's *The House on Mango Street* and Garza's *Cuadros de Familia* and *En Mi Familia* as critical texts that use home and domesticity to assert Chicana/o representation and inclusion in the US national sphere. While both authors use domestic space to include Mexicanos in the nation, they deconstruct and negotiate the association of Chicanas to home as part of their claims to national space. Their texts do so by critiquing patriarchal and nationalist constructions of gender. I argue that while their works both share a negotiated and counter-hegemonic approach to the domestic sphere, mainstream reception of their texts has frequently elided their critical and feminist critiques of gender and race, and both authors have been situated (while positioning themselves) in a domesticated role as teachers and nurturers of Chicana/o culture. Because Cisneros's and Garza's texts focus on home and domestic space from the vantage point of young narrators, their texts have been widely read and acclaimed in educational contexts, doing necessary pedagogical work to empower Latina/o students, as well as to educate non-Latina/os about Latina/o culture. As such, their texts function as important and critical tools of multicultural literacy in educational settings (Brochin-Ceballos and Fránquiz 2006). Yet the reception of their books have been embraced and co-opted by mainstream conservatism to very different ends than each author intended. Celebratory multicultural read-ings of *The House on Mango Street*, *Cuadros de Familia*, and *En Mi Familia* have frequently eclipsed the authors' political, activist, and Chicana feminist represen-tations of domesticity in their works. By "celebratory multiculturalism," I refer to readings of literature that elide specific gendered, racial, and ethnic histories, and instead frame texts as solely universal narratives (Lowe 1996; McLaren 1994). Such celebratory readings, while they importantly lead students to understand the similarities between various groups, overshadow the important work of teaching about inequality to create social change. Critical forms of multicultur-alism, on the other hand, situate representations of gender, race, and class in the context of social struggle and specific histories, leading students to assess and critique the structural factors that have led to gender and racial inequality in our society (Palumbo-Liu 1995, 15).

The Chicana/o literary and visual project of representing domestic space to claim inclusion in the nation has a fraught political history. In response to the exclu-sion of Mexicanos from US society and from dominant portrayals of Chicana/o families, many Chicano/a Movement nationalist manifestos and images of the late 1960s and 1970s used family and home to combat demeaning and dehumanizing rhetoric. Yet much of these representations configured Chicanas as cultural repro-ducers of the nation, responsible for nurturing the traditions, cultures, and *familias* of *La Raza*, as both home and nation (Blackwell 2011; Fregoso 2003; Rodríguez 2009). Chicano/a Movement representations reinforced masculine power within the structures of culture, nation, and the Mexican American family (Espinoza 2001; Huaco-Nuzum 1998; Saldívar-Hull 2000). In response, many activist women during the Movement, such as Ana Nieto Gómez, and groups, such as Hijas de Cuahtémoc, challenged male dominance and patriarchal authority by assert-ing leadership roles, organizing conferences, and creating a vibrant print culture that documented Chicana stories and histories (Blackwell 2011).[7] Several Chicana movement artists, such as Judy Baca, Barbara Carrasco, and Yolanda López, as well as the Chicana art collective, the Mujeres Muralistas, responded to the nationalist focus of the Chicano/a Movement by producing visual images and new symbols to represent Chicana subjectivity and to counter stereotypical images (Latorre 2008). Chicana feminist writings in 1980s and 1990s, exemplified by Anzaldúa's *Border-lands*, Cherríe Moraga's writings, Ana Castillo's essays, among many others texts, also critiqued patriarchal constructs of family and nation.[8]

Cisneros and Garza have different experiences and relationships with Chicano/a cultural nationalism, and as a result approach domestic space and family in differ-ent ways from each other. Garza developed many of the illustrations and focus on family that comprise *Cuadros de Familia* and *En Mi Familia* as direct responses to the Chicano/a Movement of the late 1960s and 1970s, while both Garza and Cis-neros created and published their texts in the 1980s and 1990s, decades character-ized by both a flourishing of Chicana feminist critiques of a resurgence of cultural nationalism.[9] Garza frequently cites Chicano/a nationalism as a direct influence on her art work, and her children's books emphasize the Chicano/a nationalist perspective of valuing the domestic realm as a bastion against Anglo domination and racism. Yet her works depict egalitarian gendered relations within the domestic, deconstructing the association of women with the domestic sphere and as reproducers of the nation. In this sense, Garza depicts the domestic realm from a "domesticana" vantage point, a term coined by Amalia Mesa-Bains to describe the artistic practice of affirming Chicano/a cultural traditions from the space of the domestic, while also breaking from the patriarchal past (2003).

Cisneros's *The House on Mango Street*, in contrast, presents a Chicana feminist critique of home, depicting domestic space from a "postnationalist" perspective that critiques cultural nationalist, patriarchal, and heteronormative ideologies of family and gender (Hernández 2009). By emphasizing the intersectionality of race, gender, and sexuality in Chicana experiences of home, her work shares Chicana feminism's critique of both Anglo American feminism's narrow focus on gender identity and Chicano/a cultural nationalism's exclusive focus on masculine ethnic identity. Ellie D. Hernández argues, "Chicana feminism developed the first postnationalist social critique by rejecting the terms of exclusion in organized 'national' movements and by offering a new set of terms" (2009, 51). Additionally, her text challenges Chicano/a nationalism's focus on the material and metaphorical reclamation of the United States through land, particularly the concept of Aztlán.[10] By utilizing the symbol of the house, and not the land, Cisneros's text shifts from the heroic symbols of Chicano/a nationalism, to represent the ideological, cultural, and economic limits imposed on a young Chicana (Kaup 1997, 363). Garza's illustrations also depart from the heroic symbols of the Chicano/a Movement by focusing on everyday life and families along the US-Mexico border.[11] While Cisneros's and Garza's texts approach home and domesticity differently, their works share a counter-hegemonic approach to the domestic sphere with the aim of creating public space for Chicana/os in the United States.

Young Adult and Children's Literature: Domestication and Power

The ability of Cisneros's and Garza's texts to function as counter-hegemonic narratives has been both strengthened and diluted by the marketing and reception of their texts within the genres of adult and children's literature. Because they are read within the context of young adult and children's literature, Cisneros's and Garza's works reach a broad audience and receive national attention, thereby doing important and necessary pedagogical work. Yet the marketing of their texts for children and young audiences has, in several respects, "infantilized" their works (Saldívar 2012, 153). Similar to many Latina/o authors who now publish children's and young adult literature, both Cisneros and Garza did not initially create their literature and art with young audiences in mind. Cisneros explains that she is consistently surprised by the promotion and appeal of *The House on Mango Street* with young audiences. Cisneros explains, "It seems to be marketed as a young people's book, but my readers range anywhere from second graders to university students to housewives . . . it always surprises me when children like the story (Satz 1997, 166). Because *The House on Mango Street* represents rape and incest, themes not typically present in young adult literature, Cisneros was initially perplexed by the marketing of her text in this genre. Readings of Cisneros's text in the young adult category have also frequently overshadowed the text's representations of rape and sexual abuse. The childlike voice of the narrative has been central to its appeal in a young adult market, yet Cisneros explains that the voice of Esperanza was a response to the elision of Latina voices in dominant culture. Cisneros wanted to create a narrative voice that emphasized Esperanza's marginalized position: "the language in Mango Street is . . . very much an anti-academic voice—a child's voice, a girl's voice, a poor girl's voice, a spoken voice, the voice of an American-Mexican" (1994b, xv). With the publication of *Hairs/ Pelitos*, a bilingual children's book based on the similarly titled vignette in *The House on Mango Street*, Cisneros offered literature explicitly for children in 1997, thereby suggesting the promotional and financial opportunities in creating work for young audiences, a topic that I explore below.[12]

Like Cisneros, Garza did not intend for her art to be marketed only to young adults and children. In the decades prior to the publication of her first children's book in 1990, the artist exhibited her paintings in solo and group exhibits primarily in regional art museums and galleries with a focus on Latina/o arts, including Galería Sin Fronteras in Austin, the Mexican Museum in San Francisco, Galería Posada in San Francisco, the San Francisco Museum of Modern Art, and the San Diego Museum of Art, among many other university and regional galleries across the United States.[13] As a result of many museum visitors either taking their children to her shows or expressing to Garza the power of her imagery in affirming and helping parents to teach Chicana/o cultural traditions to their children, Garza decided to present her art directly to children's audiences in the form of children's literature books in 1990 (Cortez 2010, 83). Garza also turned to this format because museum visits by children constituted only brief encounters with her artwork (Cortez 2010, 83).[14] It was not until the publication and national distribution of her first children's book, *Cuadros de Familia,* that Garza's art work also began to reach national and mainstream audiences, with many national museums now interested in displaying and collecting her work, including the Smithsonian Hirshhorn and American Art Museums in Washington, DC, the Whitney Museum of American Art in New York, the National Museum of Mexican Art in Chicago, and the Oakland Museum of California, among many others.[15] While the national eye therefore brought Cisneros to children's literature, Garza found that the children's literature format of her work gave her national recognition as an artist.

Seeing the positive impact of her art on children and the potential for expanding museum audiences with children's programming, Garza began to create pedagogical components for young audiences in her exhibits. Garza explains: "I cannot escape from being a teacher when I'm doing my exhibitions. Because once you're a teacher, you're always a teacher, and a lot of times museums are trying to expand their audience, which is one of the reasons they ask me to exhibit in their galleries" (qtd. in Cortez 2010, 83). Garza's inclusion of pedagogical aspects include her leading workshops for children, such as *papel picado* sessions for "Papel Picado: The Paper Cutouts of Carmen Lomas Garza," an exhibit at the Galería de la Raza in San Francisco in 1999; these sessions soon led Garza to write art manuals for children on the topic, including *Making Magic Windows: Creating Papel Picado with Carmen Lomas Garza* and *Magic Windows: Ventanas Májicas*, both published by Children's Book Press in 1999. For the first retrospective on Garza's art, "Carmen Lomas Garza: A Retrospective," at the San Jose Museum of Art in 2001, Garza also helped create a teacher resource handbook titled "Carmen Lomas Garza: A Teacher Resource Handbook," aimed at primary school teachers, to accompany the exhibit catalogue. Further examples of Garza's desire to focus on children's audiences in the museum include the interactive traveling exhibit *In My Family/En Mi Familia* in 2003, which began at the Austin Children's Museum and is now part of the museum's permanent collection.[16] For this show, Garza created a three-dimensional, bilingual, hands-on exhibit for kids and families, based on several illustrations from *En Mi Familia*, including *La Tamalada* (1987).

Cisneros and Garza's experiences with children's audiences suggest that they found great pedagogical value in reaching young people with their literary and artistic representations. Discussing the many Chicana/o authors who either turned to—or created works explicitly for—the field of children's literature in the 1980s and 1990s, Tey Diana Rebolledo claims: "It soon became clear that there was a need for books that provided cultural knowledge and role models for children. In elementary and middle schools, most books represented mainstream children and children's lives. Children of color would never see themselves reflected in these narratives. Some small presses, such as Children's Book Press, Bilingual Review Press, and Arte Público, began to publish books by authors of color, most with beautiful illustrations by artists of culture. Writers such as Pat Mora, Rudolfo Anaya, Carmen Lomas Garza, Sandra Cisneros, Lucha Corpi, Gary Soto, and Gloria Anzaldúa understood the importance of cultural transmission to children through books written for them" (2006, 280).[17]

Yet the publishing industry's positioning of Latina/o authors as young adult and children's literature writers has to some extent "infantilized" Latina/o authors (Saldívar 2012, 153), with many Chicana/o authors turning to writing and marketing their texts to young audiences out of financial practicality. Author Lucha Corpi explains: "There are a lot of Chicana writers who write books for children right now.... But I think that is more because publishers especially want Chicanas and Latinas to write children's books as they sell extremely well at the moment" (qtd. in Ikas 2001, 85). Poet and novelist Pat Mora further expresses the financial advantages of writing children's books: "I think that my motivation for nonfiction and children's books includes an element of practicality. Poetry might be an impractical choice in the sense that it is impractical financially" (qtd. in Ikas 2001, 136). Like Corpi and Mora, Cisneros and Garza—while they may not say so directly—clearly found that promoting their respective works to young adult audiences provided them with financial support they may not have otherwise had if they had solely created and marketed their works to adult audiences. In what follows, I explore how the specific struggles and social histories that are central to Cisneros and Garza's representations of domestic space and family, particularly their critique and engagement with gendered and patriarchal representations, have been obscured by the marketing of their texts within the young adult and children's literature genres.

Domestic Space and *Familias* in Chicana/o Nationalism

Cisneros's and Garza's depictions of domestic space both reference and critique Chicano/a cultural nationalism, particularly ideological configurations of family and the domestic sphere. Many Chicano/a Movement documents, particularly *El Plan Espiritual de Aztlán*, stressed the importance of the family in the fight against racial injustice and Anglo American racism, as well as the importance of literature and art as pedagogical tools to teach Mexican American and Mexican history, along with the colonization of the US Southwest, to Chicana/o youth (Rodríguez 2009). Part of the plan states, "Cultural values of our people strengthen our identity and the moral backbone of the movement. Our culture unites and educates the family of *La Raza* towards liberation with one heart and one mind. We must insure [sic] that our writers, poets, musicians, and artists produce literature and art that is appealing to our people and relates to our revolutionary culture. *Our cultural values of life, family, and home will serve as a powerful weapon to defeat the gringo dollar value system and encourage the process of love and brotherhood*" (Chicano Liberation Youth Conference 1972, 405, emphasis added). Explaining the link between *La Raza* and family, Maylei Blackwell explains, "*La familia* functioned as an allegory of *La Raza* and as a structuring metaphor for the Chicano Movement as a whole" (2011, 98). By conflating *la familia* with *La Raza*, Chicano/a cultural nationalism created idealized notions of family that departed from the lived experiences of men and women who have created heterogeneous family structures and alternate kinship networks for decades on both sides of the border (Rodríguez 2009; Ruiz 1998; Sánchez 1993).[18] Ultimately, Chicano/a nationalism emphasized patriarchal and heteronormative masculinity and carnalismo (brotherhood) in the household and Chicano/a nation (Blackwell 2011; Hernández 2009; Rodríguez 2009).

Chicana/o Movement writing and images, which produced and reified normative family structures, valorized male authority in the household and frequently depicted women as biological and cultural nurturers and reproducers of the family and nation. For example, sociologist Alfredo Mirandé configured Chicanas as the conduits of cultural reproduction in service of nationhood: "At the center of the family and the mainstay of the culture and its traditions, the Chicana has helped to counter the encroachment of colonialism. She perpetuates the language and values of Chicanos" (1977, 775). Mirandé continues, "In an environment where Chicano institutions have been rendered subordinate and dependent, the family has been the only institution to escape colonial intrusion" (1977, 775). Mirande's view on family promotes "political familism," or the "phenomenon in which the continuity of family groups and the adherence to family ideology provide[s] the basis for struggle" (Baca Zinn 1975, 16). Central to Mirande's "political familism," and other texts of the Chicano/a Movement, were idealized constructions of Chicanas as mothers of the nation, configuring women as reproducers of conservative and normative constructions of culture, family, and tradition (Blackwell 2011, 98).

Cisneros's and Garza's texts both critique and negotiate Chicano/a Movement cultural nationalism. Garza's artistic career illustrates her direct involvement with the Chicano/a Movement of the late 1960s and early 1970s. When Garza was in college from 1967 to 1972 at Texas A&I University in Kingsville, Texas, the Chicano/a Movement was already active in Crystal City, Texas, and the Mexican American Youth Organization (MAYO) had a strong presence in Kingsville, leading a high school walkout in 1969. Garza organized her first exhibit of Chicana/o art at the MAYO conference at La Lomita in Mission, Texas, in 1969, which included her works "Peace" (1967), "Los Mesquites" (1970), and "Self-Portrait" (1969).[19] Garza began to create art because she wanted to redress the racism and segregation she encountered growing up: "This issue about feeling pride in our culture was really crucial because so much damage had been done to us growing up in South Texas in the public schools, in the society in general, being made to feel ashamed of our own culture, our own language, because of discrimination, because of the hardships of being a minority" (1997). Garza continues: "My answer to . . . what I could do within the Chicano movement was . . . my artwork. . . . With the Chicano movement there was a big push to get to know our family histories and our historical background . . . [of] the Southwest and Mexico because we weren't taught that in the schools. We weren't taught, basically, the history of Mexico" (1997).

Even though Chicana feminist activism was present in South Texas in the late 1960s and 1970s, Garza distances herself from the feminist movement, emphasizing Chicano/a nationalism as the primary influence on her artistry, while also creating a binary between feminism and the Chicano/a Movement.[20] She states: "I know what my father has gone through. I know what my husband and my brothers have gone through, and I know what my nephews are going through with discrimination and racism. You know, I have to support them. They are my family." She continues, "I personally have not been an active member of the feminist art movement, or an aggressive participant in the feminist art movement. Because there's so much work to be done within our own movement of the Chicano movement" (Garza 1997). Representing a tension between an ethnic and feminist standpoint, Garza's description of the feminist movement echoes Chicano nationalist critiques of feminism at the time: that to focus on women's issues was to betray the Chicano/a family and community.[21] Chicana feminists, however, focused on the intersectionality of identity—that race, class, and gender were part of Chicano/a experiences and marginalization in the nation. Garza's promotion of Chicano/a nationalism indicates that Chicana artistic responses to the Movement were not monolithic; just as there is not a singular Chicana experience, there was not just one way of being a Chicana activist in the Movement (Blackwell 2011, 51). Recalling a high school experience of being placed in a home economics course, a situation confronted by many Chicanas during the 1950s and 1960s, Garza recalls how she asked her parents to help her circumvent the requirement so she could take biology: "All they are going to do is make an apron, sew an apron, cook a cake, make some eggs, learn how to clean. I already know how to do all of that . . . help me get the biology class" (Cortez 2010, 3). Here, Garza clearly voices a desire for educational opportunities beyond domestic labor in the home and public sphere, in this sense presenting a feminist critique of limited educational opportunities available to Chicanas.

Although not articulated as such, Garza's activism was rooted in her family's political activism, particularly her mother and father's involvement with the GI Forum in Kingsville, Texas, the local chapter of the national organization focused on assisting war veterans in the fight against discrimination in housing, education, health care, and employment. Garza's father was an active participant in the GI Forum, and her mother was a member of the Forum's Ladies' Auxiliary (Cortez 2010, 7). Both parents organized voter drives, supported Latina/o candidates, and fundraised to help students of the community obtain higher education (Cortez 2010, 8). Garza, while she might not align herself with feminism, witnessed in her mother the "everyday strength of women at the center of familial and community life whose sensibilities drew from a structure of feeling or commonsense beliefs about more egalitarian gendered roles based on a long legacy of working-class women's labor participation, activism, and, in some cases, radicalism" (Blackwell 2011, 50). When Garza moved to San Francisco in the 1970s, she also worked at and later managed Galería de la Raza, an art space that was home to many artists who produced art with Chicana feminist political messages.[22]

While Cisneros does not directly invoke Chicano/a nationalism as part of her inspiration for writing *The House on Mango Street*, she frequently references the exclusion of Chicana/os in the nation and in US literature as an impetus for her writing. This focus on home and Chicana/o cultural experiences connects to the Chicano/a nationalist focus on depicting family to combat demeaning portrayals. In an interview with NPR's *Morning Edition* to mark the twenty-fifth anniversary of *The House on Mango Street*, Cisneros explains her impetus for writing the text: "I had started Esperanza . . . at the University of Iowa, feeling very displaced and uncomfortable as a person of color, as a woman, as a person from working-class background. And in reaction to being there I started to write *Mango Street* almost as a way of claiming this is who I am. It became my flag" (2009b). Invoking the language of nationhood, Cisneros articulates the story of Esperanza and her experiences of home and family as central to her claiming space for Mexicanas in the US nation. Yet Cisneros cites Chicana/o literature's male dominance as one of her inspirations for writing. She explains, "At the time I wrote *House* around the end of the 70s and the early 80s, I was reading Chicano literature written by men" (2011).

A postnationalist feminist politics therefore underlies Cisneros's reasons for writing her text. In interviews, Cisneros critiques the "vendida logic," or the idea that Chicanas who are feminists are race traitors—a tension evident in Garza's constructed binary between feminism and the Chicano/a Movement. Cisneros states that because of this vendida logic she initially experienced guilt for her feminist portrayals in many of her writings: "For a long time—and it's true for many writers and women like myself who have grown up in a patriarchal culture, like Mexican culture—I felt great guilt betraying that culture. Your culture tells you that if you step out of line, if you break . . . norms, you are becoming Anglicized" (Satz 1997, 170). In response, Cisneros emphasizes the intersectionality of identity, with race, gender, and class marginalization as the foundation for her representations of Mexican American women's experiences in *The House on Mango Street*. Cisneros describes her thinking: "I knew I was a Mexican woman. . . . My race, my gender, and my class. . . . That's when I decided I would write about something my classmates couldn't write about" (qtd. in Aranda 1990, 65). Cisneros's explanation of Chicana experiences as inflected by race, gender, and class asserts a Chicana feminist viewpoint and critiques the Chicano/a nationalist emphasis on ethnicity and race to the exclusion of gender, class, sexuality, and other identity categories. Although Cisneros explains that in the 1980s "Gloria Anzaldúa and Cherríe Moraga [were] cutting their own paths through the world somewhere, but [I didn't] know about them" (2009a, xv), her works share Anzaldúa's and Moraga's, and other Chicana feminists' of the 1980s and 1990s, focus on the multiplicity of identity, thereby destabilizing hegemonic constructions of masculinity at the heart of cultural nationalism.[23]

Despite their distinct approaches to Chicana feminism, both Cisneros and Garza approach domestic space from what Pérez terms "feminism-in-nationalism" or "third space" feminism (1999). Since Chicanas have been marginalized in nationalist rhetoric and imagery, many Chicana authors and artists write within the "gaps, interstices, silences, and crevices" of dominant power to reconfigure nationalist constructions of gender (Blackwell 2011, 109; Peréz 1999). Garza's approach to working in the "gaps" of nationalism has come not from a postnationalist politics, as has Cisneros's, but rather from a "domesticana" perspective. Mesa-Bains's concept of domesticana suggests how Chicana artists utilize the materials of the domestic in order to reconfigure gender and power within domestic space. Mesa-Bains's installation *Venus Envy Chapter One (or the First Holy Communion Moments before the End)* (1993), for instance, uses materials found in domestic interiors and religious shrines—rosaries, a communion dress, a vanity, a mirror, and dressing table—in order to emphasize the social and cultural institutions that shape Mexican American women's subjectivity, while also deconstructing patriarchy. A domesticana aesthetic, therefore, depicts domestic space in order to deconstruct gender roles within the home and to forge new models of Chicana identity. While domesticana aesthetics might appear to feign complicity with dominant structures and values, they ultimately transgress and reposition these values by calling attention to the institutions that shape them.

Postnationalist Domesticity in *The House on Mango Street*

Cisneros's *The House on Mango Street*, a collection of forty-five vignettes, or short prose-poems, is narrated from the point of view of a young Chicana named Esperanza Cordero, who desires a "house of her own." While female-authored domestic narratives have traditionally used the space of the house as the symbol of gender oppression, Cisneros uses the symbol to represent racial marginalization and the ideological, cultural, and economic limits imposed on Esperanza as a first-generation Chicana growing up in the United States. The text therefore revises Virginia Woolf's "a room of one's own"—a response to gendered marginalization—by focusing on Esperanza's particular experience as a gendered and racialized subject in US society. The narrative illustrates Esperanza's development from childhood to adolescence within the context of racial discrimination and gender subjugation. Esperanza's desire for a "house of one's own" is a response to both the gendered patriarchal constraints signified by her father and the crowded living conditions of her impoverished neighborhood. The narrator first articulates her desire for space in the nation as a response to society's exclusion of her family from obtaining the "American Dream." In a now-classic passage from the text, Esperanza states:

> They always told us that one day we would move into a house, a real house
> that would be ours for always so we wouldn't have to move each year. And our

house would have running water and pipes that worked. And inside it would have real stairs, not hallway stairs, but stairs inside like the houses on T.V. . . . Our house would be white with trees around it, a great big yard and grass growing without a fence. . . . But the house on Mango Street is not the way they told it at all. It's small and red . . . Bricks are crumbling in places . . . There is no front yard . . . Everybody has to share a bedroom . . . I knew then I had to have a house. A real house. One I could point to. But this isn't it. The house on Mango Street isn't it. (1991a, 4)

The "they" in this passage references both Esperanza's parents and the nation that has sold the myth of the American Dream to Esperanza and her family. Esperanza is aware that her family's house on Mango Street does not mirror the myth that has been sold to her on TV, a distinction between Esperanza's real house and dream house that the narrative configures through spatial metaphors: instead of a two-story, large house with "real stairs," several bedrooms, and a "big" yard, Esperanza's house is "small," "crumbling," with "hallway stairs" and "no front yard." The description of Esperanza's "real" home signals how, even as Esperanza and her parents might desire the American Dream on an ideological level, she and her family remain materially excluded from it (Quintana 1996, 57). Like many migrant families, Esperanza and her family have moved and lived in various houses in Chicago, most likely due to job necessities and lack of economic security (McCracken 1989, 64). Here, I use the term "migrant" to refer to Esperanza's family's "subordinate position with respect to that of the citizen" (Schmidt-Camacho 2008, 5). As "migrants," Esperanza describes how her family has been unable to find a stable and adequate home: "We didn't always live on Mango Street. Before that we lived on Loomis on the third floor, and before that we lived on Keeler. Before Keeler it was Paulina, and before that I can't remember. *But what I remember most is moving a lot*" (1991a, 3, emphasis added).

Early reviews of *The House on Mango Street* critiqued Cisneros's representation of Esperanza's yearning for a stable house as a materialistic desire conforming and reifying the myth of the American Dream, and as supporting an assimilationist mythology that requires marginalized communities to conform to US society and dominant culture (Morales 1993; Rodríguez 1984). These criticisms overlook how Cisneros's narrative deconstructs the myth of the American Dream by showing Esperanza's alienation from it. Such early criticisms also failed to consider the important feminist message of Cisneros's text as it calls for a woman's personal space, a "house of one's own" free from patriarchal constraints, domestic abuse, and the policing of female sexuality. In a key scene of the narrative, Esperanza articulates her desire for a space of her own as one free from the patriarchal dictates and architecture of her father: "Not a flat. Not an apartment in back. Not a man's house. Not a daddy's. A house all my own. With my porch and my pillow, my pretty purple petunias. My books and my stories. My two shoes waiting beside the bed. Nobody to shake a stick at. Nobody's garbage to pick up after. Only a house as quiet as snow, a space for myself to go, clean as paper before the poem" (1991a, 108).

The House on Mango Street also depicts domestic space from a postnationalist perspective, reconfiguring the idealized homes and *familias* of Chicano/a nationalism with a Chicana feminist critique of home. With many depictions of women imprisoned within the domestic sphere, the narrative illustrates how Chicanas have been betrayed by the ideology of family. Early on in the narrative, Esperanza tells the story of her great-grandmother who was held captive by her husband, despite her challenge to the marriage: "My great-grandmother. I would've liked to have known her, a wild horse of a woman, so wild she wouldn't marry until my great-grandfather threw a sack over her head and carried her off. Just like that, as if she were a fancy chandelier (1991a, 10–11). The story of Esperanza's great-grandmother reveals how women in her family have been treated as objects of property, with the great-grandmother carried off as a "fancy chandelier," no longer an active subject—"a wild horse of a woman"—but now a commodity. Several examples of domestic confinement and captivity permeate the text, and a repeated motif in the book are images of women sitting in windows, standing in doorways, and longingly gazing out from these spaces (Olivares 1988; Saldívar-Hull 2000). For instance, Esperanza describes her grandmother as "look[ing] out the window all her life, the way so many women sit their sadness on an elbow" (1991a, 11). Esperanza also depicts the character Rafaela as "still young but getting old from leaning out of the window so much . . . locked indoors because her husband is afraid Rafaela will run away since she is too beautiful to look at" (1991a, 76). Esperanza also signals her desire to break from the patriarchal past of her great-grandmother with the metaphor of the window. She explains, "I have inherited her name, but I don't want to inherit her place by the window" (1991a, 11). Later in the text, when concerned about the physical abuse endured by her friend Sally, Esperanza also uses the image of open windows as a metaphor for women's escape from abusive gender roles: "And if you opened the little window latch and gave it a shove, the windows would swing open, all the sky would come in" (1991a, 82–83).

Depictions of physical and sexual abuse permeate *The House on Mango Street*, deconstructing the idealized, romanticized image of the family as a safe haven for Chicanas. Esperanza depicts how her friend Sally—"the girl with eyes like Egypt and nylons the color of smoke"—is physically abused by her father because her father "says to be this beautiful is trouble" (1991a, 81). Esperanza describes Sally's explanation of her father's abuse: "he hit her with his hands just like a dog, she said, like if I was an animal" because "he thinks I'm going to run away like his sisters who made the family ashamed. Just because I'm a daughter, and then she doesn't say" (1991a, 82). Dehumanized as an animal, treated "just like a dog," Sally confronts physical punishment and abuse because of her gender—"just because I'm a daughter" (1991a, 82). Esperanza herself experiences direct physical abuse and violence to her body, with the narrative's somber moment of a rape scene, which also includes the racialization of her identity: "The one who grabbed me by the arm, he wouldn't let me go. He said I love you, Spanish girl, I love you, and pressed his sour mouth to mine. . . . They all lied. All the books and magazines, everything told it wrong. Only his dirty fingernails against my skin, only his sour smell again" (1991a, 100). Here, the "they" represents the mythology of gender roles and patriarchy dominant in popular media, particularly romance novels and telenovelas, sites that represent hegemonic gender roles in many of Cisneros's texts.[24]

As a result of physical and sexual abuse experienced by Esperanza and other women of her community, Esperanza turns to alternative models of kinship and *la familia* through *comadrazgo*, or a female-based model of kinship based on Catholicism's godparent kinship system. The text's focus on comadrazgo deconstructs Chicano/a cultural nationalism and patriarchy. Comadrazgo has functioned historically as a support system aiding women's survival in the absence of males (Fregoso 2003, 89–90). Rosa Linda Fregoso describes comadrazgo as an "alternative to the patriarchal kinship basis of familia," which deconstructs the power of masculinity and male dominance (2003, 90). Vicki Ruiz describes alternative kinship networks among female agricultural workers in the early twentieth century, where "Mexicanas created their own worlds of influence predicated on women's networks, on ties of familial and fictive kin. *Comadrazgo* served as one of the undergirdings for general patterns of reciprocity as women cared for one another as family and neighbors" (1998, 16). *The House on Mango Street* depicts women who turn to comadrazgo, not because men are absent in their families and communities, but due to male dominance and patriarchal marginalization of women in the domestic household. We see how Esperanza—even as a young girl, along with the other women in the Mango Street community, particularly through her relationships with Sally and her best friend, Alicia—forges close networks and bonds that help her emotionally survive her sexual abuse and the physical abuse experienced by her friends. Additionally, comadrazgo functions as an alternative kinship system "between younger women and older, compassionate and understanding women who have also resisted and survived la vida dura" (Fregoso 2003, 101; Miranda 2003). For example, Esperanza meets many female elders, specifically curanderas, who function as her mentors, particularly Elenita and "The Three Sisters," who advise her to come back to Mango Street and to not forget her home and identity (1991a, 63–64, 105). One of the "Three Sisters" tells Esperanza: "When you leave you must remember to come back for the others. A circle, understand? You will always be Esperanza. You will always be Mango Street. You can't erase what you know. You can't forget who you are" (1991a, 105). The curanderas therefore support Esperanza's desire to leave Mango Street only on the condition that she returns to it. Here, the text illustrates the expected filial obligation of Esperanza to her community, as the daughter of Mango Street, which signifies the nation.

Yet by the end of *The House on Mango Street*, Esperanza desires to leave her home and community because she is only able to see her family and neighborhood as spaces of patriarchal confinement; in this way, her perspective departs from the female elders' view of her expected filial obligation to home and culture. In the final vignette of the text, a familiar passage reappears from the first vignette, yet with an important modification: "We didn't always live on Mango Street. Before that we lived on Loomis on the third floor, and before that we lived on Keeler. Before Keeler it was Paulina, *but what I remember most is Mango Street, sad red house, the house I belong but do not belong to*" (1991a, 109, emphasis added). The passage shifts from Esperanza's memory that she moved a lot— "what I remember most is moving a lot"—to remembering the house itself on Mango Street, specifically the house "I belong but do not belong to" (1991a, 109). Here, the house represents Esperanza's family, community, and nation. From this line, we can infer that Esperanza articulates that she feels she belongs because of shared cultural and familial identities, but that she also feels excluded due to her desire to resist the patriarchal models of earlier generations and search for new models of home and family. The character's aim to leave her community has led many critics to claim Cisneros's text as assimilationist, thereby framing the author and the narrative according to the "vendida logic." Cisneros explained, "According to their perspective, to be alone, to be exiled from the family, is so anti-Mexican" (qtd. in Satz 1997, 182).

The ending of the text emphasizes that Esperanza, after leaving home and completing an education and establishing a "house of one's own," will in fact return to Mango Street to help her community. Esperanza first tells her friend Alicia: "No, this isn't my house I say and shake my head as if shaking could undo the year I've lived here. I don't belong. I don't ever want to come from here." Yet Alicia replies, "No . . . like it or not you are Mango Street and one day you'll come back too" (1991a, 31–32). Alicia, like Esperanza, wants to forge alternative choices for herself outside of patriarchal confinement to the domestic. Alicia already attends the university, "tak[ing] two trains and a bus, because she doesn't want to spend her whole life in a factory or behind a rolling pin" (1991a, 31–32). Alicia proceeds to explain to Esperanza that it is the responsibility of women like them, who will complete a formal education, to change Mango Street. Ultimately heeding Alicia's advice to come back to Mango Street, Esperanza states in the concluding lines of the text, "Friends and neighbors will say, What happened to that Esperanza? Where did she go with all those books and paper? Why did she march so far away? They will not know I have gone away to come back. For the ones I left behind. For the ones who cannot out" (1991a, 110).[25] Esperanza's declaration that she will come back to help the ones "who cannot out" signals, on the one hand, a philanthropic desire to help those in her community once she obtains an education; this is the idea voiced by her friend Alicia. Yet on the other hand, the text illustrates that Esperanza's desire to return home is due to the cultural expectation that she return to her community and family. In the end, Esperanza is construed as perpetually obligated to her family and nation: "she can no sooner 'forget' Mango Street than she can 'disown' her parents" (Cruz 2001, 934). In this sense, the ending of Cisneros's text wages a critique of cultural nationalism by alluding to the burden placed upon Esperanza as the expected, loyal daughter of Mango Street.

Domestic Confinement: Celebratory Multicultural Readings of Esperanza's "House of One's Own"

Celebratory multicultural readings of *The House on Mango Street* have worked to decontextualize the "contextual lenses [of] ethnicity, race, gender, and class" (Cruz 2001, 922) that frame Esperanza's claims to national space, overlooking the text's various critiques of racial and gender marginalization. Cisneros's text appeals to many audiences due to its relatively "simple" narrative structure and voice, which has led to the text's accessibility and usage across multiple educational levels. Yet mainstream readings of Cisneros's *The House on Mango Street* co-opt the simplicity and accessibility of the text's youthful narrator by understanding Esperanza's voice as speaking to readers in a "dispassionate tone" (Poey 1996, 72). That is, instead of having an explicitly critical and disgruntled narrator that criticizes the racial and economic marginalization confronted by Latina/os in the United States, the narrator of *The House on Mango Street* has a childlike simplicity that appears non-threatening to mainstream audiences (Poey 1996, 211).

Mainstream reception of Cisneros's text has also tended to celebrate young Esperanza's desire for home and the American Dream as a right that is equally available to all citizens (Cruz 2001, 921). Scholar Felicia J. Cruz, for instance, found that while teaching *The House on Mango Street* to her mostly white, middle-class undergraduates, her students "inscribed Esperanza's dream in a foundational democratic rhetoric and declaration (that the pursuit of freedom, liberty, and happiness is the right of all American citizens)" (2001, 921). The consequence of this reading is that it became very difficult for students to "apprehend, much less feel, the extent to which Esperanza—and, by extension, her community— exists at a far remove from white, middleclass standards and styles of living" (Cruz 2001, 921). Emphasizing a "house of one's own" as a "natural" right, while it importantly affirms the tenets of democracy, overlooks the many structural inequalities that have made it difficult for various communities to obtain equal access to US citizenship and rights, a situation made evident by young Esperanza's search for a "house of one's own."

Celebratory multicultural readings also emphasize the universality of the narrative, placing the text within the well-established Western literary convention of the *bildungsroman*, or the coming-of-age novel (Poey 1996, 2002).[26] *The House on Mango Street* shares many traits of the bildungsroman: the depiction of a young person's development in relationship to and in opposition to others; a protagonist who moves through various stages of maturity; a protagonist who desires physical removal from family and community; and a protagonist who confronts many obstacles, leading to a deeper understanding of the individual self within the social order. Yet the text departs significantly from the genre's characteristic focus on individualism and male characters because the narrative concentrates on Chicana subjectivity, matriarchal structures, and collective community (Poey 1996, 2002). Cisneros's narrative inscribes Esperanza's race, gender, and class as central to understanding the specific social order that she confronts in the novel. Additionally, while the story is narrated predominantly by Esperanza, the text is comprised of forty-six vignettes that describe and express her interior world from a wide spectrum of characters that make up the Mango Street community, thereby illustrating the text's departure from the genre's emphasis on individualism, instead focusing on community, even as the text conforms to the genre by showing Esperanza's desire to depart from her community at the end.[27] The reading of Cisneros's *The House on Mango Street* as a bildungsroman enables the text to be embraced across literary and cultural studies frameworks, thereby giving the text visibility in educational settings. Yet such readings and the mainstreaming of the narrative have elided the text's pointed critique of the gendered, racial, and economic marginalization confronted by Latinas in domestic space, as both household and nation.

"Deceptively Simple": Domesticana Negotiations and Egalitarian *Familias* as Protest

Carmen Lomas Garza's children's books *Family Pictures/Cuadros de Familia* (1990) and *In My Family/En Mi Familia* (1996), similar to Cisneros's *The House on Mango Street,* represent a young Chicana's vision of gendered and racialized space in a racially segregated society. Yet unlike *The House on Mango Street,* Garza's children's books do not reference the outside world of gendered and racial marginalization. Instead, they depict idyllic relationships between fathers and daughters, between mothers and daughters, and between daughters and other family members, thereby departing significantly from the physically, sexually, and emotionally abusive father-daughter and husband-wife relationships that permeate Cisneros's *The House on Mango Street.* These affirmative scenes of Chicana/o families and domestic spaces, set mostly in South Texas, however, are "deceptively simple" (Noriega 2010, ix), in that they function as responses to the dehumanization and racial segregation that Garza encountered as a young girl growing up in Kingsville, Texas. Garza explains, "If you see my heart and humanity through my art then hopefully you will not exclude me from rightfully participating in society" (qtd. in Mesa-Bains 1991, 13).[28] Here, Garza views her art as part of a larger project to counter dehumanizing images and negative rhetoric about Latina/os prevalent in the dominant media. With her art, her ultimate aim is to garner political equality, inclusion, and respect for Latina/o communities in the US nation.

Garza's *Cuadros de Familia* (1990) (fig. 6), a collection of fourteen illustrations with accompanying bilingual text, visualizes and narrates family practices, celebrations, and domestic rituals along the US-Mexico border from the perspective of the young protagonist Carmen, who is autobiographically Garza as a young girl. *En Mi Familia* (1996) (fig. 7), published six years later and including thirteen illustrations and bilingual text, continues the young protagonist Carmen's perspective of her family and community on the US-Mexico border, as well as of her extended family in other regions of the United States, including Northern California.[29] Both children's books are aimed toward children ranging from ages six to twelve, and they both contain a bilingual narrative that depicts young Carmen's perspective of domestic interiors and family scenes. By depicting Chicana/o families and communities within a bilingual narrative and borderlands cultural context, Garza's children's books affirm and value biculturalism and multilingualism for many Mexicanos in South Texas and in the United States; the Spanish and

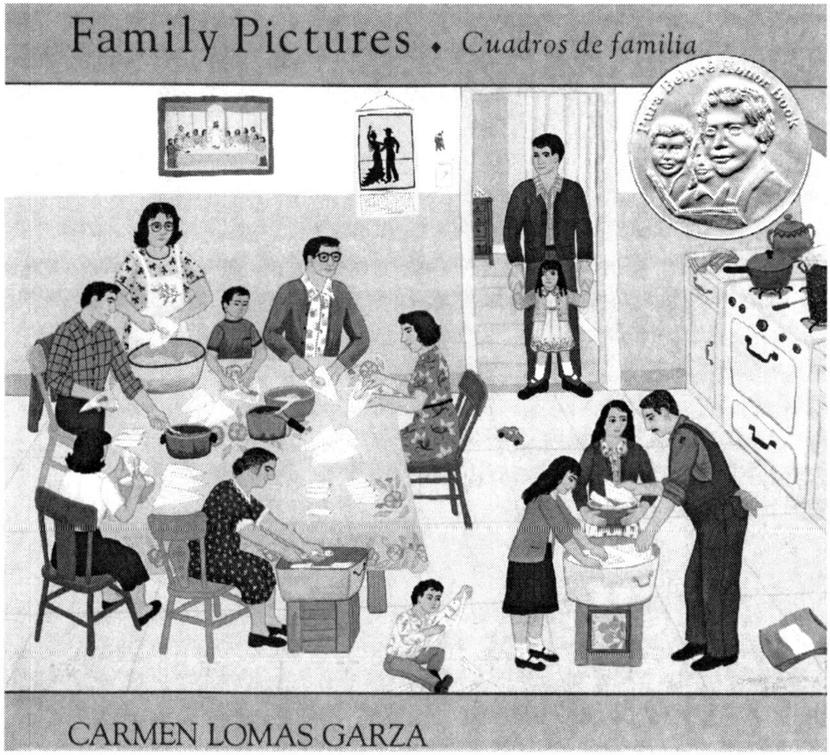

Figure 6. Cover of Carmen Lomas Garza, *Family Pictures/Cuadros de Familia* (1990). Permission arranged with Lee & Low Books Inc., New York, NY.

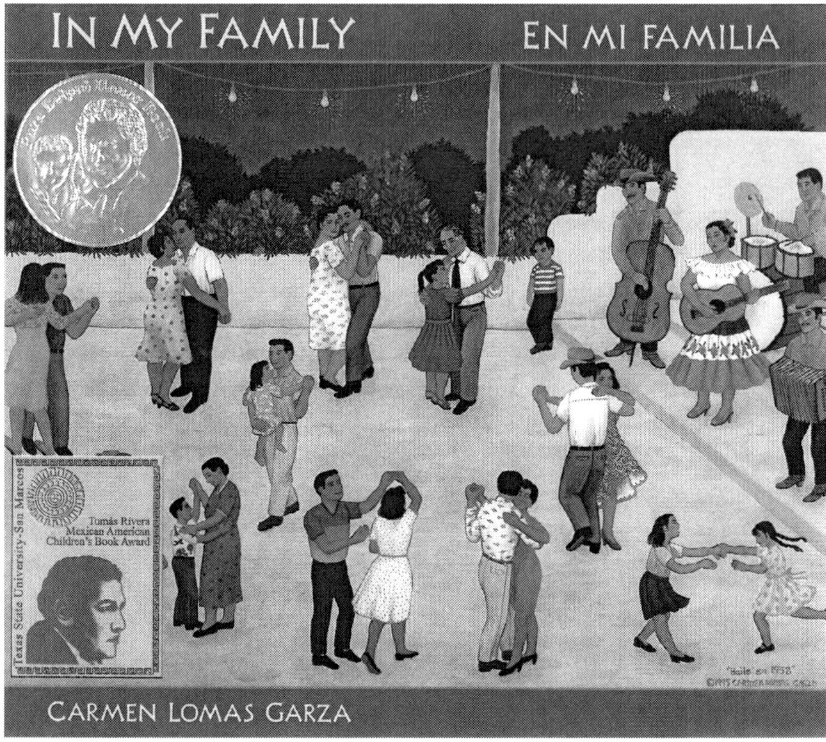

Figure 7. Cover of Carmen Lomas Garza, *In My Family/En Mi Familia* (1996). Permission arranged with Lee & Low Books Inc., New York, NY.

English narratives also create accessibility for Spanish-speaking audiences, while also valuing and affirming Spanish to English-speaking audiences.

By focusing on family, Garza's representations uphold the nationalist focus on family "as a crucial symbol and organizing principle that [has] by and large frame[d] the history of Mexican Americans in the United States" (Rodríguez 2009, 2). Yet distinct from cultural nationalism, Garza's illustrations and accompanying narratives present an egalitarian vision of gender roles and a critique of hegemonic masculinity. For instance, two of her paintings—*La Tamalada* (1987) both inside and on the cover of *Cuadros de Familia* (fig. 6) and *Empanadas* (1991) in *En Mi Familia*—depict Carmen's family and extended family in the process of making tamales and empanadas, respectively, and feature Carmen's spatial relationships with her mother, father, aunts, grandparents, brothers, and sisters. The accompanying text of *La Tamalada* reads, "This is a scene from my parent's kitchen. Everybody is making tamales. My grandfather is wearing blue overalls and a blue shirt. I'm right next to him with my sister Margie. We're helping to soak the dried leaves from the corn. My mother is spreading the cornmeal dough on the leaves and my aunt and uncle are spreading meat on the dough.

My grandmother is lining up the rolled and folded tamales ready for cooking. *In some families just the women make tamales, but in our family everybody helps"* (1990, 22, emphasis added). Immediately noticeable in both *La Tamalada* and *Empanadas*, even without the accompanying narrative, is that an egalitarian food-making process has replaced a gendered and sexual division of labor—everyone is helping with the making of tamales and empanadas. Additionally, the image and accompanying text of *Empanadas* depict Carmen's Uncle Beto, along with her Aunt Paz, both wearing aprons and participating in the making of empanadas. The imagery of Uncle Beto engaged in domestic tasks challenges the gendered division of labor constructed in Chicano/a nationalist imagery. It also contrasts with mainstream media depictions of Chicano masculinity, specifically the stereotypical view of Latino males as "macho." Garza's works deconstruct dominant media constructions of Latino masculinity by frequently featuring men and young boys cooking in the domestic sphere, along with young boys learning about spirituality and healing.

In contrast to Chicano/a nationalist depictions of family and women, Garza's children's books do not depict women as peripheral characters, but as the central focus of several paintings, often engaged in domestic work such as teaching cultural traditions, healing, and cooking. While this focus on women as nurturers of the domestic sphere may risk alignment with Chicano/a nationalist imagery, Garza's focus on the domestic departs from cultural nationalism with a domesticana viewpoint that depicts Chicanas as active agents in the domestic realm, not as passive recipients of the culture. Domesticana strategies, as Mesa-Bains explains, are "in part, a way of calling into question the patriarchal control in the domestic sphere and subverting its representation through their visual practices" (2003, 302). Mesa-Bains continues, "The vernacular of the domestic is played out amid the contradictions of working-class women whose histories in labor activism and struggle would indicate an independence no longer bound by patriarchy of the home and family. Yet the tension remains between the lived reality of resilience and capacity and the submission to the culturally ascribed role of the female in a male-dominated context" (2003, 302). This tension between a critique of the patriarchal model and acknowledgement of existence within it, according to Mesa-Bains, has led Chicana artists to utilize the materials of the domestic to negotiate and counter power relations within the private realm.

For instance, in *Curandera*, included in *En Mi Familia*, Garza depicts the resistant forms of knowledge and modes of survival enacted by the figure of the curandera. The painting depicts Doña Maria, a curandera, performing a cleansing on Carmen's sister Mary Jane. Mesa-Bains explains, "These healers are Chicana curanderas who clean away with their brooms and smoke the marks of discrimination and return the body and mind to a wholeness" (1991, 27). In contrast to Chicano cultural nationalism that emphasizes women's central roles as nurturers of *la familia* due to their biological and cultural reproduction, the figure of the curandera underscores women's knowledge and location in the domestic detached from women's roles as wives and mothers. Curanderas embody a matriarchal heritage and gender structure that privilege native indigenous culture, and in this way, the figure of the curandera resists both patriarchy and colonialism.

Garza's focus on the role of adult Chicanas who carry out cultural traditions illustrates what Caren Kaplan argues in another context, how "cultural marginality necessitates the recognition of specific skills" (1987, 187). In Garza's paintings, the "view of cultural marginality" is the specific knowledge of the Chicana elders and adults in her community who have developed specialized skills to combat dehumanization. Garza illustrates Carmen in, what Raúl Villa has suggested in another context, "the active discovery of potential skills or models of action she may draw upon for her own cultural survival" (2000, 224). Garza's depictions therefore illustrate how women adapt and survive in the present. Furthermore, since these are illustrations from young Carmen's perspective, they suggest how a younger generation of women might adapt and innovate on these domestic practices. Garza's paintings therefore depict young Chicanas, not as passive recipients of culture, but as active agents directly engaged in interpreting and creating culture.

BURDEN OF REPRESENTATION: NEGOTIATING MUSEUM SPACES

Garza's focus on family celebrations and everyday cultural practices, which appear to be idyllic and "deceptively simple," has placed a burden of representation on her artistry throughout her career.[30] Given, as Chon Noriega explains, "their pleasing and deceptively simple appearance," Garza's work has been frequently framed as apolitical, even though her works "bear the weight of violent and exclusionary practices that have had institutional and societal force" (2010, ix). For example, a reviewer of Garza's solo exhibit "Directions, Carmen Lomas Garza" at the Hirshhorn Museum and Sculpture Garden at the Smithsonian in 1995 critiqued her for *not* depicting negative images. According to Garza, the critic "felt that I was doing artwork that was too pretty and too clean and I was not depicting all the bad things about my culture—the wife-beatings, the poverty, the horrid living conditions, all of these things. There's no cockroaches on the walls on my paintings and there's no wife beatings. It was awful. It was so racist" (Kalstrom 2007). Such reviews overlook the political impetus behind Garza's affirmative representations, functioning as responses to the dehumanizing rhetoric, images, and politics confronted by Latina/o communities. The supposed simplicity and cleanliness of Garza's imagery has led her work to be widely embraced by mainstream museum institutions seeking to promote Latina/o art through a sanitized view of Latina/o culture. For instance, Garza's mixed media installation "Day of the Dead/Offering to Frida Kahlo" was the only art piece by a Chicana artist included in the major "Hispanic Art in the United States: Thirty

Contemporary Painters and Sculptors" exhibition in 1987. Even when Garza's work has been included in exhibits with a Chicana/o art focus, her images have been praised over other Chicana/o artists for depicting positive and affirmative representations of Chicana/o culture. For example, four pieces by Garza were included in the first major traveling exhibit of Chicana/o art in the United States, "Chicano Art: Resistance and Affirmation, 1965–1985 (CARA)" in 1990, including *Lotería/ Tabla Llena, Curandera, La Virgen de San Juan de Los Lagos,* and *Cama para Sueños.*

When the National Museum of American Art (NMAA), the institution responsible for coordinating the showing of CARA at the Smithsonian, wanted to use *Cama para Sueños* as the frontispiece of the CARA exhibit, debate over the use of this piece ensued between the NMAA and the CARA exhibit organizers. *Cama Para Sueños,* also included in Garza's children's book *Cuadros de Familia,* shows Carmen's mother inside the house performing domestic tasks and attending to the needs of her daughters, while Carmen and her sister sit on top of the roof, daydreaming and pointing toward the sky and constellations. The image represents the daughters' future aspirations and break from the mother's domestic past, yet a future enabled by their mother's domestic labor and nurturing of their artistic imaginations. *Cama para Sueños* was also the inspiration for a now-famous scene in Gregory Nava's 1997 film *Selena,* in which, just as in the painting, we see the daughter, in this case Selena, sitting on the roof of her house, looking at the moon, dreaming and talking to her sister about her future, while below, visible from the window, we see Selena's mother preparing their beds in the domestic household.[31]

Andrew Connors, the curatorial associate at the NMAA responsible for coordinating the show at the Smithsonian, strongly felt that *Cama para Sueños* should be used as the logo for the CARA exhibit because "it doesn't talk about issues, it doesn't talk about the pachucos, or resistance. It really only talks about affirmation" (qtd. in Gaspar de Alba 1998, 181). Connor further states, "And our point . . . was that we had to get people into the exhibition first and then you can teach them, but if you don't get them in with an appealing image, you have no opportunity to teach them. . . . I think [the image] really implies what this exhibition is about . . . many people come with a sense that this is where artists were at a particular time in history, and now there is an opportunity, a potential for opening doors into something for the future, and to have Carmen and her sister up there pointing to the stars, pointing to the future, I think is a very hopeful sign" (qtd. in Gaspar de Alba 1998, 181). Yet the curators of the CARA exhibit at the UCLA Wright Gallery in Los Angeles had already chosen and used a CARA logo, created by Willie Herrón and Patrice Roberts, which includes the acronym "CARA" with disembodied eyes staring through the letters with an image of a chain link fence behind the acronym. In the preface to the exhibition book, the curators explain that "the eyes of the CARA face—its visible gaze that reflects back on its viewer—conceptually embody the reflexive nature of [the] entire planning and implementation process" (1991, 29) As scholar and curator Teresa McKenna states, "The vision of CARA was a vision that was Chicano, and it was civil rights oriented. . . . *Cama para Sueños* was not the most political piece in the exhibition . . . and so, therefore, that choice was an affront to what CARA was all about" (qtd. in Gaspar de Alba, 1998, 186). McKenna further explains, "Even Carmen Lomas Garza was initially unwilling to let us use it, because she said it did not represent the exhibition well, that it was not typical of the exhibition" (qtd. in Gaspar de Alba, 1998, 186). McKenna's concerns about the use of *Cama para Sueños* as the CARA logo at the Smithsonian reflect a politics of representation: the CARA curators believed that the NMAA's desire to use Garza's *Camas para Sueños* as the frontispiece for their exhibit would elide a painful history of segregation and marginalization, while the coordinators of the NMAA wanted to use Garza's painting because they viewed it as safer, positive, celebratory, and inviting. Both claims overshadow Garza's reasons for depicting affirmative scenes of Chicana/o communities and domestic practices on the border, precisely because they are responses to a marginalized and discriminatory past that she endured in South Texas.

"I Am Not a Naïve Artist": Challenging
Celebratory Readings of Garza's *Familias*

Similar to the reception of Cisneros's *The House on Mango Street* as a simple text, Garza's art within her two children's books have been praised as simple, charming, and folklike. The framing of Garza's texts as simple makes sense when read within the context of children's literature because many library and parent's reading organizations stress simplicity and accessibility of children's texts as markers of quality. Yet the overall reception of her art work as simplistic and representing folk and naïve styles obscures her professional training as an artist, as well as the politicized content and specific context of race, gender, and class marginalization underlying her representations. Many reviews of Garza's illustrations in her children's books label them as "simple." In reviews of *Cuadros de Familia*, the *School Library Journal* describes Garza's illustrations as "charming," while *Parents' Choice* describes Garza's paintings as having a "flat, naïve style."[32] Garza explains, "People call my work naive, folk or primitive. It's not naive, because I've been trained professionally, and it's not folk art because I'm not working in a specific tradition, and it's not primitive because I don't live in a primitive society."[33] Art historian Tomás Ybarra-Frausto also explains that although Garza's art includes both a "naïve earnestness" and "folkloric element," her work is "neither instinctive nor primitive." He continues, "The artist is technically adept and academically trained. . . . Although her work does not posit an overt political statement, it originates from a conscious desire to respond to the contemporary situation of the Chicano by projecting positive images derived from its culture" (1980, 3). Within the context of her children's books, reviews of her art as simple and accessible belie how Garza's affirmative depictions of Chicana/o families and domestic spaces in South Texas function to garner social and political respect for Latina/o communities.

Celebratory multicultural readings of Garza's children's books praise them for their ability to create common ground among diverse cultural communities, precisely due to Garza's focus on family celebrations and home. The use of Garza's works to create equality and a shared sense of history in the classroom is an important goal in a multicultural curriculum, yet such universal framings elide the specific history of discrimination and disenfranchisement, which undergird Garza's representations of *familias* and domesticity. Using Garza's illustrations to only discuss universal experiences in the classroom ends up "managing ethnic difference," rather than teaching about social struggles to create paths for social change (Palumbo-Liu 1995, 11). For example, in 2005, the first lady of Iowa, Christia Vilsack, chose *Cuadros de Familia* as the state's book of the year, distributing 45,000 copies of the text to various state education agencies and organizations. Vilsack's choice to use *Cuadros de Familia* as the book of the year signals the text's esteemed status in educational curriculum and a genuine desire to include Latina/o stories and experiences in Iowa schools. Yet Vilsack's reasoning for the selection of the book echoes celebratory multiculturalism's emphasis on managing ethnic difference in the classroom. She explains, "The bilingual book gives every family a chance to talk about their special family and cultural traditions. . . . Like German, Scandinavian, Dutch, Italian, Irish, and Southeast Asian immigrants, who joined the Native Americans here in Iowa, Latino families are blending into communities across our state and contributing to a changing Iowa" (qtd. in Cortez, 83–84). Vilsack suggests that the acceptance of Latina/o families in Iowan society is premised on their "blending into" or assimilating into US culture, even as Vilsack notes the importance of the "bilingual book" as an important aspect of the text. Vilsack also conflates Latina/o experience with European and South Asian immigration, as well as Native American experience, rather than acknowledge crucial distinctions between the immigrant histories, experiences, and treatment of these groups in the United States, as well as important differences among diverse Latina/o immigrant groups and communities.[34] Unlike European immigrants and other recent immigrants to the United States, many people of Mexican descent trace their family history and land ownership prior to the conquest of the US Southwest. The experiences of recent Latina/o immigrants also depart from those of European immigrants due to the nation's racialization of nonwhite communities. Therefore, similar to the reception of Cisneros's *The House on Mango Street*, readings of Garza's texts within celebratory multiculturalism erase important "contextual lenses" (Cruz 2001, 922) that frame the experiences of Mexican descent communities in the United States.

Reviews of Garza's children's books also praise her texts within a universal-izing multicultural rhetoric, eliding important distinctions between ethnic com-munities. Susan Thomsen states, "This would be a great book for families to look at together—and talk about their own traditions."[35] Other reviewers praise Garza's texts' abilities to create conversations among students about their specific cultures, stating how the texts are "an excellent example of an autobiography or personal experience narrative for students to read while using background knowledge to make schema connections of all kinds, especially text to self con-nections."[36] While these statements, on the one hand, render Garza's texts as powerful because they emphasize the use of Latina/o experiences to empower all groups, they eclipse the specific critical negotiations made by Garza's chil-dren's books in asserting Latina/o presence—through biculturalism and bilin-gualism—in the nation.

Concluding Remarks

Garza's and Cisneros's representations of domestic space are crucial and neces-sary interventions in US nationalist discourse and rhetoric that has sought to exclude Latina/os in the US national sphere. In 2011, nativist and anti-immigrant policies in states such as Arizona and Texas reached historic heights, with the banning of Latina/o literature and ethnic studies curriculum in the public schools, as well as backlashes against undocumented Latina/o immigrants in this country, including with SB 1070, or "Support Our Law Enforcement and Safe Neighborhoods Act," portions of which passed in Arizona in 2010, among many others.[37] Situating *The House on Mango Street* within this moment of nativ-ist backlash against Latina/o immigrants and communities, Cisneros states, "I think the situation's gotten worse for Esperanza, I'm sorry to say. . . . When I wrote that book, I wrote it from someplace, as a very optimistic young woman in her early 20s hoping things would get better in the United States for people of Mexican descent. But, you know, I could never dream what would happen post-9/11 and with the community being under siege as it is right now with Mexican people really being vilified at this time of American history" (2011).[38] Garza also responds to the surge of nativist policies against Latina/o communities, framing her art as a reaction to the nativist narrative that Latina/os are recent immigrants to the United States: "You have to remember that a lot of our families have been in the United States for many generations, going back to before it was the United States, and for some even further back because a lot of us have Native American ancestry from not just South but also North America. My maternal family is native to South Texas and my father's family comes from Mexico and further back. . . . Everyone thinks we're recent immigrants, but we've been here for a long time. So, that has always been one of my focuses: to re-celebrate our traditions, our history, and to raise awareness."[39] Garza views her artistic representations of

Mexicana/o traditions and celebrations along the US-Mexico border as crucial tools to educate the public about the long history of Mexicana/os in the United States, particularly by demonstrating the physical and cultural presence of people of Mexican descent in the United States prior to both the Spanish and Anglo conquest of the US Southwest.

Cisneros and Garza share similarities with early authors Jovita González, Cleofas Jaramillo, and Fabiola Cabeza de Baca in their use of home and domesticity to assert the inclusion of Mexicana/os and Chicana/os in the US national sphere. Yet unlike these early Mexican American authors, Cisneros and Garza present heterogeneous constructions of home and domesticity, negotiating the exclusionary logic of previous nationalisms. In the next chapter, I explore how artist Patssi Valdez also creates work at the site of domesticity to negotiate and counter various nationalisms, as exemplified by the Chicano/a Movement, museum spaces, and Hollywood films, particularly through the sites of self-fashioning and glamour in performance and visual art. Valdez's work critiques the natural association of Chicanas to domesticity with self-fashioning in the public sphere, exposing the construction of gendered and racial identity through her paintings of domestic interiors.

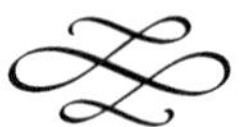

CHAPTER 5

Patssi Valdez's
"A Room of One's Own"

SELF-FASHIONING, GLAMOUR, AND DOMESTICITY
IN THE MUSEUM AND HOLLYWOOD

As traffic sped by on Whittier Boulevard in East Los Angeles in 1974, Gronk, a member of the Chicano art collective Asco, taped fellow member Patssi Valdez to the exterior of a liquor store.[1] On Valdez's left, and not shown in the most popular photo-documentation of this performance piece, *Instant Mural*, is Asco affiliate Humberto Sandoval, whose body was also bound to the wall by Gronk (fig. 8). Their taped bodies were part of Asco's commentary on the many Chicano movement murals of East Los Angeles in the 1970s. Asco felt that the Aztec symbols and Mexican nationalist iconography of these murals did not represent their experiences as young urban Chicana/os growing up in East L.A. Instead of drawing upon nationalist emblems, Valdez, Gronk, and the other original members of Asco—Willie Herrón and Harry Gamboa Jr.—fashioned their political statements using a pastiche of visual subcultures, including mod, glamour, and later punk.[2] Valdez's look and demeanor in *Instant Mural* evokes East L.A. glamour, which itself derives from pachuca fashion, a female version of pachuco or zoot-suiter style from the 1940s. In the pachuca tradition, she wears short shorts, black platform shoes, coiffed hair, and dramatic eye makeup, elements of dress that counter cultural and gendered ideologies that have cast Chicanas as demure and submissive (Fregoso 2003; Ramírez 2009).[3] With fishnet stockings and eye-catching jewelry, Valdez combines East L.A. glamour with a punk aesthetic that anticipates the Chicana punk look that would emerge in East L.A. later in the decade. Valdez's image in the photo-documentation demonstrates Chicana punks' investment in disrupting accepted notions of femininity. It also embodies punk's playful disregard for the serious and sacred.[4]

Valdez's use of fashion and performance to comment on gender and sexual norms pervades her paintings and set designs of domestic interiors for theater and film today. Valdez is now a well-known painter and set designer whose solo

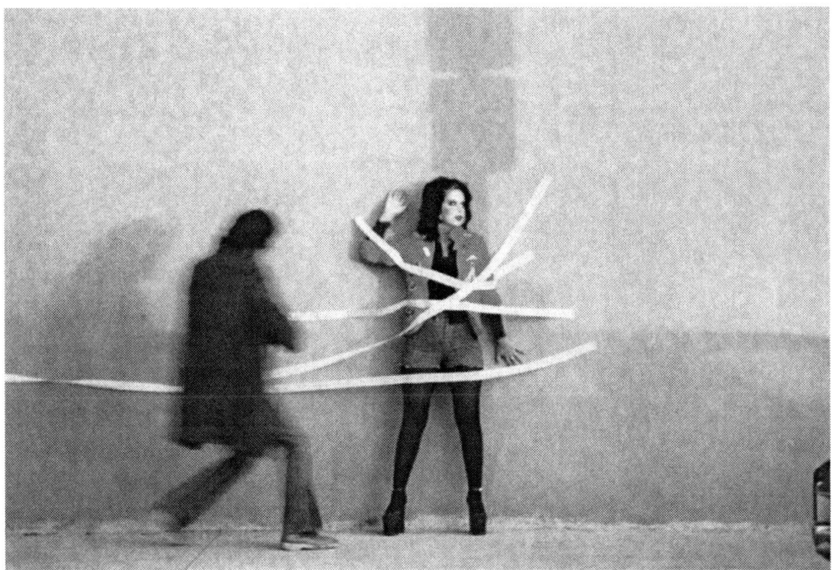

Figure 8. Asco, *Instant Mural*, 1974. Pictured are Gronk and Patssi Valdez. Photograph by Harry Gamboa Jr., courtesy of the artist.

art extends her earlier focus on glamour and beauty in Asco to the sites of the domestic, costume, dress, and masquerade. This work can be viewed in major museum exhibitions and collections, including at the Smithsonian, and her set designs of domestic interiors can be seen in the few big-budget Chicana/o-directed motion pictures of Hollywood, such as Gregory Nava's *Mi Familia* (1995) and Jose Luis Valenzuela's *Luminarias* (1999). Several academic and mainstream publications in the last ten years have also included Valdez's paintings on their covers.[5] Valdez's art work has also been featured at the National Council of La Raza Alma Awards, which honor outstanding Latina/o artistic achievement in television, film, and music, as well as at the Latin Grammies. The popularity of Valdez's visual art in these spaces has created a recognizable Chicana artistic representation of domesticity in the mainstream.

While these new artistic mediums and spaces, in addition to focusing on the domestic, might appear to depart from her multimedia and urban site-specific work with Asco, her paintings and set designs share similarities with her earlier work. They each use the sites of fashion and dress to comment on the role of glamour and domesticity in the construction of Chicana subjectivity. They also interrogate glamour and gender identity through a focus on the domestic. In Asco, Valdez focused on fashion and glamour to make her statements on domesticity, and as a solo artist, Valdez turns to interrogating the space of the domestic itself, while still concentrating on the tropes of dressing and performance that were central to her work with Asco. Valdez's Asco performances commented on the multiple layers of urban life, and her art today is centered on the everyday textures of domestic life. Her paintings "stage a highly personal theatre."[6] Taken together, Valdez's body of work can be considered an artistic interrogation of space and domesticity.

In this chapter, I argue that Valdez's performances with Asco and her solo art demonstrates a politics of negotiation that critiques gendered ideologies and the racialized public/private sphere she confronted as a Chicana in East Los Angeles and in the mainstream art world. While many critics have either placed Valdez in a passive role in Asco or deemed her solo works of domestic interiors as "apolitical," I suggest that her body of work illustrates a process of "self-fashioning" that has functioned as an act of political negotiation and critique. The term *self-fashioning* highlights the intersections of dress with bodily performance and the possibility of these sites in the negotiation of gendered and racialized ideologies. My use of the term comes from Jennifer Craik, who employs the concept to refer to the process of clothing the body as "an active process or technical means for constructing and presenting a bodily self" (1994, 1). That is, dress constructs an identity rather than disguising a natural body or real identity (5). In this sense, codes of dress communicate the relationship between a particular body, its lived experience, and the space it occupies (4–5). Laura E. Pérez, in her analysis of Chicana visual artists of the 1980s and 1990s, underscores that dress in Chicana arts "call[s] attention to both the body as social and to the social body that constitutes it as such, specifically through gendered and racialized histories" (2007, 51).

The chapter claims negotiation as a political act, suggesting that Valdez actively negotiated her silence and invisibility in Asco and the art world by creating a space for herself visually. Even though Valdez is the object of the gaze in many Asco performances, she resists and exploits that gaze through self-fashioning. My analysis of Valdez's body of work also conceptualizes agency outside of a binary system of either/or, focusing instead on situational agency. Self-fashioning, through visual references to pachuca glamour and punk in Asco and to dress and the domestic in her visual work, has provided Valdez with a negotiated agency with which to exploit the very gendered ideologies that visually put her at the center of Asco, and as a Chicana artist in mainstream museums, particularly as these spaces have excluded Chicana artists from consideration and representation. Given the male- and Anglo-dominated and defined culture and context in which Valdez has lived and displayed her works, her challenge to hegemony has not been an easy process. As an artist in Asco, Valdez confronted gendered divisions of labor, and as a Chicana growing up in East Los Angeles, she encountered racial discrimination. Within the museum, Valdez continues to encounter mainstream museum representational practices that have historically excluded Chicana artists.

I begin the chapter with Valdez's work with Asco to challenge the prevailing view that her significant artistic contributions did not occur until her solo work in the late 1980s and her critical recognition as a painter in the early 1990s.[7]

Scholarship has frequently elided Valdez's artistic contributions to Asco, presenting views of fashion, dress, and the female body within an active male/passive female binary. Even though each member of Asco used fashion, along with performance and politics, to broadcast their commentaries on race and gender, scholarship on the group has attributed fashion mostly to Valdez. Since fashion is often considered a passive, superficial, and frivolous activity carried out only by women, it has been both relegated to the female body and undervalued as a strategy of contestation (McRobbie 1994). Using fashion to make her statements in Asco, Valdez has frequently been perceived as the object of the gaze and not as an active participant in the construction of Asco images and political messages.[8] Women are often treated as the object of the gaze, since the act of looking, as Laura Mulvey explains, "has been split between active/male and passive/female" (1989, 19). Craik suggests that fashion is a particularly charged space where women become objects of the gaze and of male sexual desire (1994, 46). Studies of subcultures have also relegated women to the margins, figuring them as passive and static objects (McRobbie 1991). Asco criticism has perpetuated this view of Valdez as a passive contributor to the group by focusing primarily on the male members' contributions to the group through performance and subcultural styles, while also rendering Valdez's fashion as a natural extension of her female identity (Chavoya 1998; Hernández 2007). A pertinent example is an article in the June 2007 issue of *LA Weekly*, titled "The Art Outlaws of East Los Angeles," Daniel Hernández writes, "In old Asco photographs . . . [t]here she is, in short skirts and high heels, gloves, extreme eye makeup." With the phrase "there she is," the author attributes Valdez's presence as individualistic and passive and not as an active source of the group's public reclaiming of space. In other Asco criticism, Valdez's fashion and style is deemed natural and personal because she is female, rather than as constructed artistic statements as part of Asco's performances.

My discussion of Valdez's paintings of domestic interiors in the latter part of the chapter also challenges the initial and similar view of Valdez's solo art as representing passivity and gendered femininity. Reviews of Valdez's first major solo exhibit of her paintings at the Daniel Saxon Gallery in 1992 critiqued Valdez's shift from multimedia and site-specific, performances to the more static medium of painting. Art critics were not ready to view Valdez's work independently from Asco and were also critical of her new focus on domestic interiors. Susan Wiggins's review in *ArtWeek* exemplified this point: "Distant Memories is pronounced . . . with paintings so apolitical and free of self-reference that one can only wonder about the reasons for the change."[9] Wiggins, like other critics at the time, used a rigid public/private binary to understand Valdez's art. As a result, reviewers failed to consider how Valdez's depictions of domestic spaces were "political" as they functioned as commentaries on gendered ideologies. They also overlooked how these new works extended her work with Asco because they incorporated elements of performance, fashion, and dress. In order to illustrate how Valdez's visual art of domestic space continues her political focus and self-fashioning that were central to her work with Asco, I analyze Valdez's paintings *The Dressing Table/La mesa del vendaje* (1989), *The Kitchen/la cocina* (1989), *La Cocina* (2002), and *Patssi's Kitchen* (2002). These paintings interrogate the sites of domesticity that have shaped cultural constructions of beauty and gender, including the dresser, kitchen, and bedroom. I also analyze Valdez's set designs for Gregory Nava's *Mi Familia* to demonstrate how she extends her focus on self-fashioning and performance with Asco to other mediums. I suggest that these set designs function as alternative representations to patriarchy and nationalism within the cinematic space of the film.

Despite Valdez's iconic role in visual culture in the last four decades, scholars have only recently begun to acknowledge and examine her significant contributions to Asco and her work as a solo artist. Essays by art historian and artist Amalia Mesa-Bains (1999) and museum curator and scholar Tere Romo (1999) in the limited-circulation exhibition catalog of Valdez's 1999 retrospective *A Precarious Comfort* at the Mexican Museum of San Francisco were, until recently, the only texts that had examined Valdez's significant role in Asco and her work as a solo artist. Other available texts included a handful of unpublished interviews, notably a 1999 Smithsonian interview conducted by Jeffrey Rangel (Valdez 1999), as well as brief coverage of Valdez in other museum catalogs, local newspaper reviews, and Latina/o-themed magazines. Two exhibits on Asco in the 2000s—"Phantom Sightings" at the Los Angeles Contemporary Museum of Art (LACMA) in 2008, curated by Rita González, Howard N. Fox, and Chon Noriega, and the retrospective "Asco: Elite of the Obscure" at LACMA in 2011—led to new interest in Valdez. Brief essays by Romo, Ramón García, Colin Gunckel, and Josh Kun in the exhibit catalogue expand the discussion on Valdez's contributions to Asco and her work as a solo artist in the 1980s. Yet by focusing mostly on Valdez's performances in Asco and her solo art in the 1980s, this new criticism has shifted attention away from Valdez's contributions as a painter and set designer of domestic interiors from the 1990s to today.

Even with the scholarly elision of Valdez's active presence in Asco prior to the LACMA exhibits, Valdez's image had frequently been used to exemplify the group's aesthetics and concerns. Valdez's taped body in *Instant Mural*, which opened this essay, has been cited in nearly every piece of scholarship on Asco in the fields of Chicana/o studies, art history, and performance. The photo-still of Valdez's image in *Instant Mural* graces the cover of Chon Noriega's *Urban Exile: Collected Writings of Harry Gamboa Jr.* (1998), the first full-length published text devoted to an Asco member.[10] In the exhibits "Phantom Sightings" in 2008 and "Asco: Elite of the Obscure" in 2011, *Instant Mural* was everywhere: from the exhibition itself to promotional brochures, newspaper and Internet reviews, and blog postings.[11]

Valdez's image in *Instant Mural* and her role in the group, however, have not always been praised or understood. Her contributions have frequently been critiqued as exemplifying female oppression. As Valdez explains, some Chicana feminists and artists were angry at her for her work in *Instant Mural* and other Asco performances: "Some of those difficult [images] really pissed off some women. Where I have chains or I'm wrapped up. A lot of feminist Chicanas were really angry at me for that" (1999). Such views led to the exclusion of *Instant Mural* from "Chicano Art: Resistance and Affirmation," the first and largest traveling exhibit of Chicano art curated by Chicano scholars and artists, which began at the Wight Gallery at the University of California, Los Angeles, in 1990. Gronk recounts that he submitted *Instant Mural* to be included in the show among other Asco pieces. Renowned Chicana muralist and arts activist Judy Baca, whose work was also in the show, did not want to include the piece of Valdez's body taped to the wall. Gronk recalls, "One of the reasons for her was, perhaps, because I was taping a woman to the wall—Patssi Valdez—and she thought that that was like really not a good thing for an image to be in the exhibition" (1997). Baca, who confronted the sexism of the Chicano/a movement as an artist, most likely did not want to include an image that she felt perpetuated women's subjugation to men.

In contrast to these earlier negative receptions, a newer generation of Chicana/o artists has celebrated Valdez's fashion and demeanor in *Instant Mural* and other Asco performances. Contemporary Chicana artist Sandra de la Loza explains: "Well, I think just so many people like Patssi from that generation . . . continue to be very inspiring . . . visually in terms of their fashion and of course in their art work, and just the kind of boldness and unapologeticness in their art work and their being."[12] De la Loza's words highlight the important role of fashion in Valdez's visual iconography, a facet I explore in both Valdez's work with Asco and as a solo artist today.

Chicana Self-Fashioning and Hollywood Glamour in the Los Angeles Cityscape: The Asco Years

Valdez first accessed creativity and the possibility of an arts career while taking art classes at Garfield High School. Art class functioned as an empowering outlet for Valdez, suggesting that she might someday go beyond the limited job opportunities available to her in East Los Angeles. She found relief in these classes, even taking three a day one year. She describes her high school art teacher, Mr. Ramírez, as a "real artist" because he used to exhibit on the West Side in La Cienega. Galleries on the West Side were considered spaces of high art, while the few Eastside galleries were deemed outside the rigid confines of the art world. With this description of her art teacher, Valdez comments on economic divisions in the industry: from her experiences, she knew that one could only make a living from art by traveling outside the boundaries of East L.A., a space largely marginalized in a racially and economically segregated art world (Valdez 1999). Valdez's narrative also indicates a model of the artist as male. Knowing no female artists in her immediate community, and with few artist role models of any gender in East L.A., Valdez initially did not consider art a viable career for herself. In fact, while Valdez experimented with painting and had a closet filled with paintings in high school, she was reluctant to show this work publicly (Gronk 1997).

Valdez began working as a hairdresser at her mother's beauty shop in East Los Angeles after graduating from Garfield High in 1970.[13] This work provided her with the economic means to support her interests in art: "I did it on weekends so I could earn money to support my art habit. [During] the Asco years I was a hairdresser" (Valdez 1999). During the same period, she took classes in theatrical makeup at East Los Angeles College and attended the Elegance Academy of Professional Make-Up, where she learned to apply makeup and style hair. The shop gave Valdez an income, and it also gave her power and autonomy. It helped pay for her "art habit" after high school and provided some of the funds she would later use to attend art school. In this way, her mother's beauty shop functioned as an outlet against a racialized and gendered regime that has often limited working-class Chicanas to domestic or factory work. The curriculum for Chicana high school students in the 1960s and 1970s emphasized home economics and typing classes to prepare them for a racialized and gendered division of labor. As Dionne Espinoza explains, Chicanas "were ostensibly trained to be secretaries, but the gender, race, and class regimes of the state promised to keep most of them in the positions of domestic or factory workers" (2001, 33). Valdez recalls that her home economics teachers at Garfield High even told the Chicana students that they would one day be cooking and cleaning in the homes of affluent whites.[14]

While the beauty shop has often been viewed as a site that reinscribes gender, for Valdez, as well as for other women of color, it has frequently functioned as a site of empowerment and negotiated agency, offering a significant yet limited avenue of economic independence. Writing about Dominicans in New York City, Ginetta E. B. Candelario suggests that the "Dominican beauty shop—while not entirely providing autonomous or especially well-paid work—offers greater flexibility, earnings, and community status than the leading employment alternatives in the low-wage service industries available to Dominican immigrant women" (2007, 185). Similarly, for a working-class Chicana in East Los Angeles in the 1970s, who confronted limited opportunities in the low-wage service sector, beauty shop employment offered economic advantages, and particularly for Valdez provided her the means to pursue her interests in art. That Valdez's mother was the owner of the shop is significant as well. In her mother, Valdez found an alternative image of women that was not confined to the domestic, despite the prevailing social view of women as devoted mothers, wives, or domestic workers occupying their "proper" places within the home. As an entrepreneur with access to her own income, Valdez's mother disrupted such domestic ideologies. Valdez explains, "My mother . . . showed me how to be [my] own boss and run a successful business. I owe my business sense to her."[15]

As hairdressers, both Valdez and her mother were responsible for creating glamour for working-class women in East Los Angeles. Valdez explains that she developed her interest in glamour from her mother: "Well, I have a glamorous mother. . . . The first thing was you showered and the makeup came. Then the hair and the clothes. My mother was always well-groomed. I . . . thought it was normal that women just did this" (1999). As socializing agents in the public sphere, beauty shops both reflect and create gender norms of femininity that circulate in the private sphere, as indicated by Valdez's statement about her mother's beauty routine at home. Candelario also suggests, "As an openly and avowed gendered space, the beauty shop is explicitly dedicated to producing certain kinds of female beauty while at the same time implicitly providing a space where *certain kinds* of women come together regularly" (2007, 178, emphasis in original). Within the context of East L.A., the beauty shop upholds Chicana/o beauty against a dominant society that privileges whiteness. It offers hair care products suitable to the specific and diverse needs of Chicanas across generational lines. As Laura Gutiérrez Spencer explains, "For many working-class women, women of color, and women of the middle and upper classes, the application of makeup serves as a daily ritual in which the woman, either consciously or not, has a hand in authoring or defining the image she presents to the world" (1994, 69). For Valdez, the beauty shop was a place to create not just the latest hairstyles, but also subcultural looks. In this way, it was a space that enabled her to both inscribe and transgress normative femininity.

After she graduated from high school and spent time working in her mother's beauty shop, Valdez began to see a career in the arts as a possibility. This period coincided with Valdez's work with Asco, and she recalls that she began to consider the prospect of pursuing formal art training when she was at a party with artists from Otis Art Institute. At the gathering, she recalls thinking to herself: "If this is going to be your life's work and you're going to function in this circle, you better get your butt in school and you'd better learn what these terms mean. Because you're going to need to know this stuff if you want to go where you need to go! And so I knew . . . I needed to go to school. I just needed it" (1999).

In 1980, Valdez quit her job as a hairdresser to attend Parsons School of Design in New York City. She even sold her red convertible, which she had purchased with her income from the beauty shop, in order to attend art school full-time. The move to New York also meant that Valdez quit Asco. In New York, Valdez recalls, she initially was not taken seriously as an artist because of her dress. One day, when she showed up for class "all dolled up" and wearing high heels, her teacher demanded, "Miss Valdez? . . . Do you expect to make art looking like that?" (1999). The instructor's response to her look suggests that fashion and glamour are deemed feminine and frivolous, while the art class and art student are considered masculine and serious. Even at Parsons, one of the nation's premiere fashion design schools, there was a gendered and racialized division between fashion (as design) and the visual arts (as art). Valdez's hyperfeminine East L.A. glamour was pitted against the professional veneer and modest fashion of the New York City student of high art. The relation between the L.A. and New York City art scenes was conceived as a low/high binary that was also inflected by race. Valdez's East L.A. dress was considered excessively feminine and garish, leading the instructor and other students initially to dismiss her as an artist. According to her art teacher and fellow students, artists did not "look" like Valdez (Valdez 1999).

Valdez eventually returned to Los Angeles and entered the Otis Art Institute, affiliated with Parsons, where she graduated with a BFA in 1985. She found artistic creativity, encouragement, and autonomy in both the visual arts and fashion, which were important intertwined elements in her artistic trajectory. While her art instructor in New York City positioned fashion/beauty against art within a low/high art binary, Valdez's training as an artist in multiple fields—the beauty shop, design, and the arts—resists this narrative. During her years in Asco in the late 1970s, before she attended art school, Valdez drew on her training in self-fashioning at Garfield High and in her mother's East L.A. beauty shop to negotiate racial and gender invisibility in the Los Angeles cityscape.

Valdez's synthesis of art and fashion as a means to challenge hegemonic narratives began within the segregated spaces of Los Angeles in the 1970s. Here, Valdez confronted the racialized and gendered exclusion of Chicana/os from Hollywood film and fashion advertising. It is no surprise, therefore, that Valdez's most glamorous creations took place in Asco's No Movies, which were not actual movies but rather single 35mm images that resembled stills from a movie with an implied narrative. Essentially, No Movies were fake publicity stills (Noriega 1998, 12) and often invoked classic movie scenes from the studio era. No Movies incorporated many specific artistic modes, including performance pieces, published interviews, mail art, and media hoaxes, intended to critique the commercialization of Hollywood film (Mesa-Bains 1999, 35; Noriega 1998, 7). They did not have an intended audience or an exhibition space for their performances; rather, these works were a low-budget response to the high costs involved in producing film. As they circulated in the underground art scene and did not enter the gallery or museum space until much later, they have only recently received critical attention. Many scholars have noted important similarities and differences between Asco's No Movies and Cindy Sherman film stills, which Sherman began in 1977, two years after one of the first Asco No Movies, *Asshole Mural* (1975). While No Movies and Sherman's film stills share several conceptual and formal similarities, Sherman's film stills critique normative gender codes by working within already established narratives of racial inclusivity, while Asco's No Movies deconstruct an institution from which they were excluded (Chavoya 1998, 10).

Most scholars have focused on No Movies as counter-hegemonic sites that critique Hollywood's racialized exclusion of Chicana/os. As Max Benavidez explains, "Because Hollywood discriminated against Chicanos in terms of both industry access and representation, Asco reconceptualized and inverted the idea of the Hollywood movie" (2007, 45). Critics have also cited Gronk's explanation of the No Movie: "The idea was to reject the reel by projecting the real," which captures the goal of the form as a response to stereotypes of Chicana/os on screen (Gronk 1997). David E. James further argues that No Movies were Asco's radical critique of Hollywood's media and geographic exclusion of Chicanos. As James explains, while the Hollywood sign has been visible from several Chicana/o communities in Los Angeles, the racial and economic inequities of Los Angeles have excluded them from the industry (1999).

This focus on No Movies as a response to Hollywood's racial and economic exclusion of Chicana/os, however, elides the form's important transgression of hegemonic gendered narratives. Asco's No Movies not only engaged racialized exclusion, they deconstructed Hollywood's idealization of feminine beauty as white. Publicity stills of popular Hollywood icons, such as Marilyn Monroe and Grace Kelly, from the 1940s and 1950s (the heyday of Hollywood glamour) represent the construction of and emphasis on whiteness as the normative definition of beauty in Hollywood—a look characterized by anglicized features, light skin, and svelte figures. At the time of Asco's performances in the late 1970s, popular white female actors such as Carrie Fisher and Teri Garr dominated movie screens, and models such as Christie Brinkley and Brooke Shields adorned fashion magazine covers. Idealizations of whiteness in Hollywood and popular representations have led to a system of representation in which some of the most famous Latina stars at different moments in Hollywood history, such as Rita Hayworth in the 1930s and 1940s and Jennifer Lopez in the 1990s, have exploited racial narratives to obtain visibility. They have done so by either downplaying or emphasizing their ethnicity, depending on the historical moment (Ovalle 2011).[16]

Valdez's use of self-fashioning to comment on Hollywood's exclusion of Latina beauty is evident in Asco's 1977 No Movie titled *A La Mode* (fig. 9). The "movie still" was taken in the famous Los Angeles restaurant Phillipe's, an unglamorous space known for its French dip sandwich, ten-cent coffee, sawdust, paper plates, ceiling fans, and long wooden tables. The photo captures the moment after Gronk, Valdez, and Gamboa Jr., after ordering coffee and apple pie, struck poses around and on top of a restaurant table. The performance was titled *A La Mode* because, as Gronk explains, underneath Patssi sits a piece of pie and "so in a sense, she became a scoop of ice cream" (1997). This explanation raises larger questions about the objectification of Valdez's body or, at the very least, the site of her body as an object to be consumed. With knowledge of Gronk's reason for choosing the title, the viewer might be tempted to read the title as referring to food, and Valdez as an object of consumption. Without Gronk's explanation, however, the viewer might simply interpret the image in context of the title's reference to glamour and fashion (*la mode*). Whether or not Valdez would

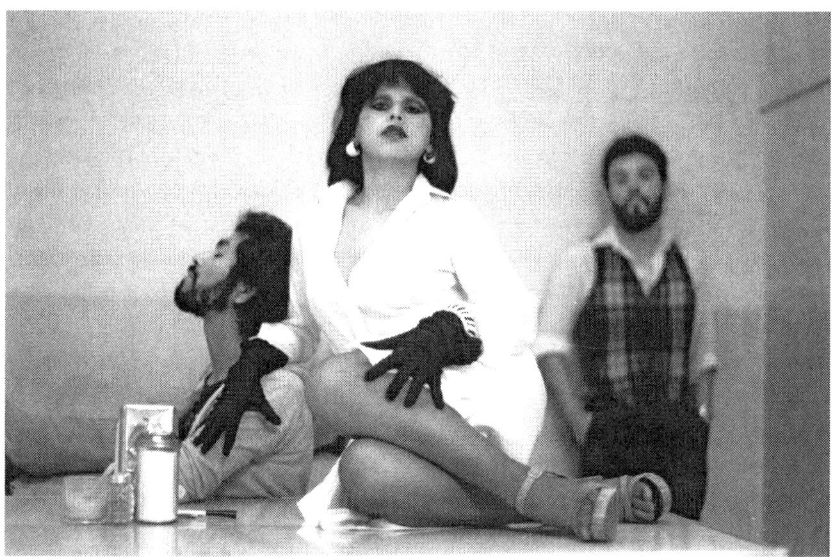

Figure 9. Asco, *A La Mode*, 1977. Pictured are Gronk (left), Patssi Valdez, and Harry Gamboa Jr. Photograph courtesy of Harry Gamboa Jr.

have titled this image *A La Mode* in order to evoke her own body as a scoop of (vanilla) ice cream remains unclear.

What remains evident is that Valdez's posturing in *A La Mode* deconstructs and repositions Hollywood glamour by referencing transnational Latina glamour. She mimics the sex-kitten poses that were prevalent among Mexican actresses during the golden age of Mexican cinema, including Lupe Vélez, Maria Montez, Dolores Del Rio, and María Félix, all of whom Valdez no doubt encountered on screen while she was growing up in East Los Angeles. Her pose also references those of 1960s Hollywood glamour icon Sophia Loren, to whom Gronk and other scholars have frequently compared Valdez. Describing Valdez as a high school student, Gronk states, "She had an exotic look to her, sort of like a Sophia Loren kind of quality to her at the time" (1997). Gronk's comparison of Valdez with the Italian-born actress emphasizes how both women are part of nonwhite groups that have been exoticized and hypersexualized in Hollywood film.

Even though Valdez's reference to sex-kitten poses in *A La Mode* might seem to uphold hegemonic definitions of gender and beauty, her bold posturing and provocative gaze also reconfigure them. In contrast to actresses in typical Hollywood studio-era movie stills, Valdez does not lean in demurely toward the viewer or tilt her head seductively. Rather, she controls the viewer's gaze by blocking her midriff with her left hand. She also sits with head and shoulders tilted back. Her eyes are constantly above ours and thus we never meet hers. Valdez controls the gaze through a triangulation of desire that is created between Gamboa Jr., the viewer, and Valdez. While Valdez's gaze is directed above the viewer,

Gronk and Gamboa Jr. look away from her: Gronk faces right, almost becoming a statue, while Gamboa Jr., standing in the background, directs his gaze toward the onlooker. This triangulation trains the viewer's attention on Valdez, whose prominence is accentuated by the contrast between the sharp focus on Valdez and soft focus on Gamboa Jr. Instead of leaning on the men around her (think Marilyn Monroe performing "Diamonds Are a Girl's Best Friend" in the 1953 film *Gentlemen Prefer Blondes*), she places her black-gloved right hand on Gronk's shoulder and uses him to hold herself up, as if he were a prop.

By countering the passivity of Hollywood glamour, Valdez's self-fashioning captures the bold attitude and active demeanor of Chicana punks in East Los Angeles in the 1970s. Her heavy eye makeup, dark lipstick, and black gloves evoke the punk style of Alice Bag, who formed The Bags in 1977, and Teresa Covarrubias of The Brat, which formed in 1979.[17] The production of the Asco performance *A La Mode* in 1977 further emphasizes the ways in which Valdez's dress illustrates an affinity with punk style. Her look, however, departs from the "very punk" aesthetics of Alice Bag and Teresa Covarrubias as represented by their spiky hair and chain jewelry. As Valdez explains, "I was influenced by all of this [punk and rock 'n' roll] and none of this to create and define my style [as] my own."[18] By mixing and repositioning a variety of subcultural styles, including Hollywood glamour, transnational Latina glamour, punk, and new wave, Valdez uses bricolage to create her image (Hebdige 1981). Punk aesthetics were just one medium that provided Valdez with a way to refract the gaze of Hollywood glamour.[19]

In Asco, and later as a solo artist, Valdez used fashion that was influenced by a variety of subcultural movements, including punk. She explains, "Punk was very much the fashion of the times and I was there with Eddie Ayala the singer of Los Illegals at the time . . . I was in the world of my fashion-conscious friends, the world of art and politics, and that of rock and roll and punk rock."[20] Asco member Herrón was directly involved in the East L.A. punk scene when he joined the band Los Illegals in 1979, replacing original singer Eddie Ayala. Herrón cofounded the club Vex in 1980 with Joe Vex (Suquette) and Sister Karen, a nun from the Eastside who had helped establish Self Help Graphics.[21] The collaboration between Herrón, Joe Vex, and Sister Karen, along with Herrón's active interest in Chicano public arts activism, led to a punk rock space informed by both punk music and visual arts.[22] Valdez and the other Asco members had varying relationships to the East L.A. punk scene in the late 1970s and early 1980s.[23] By 1980, Valdez had already left Los Angeles to attend art school in New York City. Yet her self-fashioning while in Asco, particularly in the performance *A La Mode* (1977), and her solo work after Asco, suggests that a broader punk subculture and aesthetics, along with new wave and glamour, influenced her art.[24]

The view of punk as an empowering and critical discourse for Chicana artists was evident in the show "Vexing: Female Voices from East L.A. Punk" at the Claremont Museum of Art in 2008. "Vexing" was a documentary-style exhibition that looked at the role of women who were at the forefront of the punk movement in East Los Angeles that was defined by a mixture of music, visual art, fashion, and culture. "Vexing" included Valdez and another important Asco affiliate, Diane Gamboa, whose fashion and style in the early 1980s also share similarities with the self-fashioning of Chicana punk rockers. Gamboa, who joined Asco later, documented the East L.A. punk scene through photography, and used clothing as a form of social commentary through her paper fashions—fashions literally made from paper and found materials that she presented in "Hit and Run" fashion shows, which often took place at punk venues.[25] While "Vexing" included Gamboa and Valdez, the exhibit did not concentrate on the role of self-fashioning in East L.A. punk, and it replicated the view that Valdez's artistic contributions did not occur until she began her solo work after leaving the group.[26] Michelle Habell-Pallán explains how East L.A. punk in the late 1970s and early 1980s functioned as a "visual and sonic language" that enabled working-class Chicanas to respond to marginalization and abuse in their homes, as well as to defy cultural constraints (2005, 156). Punk's ability to subvert dominant culture, Habell-Pallán explains, appealed to working-class Chicanas who experienced racial and economic marginalization. With punk, Chicanas could see themselves as empowered subjects.

While still affiliated with Asco in the 1970s, Valdez created solo works that extended the references to glamour and punk that were central to her self-fashioning in the group. Her multimedia collages, paintings, installations, and videos illustrate how Valdez used punk and new wave aesthetics to control the gaze of society. In *Self-Portrait with Barbed Wire*, a mixed-media photograph produced in the late 1970s, Valdez repeats a photograph of her face within overlapping square grids that are overlaid with barbed wire. The work's incorporation of barbed wire cites punk's "nihilistic bravado of self-mutilation" and "cut-up graphics" (Arnold 2001, 46); it also functions as a powerful commentary on the confinement of Chicanas according to gendered expectations (Romo 1999, 27).[27] *Take-One* (1976), an acrylic on canvas, is another powerful example of Valdez commenting on the male gaze she encountered and sought to control while in Asco; in it, she produces a photo-realist production of a black-and-white No Movie still of herself and Billy "Star" Estrada as a glamorous couple in a Hollywood movie. In the painting, Valdez wears a black dress, white sunglasses, and oversize floppy hat, citing Hollywood and pachuca glamour. These solo works indicate that Valdez used fashion and glamour, as she did with Asco, to negotiate the normative discourses of gender and femininity that she confronted as a Chicana in East Los Angeles, an emphasis on self-fashioning that she continued in her solo career after she left the group.[28]

DRESSING AND DOMESTICITY IN THE MUSEUM AND HOLLYWOOD

Valdez's first major solo gallery exhibition of her painted domestic interiors in 1992, titled "Distant Memories" at the Daniel Saxon Gallery in West Hollywood,

Los Angeles, was initially misunderstood by critics. This was not Valdez's first solo exhibit, but the first major solo showing of her paintings of domestic space. She had previously displayed her photo collages, photographs, installations, and some paintings in three solo exhibits in Los Angeles, San Francisco, and Europe prior to the Daniel Saxon showing.[29] Her photo-collage *Downtown* was also part of the monumental traveling exhibit "Chicano Art: Resistance and Affirmation" (CARA) that began at the UCLA Wright Art Gallery in 1990.[30]

By the time of the Daniel Saxon showing, Valdez had already established an artistic career outside of Asco. She had received a National Endowment for the Arts Fellowship in Painting in Washington, DC; a Brody Arts Fellowship in Visual Arts; an artist residency at Self-Help Graphics; and a medal of recognition from Nantes, France, for her involvement in the "Le Démon des Anges" show, the first exhibition of contemporary Chicana/o artists that traveled throughout Europe. However, within the local Chicana/o art scene in Los Angeles, her notoriety dovetailed on the heels of her Asco work as well as her affiliations with other Asco members, most notably Gronk, who was also establishing a solo artistic career. In fact, Gronk was the first artist to exhibit at the Daniel Saxon gallery, when owner Saxon and then-partner Candice Lee asked Gronk to do a solo exhibit after viewing his work at the Los Angeles Museum of Contemporary Art in 1985. After Gronk's exhibit, the Daniel Saxon Gallery soon established itself as a gallery for several prominent Chicana/o artists in Southern California (Gronk 1997).[31]

Though Valdez was already established as a solo artist both in Los Angeles and internationally, the Daniel Saxon Gallery exhibit was her first major showing that drew attention from art critics for her work as a painter of domestic interiors and still-lifes. Although Gronk's affiliation with the Daniel Saxon Gallery may have helped Valdez get a showing, Saxon probably showed her work due to Valdez's already established reputation as a Chicana artist in Los Angeles. Even if Valdez's connection to Gronk did help her get the show, the aid was mutual. Valdez helped Gronk several years earlier, when she was asked to exhibit in the "Le Démon des Anges" show in France, and Gronk was later asked to join.

Nonetheless, reviews of the Daniel Saxon Gallery showing illustrate that critics were not yet ready to view Valdez's work independently from Asco. In fact, reviewers of the Daniel Saxon Gallery exhibit were perplexed by Valdez's shift from the multimedia and site-specific, performance work with Asco to the more static medium of painting and her new focus on domestic interiors. In a review of the exhibit in *ArtWeek*, for example, art critic Susan Wiggins explains, "Distant Memories is pronounced . . . with paintings so apolitical and free of self-reference that one can only wonder about the reasons for the change" (Wiggins 1992). In Wiggins's review, Valdez's work with Asco—rooted in the urban public sphere and charged with an articulated political aim—is perceived as "political," while her new solo work as a painter focused on the domestic sphere is treated as "personal" and therefore "apolitical." Like other initial reviewers, Wiggins used a rigid public/private binary to understand Valdez's new domestic interiors, and in doing so overlooked the impact of broader power structures in the public sphere on women's lives in the private sphere. Within this gendered public/private binary, the public sphere is coded political and male, while the private sphere is figured as apolitical and female. Such reviews overlook how Valdez's current paintings draw upon the sites of fashion and dress that were central to her work in Asco.

These criticisms of Valdez's paintings of domestic interiors elide how the space of the domestic has consistently played a role in Valdez's work and the political critiques of gender and beauty that take place in her representations of domestic interiors. First, Valdez's artistic statements through self-fashioning in Asco had a relationship to the domestic as she drew upon materials from the home. Valdez's costumes in Asco were often home-made and based on found materials, such as fabric, glitter, and paper. With these paper fashions, Valdez notes, "I was role playing. And then I didn't have money for gowns or anything so I'd make them out of stuff that I found" (Valdez 1999). In Asco's 1972 *Walking Mural*, for instance, Valdez wore a black and silver aura made out of paper, and in her 1974 performance of "The Universe" in Asco's *Dia de Los Muertos*, Valdez wore a headdress assembled with cellophane, cotton balls, and glitter. In Valdez's 1984 photograph "Portrait of Billie," her subject is featured wearing an elaborate hand-painted paper costume created by Valdez. After her years in Asco, Valdez began to work within the medium of installation, and these materials also draw from objects found in the home, as well as a wide range of influences, including store display, Chicana/o theater, and the Mercado (Mesa-Bains 1999, 40).[32] In this way, Valdez's installations draw upon traditional materials from the domestic but also from the mass market. Valdez explains how her materials are "plastic and bought in mass quantity, mass produced religious objects . . . from K-Mart or something" (Valdez 1999). Ultimately, the materials Valdez chose for her installations were determined by economic necessity—the use of foil papers, plastics, netting, and glitter were all materials that were cheap and readily available.

Second, by drawing upon the materials of the domestic in her performances, Valdez incorporates a visual vocabulary that Mesa-Bains has defined as "rasquache domesticana," which enables her works to function as commentaries on the institutions that have structured Chicana femininity. As Mesa-Bains notes, "For the Chicana artist, the position of the underdog and the strategy of making do is situated in the domestic. She employs the materials of the domestic as she contests the power relations located within it. The visual production emerges from the everyday practices of women's life with style and humor" (Mesa-Bains 2003, 302). Because "domesticana" employs materials of the domestic sphere rooted in women's work within the home, it might appear to feign complicity with dominant structures and values. Yet "domesticana rasquache," similar to "rasquache," ultimately subverts and repositions these values by calling attention to the structures and institutions that shape them.

In Valdez's solo installation work after her Asco years, the site of the domestic played a central role. These installations began Valdez's artistic process of detailing identity through the arrangement of objects and mementos within the domestic sphere, a process that Jennifer A. González refers to as an "auto-topography" (1999, 185). These installations illustrate Valdez's process of carving out a "room of one's own" through domestic space. They express a trait that became central to her paintings: the incorporation of juxtaposition and paradox. The installations illustrate Valdez's skillful use of space: her use of three-dimensional space in her installations becomes reworked in the two-dimensional space of painting. These installations also begin Valdez's use of a "rhetoric of objects," which González elsewhere defines as "the use of material culture within a context of presentation or display (such as commercial market, museum, private collection, or art installation) for the sake of producing a visual and material argument at a particular historical moment and within a legible semantic 'code'" (1999, 186). Similar to her installations, Valdez's paintings use a "rhetoric of objects" to call attention to the construction of gender roles in the domestic.

The early reviewers of Valdez's paintings of domestic interiors also failed to see how these paintings continue Valdez's early project of negotiating Chicana identity and constructions of womanhood while in Asco. Because her new work is overtly domestic, her paintings are quickly deemed to be apolitical. Yet by shifting to a direct focus on domestic space, Valdez's paintings begin to interrogate the spaces that structure Chicana femininity and glamour. In her painting *The Dressing Table/La mesa del vendaje* (1988), for instance, Valdez incorporates self-fashioning by commenting on gender performativity and the cultural institutions that shape Chicana femininity (fig. 10). The painting calls attention to the prosthetics necessary to perform femininity and to the role of the domestic sphere in shaping gender and beauty norms. With the image of the naked woman in the far left plane of the painting—who is reflected in a mirror in monochromatic blue- and white-tones, alongside the several objects, or prosthetics, on the dressing table in the center of the painting that are necessary to "put on" femininity—Valdez emphasizes gender as a performance and as drag (Butler 1990). With the image of the Black Virgin, the rosary, the cross necklace, the milagro, and votive candle on the dresser juxtaposed against the red makeup compact, perfume bottles, evening bag, rosary-as-necklace, Valdez foregrounds both the site of religion and the domestic in constructing femininity. Significantly, Valdez's dresser functions as an altar. By juxtaposing beauty and glamour against religious devotion, Valdez illustrates the contradictions posed by cultural institutions that shape Chicana identity—whether they are economic, religious, or familial. One contradiction is the virgin/whore dialectic produced by patriarchal Catholicism, whereby Chicanas are expected to be pious, virginal, and devoted on the one hand, and sexual and desirous on the other. Valdez visualizes

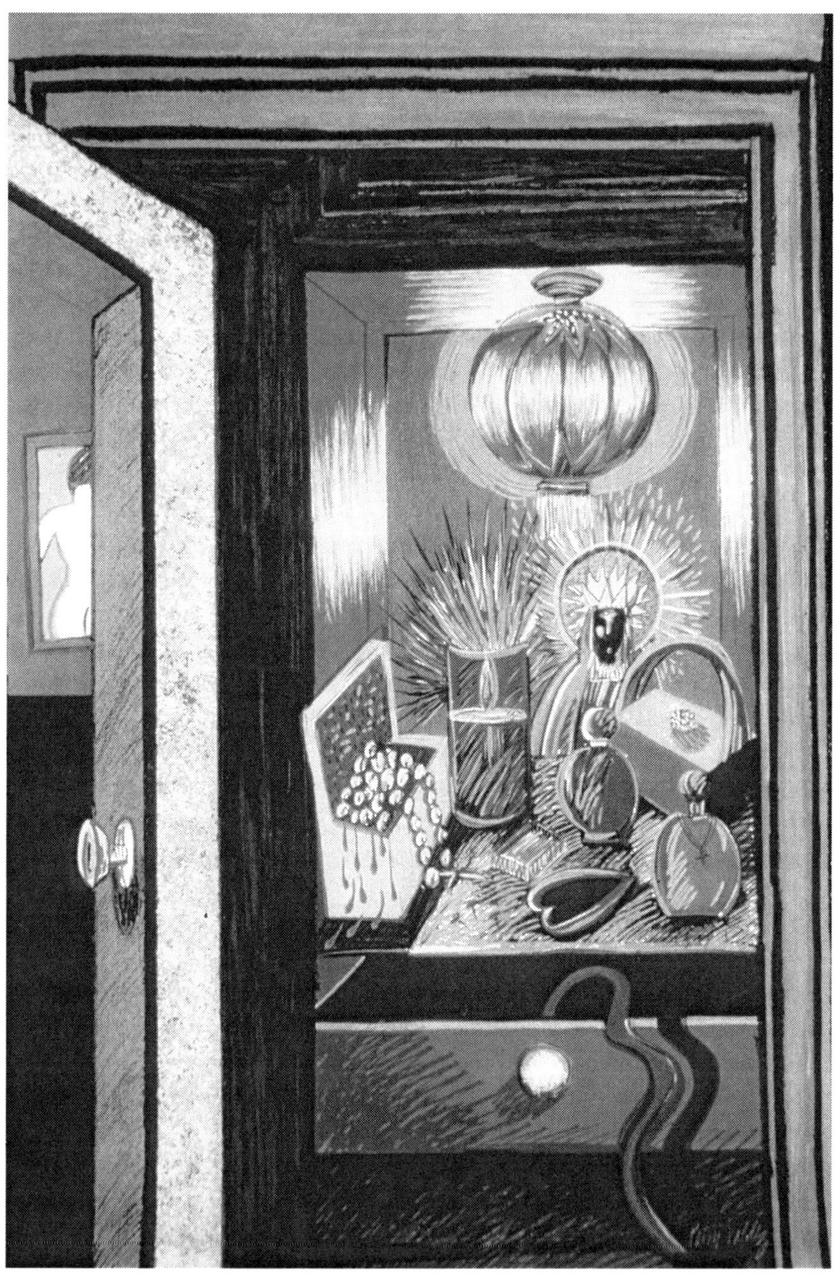

Figure 10. Patssi Valdez, *The Dressing Table/La mesa del vendaje*, 1988. Serigraph, 37 x 25 inches. Courtesy of the artist.

this contradiction by placing objects of beauty and desire next to religious motifs on the space of the dressing table. As González explains in another context, "This overlay of spaces, public and private, sacred and profane, is clearly meant to demonstrate their mutual influence and interdependence in the formation of subjectivity and in the process of identification, particularly for women of Mexican descent living in the United States" (1999, 187).

With the figure of the Black Virgin on the dresser (which is the same size as the nude woman in the far left plane of the painting), Valdez reclaims a specific female icon as a point of identification—that of a mestiza beauty—thereby claiming a *mestiza* or borderlands identity lost within colonization and conquest (Anzaldúa 1987). The Black Virgin emphasizes the indigenous cultural roots of Mexican culture in contrast to the emphasis placed on "Spanishness," in other words "whiteness," which dominates traditional iconography and understandings of La Virgen de Guadalupe. In this way, *The Dressing Table/La mesa del vendaje* acts as, what González has described in another context, an "iconographic revision" (1999). In Valdez's painting the image of the Black Virgin becomes the site in which a new image of womanhood is projected. First, the Black Virgin counters the construction of gender and femininity as white in mainstream visual representations. Second, the Black Virgin articulates La Virgen de Guadalupe's social function as a site of "mestiza consciousness" crucial to living in a nonbinary frame of gender and ethnicity (Anzaldúa 1987). Ultimately, *The Dressing Table/La mesa del vendaje* narrates the process of dressing as enabling new ways to construct gender and ethnic identity.

Valdez's *The Kitchen/la cocina* (1988) is also far from apolitical. Rather, the painting narrates a dystopic view of home in a dark and turbulent palette of intense reds, blues, and blacks in an unstable picture frame (fig. 11). This painting represents Valdez's early domestic interiors and her commentary on domestic abuse and violence in the home. From 1988 to 1995, Valdez's paintings paralleled the psychic turmoil Valdez underwent as she embarked on a therapeutic path toward emotional and spiritual healing. Valdez has commented that her domestic interiors act as metaphors for her interior self and reflect her coming to terms with a difficult childhood and home life. She explains, "My childhood was a combination of sexual abuse, alcoholism, and domestic violence. In the midst of all that, I tried to maintain my sanity" (qtd. in Romo 1999, 10). Valdez therefore describes her paintings as a way to cope with those memories: "I started going inside of me. And then I started to paint. It went roughly from my childhood. That was probably my first painting 'Kitchen.' . . . So I started to paint my own childhood. Memories of my . . . home, the things that took place in these rooms. The feelings that were in these rooms" (Valdez 1999).

The painting *The Kitchen/la cocina* references the violence Valdez experienced in her own home life—her father was abusive and left the family when she was young. It also represents Valdez's coming to terms with feeling silenced in Asco.

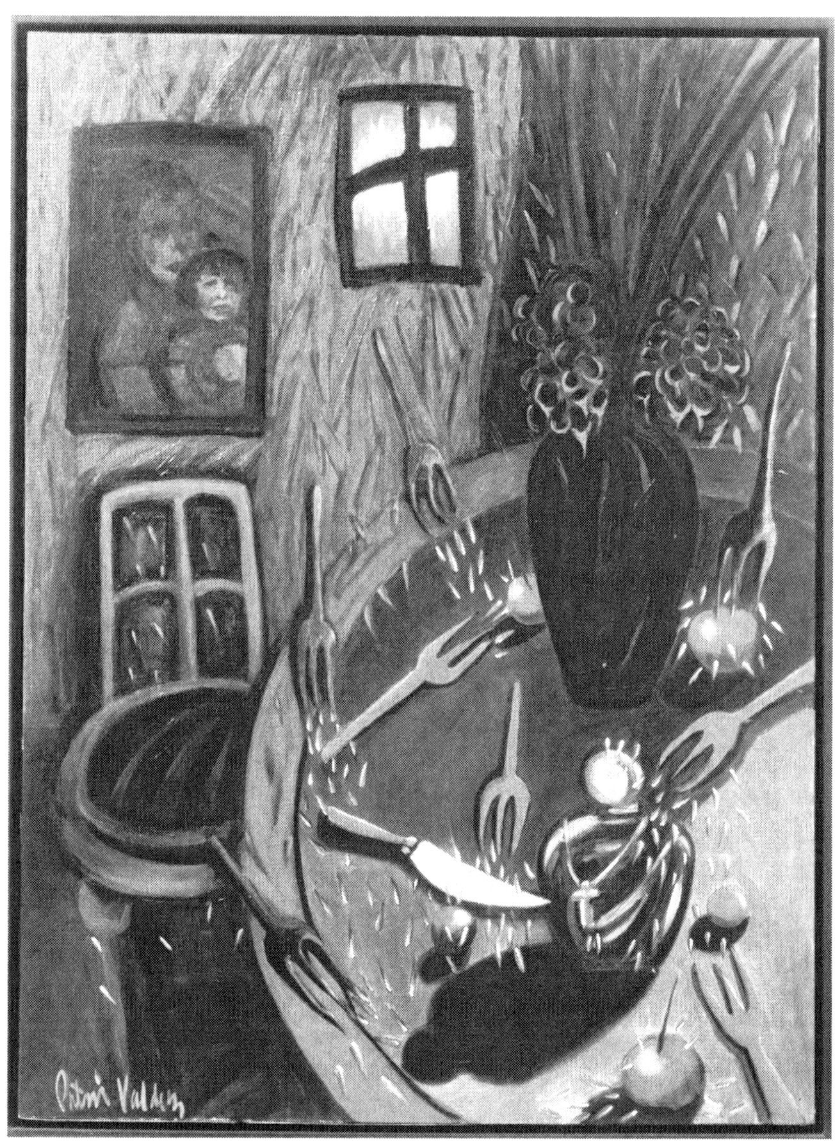

Figure 11. Patssi Valdez, *The Kitchen/la cocina*, 1988. Acrylic on canvas, 48 × 36 inches. Courtesy of the artist.

Valdez has often expressed that she felt unable to speak for herself in the group, and these early paintings suggest her search for a voice that she could broadcast to the public. Critic Lorenza Muñoz notes, "Performance art was a good way to express several different emotions at the same time, but with painting, Valdez found focus was important. This led to a difficult period of self-examination during the mid-1980s" (1999).

The Kitchen/la cocina shares affinities with Chicana literary representations of homes as sites of violence and sexual abuse.[33] Since the kitchen functions as a space that provides for the family's basic needs, specifically alimentary needs, the kitchen has strong associations with the body. Yet conversely, the kitchen's linkage to the body is also what makes it the most volatile, for any repression of those needs can create violent situations. As Samantha E. Cantrell explains, "[T]he kitchen's volatility can sometimes culminate in metaphorical or actual violence" (2004, 144). In Valdez's *The Kitchen/la cocina* violence is not carried out by actual physical bodies, but by material objects that represent institutions, such as patriarchal Catholicism and the Church, that have historically precluded Chicanas from speaking out against sexual abuse and violence. The painting depicts the influence of the Church in silencing Chicanas through the inclusion of religious symbols—the cross necklace on the milagro, along with the cross on the wall that doubles as a kitchen window, which is repeated again in the chair back. The contrasting family portraits in this scene—the mother lovingly holding her daughter in the photo on the wall and the scene of domestic violence narrated through phallic symbols, such as the piercing forks and knife directed toward the milagro with a cross in the middle of the table—serves to intensify and dramatize the violence about to ensue. As the mother and daughter within the portrait on the wall (whose focus seems to be directed toward the table in the kitchen) anxiously await the scene of violence about to occur, so does the viewer. With the image of the knife and red forks about to pierce the milagro adorned with a cross in the middle of the table, *The Kitchen/la cocina* suggests that the Church is unable to protect the mother and daughter from the impending violence. These references to the Catholic Church particularize this scene of domestic violence and abuse for Chicanas. Josie Méndez-Negrete indicates the socioeconomic and political obstacles that Chicanas and Latinas confront when dealing with domestic violence and sexual abuse, noting "Structures of inequality further complicate the way we understand ourselves and . . . our sexual lives" (2006, 196).

While the kitchen is a site of uneven gender roles, these social relations have often been disguised by emotional and nostalgic rhetoric about the home as hearth. In US culture, the kitchen is traditionally depicted as a utopian space and place for gathering and nurturance of the family. The Norman Rockwell version of the kitchen, exemplified by Rockwell's 1943 painting *Freedom from Want*, evokes smells of cooking, the warmth of the oven, an image of a happy family gathering for a meal, and the iconic role of a motherly figure in an apron preparing and presiding over food.[34] Within a Chicano/a nationalist framework, the domestic has frequently been represented, as Fregoso explains, as "an indispensable support system capable not only of meeting the needs of its members but also of sheltering them from violence, exploitation, racism, and abuse perpetrated in the external, public sphere of the Anglo capitalist world" (2003, 173). Yet this valorization of home and nation has been predicated on gender hierarchies and patriarchal definitions of female sexuality. In contemporary Chicana literature and cultural production, therefore, the domestic has become a site for the renegotiation of patriarchy, cultural values, and heterosexist family structures. This challenge to patriarchy is made evident in Valdez's *The Kitchen/ la cocina*, as the painting focuses on the domestic violence and abuse that affects women in the home.

In Valdez's later paintings, including *La Cocina* (2002) and *Patssi's Kitchen* (2002), the artist's depictions of the kitchen lack references to domestic violence that were prevalent in her earlier paintings. In these paintings, the patriarchal relegation of women to traditional female roles of *Kirche, Kuche, Kinder* (church, kitchen, children)[35] has shifted to a space where Chicanas assert control and independence. First, the title of the painting, *Patssi's Kitchen*, emphasizes the idea of power and ownership. This painting, similar to Sandra Cisneros's 1984 *House on Mango Street* and her narrator Esperanza who desires a "house of one's own,"[36] signals the desire for independence and socioeconomic mobility for contemporary Chicanas. Second, the domestic interiors are represented in lighter and brighter colors. Valdez's new kitchen paintings incorporate wider shots that depart from the feeling of claustrophobia that defined her earlier paintings. These recent kitchens are situated within a square frame, objects are (more) stable, and colors have shifted from a palette of dark reds, blues, and blacks to one of pinks, oranges, browns, lighter blues, and yellows. They are "rooms with a view" where the domestic simultaneously enters and is open to the outside realm.

Instead of the presence of family portraits in *The Kitchen/la cocina* and the inclusion of barely noticeable figures in *The Dressing Table/La mesa del vendaje*, the new kitchen paintings lack bodies entirely. Even though these early paintings include portraits and the presence of people, the dark tones and subject matter give them a solitary feel. The new paintings, on the other hand, even though they lack bodies, imply, by the inclusion of images of open drawers and cabinets, heat from warm coffee and food, and Valdez's signature brooms, the presence of bodies. Explaining this shift from solitary to inhabitable space, Mesa-Bains explains how these new paintings "begin to reflect the move from a house of urban survival to a home of lived experience" (1999, 43). In *La Cocina* and *Patssi's Kitchen*, recognizable realistic elements, including windows, tables, and brooms, merge with magical realist characteristics, including windows thrown open, tables askew, and flying brooms.[37]

The kitchens of both of these paintings have an active presence where, at any moment, resistance or rebellion—perhaps by female inhabitants—seems plausible or even about to occur.

These new kitchen paintings make powerful arguments for the role of domestic space as a comforting and secure realm for Chicanas against the forces of oppression inside and outside the home. These paintings depict the domestic in similar ways to representations of home by Chicana author and poet Pat Mora, who narrates home as a safe and nourishing space in the face of Anglo American racism and hostility. Mora's narratives depart from the nationalist discourses of home that upheld gender hierarchies and denied women agency. Instead, by affirming solidarity among women—a kinship that is not based on patriarchal structures—Mora's representations of home rewrite home and *la familia* in feminist terms. Mora's recent collection of poetry, *Adobe Odes* (2006), for instance, extols the kitchen as a site of food, family, place, and religious icons that nourish Chicanas amid Anglo American racism and hostility toward Mexican American language and culture. Her kitchens are sites for the passing down of Chicana/o cultural traditions as a way to resist assimilation. Visual artist Carmen Lomas Garza and her paintings *La Tamalada* (1990) and *Empanadas* (1991) also illustrate the kitchen as a site of nourishment in response to Anglo racism and structural inequalities on the US-Mexico border.

Domestic Space and Performance: Set Designs for *Mi Familia*

Lacking bodies or actors, Valdez's paintings are essentially performance spaces; they are scenes where actors have just left or are about to enter the room. Valdez comments on the role of performance in her paintings: "My goal is to keep the paintings alive, to give them a sense of movement. I want to evoke a feeling that people just left the room" (Valdez 1999). Writing about the home as performance, Beatriz Colomina claims, "The house is the stage for the theater of the family, a place where people are born and live and die. Whereas a work of art, a painting, presents itself to ritual attention as an object, the house is received as an environment, as a stage" (2000, 318). In performance terms, then, Valdez's paintings imbue the house as not a static object but as a lived-space in movement. Valdez's rendering of the domestic as a performance space is most evident in her 1994 painting *The Magic Room*, now in the permanent collection at the Smithsonian American Art Museum.[38] Similar to the magical realist elements of her kitchen paintings, this is a magic room where deep red and heavy theatrical curtains frame a scene in which wine glasses topple over, unsteady chairs float, a carpet swirls in vibrant colors, gymnastic rings swing, forks cling to the table, and party favors suspend in the air. The perspective of the painting emphasizes the theatricality of the scene: it is as if we are looking at it from the perspective of an audience member sitting high up in a balcony.

Paintings such as *The Magic Room*, with their uninhabited and performative domestic spaces portrayed in vivid colors, led director Gregory Nava to ask Valdez to work as a design consultant on his 1995 film *Mi Familia*,[39] one of the few big-budget Hollywood films by a Chicana/o director, and one that included a cast of well-known Latina/o actors: Edward James Olmos, Esai Morales, Jimmy Smits, Lupe Ontiveros, and Jennifer Lopez.[40] Valdez's set designs for *Mi Familia* are extensions of her previous performance work in Asco and her work as a set designer and design consultant in theater. Prior to and while making *Mi Familia*, Valdez was a set and costume designer for several Latina/o theater productions, including Culture Clash's *Carpa Clash* (1993) and Luis Alfaro's and Diane Rodríguez's *Diva L.A.: A Salute to L.A.'s Latinas in the Tanda Style* (1995), both produced at the Mark Taper Forum in Los Angeles.

Valdez's self-fashioning in Asco functioned as commentary on the exclusion and simultaneous exoticization of Latinas in Hollywood film. On her relationship to Hollywood, Valdez explains, "When I was in high school, I had these dreams.... I guess [I was] highly influenced by Hollywood.... Now I look back [at] ... Latina actresses like Seidy Lopez ... and I think, 'God, how lucky' because some part of me feels like I was like Seidy. And that I could have been an actress" (1999). Given Valdez's feelings of invisibility, her set designs for Nava's *Mi Familia* can be read as part of a desire to intervene in existing Latina/o representations (R. González 2000). Several Latina/o actors in the film, such as Jimmy Smits, expressed that they were further compelled to be part of the film given the historic lack of Chicana/o representations in Hollywood (McKenna 1995).

Valdez's life relates to the subject matter of *Mi Familia*. She states: "I grew up in East L.A. in the '50s, so this is a world I knew very well" (Qtd. in McKenna 1995). Nava's *Mi Familia* follows sixty years and three generations of a Chicana/o family living in East Los Angeles, the Sánchez family, and depicts each generation's struggles with social barriers and racism in a segregated East Los Angeles. The film is told from the point of view of Paco Sánchez, played by Olmos, who is the aspiring writer of the family. The narrative begins in the early twentieth century, with the first generation of the family in rural Mexico, and follows the parents as they immigrate to Southern California in the 1920s, an environment dominated by structural inequalities and xenophobia toward Mexican-descent communities. *Mi Familia* can be read as a cinematic representation of familiar aspects and tropes of Chicana/o history, what Fregoso describes as "indigenous music and iconography, circular migrations, Californio territorial claims, service workers, repatriation during the thirties, state repression, pachuco resistance, political activism, and incarceration" (2003, 71). Importantly, given the film industry's and popular media's either complete historical evasion of or use of distorted stereotypes to depict Chicana/o culture and identity, *Mi Familia* is a necessary film that intervenes in the dearth of representations of Latina/os in Hollywood.

Mi Familia can also be read as a response to a New Right discourse of family values in the 1980s and 1990s that positioned a disintegrating US nuclear family as the culprit for society's social ills (Fregoso 2003). For working-class communities of color, New Right conservatism emphasized broken family structures as responsible for larger social problems, rather than symptomatic of larger structural and racial inequalities. *Mi Familia*'s celebration of family at the center of Chicana/o culture can therefore be read as a reaction to a Republican social agenda that demonized Chicana/o families while upholding the myth of a moralistic US family (Fregoso 2003). In fact, in discussions about his film, Nava engages with conservative discourse by emphasizing how Chicana/o families are similar to other US families: "We all have more in common than we realized. The family is one of those things" (qtd. in McKenna 1995). Nava also explains his emphasis on family as a reaction against popular media stereotypes of Chicana/os as gang members, stating "[I]nstead of putting gangs at the center of Latino culture, which the media have done, the family is at the center" (qtd. in McKenna 1995).

As many have argued, *Mi Familia* privileges a male discourse in regards to Chicana/o history and family, and thereby "downplays the significance of female voices within la familia" (Fregoso 2003, 75; Rodríguez 2009). Within this framework, the film privileges a Chicano/a family romance steeped in "heterosexual marriage, nuclear bloodlines, and gender hierarchies" (Fregoso 2003, 72; Huaco-Nuzum 1998). Fregoso, Huaco-Nuzum, and Rodríguez argue that the film evades alternative family structures and ignores the diversity of actual family life in Chicana/o households (2003, 1998, 2009). In doing so, the film perpetuates a patriarchal and heteronormative *familia* at the center of Chicana/o culture and history. In interviews, Nava defines family within a familiar nationalist discourse that situates family as a protective shelter against racism. He states, "Because Latino culture in L.A. has been poor and oppressed, these people have always looked to their families for protection and strength" (qtd. in McKenna 1995). Because Nava's Sánchez family functions as "paradigmatic for a nation," it therefore becomes a generalized representation of all Chicana/o families (Fregoso 2003, 71).

Valdez's set designs for *Mi Familia*, however, can be read as providing a female-centered visual narrative within the dominant discourse of a patriarchal *la familia* in the film. They were frequently noted and discussed in reviews of the movie, indicating the prominent and important role of her designs in shaping a visual iconography of the domestic and family for the film. In fact, reviewers consistently note how the Sánchez family home becomes another prominent character, if not the main character. Roger Ebert states, "[I]n actuality, the chief character is the house, a living organism that expands, contracts and takes on different characters as time goes by. As the tale progresses and the family expands, the house grows too. By the time the story jumps to the 1980s, the colors have become intensely dark, and the house has begun to sag because there's so much living in it" (1995). Production designer Barry Robison explains how the Sánchez home in the 1950s was partly inspired by Valdez, as well as the work of Diego Rivera and Frida Kahlo, which led him to use a color palette dominated by pastel and folk-art colors. The Sánchez home of the 1980s, however, is almost entirely influenced by Valdez's paintings. Robison explains, "We all carried around color Xeroxes of her paintings because Greg [Gregory Nava] wanted a literal interpretation of her work, he wanted her paintings to come to life in everything, from the sets to clothes and make-up" (qtd. in McKenna 1995). Valdez explains how Nava was drawn to her paintings because of the way they used light: "Greg told me that the thing that struck him about my paintings was the way the light comes through the windows into the rooms, light is either warm or cold in my paintings, and it's an intensely emotional interpretation of light" (qtd. in McKenna 1995). Thus, the Sánchez family home in the 1950s is filled with bright light to reflect a more innocent time, while the home in the 1980s becomes dominated by heavier light and muted colors, thereby reflecting the intensity of the plot as it unfolds.

As indicated in the critical reception of the film, Valdez's set designs function more than mere backdrops to the film's narrative, but hold a strong presence as they powerfully contribute to the representation of Mexican American family and home in *Mi Familia*. Valdez's set designs for *Mi Familia*, like her installations, use materials of both the domestic sphere and the mass market, and create a look that can be classified as "rasquache domesticana" (Mesa-Bains 2003). The Sánchez family home of the 1980s overflows with archetypal objects of a working-class Chicana/o home, including proud presentation of ceramics, lace tablecloths, plastic furniture covers, and family photos (R. González 2000). By emphasizing working-class culture and female roles within the home, the designs can be considered alternative sites to the patriarchal and nationalistic representations that are at the center of the film's narrative. While "rasquache" generally "makes do" with materials found in the home, "rasquache domesticana" invokes its specific power by critiquing institutions that have structured Chicana femininity. As discussed earlier, domesticana strategies are in part a mode of exposing patriarchal control in the domestic sphere while subverting gendered ideologies through visual practices. While Valdez's set designs may not explicitly "subvert" representations of patriarchal and heteronormative *familia* in the film, they serve as a visual reminder of the ideologies that structure women's roles within the home. They also emphasize visually how Chicanas have used domesticity to assert power in an otherwise marginalized sphere.

Concluding Remarks

Patssi Valdez is one of the most influential yet understudied female artists of the Chicano/a movement and contemporary period. Her self-fashioning in her performances with Asco and in her solo art function as powerful sites that represent her searching for a "room of one's own" in patriarchal spaces and mainstream discourses, a desire for space through acts of negotiation.[41] Yet Valdez's vision and artistic contributions continue to be underestimated. The omission of Valdez from Chicano/a studies and art history reminds us that self-fashioning and domesticity, often considered the domain and site of the female body and not a legitimate art form, must be taken into consideration when viewing the cultural production of Chicana artists. It also reminds us of the importance of reading cultural production outside of a binary model of resistance/affirmation. Only when we do so will the self-fashioning and domestic spaces of Chicana artists continue to be seen and heard.

In my final chapter, I turn to actor and director Diane Rodríguez, a pivotal figure of Latina/o theater and performing arts whose body of work has also yet to be fully theorized and explored in Latina/o theater and cultural studies. Like Valdez's, Rodríguez's artistic expressions of Chicana domesticity cannot be easily read within a framework of resistance/affirmation. As a performer and director, Rodríguez works with hegemonic scripts that are not of her own making, and many of these scripts represent the naturalization of domesticity on the Latina body. Her career therefore illustrates what an artist can do when they are working with texts that are not their own, but who seek to be part of the construction of that script. Whether it is through her performance of lines or direction of a play, Rodríguez has negotiated dominant scripts that have sought to ascribe domesticity to the Chicana/Latina body, or the repeated placement of Latinas in the home in a discourse that portrays their bodies as biologically, racially, and socially suited to the domestic sphere. Acts of negotiation have therefore been crucial for Rodríguez to get her work "out there" as an actor in Hollywood and as a director of Latina/o theater.

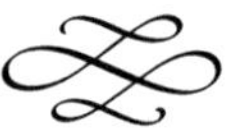

CHAPTER 6

Redirecting Chicana/Latina Representation

DIANE RODRÍGUEZ'S PERFORMANCE AND STAGING OF THE DOMESTIC

In December 2003, Home and Garden Television (HGTV) featured director and actor Diane Rodríguez's home in Echo Park, Los Angeles, in a segment titled "Mexican Holiday Décor" for their annual program *Handmade Holiday with Kitty Bartholomew.*[1] In the episode, the host, Kitty Bartholomew, guides audiences on a multicultural tour of twelve houses, spotlighting homeowners who have created "handmade objects reflecting their heritage and family traditions" for the holiday season.[2] Only three homes are assigned an ethnic and racial designation, including Rodríguez's and two others with the labels "African American Holiday" and "Japanese Style Wrapping."[3] The piece on Rodríguez's home features panoramic and close-up views of her various decorations; Bartholomew's voiceover describes them as quintessentially Mexican, using descriptions such as "typical of a Mexican color palette" and "Mexican folk art." While the camera pans across these various objects, Spanish flamenco guitar plays in the background, and in one scene, Rodríguez demonstrates the craft of decorating a small Christmas tree. As the camera focuses on Rodríguez topping the tree with a bright, colorful star, Bartholomew exclaims that it "is reminiscent of a colorful Mexican piñata!" At the beginning of the segment, Bartholomew provides an explanation for Rodríguez's decorative choices: "Homeowner Diane Rodríguez resides in Los Angeles and since it's so close to the Mexican border it's easy for her to find décor that celebrates her heritage."[4]

The holiday special's depiction of Rodríguez's home and décor references popular discourses of Latina/o cultures and domestic spaces that I have described throughout this book. The HGTV special renders Latinas in the United States as nurturers and laborers of the domestic household and domestic nation, while locating Mexican culture and identity outside of the United States' literal and figurative borders. First, the program elides Mexican culture and identity as a hybrid, living cultural form in the space of Los Angeles and the nation. When Bartholomew asserts that it's "*easy* for [Rodríguez] to find décor that celebrates her heritage" since "it's *so close* to the Mexican border" (emphasis mine), she implies that Southern California's proximity to Mexico makes it easy to find Mexican items in Los Angeles. Yet with the statement, she locates Mexican culture south of the US-Mexico border, and not as a lived experience and identity shared by those of Mexican descent in the space of Los Angeles. Furthermore, while Rodríguez's voiceover expresses the plurality of cultures that informs her holiday décor, Bartholomew's narrative isolates Rodríguez's décor as typically "Mexican," particularly through her labeling of the Christmas tree star as a "colorful Mexican piñata" and other references to her décor as "typical of a Mexican color palette." This view contrasts with Rodríguez's description of her decorations in her voiceover, where she states: "The decorations, most of them are from Mexico, but a lot of what I have in my home is not strictly Mexican."[5] Rodríguez continues, "That's the tradition of Southern California: we have all this color to pull from, we have all this color swirling around us."[6] In my interview with the artist, Rodríguez describes how she "took Mexican folk art and color and mixed it with Asian, Moroccan, and Afghan art to create a pastiche of a Southern California look."[7] Here, Rodríguez expresses a postmodern view of Mexican American identity and culture, affirming what Victor Hugo-Viesco explains in another context: "Neither assimilationist nor separatist, th[e] site of contemporary Chicano cultural production affirms its cultural heritage and its history of place in Los Angeles while creatively engaging in the adaptation of the diversity of cultural forms that cross the city" (2005, 486). Additionally, with the Spanish flamenco guitar soundtrack, the special evokes Spanish Fantasy Heritage discourse, which conflates Mexican and Spanish cultures and fixes Latina/os in an "idyllic nation-based past," privileging Spanish identity and eliding *mestizaje*, or cultural and racial mixture (Habell-Pallán 2005, 10). Finally, by marking only three homes out of the twelve with an ethnic and racial designation, the special signifies the other homes, presumably Anglo American, as normative representations of US identity and culture.[8]

The HGTV special's portrayal of Rodríguez's relationship to home décor references the naturalization of Latina domesticity, or the dominant culture's repeated placement of Latinas in the home. Such discourses portray Latinas as biologically, racially, and socially suited to the domestic sphere. Rodríguez is presented as a homeowner and not an artist on the program, implying that her holiday decorations develop organically from her gendered and racialized identity. While the majority of HGTV programming constructs women's relationship to home as natural and effortless (a consistent thread that is also evident throughout the other segments of *Handmade Holiday*), the special frames Rodríguez's domestic interior as developing from her ethnic identity as a woman of Mexican descent. In the opening of the segment, Bartholomew states, "[Rodríguez has] honored her Latina heritage with her colorful holiday décor." This statement links Rodríguez's "Mexican" decorations with her innate knowledge of them as a Latina, and not as a Latina artist.

Despite HGTV's suggestion that Rodríguez's decorations developed organically from her Mexican heritage, her participation in the special grew out of an artistic and commissioned collaboration with Chicana visual artist and friend Patssi Valdez. Rodríguez explains, "[Artist Patssi Valdez and I] have a friend who works for HGTV, Ken Short, he's an art director and they were doing a Christmas special and Ken asks if we can do this for him, and I thought, oh my god, I'm in the middle of directing a play, I can't! And, he said, what if I got Patssi and we do it together, and since Patssi and I are such good friends, then we'll do it, and we did it in like a day!"[9] When Rodríguez says "we did it in like a day," she refers to the time it took to tape the program, as both Rodríguez and Valdez worked on creating and gathering objects for the special in advance of the taping.[10] Rodríguez also describes her demonstration of the holiday craft as a performance: "[W]hen they came to shoot it Patssi got sick . . . so I did the whole thing by myself, and I was the one who was going to be on camera. . . . We were supposed to do a craft, which was decorating a tree, a Christmas tree, a small one, and Patssi told me in a second what it was, . . . and in the middle of shooting [it], I thought I don't know what I'm doing! *I've never done this in my life! . . .* but they were shooting it and *I just improvised* and it came out great, but it's very funny!" (emphasis added).[11] With the term "improvise," Rodríguez indicates how as the cameras rolled in that moment, she performed a craft that she had not created or demonstrated prior to the special, most likely drawing on her training in acting and directing to perform the decoration. Any easiness that Rodríguez therefore ascribes to her collaboration with Valdez refers not to their innate talents to decorate homes as Latinas, but rather their abilities as Latina visual artists in set design and performance to create what HGTV frames as "Mexican Holiday Décor."

HGTV's naturalization of Latina domesticity, along with the artist's participation, echoes the artist's experiences as an actor in Hollywood television and film. As both an actor and director, Rodríguez has frequently confronted dominant narratives of Latina domesticity that have sought to render Latinas as biologically, racially, and naturally suited to motherhood and home. In Hollywood specifically, Rodríguez has consistently been typecast as the Latina domestic, the devoted wife, and suffering mother. Due to this frequent typecasting, Rodríguez made a strategic decision to negotiate these roles by focusing on theater directing, a position she believed would enable her to actively stage and produce complex images of Latina/o communities. Rodríguez states that she works almost exclusively as a director because "it gets me out of there. . . . I couldn't stand to see myself in a maid's uniform," referring to the role of the domestic laborer in which she found herself frequently cast.[12]

In this chapter, I closely read Rodríguez's career trajectory, from her performances in the activist theater troupe El Teatro Campesino, to her roles as a character actor in Hollywood cinema and television, to her direction of Latina/o theatre. I argue that her acting and directorial work function as a process-related, ephemeral, and enacted negotiation of various hegemonic scripts that have sought to ascribe domesticity to the Latina body. These negotiations, on the one hand, support and further the stereotype of Latina domesticity, but on the other hand, challenge them. As she has consistently confronted dominant narratives in her career, Rodríguez has used performance and direction to negotiate those narratives, whether it is through her performance of lines or direction of a play. Regardless of the hegemonic script, Rodríguez's approach has been to destabilize the dominant discourse of Latina domesticity. Rodríguez's artistic career is therefore an example of what an artist can do when they are working within structures that are not of their own making, but who seek to be part of the construction of that script. Since performance and direction are inherently collaborative endeavors, Rodríguez's career illustrates how she has modified the tools of others to "dismantle the master's house" (Lorde 1984).

In each of this chapter's sections, I explore how Rodríguez takes an existing narrative and intervenes in it with either performance or direction. I read her performances and direction of Latina domesticity as acts of "disidentification," a term coined by Jose Muñoz to describe how racial outsiders negotiate the majority culture not by aligning themselves with the dominant narrative but by transforming it for their own cultural purposes (1999). As Muñoz states, "[D]isidentification is about cultural, material, and psychic survival. It is a response to state and global power apparatuses that employ systems of racial, sexual, and national subjugation. . . . Disidentification is about managing and negotiating historical trauma and systemic violence" (1999, 161). I also utilize Charles Ramírez Berg's theorizations of acting as an embodied performance that has the potential to transgress stereotypes on screen (2002). Berg proposes the concept of "performative excess," in which Latina/o actors offer more than the Hollywood stereotype and therefore subvert the stereotype through the process of acting (2002, 89). Finally, I suggest that Rodríguez's directorial choices function as a "redirection" of the confinement of Latinas to domesticity that she experienced as an actor early in her career. By "redirection," I refer to Ellen Donkin and Susan Clement's suggestion that a director can use her role to "completely upend the text, encourage her actors to develop subtexts the playwright never dreamed of, enlist her designers in the creation of a destabilizing visual counterpoint, or cast performers whose very presence throws the text into question" (1993, 2). The term "redirection" highlights the choices a director makes to shift the tone and focus of the play script. I also use the term to signal a director's engagement with a dominant narrative that is outside of the script. I suggest that with redirection in Latina/o theater, Rodríguez negotiates narratives about Latinas and domesticity she encountered in mainstream media, as well as creates a space for complex and diverse images of Latinas in visual representations.

THE PERFORMANCE OF LATINA DOMESTICITY

Throughout her career, Rodríguez has confronted Hollywood and US racial definitions of Latina identity and Chicano/a nationalist definitions of gender, both of which have sought to limit the roles of Chicanas and Latinas in visual representation. As one of the original members of El Teatro Campesino, a theater troupe founded under the cultural arm of the United Farm Workers Movement in the 1970s and 1980s, Rodríguez performed in *actos,* or short skits, on flatbed trucks in the fields for farm workers and in union halls; the troupe later toured community theater spaces across the United States and Europe. Many of the *actos,* which included migrant farmworkers themselves as performers, dramatized the struggles and activist causes of the farmworkers, with the ultimate goal of illustrating how racial and socioeconomic inequalities can be transformed through collective union organizing (Broyles-González 1994; Habell-Pallán 2005, 40). Other El Teatro performances affirmed and celebrated cultural traditions and religious icons, relying on a shared working-class Chicana/o aesthetic, experience, and cultural heritage (Broyles-González 1994). As a site of "alternative constructions of [US] nation and citizenship," El Teatro led its laboring audiences to challenge hegemonic power relationships by depicting images of Latina/os as controlling their future and destiny (Habell-Pallán 2005, 36).

As a performer in Chicana/o activist theater, Rodríguez experienced gendered stereotypes. In El Teatro Campesino, Rodríguez and the other female performers confronted limited gendered roles due to the cultural nationalism and patriarchalism of the Chicano/a Movement (Broyles-González 1994). The women of the troupe frequently performed as mothers, daughters, and wives—roles that the majority rural Mexicano audiences could relate to—and these characters were often further narrowed to reflect cultural assumptions of women as either saints, martyrs, virgins, or whores. Rodríguez explains how, because of these limiting parts, she often chose to play more "androgynous" characters in El Teatro Campesino:

> It is true, the Teatro repertoire of women's roles, the wives, the girlfriends, the loose women, the Virgins, was tiresome and limiting. I was never very good at playing any of them. Looking back, I realize it was my way of resisting those roles. I was most comfortable playing androgynous characters: La Muerte in *La Carpa de los Rasquachis* or Satanás in *La Pastorela,* a shepherd's play. These roles offered more versatility and power. We women complained but, in the end, we accepted the roles. All of us could have walked away, but we didn't. I take full responsibility for what the group was delivering. I was a willing participant. (Qtd. in Broyles-González 1994, 317)

By indicating that she was "never good at playing" the limited gendered roles of virgin and whore in El Teatro, Rodríguez does not suggest that she was a bad actor. Rather, she locates her resistance to the hegemonic gendered binary, explaining how she was not fully engaged in those roles, since they lacked "versatility" and "power." Her explanation that she continued to play these limited gendered characters reveals women's secondary status within El Teatro Campesino, which reflects the larger context of female marginalization within the greater Chicano/a Movement (Latorre 2008). If Chicanas were to place priority and emphasis on feminist issues in the movement generally, they were often deemed *malinchistas* or traitors (Blackwell 2011, Espinoza 2001).

Similar to her performances with El Teatro, much of Rodríguez's later and current theater work has been rooted in social activism, utilizing the genres of activist theater and comedy to create new images of Latina/os on the US stage. In the late 1980s, Rodríguez co-founded Latins Anonymous, an L.A.-based comedy troupe that incorporated satire to critique the typecasting of Latinas and Latinos in Hollywood; the project was a response to the limited roles Rodríguez persistently encountered while pursuing an acting career in Los Angeles. In her role as co-director, and as director of the Latino Theatre Initiative at the Mark Taper Forum from 1995 to 2005, a mainstream theater space and nationally recognized institution, Rodríguez created visibility for Latina/o drama in Los Angeles by ushering in new Latina/o playwrights, producing Latina/o stories, and providing programming pertinent to Latina/o communities (Rodríguez 2011, 2). As co-director of the Latino Theater Initiative, Rodríguez helped oversee several of the eleven total Latina/o plays produced on the Taper's main stage during the course of the initiative (Rodríguez 2011, 3).[13] Significantly, Rodríguez worked with Luis Alfaro, the co-director of the Latino Theater Initiative from 1995 to 2003, to produce and develop new plays by Latina artists, including many influential and well-known Latina female playwrights (Rodríguez 2011, 19).[14] As a theater director, Rodríguez has also directed several plays by Latina/o authors whose works question stereotypical views of race, gender, and sexuality.[15] Finally, since 2005, in her role as the associate producer and director of new play production at the Center Theatre Group and as an associate member of Cornerstone Theater, Rodríguez advocates for Latina/o actors and playwrights by spearheading theater partnerships and artist residencies.[16]

Alongside this career of activist performance, directing, and advocacy work in US Latina/o theatre, Rodríguez has also pursued an acting career in Hollywood television and film. In contrast to the level of agency she has had shaping and countering stereotypical images of Latina/os as a theater professional, Rodríguez has played every conceivable Latina stereotype in Hollywood film and television, underscoring the industry's frequent typecasting of Latinas as maids, unskilled laborers, and criminals. For example, in the big-budget film *Psycho III* (1986), Rodríguez played a nun, and in *La Bamba* (1987), Rodríguez performed in a minor nonspeaking role as Richie Valens's aunt Ernestine. In the block-buster *Terminator II: Judgment Day* (1991), Rodríguez performed the character of an indigenous healer. In the early 1990s, Rodríguez played a recurring role as a Mexican maid on a short-run soap opera, *Sunset Beach*. Then, in the short-lived television show *L.A. Doctors* (1998), Rodríguez played a Mexican nurse in an alternative treatment clinic in Mexico. In the television movie *On the Line* that same year, Rodríguez portrayed Mrs. Gómez, a traditional Latina mother to a daughter in a violent Los Angeles girl gang. A decade later, in a 2004 episode of *ER*, Rodríguez played Rosario, an aunt who kidnaps her niece from Mexico and forces her into sexual slavery. When we read these minor, stereotypical, and mostly nonspeaking roles against Rodríguez's activist work as a theater profes-sional invested in countering dominant images and creating space for diverse Latina/o representations, they are striking. When asked about her role as a maid on *Sunset Beach*, Rodríguez explains that she quit this job after receiving a phone call from a friend telling her she should not have to accept the maid role consid-ering her theater experiences and Chicana activism.[17] If Rodríguez had turned down the gendered and racialized roles available to Latina/o actors in television and film, it is likely she would not have had as prolific a career in the industry. As noted earlier, as a result of this typecasting, Rodríguez chose to concentrate her efforts on building her career as a theater professional.

Even as a performer in US Latina/o theater, Rodríguez has been frequently rel-egated to gendered roles associated with motherhood and biological reproduc-tion. Rodríguez explains how "it was very depressing" to play a Latina domestic in Lisa Loomer's play *Living Out* (2003), even though the work critically explores the fraught relationships between two white mothers and their domestics in Santa Monica, California. She also describes her performance of Minerva, a wife and mother who overeats and becomes obese in Luis Alfaro's *Breakfast, Lunch, and Dinner* (2002–2003) as "challenging" because the character is confined to the home and "never leaves the house," even though the play also critiques hegemonic gender and culture roles.[18] Rodríguez suggests that both parts were difficult to portray because these women were confined to the home and margin-alized in their communities; she also linked the challenge of playing these parts to the frequent typecasting of her body in the domestic role in Hollywood.[19]

Rodríguez's experiences in Hollywood reveal the combination of both gen-dered and racialized marginalization. The hegemonic representations of Latinas in Hollywood invoke stereotypes of Latina/os (Noriega 1992; Ramírez Berg 2002) and reflect a racialized social structure (Dávila 2001; Molina-Guzmán 2010; Ovalle 2011). As Priscilla Ovalle argues, "Hollywood film embodies and renders visible the racial, sexual, and gendered ideologies of the United States and these representations function as recognizable—if exaggerated—versions of the US social/racial hierarchy" (2011, 5). To this end, popular US media constructions of Latina beauty and desirability are often shaped by colonial frameworks of racialized and gendered bodies that emphasize whiteness over blackness (Dávila 2001). Within this racialized hierarchy, Ovalle argues, Latinas occupy an ambiguous racial space and fluctuate "between the normalcy of whiteness and the exoticism of blackness" (2011, 7).

Latina actors with darker and indigenous features have been typically confined to marginal, domestic roles, while Latinas with lighter skin who conform to Hollywood beauty standards have been assigned major and leading roles on screen, and have had more flexibility within the racialized hierarchy (Ovalle 2011).[20] Contemporary Latina actors who performed as domestics in secondary, not lead, roles in primetime television include Shelley Morrison and the late Lupe Ontiveros; both actors have darker features and unconventional looks by Hollywood's standards. Morrison, best known for her character Rosario, Karen Walker's Salvadorian maid, on *Will & Grace* from 2001 to 2006, has portrayed a maid or housekeeper in over thirty roles in Hollywood.[21] When Morrison received the call for the part on *Will & Grace*, she had recently informed her agent not to offer her any more "maid parts."[22] Like Rodríguez, Morrison indicates her frustration with playing the part of the domestic, yet most likely accepted the part in order to advance her Hollywood career. Additionally, Morrison's performance of the character Rosario utilizes the stereotype to challenge and subvert it.[23] Lupe Ontiveros, perhaps the most well-known Latina actor in the marginal domestic role, portrayed more than 150 Latina domestics in film and television.[24] Commenting on her many performances in the domestic role in 2002, Ontiveros stated, "I'm proud to represent those hands that labor in this country. I've given every maid I've ever portrayed soul and heart" (qtd. in Navarro 2002). Ontiveros noted here and in other interviews that she responded to the casting of her body in the stereotypical and often dehumanizing maid role by imbuing the domestic character with humanity. Ontiveros played many of her domestic characters with power, sarcasm, and feistiness, suggesting how she negotiated the dominant script of Latina representation throughout her long career.

The frequency of Latina maid characters on primetime television, on the one hand, reflects the shifting racial demographics and a modern global economy that increasingly depends on the labor of Latina immigrants (Navarro 2002; Segura and Zavella 2007). Yet it also reflects a consistent stereotype in Hollywood film and television that portrays Latinas as low-wage workers and not as professionals. Furthermore, the majority of the maid roles stereotype Latinas within a gendered and racialized discourse about their assumed fertility, domesticity, sexuality, and subservience (Molina-Guzmán 2010, 10). The casting of the Latina body in the role of the domestic references a nativist discourse about reproductive labor, motherhood, and citizenship (Kim 1999, 108; Romero 2003, 833). For example, in dominant rhetoric, Mexican immigrant women have consistently represented long-term settlement and the "dramatic growth of a 'minority group'" (Chávez 2007, 68; De Genova 2006; Gutiérrez 2008). During the debate over Proposition

187 in California in 1994, a measure that sought to deny undocumented immigrants healthcare and education,[25] several national television programs claimed that Mexican women and children were responsible for the state's economic woes due to their cultural and biological reproduction. Proponents of Proposition 187 charged Mexican and Latina immigrants with invading the nation through their fertility (Chávez 2007, 2001; Gutiérrez 2008). Bette Hammond, an activist proponent of Proposition 187, articulated this view of Latinas as invading the nation to soak up social services: "They come here, they have their babies, and after that they become citizens and all those children use social services" (qtd. in Chávez 2007, 68). Such rhetoric resurfaced during the 2010 midterm elections, when right-wing politicians once again referred to the children of undocumented Latina immigrants as "anchor babies." In reference to this discourse about Latina fertility and cultural invasion, many Hollywood film and television portrayals strip Latina domestics of their own domesticity and reproductive labor, instead emphasizing their facilitation of a wealthy white family's domesticity and reproduction.[26]

Amid this larger, long-term stereotyping of Latinas in the domestic role, many Latina actors have challenged and engaged with the typecasting of their bodies in their performances. As George Lipsitz suggests, "Even demeaning portrayals of working-class people contain contradictions, allowing for negotiated or oppositional readings" (1986, 370).

In what follows, I explore Rodríguez's negotiation of the domestic role as a Mexican maid in the Hallmark Hall of Fame movie *Stones for Ibarra* (1988), directed by Jack Gold. I closely read her involvement in the television movie as a performance that negotiates the dominant script of Latina domesticity through "disidentification" (Muñoz 1999) and "performative excess" (Berg 2002). The film exemplifies the stereotypical scripts often assigned to Latina characters; Rodríguez's character supports a white couple's domesticity and represents an essentialized view of ethnic female identity that presumes a Mexican woman's domesticity and subservience. Similar to the HGTV special, *Stones for Ibarra* utilizes a Spanish Fantasy Heritage discourse that configures Mexicans and Mexican Americans as premodern, while positioning Mexican American cultures outside of the borders of the US nation. Both programs echo contemporary rhetoric about Latina/o immigrant communities, specifically a welcoming of Latina/o immigrants as laborers, but a denial of their citizenship within the literal and figurative borders of the US home. Within this narrative, the Latina domestic labors in the US home, yet is excluded from the nation.

Negotiating Latina Domesticity in *Stones for Ibarra*

The 1988 Hallmark Hall of Fame film *Stones for Ibarra*, directed by Jack Gold, was adapted from Harriet Doerr's original novel of the same name.[27] Published in 1984, the novel quickly became a bestseller and received several prestigious book awards, including the 1985 National Book Award for First Fiction and one of the three Bay Area Book Reviewers awards in 1984, as well as other accolades.[28] Partly autobiographical, *Stones for Ibarra* tells the story of a married, middle-aged Anglo American couple, Sara and Richard, who decide to leave their comfortable life in San Francisco and move to a fictionalized rural Mexican village named Ibarra; their move to Ibarra is a result of the husband's desire to reopen his grandfather's copper mine, which the grandfather closed during the Mexican Revolution of 1910.[29] The narrative centers on Sara and Richard's many encounters with the Mexican villagers of Ibarra and highlights the tensions between the US couple's "modern" and "civilized" ways and the Mexican villagers' "premodern" and "primitive" beliefs. As the story progresses, the husband falls deathly ill with leukemia, and when he is not cured by the local doctor, Sara relocates him to a California hospital, where he ultimately dies. In the final scene, Sara returns to their house in Ibarra and is joined by many of the Mexican villagers, who bring stones to honor Richard. Almost immediately, Doerr was praised for presenting an authentic vision of Mexico and for giving her readers "a remarkable picture of a declining Mexican village of one thousand souls" (Broyard 1983). Hailed by some as "one of the best American novels in the last 50 years" (Fish 2003), critics put Doerr in the ranks of novelists such as Gabriel García Márquez, Katherine Anne Porter, and Graham Greene.[30]

Stones for Ibarra first aired January 29, 1988, on the CBS network.[31] The film, like the novel, follows the San Francisco couple Sara and Richard—played by Glenn Close and Keith Carradine—who journey to the small, fictionalized Mexican village of Ibarra to escape the busy city life of San Francisco. In the film, Rodríguez plays María de Lourdes, a Mexican maid who works for the US couple in Mexico. The film was praised for "brilliantly maintain[ing] the balance between imagination and reality, the Mexicans and the Americans" and bringing "something very special" to the depiction of Mexico (O'Connor 1988). While the film did not receive as much critical acclaim as the novel, it was still attributed with presenting an "authentic" vision. Filmed on location in Tucson, Arizona, *Stones for Ibarra* is cast primarily with Latina/o actors in minor roles, many of whom have had an extensive career in Hollywood, including the late Lupe Ontiveros, Ray Oriel, the late Trinidad Silva, Alfonso Arau, Jorge Cervera Jr., and Angie Porres. In fact, the lead actors, Glenn Close and Keith Carradine, are the only non-Latina/o cast members in the film. Given Hollywood's history of using any ethnic-looking actor or Anglo actor in Latina/o parts, the film's casting of Latina/os actors in Latina/o roles is an improvement. All of the Latina/o characters and their actions in the film, however, are in service (literally as maids and mine workers) to the white US couple and their narrative, since the film largely centers on the story of Sara and Richard.

The movie exemplifies the stereotypical roles that Hollywood assigns to Latinas and Latinos. The Mexican characters of the village of Ibarra include a violent "macho" town drunk, a fair-skinned and youthful beautiful señorita, mischievous Mexican maids, rowdy mine workers, and an aspiring young Mexican man (with lighter features) whose dream is to migrate to the United States. While such characterizations of class according to skin color stem from a racial caste system and racial ideologies in Mexico, the film's typecasting of US-born Latina/o actors according to skin color also reflects US racial ideologies. Furthermore, even though the film is set in Mexico, Spanish is not spoken in the movie, except in the case of proper names, such as names of villages, and titles, including señores and señoras. In fact, many scenes show Close's character ostensibly receiving Spanish lessons from a nun, yet the lessons are spoken in English by the actors. Additionally, the film is shot in brown, gray, almost sepia tones, emphasizing the construction of Mexico as a premodern and uncivilized space. The film's use of muted color represents a stereotypical, Hollywood view of Mexican poverty; the dim tones contrast sharply with the HGTV special's equation of Mexican identity and culture with exaggerated color. Additionally, Rodríguez's character does not speak in the first half of the film, emphasizing her subordinate and primitive status as Sara and Richard's maid; María Lourdes's silence corresponds with other Hollywood representations of the silent native "other."[32]

As a whole, the film conforms to the construction of Mexicans and Mexican Americans as locked in an idyllic and primitive past, and Anglo Americans as existing in a modern and civilized present, a dichotomy prevalent within the Spanish Fantasy Heritage. This construction of Mexican and Mexican American identity as premodern has been a pervasive stereotype in US culture and popular media, yet generally, the Spanish Fantasy Heritage discourse presents people of Mexican descent within a romanticized narrative, cleansed of sociohistorical circumstances and violent histories of conquest (Habell-Pallán 2005; Montgomery 2002; Nieto-Phillips 2004). Within the space of California, the Spanish Fantasy Heritage "used the cultural material of the Spanish colonial past to mask the presences of mostly poor, mixed-race, immigrant Mexicans in their midst" (Foley 2003, 1156). The Padua Hill Players in Claremont, for example, was an ensemble of Mexican American youth who, from the 1930s to 1950s, performed in plays that "circulated seemingly benign image[s] of a romantic California, one that whitewashed the violence of territorial conquest and the harsh living conditions of most Mexican Americans in California at that time" (Habell-Pallán 2005, 25).

The fictional space and time of *Stones for Ibarra*—initially set in San Francisco and then mostly in Mexico, both in the late 1950s—inform the codes of the Spanish Fantasy Heritage present in the film's depiction of its Mexican characters. The period of the late 1950s, as well as the decade in which the film was produced, the 1980s, were both characterized by an influx of Latina/o immigration in the United States. San Francisco in the 1950s experienced a bourgeoning modernization and an increase in immigration from Mexico and Central America, with many of these immigrants settling in the Mission District.[33] Previously an Irish neighborhood, the Mission shifted from an 11 percent Latina/o population in the 1950s to 45 percent in 1970, with many Central Americans from Nicaragua and El Salvador fleeing repressive dictatorships as part of this increasing percentage (Nyborg 2008, 35). Anglo fear and racism toward this increase in the Mexican immigrant population in San Francisco during the 1940s–1970s initiated the "white flight" of many Mission District residents. Additionally, the 1950s was the period of "Operation Wetback," in which an intense climate of anti-Mexican and anti–Mexican American sentiment led to a policy that deported and repatriated citizens of Mexican descent (García 1980).

The late 1980s, the time in which *Stones for Ibarra* is produced, was another moment of increased Latin American migration to the United States, with many Central and South American refugees fleeing civil wars and political instability. Furthermore, despite the Immigration and Reform Control Act (IRCA) in 1986, in which many undocumented migrants in the United States were granted legal status, a new undocumented Latina/o immigrant labor class grew in the late 1980s and early 1990s due to porous borders and employer demand for unskilled laborers. Nativism and xenophobia against many Mexicans and Mexican Americans in the United States increased during this period (Telles and Ortiz 2009, 94). Many people of Mexican descent, regardless of citizenship status, were viewed as foreigners and a threat to the cultural cohesion of US national identity and culture.

This context of increased Latin American immigration and resulting anti-Mexican hysteria in the United States is not present in the novel or film version of *Stones for Ibarra*. Yet it is clear that the couple seeks to escape the "big city" life of San Francisco, which in the 1950s includes a growing Mexican immigrant and Mexican American population. The novel and film's placement of Mexicans and Mexican communities outside of the borders of the US nation echoes nativist discourse, which excludes people of Mexican descent from US belonging and citizenship. The jacket copy of the VCR version provides an explanation for Sara and Richard's flight from San Francisco: "Sara and Richard Everton are a young American couple who escape the rat race of big city life and embark on an odyssey set in the beautiful landscapes of rural Mexico in 1959. In the village of Ibarra, they soon discover the strange mystical and spiritual nature of the poor villagers they have come to live among."[34] The hypocrisy, of course, is that Sara and Richard move to Mexico to escape the "rat race of big city life" in San Francisco, which includes the presence of Mexican immigrants and Mexican Americans, to carry out a fantasy narrative of living among Mexicans who are rendered simple, idyllic, and premodern. Additionally, by reopening his grandfather's mine in the fictional village of Ibarra, Richard becomes the village's major employer and therefore holds significant economic power; many of the Mexican mine workers and their families now rely on Richard and Sara for their economic livelihood, suggesting how the couple's move to Mexico indicates their refusal to be "colonized" by an increasing Mexican immigrant population in the United States, only to become the "colonizers" in Mexico.

Two early scenes in the film reference the Spanish Fantasy Heritage discourse, which depict benign and romanticized images of Mexican and Anglo relationships. When Sara and Richard first approach Richard's grandfather's house, Sara imagines her ancestors' past home, which includes a scene of a Mexican worker (perhaps the grandfather's butler or gardener) wearing all white, taking off his mariachi-style hat, smiling, and beckoning visitors to enter into Richard's ancestor's estate; this scene also includes an upbeat Spanish guitar soundtrack. When visitors (Sara in her fantasy, and the audience of the film) enter into the courtyard, they are greeted with a harmonious scene of Anglo men and women dressed in Victorian-style clothing playing tennis, while their Mexican workers, dressed in crisp, white clothes, tend to the yard. The film later depicts the present-day scene of the Mexican villagers of Ibarra, wearing drab work clothes, rebuilding Richard's grandfather's house; this scene includes a lively mariachi music soundtrack. The juxtaposition of the two scenes—the "Spanish" past and the "Mexican" present—emphasizes Sara's desire for an idealized and simple life of harmonious race relations, instead of her present life of uncertain circumstances rebuilding a house and opening up the grandfather's mine. In both scenes, the Mexican villagers are laborers in the white home.

An overall theme of the film is the tension between the US couple's Western beliefs and the villagers' (particularly their maid Lourdes's) indigenous beliefs. The film depicts these tensions early on by including separate scenes of the Evertons' and the villagers' (represented primarily by the maid Remedios) gossiping about one another; in these scenes, both groups seek to assert the superiority of their beliefs. For example, Ontiveros, who plays Remedios, another maid in the town, frequently gossips about the US couple as she washes clothes in the center of the village. Remedios states, "We saw it from their window. The Americans are very rich, but they are foolish. There is no end to their extravaganzas." Remedios further explains: "The Americans have no faith in anything. Everything Maria Lourdes left in cupboards and drawers to ensure their health has been thrown out. They are so wise, but so blind to the important things of their own lives." Gossip, as Lisa Lowe argues, functions as an "'unofficial' discursive structure" (1996, 113). With gossip, Remedios asserts the validity of the Mexican domestic's knowledge and belief systems.

Since the film is primarily about the US couple, the film focuses mostly on Sara's and Richard's persistent views of indigenous and *curandero* practices as irrational and based on instinct. Even though Sara and Richard persistently look down on Lourdes's indigenous remedies throughout the film, Sara gradually begins to yield to them by the end of the film. Her husband and the Mexican town doctor, however, remain unconvinced of the merits of native remedies; the irony is that Richard's health seems to be momentarily improved by indigenous cures. Also, when Richard dies at the end of the film, he is honored with stones. The film shows Rodríguez's character, Lourdes, describing to Sara the purpose of the stones, which is to honor and remember life, not death. By the end, Sara watches with great emotion and is moved by several of the Mexican villagers placing stones by their house. The film therefore, in certain respects, honors and respects the Mexican villagers' ways. Yet ultimately, these indigenous beliefs service the white couple's experiences and journey in the script.

There are various factors that mediate Rodríguez's performance of María Lourdes in the film, including Ernest Kinoy's adapted screenplay of Doerr's novel, Jack Gold's direction, and Keith Palmer's editorial changes in the final production. As Berg explains, actors tend to have the least amount of authorship on a film set (2002, 84). As a result, it is often difficult to analyze an actor's embodied performance, since, as Peter Krämer and Alan Lovell point out, "acting is an elusive art" (1999, 5). Much scholarship on film acting therefore focuses on the character as written as opposed to the character as acted (Berg 2002, 85). Berg explains: "there is the vexing problem of how to isolate the actor's contribution. After all, the actor is dressed by costumers, coifed by hairstylist, made up by makeup artists, lit by the director of photography, and presumably guided in every shot by the director. In addition, actors speak words written by the screenwriter, and the editor shapes their performances into their ultimate form. Where, then, is one to locate the actor's creative participation?" (2002, 85).

In order to analyze the character María Lourdes as acted by Rodríguez in *Stones for Ibarra*, I focus on the "signs of performance," a term by Richard Dyer (2008, 151). These signs include an actor's facial expressions, voice, gestures, body posture, and body movement (Dyer 2008, 151). I also focus on "performative excess," a phrase used by Berg to describe the process by which minority actors offer more than the Hollywood stereotype and therefore subvert the stereotype through the process of acting (2002, 89). He argues, "The more textured the performance, the more facets the actor is able to provide for the character, the more [...] viewers are called on to simply notice the Latino character, the less that character exists as a stereotype. Anything an actor can do to enrich their screen characters, to allow them to become individuals rather than to remain types, undermines their existence as a mere stereotypical sign" (Berg 2002, 89–90).

The first time we see Rodríguez's Lourdes in *Stones for Ibarra* (and she is only referred to as "Lourdes" by the American couple because, as Sara explains, there are "just so many Marías"), she is wearing long braids and peasant clothing. In the opening scene, Lourdes and another maid in the village are walking with a basket of laundry; they both stop when they see the *Americanos* driving into the village, a sight that leads both women to follow the Evertons' car with their eyes. In the next shot, we see Rodríguez's still and immobile body alongside the mobile *Americanos* in their car. Both Sara and Richard are accompanied by a local villager who serves as their guide and translator. When Sara and Richard drive into town, Sara, played by Glenn Close, watches the villagers of Ibarra first with a smile and then with a look of wonderment. With her look, she establishes the script's fantasy of Mexico as a premodern and mystical space. When many of the villagers, including Rodríguez, watch Close's character with curiosity, Close returns the villagers' gazes with a look of fear.

The film script constructs Rodríguez's Lourdes as a foreigner within Sara and Richard's home. A recurring plot of the film is Lourdes's placement of native remedies, including herbs and talismans, in the US couple's home in the attempt to cure Richard's leukemia. These items are persistently viewed by Sara and Richard as foreign, strange, and backward. In a key moment of the film, for example, Sara explains to Richard, "It's a maguey thorn. Lourdes believes it will protect the mine and the house." Richard then throws the thorn in the fireplace and replies—unconvinced by the value of these objects—"Good lord, what next?" Sara ultimately smiles in agreement and hugs Richard. This disregard and literal discarding of Lourdes's native medicinal practices by the US couple establish the film's construction of the Mexican maid's curandera practices as irrational against the rational and logical belief system of the Americans. In other scenes of the film, the villagers' indigenous Mexican beliefs are devalued by the husband. Prior to the couple's direct confrontation with Lourdes about the objects she leaves in their home, the husband is approached by a mine worker about health benefits. Richard explains he will not reimburse the man for services rendered by a *brujo* (curandero) because he will only pay for medical services provided by a "doctor." Richard states, "The mine pays for medical expenses. Not for the *brujo*. Not for the curandero." As implied by Richard and Sara in these scenes, curandero health practices threaten their American home and Western belief systems.

Other attempts by Rodríguez's character to insert and assert her native medicinal beliefs in the US couple's home are met with suspicion and condescension by the US couple, with the film script attributing mystical and supernatural qualities to Lourdes. In a later scene, Sara assigns Lourdes to watch Richard at his deathbed. Sara tells her, "When he wakes give him some water, make him drink." Lourdes says, "Yes, Señora," thereby seeming to comply with Sara's request. Yet Lourdes goes further in her assigned duties by using both *curanderismo* and Catholicism to heal Richard, proceeding to make the sign of the cross while putting a *romero* (rosemary) branch on Richard's pillow. As Lourdes proceeds to chant over Richard's death bed, the camera pans to Sara, who smiles in a patronizing manner. When Sara later walks into Richard's room with the town doctor, the Mexican doctor immediately throws aside the *romero* that Lourdes has placed on Richard's pillow, thereby discounting native medicinal practices and demonstrating different views in the Mexican community over the merits of *curanderismo*. In the subsequent scene, however, the herb reappears on Richard's bed. The film does not show Lourdes physically placing the herb beside Richard, yet the sequence of events implies that Lourdes has again placed it there. By not including a scene with Lourdes placing the herb on the pillow, the film implies Lourdes's supernatural and mystical qualities. This emphasis reinforces what Mary Romero describes, in another context, as "the stereotypical mysteriousness and spiritualism attributed to indigenous cultures and women of color as caretakers" (2003, 828).

Yet in each of these scenes, Rodríguez plays the character of Lourdes with dignity and defiance. While Rodríguez could have performed Lourdes in a stereotypical and childlike Mexican accent (which some of the actors do in the film), she consistently plays the part of Lourdes by speaking clearly and boldly, without an exaggerated inflection. And while she could have played Lourdes by bowing down to her employer meekly when responding to Sara's castigation of her, Rodríguez (as Lourdes) confronts Sara with self-assurance. Rodríguez's performance of Lourdes as strong and bold counters the film's depiction of Lourdes as childlike and mischievous. For example, in a key scene prior to Richard's death bed scene described above, Sara directly confronts Lourdes about the indigenous remedies she continues to leave in their home; this is the first time in the film Lourdes directly speaks to Sara:

> SARA: What are these? I found these under the pillow.
> LOURDES: Two blue buttons, señora.
>   [...]
> SARA Lourdes, what are these?
> LOURDES: Señora? A hairpin and a slice of bread.
> SARA: What are they for?
> LOURDES: Who knows?

During this exchange, Close, as Sara, looks in wonderment at her Mexican maid Lourdes and her premodern ways; this parallels the opening segment, when Close's character looks in wonderment at the villagers. The scene is also accompanied by a soundtrack with a native flute, emphasizing Sara's perspective of Rodríguez's character as mischievous and mystical. Lourdes's refusal to explain to her employer the purpose of the items as cures for Richard's leukemia, on the one hand, conforms to Sara's view of Lourdes as using mysticism to manipulate the US couple. Yet on the other, it suggests Lourdes's defiance of the US couple. Rodríguez's performance of Lourdes in this scene enhances this reading of Lourdes's resistance. When she replies, "Señora? A hairpin and a slice of bread," she looks at the objects strangely, implying to Sara, "you know what these are." While Rodríguez could have played the part by simply feigning a childlike innocence, especially when Lourdes responds with the question, "Who knows?" she instead plays the part with knowledge and boldness, placing the emphasis again on Sara's lack of knowledge of the items.

Rodríguez's performance of the maid Lourdes as defiant and bold, rather than as meek and childish, is most evident in the major confrontation between Lourdes and Sara over the indigenous objects. While Sara is inspecting a lamp shade by her bed (i.e., checking Lourdes's housework), she finds a thorn placed on the shade. In the next image, Lourdes is shown in another room watching Sara. When Sara calls out, "Lourdes?," we see Lourdes in the next shot moving out of the frame so Sara cannot see her, but then Lourdes reappears; this movement suggests the film's framing of Rodríguez as mischievous once again. Rodríguez, as Lourdes, then walks up to Sara with eyes facing and confronting hers, and then listens to her. Sara scolds, "Now, here is a thorn, and now here is a crack in the lamp shade to prevent me from noticing that the shade is cracked. That was probably an accident and that's perfectly all right [Close, as Sara, smiles patronizingly]. But what I don't understand is how you could possibly believe that the thorn would keep me from finding out?" Close's performance of Sara's last line emphasizes her character's patronizing and childish treatment of Lourdes. While Sara speaks during this moment, Rodríguez's character looks down and sighs, as if annoyed, but she is patient, waiting to speak. In this moment, Rodríguez might have interpreted Lourdes's scripted response by shrinking and bowing to Close as Sara, yet she plays the character calmly, suggesting her rationality. Rodríguez's character replies: "Well, Señora. Sometimes it doesn't work completely. But Señora, consider. This morning the malageña opened a new shoot. And Don Ricardo said he had good news from the bank and will not have to close down the mine." As Lourdes speaks, Sara tries to interrupt by saying, "well, that doesn't. . . ." Rodríguez, as Lourdes, then stops Sara from talking by motioning with her hand. Lourdes continues, "And consider how quickly Don Ricardo recovered from his sickness. All of this happened while the thorn was in the lamp shade." Rodríguez performs this last sentence confidently, implying the easiness of the explanation. While the written dialogue might have implied the naivety of Lourdes, Rodríguez's performance of the character instead projects self-confidence, trying to convince Sara to believe in her ways. Instead, Close, who performs Sara's unwillingness to believe in her Mexican maid's beliefs, turns away in disbelief and anger at what she believes is her domestic's stupidity, and proceeds to throw the thorn dramatically in the trash can.

Even though Rodríguez's portrayal of Lourdes suggests how she used performance to shift and negotiate the stereotyping of her character as naïve and childlike, the film ultimately creates caricatures of Latina domestics as defiant and unruly, and Mexican and indigenous culture as primitive and backward. While the film allows for Lourdes's resistance to the US couple, particularly as she refuses in many scenes to explain the indigenous remedies, the film leaves audiences with stereotypical portrayals of Lourdes and the other Mexican villagers. Furthermore, while the film appears to value indigenous practices at the end, with Sara's acceptance of the villagers' honoring of her husband's life with stones, this valuing ultimately occurs in service of the US couple's narrative and life, thereby further marginalizing the already secondary storyline of the maids' experiences in the film.

Redirecting Latina Domesticity in Migdalia Cruz's *The Have-Little*

Narratives that seek to naturalize Latinas to domesticity conflate Mexican American women with the domestic, either as laborers in the familial home space or in the domestic space of the US nation, and render Latinas as biologically, racially, and socially suited to the domestic sphere. The many images that locate Mexican American women and Latinas in domestic space—in tourist industries, public policies, government agencies, activist movements, museums, the publishing industry, cinema, television, and theater—are so widespread that Latinas' presumed role and identity in the domestic become matters of fact. While the HGTV special, *Handmade Holiday with Kitty Bartholomew*, and *Stones for Ibarra* are distinct, they both present this presumed naturalized relationship of Mexican American women to the domestic sphere. Rodríguez's Lourdes in *Stones for Ibarra* is marginalized to domestic labor as the US couple's maid in Mexico (even though she has some mobility as a curandera), while Rodríguez in *Handmade Holiday with Kitty Bartholomew* is depicted as a homeowner whose holiday décor derives naturally from her Latina identity.

In this final section, I examine Rodríguez's redirection of the hegemonic script of Latina domesticity in her direction of Puerto Rican playwright Migdalia Cruz's play *The Have-Little*. In contrast to the dominant rhetoric that naturalizes Latina domesticity, Migdalia Cruz's play exposes the gendered and racialized social structures that often restrict and confine US Latinas to the domestic sphere. In this way, the play challenges the natural association of Latinas with domesticity that Rodríguez and other Latinas have confronted in Hollywood. Yet even though the play counters the hegemonic script, Rodríguez found the play difficult to direct. Rodríguez therefore redirected Cruz's play with lighting, music, and staging to navigate narratives about Latinas and domesticity she encountered in mainstream media representations, as well as to create a space for multifaceted and diverse images of Latinas in theater.

The Rodríguez-directed production of Cruz's *The Have-Little* opened on March 16, 2002, at the Marilyn Monroe Theatre in the Lee Strasberg Creative Center in West Hollywood, California, and was coproduced by the Latino Theater Initiative and The Group, a production company at the Lee Strasberg Theatre Institute. Prior to Rodríguez's direction of the play's West Coast premiere, *The Have-Little* was produced by INTAR (International Arts Relations) Theater in New York and directed by Nilo Cruz in 1991, with a second production at Teatro Latino in Milwaukee, Wisconsin, in 1995 (Cruz 1996, 106).[35] As director of the Latino Theater Initiative, Rodríguez helped to bring the play to the Lee Strasberg Center with the aim to promote Latina/o theater and because she greatly admired Cruz's writing.[36] The center's staging of six plays by diverse playwrights between 2001 and 2003 indicates the company's commitment to representing diverse experiences on the US stage; prior to this effort, The Group had produced works mostly by US canonical playwrights, such as Tennessee Williams and Arthur Miller. As both a mainstream and alternative theater venue, the Marilyn Monroe Theatre reaches a broad audience demographic, yet one that is mostly Anglo American. Rodríguez's direction of Cruz's play at the Marilyn Monroe Theatre therefore suggests that she attempted to intervene in popular Latina representations for a theater audience beyond the community-based or political theater that had defined her earlier career.

The play follows two years in the life of thirteen-year-old Lilian, who lives in a home of extreme negativity defined by abusive personal relationships, including emotional and physical abuse from her mother, Carmen, alcoholic father, José, overly dominant friend, Michi, and heroin-addicted boyfriend, Ricky. As the narrative develops, Lilian becomes pregnant by Ricky, who later dies from a heroin overdose. By the end of the play, Lilian's mother has passed away, her father is homeless, and Michi has left the South Bronx to begin college. The dramatic action of the narrative takes place exclusively within the four walls of Lilian's home, emphasizing the entrapment that she endures. According to a review of Rodríguez's direction of the play, Rodríguez enhanced Lilian's confinement by directing the lighting designer to use low lighting and by staging each scene within cramped spaces of the kitchen and living room: "The feeling of claustrophobia is heightened by the setting of the entire play in Lilian's apartment, providing the same trapped feeling that the characters experience" (Pasternak 2002). Adding to this entrapment is the fact that Lilian never leaves the confines of the domestic sphere in the play; the closest she gets to leaving is the fire escape, which symbolizes both Lilian's marginalization and her need for escape.

By setting the play in the South Bronx of the 1970s, Cruz's play alludes to the social, political, and economic factors that marginalize Lilian to the domestic realm, even as the play centers mostly on her abusive personal relationships. Economic revitalization projects, coupled with racial discrimination in housing in New York from the 1940s to the 1970s, severely impacted the majority lower-economic Puerto Rican and African American populations of the South Bronx. The construction of the Cross-Bronx Expressway from 1948 to 1972, for example, led to the displacement and relocation of approximately 170,000 residents in the area already strained by welfare and poverty. According to Tricia Rose, "[E]thnic and racial transition in the South Bronx was not a gradual process . . . instead, it was a brutal process of community destruction and relocation" (1994, 30). As a result of racial and economic disenfranchisement, Puerto Ricans and African Americans in the South Bronx found it difficult to obtain employment, pay rent, and gain access to public schools (Rose 1994, 30; Worth 1999). These structural conditions only heightened Latinas' and African American women's already marginalized position on the US socioeconomic ladder. Cruz's play does not directly mention these factors, yet they are evident in Lilian's lack of socioeconomic mobility and subsequent confinement and marginalization to unskilled labor. Lacking opportunities and the resources necessary to obtain a good education, Lilian at fifteen works at a hospital as a laundress, folding clothes, a job that reproduces what is a traditional domestic task in the public sector.

The Have-Little also foregrounds the role of hegemonic religious ideologies in hindering Lilian's socioeconomic mobility. Lilian's mother, Carmen, consistently reminds Lilian that Catholicism is her only path to salvation, advising her daughter: "You're not smart—you're like your mother. You don't have to read to learn what you need to know. What you need to know isn't in books—it's in church. That's the only thing to help people like us" (Cruz 1996, 111). Emphasizing religion as Lilian's only option, Carmen tells Lilian that she should follow the traditional female roles of virgin, martyr, and saint, which she learned from the church. Carmen also berates Lilian for not having the same intellectual capabilities as her best friend, Michi, arguing that she should rely on the church for guidance: "When are you gonna learn? Huh? Nothing means nothing! School don't help if you're poor" (Cruz 1996, 109). The script points to Carmen's views of women's proper gendered and cultural roles, and her critique of Lilian's intellectual capabilities, as leading to Lilian's lack of self-confidence; these combined factors result in the tragic ending of the play.[37]

In the final scene, Lilian sits in her kitchen, lit only by the flames that emanate from the stovetop, while holding her dying baby Joey; Lilian's baby has a chronic cough that Lilian has not treated because she believes that the state will take her baby from her.[38] Lilian also prays, thereby following her mother's prescription to rely on religion to resolve her problems. Her final monologue reveals her sense of hopelessness, which is nonetheless cloaked in a language of hope:

> We got so much together Joey. . . . We have our radio. It's loud and keeps us company. . . . I don't think it matters. I mean, even the people that have don't always get nowhere. . . . I could be anywhere right now and I wouldn't feel no different. If it was snowing, I wouldn't be cold. I could just curl up and let my skin fall over me like snow on a tree, and not feel nuffin. Not the cold anyways. And you're just like me, Joey. . . . I can smell every picture in my head. When I close my eyes, I can go somewhere. So I don' need to go nowheres, because it's all *(Pointing to her head)* in one place. It's my place . . . it's our place. (Cruz 1996, 126)

Lilian's ultimate retreat into the private realm, in this case herself, reflects a gendered view of the private sphere as a safe haven and the public sphere as violent, a perspective that comes from her many negative encounters with the outside world. The irony is that she is unable to see her private sphere as an inhospitable and dangerous place, thereby unwittingly perpetuating her mother's gendered beliefs. Additionally, the stage directions indicate, "She rocks and speaks softly to Joey. They are both bundled up," referencing a Virgin Mary–Jesus image, indicating the impact of religious and cultural views of womanhood on Lilian's circumstances.

Cruz's choice to end her play with Lilian's confinement and hopelessness stems from her personal experiences growing up in the South Bronx during the

1960s and her own artistic and political visions as a playwright. In interviews, Cruz explains how it is necessary to write about the predicament of Latinas who have endured social and economic marginalization, as she herself has witnessed several of the problems her characters experience. She states, "My best friend at the age of eight was raped and murdered and thrown off the roof of the apartment house we lived in. My next best friend was pregnant at age 13 and dead from an overdose at 15" (Cruz 1996, 106). Cruz also explains that it is important to write about stories of marginalization, because Latinas continue to endure violence and abuse in their homes and communities, and therefore "you don't forget what it was like for you and what it is still like for people who are still there and struggling with those things."[39] Here, Cruz suggests how, even though Latinas have gained social and economic mobility in the professional sector, many are still marginalized due to a racialized economy. By showing audiences the effects of racial, social, and economic injustice on a young Latina, Cruz desires to make visible the factors of marginalization that are often concealed from theatre audiences.

The play's focus on Lilian's marginalization to domesticity, and the narrative's suggestion that young Latinas have few possibilities for transcending racial and gendered ideologies, led to Rodríguez's difficulty with directing Cruz's play. She explains, "I found [the play] the hardest to [direct] and consequently the hardest for audiences to take. . . . There's really a small group of people who are willing to see the tragedy of that and there's little catharsis. . . . I can understand why it's hardly done. Because it's so depressing. The little girl just hides. She ends up in this abandoned apartment with her little baby and has not gone to school. . . . The home became her protection. She was protected from the world and so what happened is that the piece became very . . . it choked me."[40] On the surface, Rodríguez's perception of Cruz's play echoes other Latina/o viewers who perceived Cruz's narrative as perpetuating negative Latina images. For instance, in an interview with Tiffany Ana López, Cruz explains: "I was doing a play at INTAR and a Puerto Rican woman working in the office said what a wonderful writer she thought I was but . . . she asked, 'Why are you always writing about junkies and pregnant teens? Our community has moved beyond that.' I said, 'Well, there are lawyers and doctors, but I don't know any lawyers or doctors. If that's where I came from I would write about that. These are the people I find interesting and poetic and these are the people I love.' I was taken aback by her understanding that what I should be writing about as a Puerto Rican would be so exclusive" (qtd. in López 2000, 55). Certainly in film and television, the characters Cruz writes about—barrio families of poverty and violence, drug addicts, and street people—are rendered as stereotypes (López 2000, 55). The woman's desire to see positive images therefore points to her need not to feel dehumanized as an object and victim. The conversation between Cruz and the woman at INTAR indicates the "burden of representation" placed on artists of color, specifically the expectation to create positive and uplifting images to remedy the persistence of demeaning stereotypical representations of people of color in dominant media.

Like the Puerto Rican woman at INTAR, Rodríguez was concerned that Cruz's representation of Lilian would potentially reinforce negative Latina/o images. This worry was heightened by the staging of *The Have-Little* at the Marilyn Monroe Theatre in the Lee Strasberg Creative Center, with a broad audience demographic comprised mostly of white audience members. Rodríguez explains that the play failed to take off: "It didn't have a great word of mouth. Consequently, the audiences felt small. You wish there was a glimmer of hope that people could take home with them and that glimmer I think would have translated into audiences."[41] Yet distinct from the woman at INTAR, Rodríguez explains how she sympathizes with Cruz's desire to create art that reflects her harsh, personal experiences. She explains: "I completely respect what Migdalia was doing [to] try to show her reality, so it's a real hard place to be in terms of art. You want as many people to see your work and you want it to be true." As the director of the play, however, Rodríguez wanted to produce a piece that would ultimately appeal to and bring greater audiences to the play.

Through her redirection, Rodríguez sought to give Cruz's tragic narrative of confinement some glimmer of hope, which she hoped would translate into larger audiences. As a way to counteract the hopelessness of the play, Rodríguez used music, lighting, and directed the actors to deliver portions of their monologues in optimistic tones. Rodríguez directed América Ferrera, the actor who played Lilian, to emphasize bodily movement and portray her character as ultimately desiring escape from social, cultural, and gendered confinement. In one scene, for instance, Rodríguez directed Ferrera to walk boldly across the stage, using upbeat Cuban music to emphasize her movement: "There is this one moment in which there is a transition of time [when Lilian's mother dies] and so what I did was, I wanted to see passage of time and I wanted to see travel, my god get out of here! So, I staged the scene in which I had Lilian walk at an angle very slowly to this amazing music by a Cuban artist and it was so gorgeous and it felt epic in this very small space. It felt like time was passing. It felt like she was getting older. And it felt like she was coming to peace with something."[42] With this adjustment to Lilian's movement and by adding upbeat music, Rodríguez intended to give Lilian's space grandeur and importance.

Yet the playwright did not always agree with Rodríguez's directorial choices. For Lilian's final monologue, Rodríguez wanted to use uplifting music to suggest that Lilian would one day leave her dire circumstances. Rodríguez states, "I tried to bring it up and lift it up. But you know Migdalia did not want it. We wanted to end with this sort of upbeat Michael Jackson music and she wouldn't have it. There is only so much you could do when an artist refuses . . . and her play is about the trapping of this girl. And in some ways you could bring it up and at this moment she is going to find her way."[43] Since Cruz's artistic goal is to expose the debilitating effects of cultural and gendered restrictions on Latinas, her play ends with Lilian's confinement. Yet Rodríguez was convinced that by ending Cruz's play with Lilian's domestic confinement, audiences would be left with a bleak and unsatisfying tragic ending. Since Cruz did not agree with Rodríguez's choice of music for Lilian's final monologue, Rodríguez used lighting to create a subtext of optimism in the final scene; this particular choice was met with Cruz's approval.[44] At the end of the play, Rodríguez decided to use bright light on Ferrera and directed her to deliver Lilian's final monologue in an uplifting tone. By imbuing the scene with hope, she wanted to create ambiguity regarding whether or not Lilian's baby actually dies at the end. Rodríguez explains: "I had her look very angelic and I had beautiful light on her. I had her deliver the monologue in the most hopeful of ways, and I really tried to tweak it so you don't really know if the baby is dead or not. I think in Midgalia's eyes the baby is dead, but I tried to make it so you don't really know."[45] For Rodríguez, the use of bright light on Lilian was intended to convey optimism that Lilian would one day transcend her marginalization due to society, culture, and gender. In a photographic still from the performance, bright light shines on Ferrera, as Lilian, who almost appears to be daydreaming. Furthermore, Lilian is not holding her baby as indicated in the stage directions to Cruz's play.[46]

To a certain extent, Rodríguez's use of light on Lilian for the final scene risks reifying both gendered and cultural views of womanhood. During the Victorian period, society often viewed women as "angels in the house" invested with spiritual qualities as the home itself took on religious characteristics; as "angels," women's sacred duty was to protect men from the harsh realities of the public sphere. Hispanic Catholicism and Latina/o cultures also frame women as innately more spiritual and virtuous, thereby bolstering an idealized view of women as naturally suited toward domesticity. The ideology of *marianismo* stresses women's inherent chastenesss, a characteristic that leads to the construction of women as having spiritual superiority to men (Asencio 2009; Stevens 1973). Yet Rodríguez's use of lighting to make Lilian "look very angelic" was less about gendered references and more about her desire to use lighting to create hope and optimism for a female character in an otherwise tragic play. And considering the context of Cruz's script, which critiques gendered and cultural constructions of womanhood, Rodríguez's choice to use bright light on Lilian most likely did not circumvent the play's overall critique of gendered marginalization.

While the play seeks to emphasize the gendered and religious ideologies, coupled with socioeconomic and racial marginalization, that lead to Lilian's marginalization in the play, reviewers were left mostly with an image of Lilian's individual circumstances—particularly her personal, abusive relationships—as leading to her tragic ending. Reviews of Rodríguez's direction of Cruz's *The Have-Little* at the Marilyn Monroe Theatre indicate how many did not see the social and economic factors that marginalized Lilian in the play. For instance, Kathleen Foley's *Los Angeles Times* theatre review claims that fifteen-year-old Lilian is marginalized because she "just doesn't have the emotional muscularity to rise above her circumstances" (2002, F40). She continues, "Any upward momentum requires determination, smarts, and a supportive family—or a combination of the three" (Foley 2002, F40). Foley's statements echo the myth of individualism and belief in meritocracy: all Lilian has to do to escape the confines of poverty and motherhood is to "pull herself up by her bootstraps." These comments elide how Lilian's lack of determination, "smarts," and supportive family most likely arises from society's denial of necessary socioeconomic resources, factors that would otherwise enable her to transcend her marginal position. The concluding lines of Foley's review praise the "superb design elements," which illustrate "the marginal conditions of these flawed but valiant have-littles" (2002, F40). The phrase "flawed but valiant have-littles" perpetuates the myth that solely personal circumstances, not societal and structural factors, contributed to Lilian's problems. According to Foley, the members of the Puerto Rican community of the South Bronx neighborhood of the 1970s failed, not because of racial and economic disenfranchisement, but because they were inherently "flawed" or are just not determined enough to escape their difficult circumstances.

Reviewers also critiqued Cruz's play and Rodríguez's direction for portraying excessive emotion and sentiment. The majority of *The Have-Little* takes place within the domestic sphere, mostly among women and within intensely close, abusive family relationships; in this sense, the play is a melodrama. The critique of Cruz's play as "excessively" sentimental overlooks the strategic use of melodrama and sentiment in feminist theater, in which melodrama is often used to subvert the association of the personal and private sphere with emotion and weakness (Gledhill 1987; Kaplan 1992; McHugh 1999). Most broadly, the word "sentimental" denotes a thought or attitude based on emotion instead of reason. The word, however, connotes the use of emotion to appeal to romantic feelings and the act of being extravagantly emotional. The term "sentimental" has also been used to position women's writing as "popular," part of "low" culture, and less refined (Tompkins 1994, 504). It is a term that associates emotion with weakness and the realm of femininity, thereby suggesting that women are inferior to men. Reviewer Dave de Piño, while also noting Rodríguez's direction, argues that Cruz's play contains an "excessive sentimentality." He states, "The piece is so well-intentioned you hate to find fault, but . . . the story needs to be trimmed of the excessive sentiment and melodrama. . . . The writing is fluid and mostly honest until it reaches too far to produce an emotional jolt. . . . Diane Rodríguez does nice work overall, but also gets caught up in the melodrama at times."[47] Foley also indicates the "excessive" sentimentality in Rodríguez's direction by stating, "Veteran director Diane Rodríguez occasionally errs on the side of sentiment, overplaying scenes that could have used more emotional restraint"

(2002, F40). By critiquing Cruz's play and Rodríguez's direction for use of sentimentality, both Foley and De Piño suggest that Cruz's play about a young Puerto Rican youth who confronts socioeconomic marginalization and abuse should use reason instead of emotion to narrate this experience. Such views fail to recognize that Cruz's play deliberately uses sentimentality, since rationality has been denied to Lilian and her community. They also indicate the pervasiveness of gendered ideologies that have ascribed emotion and passivity to the domestic realm.

Concluding Remarks

As a performer in Hollywood and a director of US Latina/o theater, Rodríguez has consistently negotiated dominant scripts of Latina domesticity. Her disidentifications and redirections of such narratives in film and theater suggest the strategies she took as a Latina performer and director to resist dominant ideologies in US and Latina/o visual culture, particularly as she confronted scripts that were not of her own making. Given the persistence of dominant narratives seeking to link Chicanas and Latinas to the domestic sphere through biological and cultural reproduction in political and visual rhetoric, Rodríguez's artistic interventions are crucial and necessary. The current political climate that represents Mexican immigrants and all people of Mexican descent as threatening the cohesion of the nation through discourses that racialize and gender the bodies of Chicanas and Latinas is a stark reminder of the importance of Chicana artistic representations that focus our attention on the domestic sphere. In my epilogue, I turn to visual artist Alma López's powerful digital print *California Fashions Slaves*, which presents a critique of several binaries—legal/illegal, white/nonwhite, public/private—that have framed the dominant narrative of Mexicana, Chicana, and Latina domesticity that I have analyzed throughout this book. *California Fashions Slaves* visually links our current political climate of nativist rhetoric against Latina/o immigrants with the historical periods that precede it, including the colonization of the US Southwest and the many programs that sought to disenfranchise and circumscribe Mexicanas and Chicanas to domestic labor. The digital print represents Chicanas and Latinas who work in sweatshop conditions within the borders of the United States, particularly the California garment industry. It also depicts Macrina López, López's mother and a seamstress, alongside Mexicana garment workers and union organizers from the 1930s and 1940s in a contemporary Los Angeles cityscape. By visualizing the labor of Mexicana and Chicana garment workers and activism specifically, *California Fashions Slaves* honors women's creative resistance and agency, and provides a visual representation of Chicanas outside of the colonial binary of virgin/whore and the xenophobic frameworks of domestic/foreign and legal/illegal.

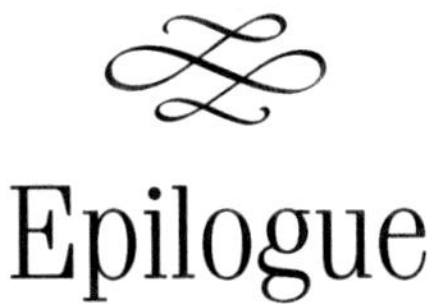

Epilogue

DENATURALIZING THE DOMESTIC

Nativist and anti-immigration policies, as exhibited by the passing of SB 1070, or the Support Our Law Enforcement and Safe Neighborhoods Act, in Arizona in 2010 and similar calls to enforce such legislation nationally, recycle and extend the racialized binaries of domestic/foreign and legal/illegal, which have framed the dominant narrative of Mexicana, Chicana, and Latina domesticity that I have analyzed throughout this book.[1] SB 1070 affirms the requirement that immigrants register with the US federal government and makes it a state misdemeanor to not have registration documents in one's possession at all times. It requires local law enforcement, during a lawful stop, detention, or arrest, to determine a person's immigration status if there is "reasonable suspicion" that the person is an undocumented immigrant (Arizona State Senate, 2010).[2] While SB 1070 focuses on the public space of the law, rhetoric surrounding the bill targeted the Latina body and domestic spheres of Latina/o immigrant communities. In this way, the bill echoes nativist discourse prevalent during the debate over Proposition 187 in California in 1994, which configured Mexicanas as invading the nation through their fertility. As many commentators have noted, SB 1070 was introduced by Arizona State Senator Russell Pearce, who worked with Kris Kobach, a Kansas attorney who has connections with the Federation for American Immigration Reform (FAIR). The organization has a long history of seeking to regulate the reproductive rights of Mexicanas and Puerto Rican women, as represented by the founder and board member of FAIR, Dr. John Tanton, whose writings have linked population growth and immigration since the 1970s (Gutiérrez 2008). As C. Alejandra Elenes argues, "Laws such as SB 1070 not only create a hostile environment for Latinas/os in Arizona but are part of a national narrative of race and gender in the United States resulting from demographic changes and fears about the 'browning' of America. In this climate, the female brown body is particularly targeted and objectified."[3] Given the persistence of rhetoric that continues to render women of Mexican descent—regardless of class and immigration status—as threatening the cohesion of the nation through their biological and cultural reproduction, the Chicana artistic project of denaturalizing the associations of Latinas to the domestic is now more crucial than ever.

In this epilogue, I turn to Alma López's digital print *California Fashions Slaves* (1997)—an iris print on canvas, and part of her series "1848: Chicanos in the US Landscape After the Treaty of Guadalupe Hidalgo" (fig.12).[4] Produced just three years after the debate over Proposition 187, on the ballot in California in 1994, the print comments on another moment of heightened anti-Latina/o and anti–Latina/o immigrant rhetoric and nativist climate. Proposition 187 sought to deny undocumented immigrants healthcare and education, a goal shaped by the popular belief that Latina/o immigrants were a menace to the California economy. Supporters of the proposition depicted Mexicans as invading the nation through their fertility and domestic spaces (Chávez 2007, 2001; Gutiérrez 2008).[5] López indicates how her print "directly relates to the whole misconception that immigrants are a drain on the economy. For me growing up everybody including my mother were hard-working people. More than anything they're

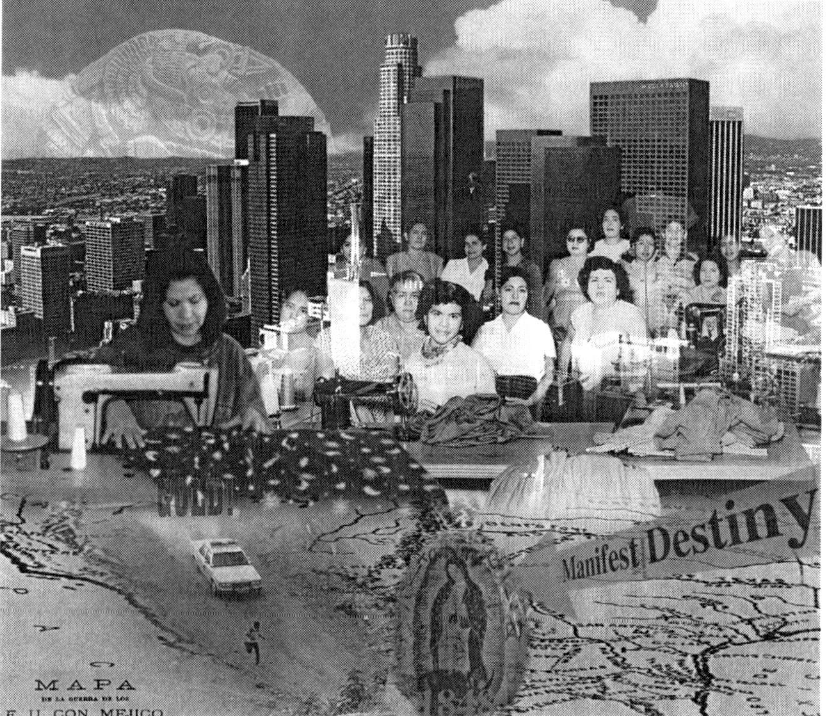

Figure 12. Alma López, *California Fashions Slaves*, 1997. Digital iris print on canvas, created in Photoshop, 20 × 24 inches. Thanks to Macrina López Ureña. Courtesy of the artist.

working poor, working really hard at less-than-minimum-wage salaries. If any-thing, they're contributing to the economy" (qtd. in Knight 2001). López further suggests how these women are "part of a working poor community racially ste-reotyped and vilified for allegedly draining the United States economy" (2002, 90). The print visually links contemporary political moments with the historical periods that precede them, including the colonization of the US Southwest and the many programs that sought to disenfranchise and circumscribe Mexicanas and Chicanas to domestic labor, such as Manifest Destiny, the Treaty of Gua-dalupe Hidalgo, Americanization, immigration policies, and globalization. The print therefore functions as a powerful commentary on the persistence of xeno-phobic rhetoric against Latinas in the United States.

California Fashions Slaves depicts Macrina López, López's mother and a seam-stress, alongside Mexicana garment workers and union organizers from the 1930s and 1940s in a contemporary Los Angeles cityscape.[6] With this imagery, López's print emphasizes the economic contributions that Mexicana laborers make to the US economy, thereby challenging the dominant rhetoric espoused by propo-nents of Proposition 187 and contemporary racialized rhetoric directed toward undocumented Latina immigrants. With the digital medium, the print also creates an empowering artistic statement that critiques the global policies that have facilitated the economic marginalization, exploitation, and violence against Latina laborers within globalization.[7] The North American Free Trade Agree-ment (NAFTA), for instance, accelerated the integration of the US and Mexican economies, leading to the creation and development of maquiladoras along the border in an unregulated and free trade system.[8] Many women who work in the maquiladoras produce the digital technology that US residents and citizens use on a daily basis, including computer and television parts for major electronic corporations (Funari and De La Torre 2006). With the digital medium, López therefore utilizes the very product that marginalizes women to consumerism and production to challenge the exploitation of Latina laborers within globalization. By visualizing the labor of Mexicana and Chicana garment workers and activism, *California Fashions Slaves* also honors women's creative resistance and agency, providing a visual representation of Chicanas outside of the xenophobic frame-works of domestic/foreign and legal/illegal. Ultimately, the print concentrates on women's empowerment as a labor class.

The print represents Chicanas and Latinas who work in sweatshop condi-tions within the borders of the US nation, particularly in the California garment industry.[9] It links the past and present by depicting the valuable labor contri-butions of Mexicana garment workers who constituted this workforce in the 1930s and 1940s, as well as the contemporary Mexican and Latina immigrant female garment workers who perform this work today. With the image of Macrina López, the print references the many Mexicanas and Latinas who per-form "industrial homework," or who sew for long hours for little pay at home, a form of work that continues to exist in California even though the state formally banned such practices. Industrial homework brings the domestic and public spheres together, in ways that exploit Mexican-descent women in the United States.[10] The effects of NAFTA, along with an increasingly globalized apparel and textile market, increased the vulnerability and the exploitation of Mexican and Latina/o immigrant women's labor in the garment industry.[11] In both the factory and home, these are jobs that typically pay minimum wages, have few if any benefits, are nonunion, are seasonal, and are subject to displacement (Segura and Zavella 2007, 13). In the early twentieth century, Mexicanas who worked in the garment industry also confronted the demands of production speed-ups and faced substandard pay, sexual harassment, and other hazardous conditions (Ruiz 1998, 148). In Los Angeles in the 1930s, for example, 75 percent of the garment workers were Mexicanas, and 40 percent earned less than five dollars per week, with long hours and home work (Sánchez 1995, 232). In response to the exploitative conditions that garment workers faced in the workplace in Los Angeles in the 1930s, 1,500 female dressmakers, the majority of whom were Mexican (the rest were Anglo, Italian, and Jewish), unionized and formed Local 96 of the International Ladies' Garment Workers' Union (ILGWU).[12] The nature of factory work within a globalized context today, particularly production speed-ups and increased emphasis on productivity, however, has made it extremely difficult for women to organize, underscoring how women's agency is often constrained by global-economic forces (Ruiz 1998, 148; Soldatenko 2000).

California Fashions Slaves portrays the women's laboring conditions through the image of mounds of crumpled fabric on a factory desk in front of the women and the high-fashion clothing hanging on the buildings behind them. With this positioning, the print indicates the labor that is necessary to turn raw materials into products for consumption. The work then contextualizes the cheap labor of the garment workers amid images of exclusion, particularly a map of the Treaty of Guadalupe Hidalgo in 1848 in the lower portion of the print, which the artist turns into a raised-relief map with digital technology—indicated by the mounds of land below the factory desk. The treaty purported to give Mexican inhabitants rights as US citizens, but denied them their legal and political entitlements as US citizens. By including a map of the Treaty of Guadalupe Hidalgo in the lower portion of the image, the print references one of the most profound material consequences of Manifest Destiny: the racial disenfranchisement of the mostly Mexican and Native American population in the US Southwest (Menchaca 2001). The placement of the image of the treaty, literally beneath the Los Angeles cityscape, links the contemporary exploitative conditions created by globalization to historical ideologies of exclusion and marginalization. By contextualizing the laboring bodies of Mexicana garment workers with references to the Treaty of Guadalupe Hidalgo and other material consequences of Manifest Destiny, the print emphasizes the profound material consequences of colonization on women.

The print underscores both the factory and land as sites of exploited work for Mexican immigrant and Mexican American communities. The mounds of clothing on the sewing table mirror the mounds of land on López's relief map of the treaty, both of which sit on horizontal planes. The brown and sepia tones of both the map and the garment workers are contrasted with images in white that reference labor, law, and capitalism, including the police car, the Wells Fargo building, the sewing machine, and the spool of white thread, all of which signify systems of racialization that privilege whiteness. With the red arrow of "Manifest Destiny," the print references the US political ideology of imperial power that sought to justify the nation's colonization of land inhabited by Native American and Mexican peoples in the US Southwest. The ideology of Manifest Destiny expressed the United States's imperial mission and natural right to expand "the boundaries of freedom" and democracy to other territories. The idealism supported American imperialism and the expansion of the nation both west and south into Mexico, leading to the conquest of northern Mexico (Rivera 2006, 59; Gómez 2008, 4). In this way, Manifest Destiny sought to position Mexican homes and communities as foreign and outside the domestic. The capitalized English word, "GOLD," in the lower-left field of the print, references another material consequence of Manifest Destiny: the appropriation of resources and land from Mexican and indigenous communities by Anglo American squatters. The print situates the word "GOLD" within a triangulation of the other images that are linked with exploitation, profit, and labor, including the white sewing machine, the white border police car, and the white Wells Fargo tower, all rendered as white to reference the economic marginalization of Mexican and native communities as a result of Anglo American conquest.[13]

California Fashions Slaves also incorporates a mass media aerial photograph of a border patrol car chasing an undocumented border crosser to emphasize the spectacle of "illegality." With this scene, López emphasizes, what Nicholas De Genova has argued in another context, "the legal production of Mexican/migrant 'illegality' [that] requires the spectacle of enforcement at the U.S.-Mexico border" (2006, 81). Since the construction of "illegality" by various immigration policies and laws are relatively invisible to the common public, producing "illegality" requires a "spectacle of 'enforcement' . . . precisely because it renders a racialized Mexican/migrant 'illegality' visible and lends to it the commonsensical air of a 'natural' fact" (De Genova 2006, 80). The aerial photograph of the border chase scene represents the "militarized spectacle of apprehensions, detentions, and deportations" (De Genova 2006, 80). It also indicates the often invasive and highly sophisticated technology that is used to survey and police the border, a surveillance system that dehumanizes Mexican migrants. Commenting on the border patrol scene in this print, Judith L. Huacuja states, "When translated out of an economic perspective of low-wage labor, the worker's body is criminalized by governing agencies—witness the mass media–sponsored aerial photograph of the *migra* chase scene in the lower left field of the digital image" (2003, 108). Additionally, this notion of surveillance parallels another aspect of the print, which is the monitoring of Mexican immigrant women's reproduction and the notion that Mexicanas are invading and threatening the United States as a nation-state through biological and cultural reproduction. With the inclusion of the mass-media photograph of the border chase scene, López marks the criminalization of Mexican immigrants for scrutiny by her viewers.

The diagonal scene of a border patrol car and officer chasing a supposed "illegal" immigrant crossing into the United States also parallels the diagonal "Manifest Destiny" arrow, and both bring the viewer's attention to the image of La Virgen de Guadalupe in the center-lower field; the direction of the arrow and the placement of Guadalupe emphasizes phallocentrism and the gendered violence of colonization. Guadalupe has a powerful presence throughout the print, and she appears in three sites: in her traditional and religious iconographic form in the central, lower field of the image; in the cloak that Macrina López sews (which also doubles as the US flag); and as a halo in the syncretic form of the pre-Columbian Coyolxauhqui in the upper-lefthand corner of the print, rising above López's mother and the Los Angeles skyline. With this configuration, the work elevates Macrina López to the place occupied by Guadalupe, and in doing so, honors the labor of garment workers and seamstresses. The placement of the traditional iconography of Guadalupe in the lower field or the "crotch" zone of the print (if we read the digital print as a "body" of work) and the red "Manifest Destiny" arrow directed toward the icon emphasizes the violence of Manifest Destiny and colonization, both as forces penetrating Guadalupe. Guadalupe's traditional form also sits beneath the tallest and most phallic image in the print—the white Wells Fargo building in the upper center field. With Guadalupe's constant presence, despite being subject to various forms of conquest and gendered violence, the print underscores the figure's role as a symbol of strength and resistance.

With the presence of Guadalupe, Macrina López, and the Mexicana garment workers and union activists—amid the trauma, conquest, and violence of the US Southwest—López's print underscores how women of Mexican descent have actively resisted their marginalization through union organizing and forming networks of survival. These women, as Segura and Zavella explain in another context, "contest or create representations of their identities in light of their marginality and give voice to their own agency" (2007, x). Through activism, they challenged the racialized and gendered ideologies that deemed their labor and bodies as cheap commodities vulnerable to exploitation. The women in the print also make visible the otherwise invisible exploitative conditions they encountered and endured. The print emphasizes the connection between activism and visibility by placing the line of garment workers outside of the factory, in the public streets of downtown Los Angeles. By depicting the bold gazes of the female garment workers who are mostly looking directly at the viewer and by including them as a group, López's print underscores the determination and agency of Mexicana garment workers who fought against labor exploitation and who countered dominant views about Mexican women's passivity.

Alma López's rendering of her mother, Macrina López, as Guadalupe in *California Fashions Slaves* powerfully deconstructs romanticized images of women's labor and domesticity. With its references both to the mother's seamstress work and the pre-Columbian moon warrior goddess Coyolxauhqui rising over Macrina López and the Los Angeles cityscape, the print denaturalizes motherhood and reproduction.[14] The print counters sentimentalized or romanticized views of women's work, but rather elevates and honors the harsh labor and working conditions that seamstresses endure. López represents her mother sewing La Virgen de Guadalupe's cloak and the image imbues the fabric as a symbol of US nationalism. The print depicts Guadalupe's cloak as having a blue background with white stars, which departs from the blue-green cloak in traditional Guadalupe iconography. With this revision, the artist represents her mother as literally sewing and supporting the nation, particularly through her labor in the garment industry as part of globalization. Luz Calvo explains, "This image underscores the unseen and under-considered labor of women who sew not only the Virgin's cloak but our clothes as well" (2000). In this way, López manipulates the visual language of Catholicism in order to unbind Chicanas from ideologies of gender and sexuality (Davalos 2008). Karen Mary Davalos explains, "The yards of fabric and the angel [are] symbolic of control and subservience since both prevented Guadalupe from moving" (2008, 88).

Furthermore, Macrina López's halo is not the typical mandorla, or full-body halo, of the traditional Catholic imagery of Guadalupe, but is instead an image of the pre-Columbian goddess Coyolxauhqui, who hovers over the Los Angeles cityscape. Coyolxauhqui, Coatlicue's oldest daughter, according to legend, directed her four hundred siblings to fight their brother Huitzilopchtli, the god of war, who ultimately defeated Coyolxauhqui and her siblings. Huitzilopchtli then mutilated Coyolxauhqui, throwing her head into the sky and casting her torso and limbs along the steps of the temple pyramid (López 2011, 272). For López, Coyolxauhqui represents "not only an incredibly violent dismembering of a warrior woman but also the need to re-member and heal not only ourselves but also our histories and cultures from this violent and misogynistic past [. . .] we have a long history of goddess warriors to guide and protect us" (2011, 272). The "Coyolxauhqui imperative," a concept coined by Anzaldúa, describes a creative route of self-healing in which an individual moves from fragmentation to complex wholeness (Keating 2009). According to Anzaldúa, "The path of the artist, the creative impulse, what I call the Coyolxauhqui imperative, is basically an attempt to heal the wounds. It's a search for inner completeness" (2003–2004, 18). With the image of Coyolxauhqui, the print underscores the material and psychic consequences of colonization on women of Mexican descent, as well as Mexicanas' and Chicanas' powerful strength, creative adaptation, and agency in response to such forces.

Given the persistence of rhetoric that continues to render women of Mexican descent as threatening the cohesion of the nation through their biological reproduction, *California Fashion Slaves* is a necessary artistic work. The print depicts a visual landscape of the gendered and racialized binaries that continue to naturalize women of Mexican descent to domestic labor and reproduction in cultural and visual representations. Yet the work also pays homage to the Mexicanas and Chicana activists who through labor activism resisted their marginalization and exploitation. With this depiction of Mexican-descent women as active agents who intervene in colonial and xenophobic frameworks of virgin/whore, domestic/foreign, and legal/illegal, *California Fashion Slaves* makes a bold challenge to dominant political rhetoric seeking to essentialize Chicanas and Latinas to domesticity, labor, and motherhood.

Notes

1. The California courts nullified Proposition 187 as unconstitutional. Congress later passed the Illegal Immigration Reform and Immigrant Responsibility Act in 1996, which, as Proposition 187 did, restricted access to healthcare for undocumented immigrants, except for emergency care. The act also increased border patrol and technology, which further militarized the border zone (Segura and Zavella 2007, 10).

2. C. Alejandra Elenes, "Mujeres, Migration & Arizona's SB1070: Codifying Patriarchy and White Privilege," *MALCS Mujeres Talk* (blog), January 17, 2011, http://www.malcs.org/mujeres-talk/mujeres-migration-arizonas-sb1070-codifying-patriarchy-and-white-privilege/. SB 1070 was introduced by Arizona State Senator Russell Pearce, who worked with Kris Kobach, a Kansas attorney who has connections with the Federation for American Immigration Reform (FAIR). This organization has a history of seeking to regulate the reproductive rights of Mexican and Puerto Rican women, as represented by the founder and board member of FAIR, Dr. John Tanton, whose writings have linked population growth with immigration since the 1970s (Gutiérrez 2008).

1. Throughout his career from 1898 to 1969, Ayres used different architectural styles, including American Colonial, elements of European architecture, and Spanish Colonial, the latter of which dominated his work later in his career in San Antonio and throughout Texas (Coote 2001, 4 7).

2. Emphasis added. Fiesta Mexicano Synopsis, 1938. Atlee B. Ayres Papers, MS 388, University of Texas at San Antonio Libraries Special Collections.

3. Fiesta Mexicano Synopsis, 1938. Atlee B. Ayres Papers, MS 388, University of Texas at San Antonio Libraries Special Collections.

4. Ayres's other fiestas include Night in Old Mexico (1936), An Evening in Taxco (1940), Cabaret Rio Caliente (1941), and Fiesta La Villita (1943).

5. Fiesta La Villita Synopsis, 1943. Atlee B. Ayres Papers, MS 388, University of Texas at San Antonio Libraries Special Collections.

6. The term "chili queen" came into use by newspaper reporters in the late nineteenth century to describe the most beautiful female chili vendor in the plazas; in the twentieth

century, many reporters applied the term to all chili vendors (Jennings 1996, 44). A few chili queens were Anglo, yet rhetoric suggests that all queens were imagined as Mexican and "Spanish." For instance, Sadie Thornhill, who is noted as being from "the Blue Grass land of old Kentucky," was described as "Spanish-looking" and having the ability to speak Spanish fluently ("Sadie, The Chili Queen," *Forest and Stream*, April 28, 1894, 358).

7. Some early historians place the origins of the chili queens as camp followers with the Spanish colonial army (Bushick 1927). Yet textual references document their origins to the 1880s (Everett 1975, 32). In Military Plaza in the 1880s and 1890s, the chili queens served chili, tamales, enchiladas, tortillas, and café to soldiers and new visitors to the area. Many of the chili vendors built mesquite fires on the square to keep the chili warm, lighted their stands with lanterns, and served chili to customers, who sat on wooden stools.

8. By the late nineteenth century, the chili queens were already well known throughout the United States as a result of the "San Antonio Chili Stand" at the Columbian Exposition at the Chicago World's Fair in 1893.

9. "Maverick's Chili Stands Closed by His New Health Department." *San Antonio Express.* July 7, 1939: 7.

10. *San Antonio Express.* July 5, 1939: 8A.

11. Descriptions of the chili queens found in online blogs and tourist promotions to San Antonio describe the chili queens as wearing "colorful costumes." As this chapter illustrates, this reference to "colorful costumes" refers to the chili queens in specialized events, as there is no documented photographic evidence that the independent chili vendors in the public plazas wore colorful costumes. Contemporary accounts that describe the chili queens as wearing "colorful Mexican costumes" are also most likely referring to the city's iconic "María's Tortillas" women, Mexican American women who at Night in Old San Antonio (NIOSA) each year make "maría's tortillas," a hand-patted and grilled corn tortilla, buttered and filled with cheddar cheese and salsa, while wearing bright and colorful costumes. "María's Tortillas," named after entrepreneur María Luis Ochoa, began at NIOSA in the 1950s. Ochoa was the housekeeper for SACS member, and onetime president, Ethel Harris in the 1940s. As Hernández-Ehrisman explains, "for many of the festival's early years, Harris pressed Ochoa to make tortilla's for the event. Apparently, this was not always the easiest relationship" (2008, 100).

12. Quote from 1890s railroad brochure (Jennings 1996, 44).

13. The term "queen" also connotes a hyper femininity laden with sexual deviance, paralleling the use of the term to refer to male homosexuals coming into use in the nineteenth century (Pilcher 2008, 182). The term "gay" referred to various modes of sexual conduct since the seventeenth century, including its application to women to indicate a prostitute, its link with men to imply womanizing, and a gay house, which referred to a brothel (Chauncey 1994).

14. For Anglo tourists and others in the city, chili con carne represented an exotic Mexican dish. For working-class Mexicans, chili con carne was basically food from the rancho. Wealthy Mexican exiles who arrived in San Antonio in the early twentieth century, many of whom opened Mexican restaurants in the formal economy, viewed chili con carne as "detestable food with a false Mexican title that is sold in the United States of the North" (Santamaria 1992). The Mexican elites instead praised foods that signified national connections with Mexico, including barbacoa, tamales, and buñuelos (Pilcher 2008, 146).

15. Prejudice against Mexican Americans flourished as several interest groups blamed Mexican immigrants for the nation's financial problems. From 1930 to 1939, approximately 2 million people of Mexican ancestry—including approximately 1.2 million who

were US citizens and legal residents—were deported from the United States to Mexico (Balderrama and Rodríguez 1995, 50–53).

16. Pilcher has provided the most extensive scholarly inquiry into the chili queens, particularly detailing the relocation of the chili queens due to Progressive Era projects and racial-economic disenfranchisement (2008). In his co-authored essay with Diane Gabaccia, Pilcher also explores the meaning of chili con carne in the public sphere and the history of immigrant street vending practices through a comparative analysis of Mexican and Italian immigrant food consumption; in this essay, Pilcher places the history of chili con carne in a history of Mexican street foods (2011).

17. In popular discourse, chili is most often associated with whiteness and masculinity, as well as images of the US Southwest, West, and frontier. Today, many chili historians recognize the chili queens as the inventors of the dish, crediting the "San Antonio Chili Stand" at the Chicago World's Fair in 1893 for popularizing the meal. Chili con carne is also considered to be the official state dish of Texas, designated as such by the Texas Legislature in 1977. As Pilcher describes, "The fate of the 'chili queens' provides a seemingly classic case of cultural appropriation whereby Anglos transformed the spicy foods of Mexican women into a symbol of the dominant, masculine culture, Texas chili" (2008, 173).

18. The Return of the Chili Queens Festival throughout the years has showcased many Mexicana female street vendors selling various foods, including tamales, gorditas, and aguas frescas. The festival has also included student mariachi, rock, and Tejano bands as part of a "Radio-Thon Four education" sponsored by LULAC. In 2011, the musical acts included Tejano music, Tex Mex, country, and pop. The festival also includes a chili cook-off on Sunday sponsored by the Chili Appreciation Society International, an organization of mostly Anglo Americans, as indicated by the member directory on their website.

19. These websites include My San Antonio, Foods and Flavors of San Antonio, The River Walk Guide, and San Antonio Event Guide. The Return of the Chili Queens Festival is also included in the following tourist guides: *Insider's Guide to San Antonio*, edited by Paris Permenter and John Bigley (2008) and *Frommer's San Antonio and Austin*, edited by David Baird (2009).

20. An online blogger describes the "Chili Queen Cook-off" at the Bonham: "It was a giant orgy of drag queens, beer, and some very good chili, and I'd do it again in a heartbeat. I was sitting with the crowd, themed after Alice and Wonderland." Soror, "Monday's Little Dance," Posted April 19, 2011, http://soror.dreamwidth.org/2010/04/19.

21. The construction of the city courthouse on the Main Plaza also solidified several decades of private property exchanges that gradually shifted the plazas from ownership by families with Spanish surnames like Treviño, Flores, and Salinas to those with non-Spanish surnames like Maverick, Lewis, and Callaghan (Arreola 2002, 135). While this shift suggests the increase in European immigration to the city and thus the diversity of the population; the ownership of the buildings by European families indicates the racial-economic transformation of the plazas (Arreola 2002, 136–146).

22. Some chili queens continued to vend in fully screened enclosures across from Market Plaza in 1948 ("Chili Queens in New Parlor," *San Antonio Light*, July 29, 1948). The chili queens also made appearances at Night in Old San Antonio (NIOSA), begun in 1948 by the San Antonio Conservation Society and held during Fiesta week in April (Fisher 1996, 223; Hernández-Ehrisman 2008, 72–75). Chili queens continued to vend at NIOSA until the 1970s ("Niosa, Always Crowded, Fun Filled," *San Antonio Light*, April 18, 1971, 11). With the construction of Interstate 35, the lively culture at Haymarket Plaza ended in 1956, yet some chili queens continued to vend throughout the 1960s and 1970s in the area,

including in March 1964 and December 1973 at the Farmer's Market downtown ("Chili Queens Will Return," *San Antonio Express*, March 14, 1964, 6-C; "Fiesta Navideña," *San Antonio Express*, December 2, 1973).

23. As early as 1909, the Board of Health recommended the city remove the stands in Alamo Plaza due to health concerns (Bechtol 1987).

24. *San Antonio Light*, March 4, 1936.

25. *San Antonio Light*, March 4, 1936.

26. "Chili Stands to be Removed," *San Antonio Express*, March 5, 1936. LULAC's agreement to the compromise is not surprising given the organization's historical approach to protecting the rights of the Mexican American community by working within established systems. For example, a year later, LULAC leaders used existing racial classifications to support the rights of Mexican Americans, requesting city health officials to change the racial classification of Mexican Americans from inclusion as "whites, Negroes, Mexicans" to "white, including Mexican, Negroes, and other races" (Orozco 2009; Pilcher 2008, 192).

27. "Chili Stands to Be Removed," *San Antonio Express*. March 5, 1936. A special committee to keep the chili queens in the plazas under sanitary conditions included Atlee B. Ayres, chairman of the arts and atmosphere; Dan G. Gerard, president of the West Side Improvement and Taxpayer's Association; M. C. Trub, president of LULAC; Solomon Casseb, member of the taxpayer's group; Mrs. H. R. Riegler, Mrs. Ed Leighton, and Mrs. F. W. Sorrell, members of the Centennial Association.

28. In a *San Antonio Light* article from 1943, the year when several chili queen vendors are officially shut down in the plazas, the reporter reveals poor living conditions in some of the chili vendors' homes where the food was prepared, including "mud in two room shacks where the food is prepared," "meat kept out twenty-four hours without refrigeration," and a "cat sitting in the cart calmly chewing on the coming night's menu." What is clear from this article is that the living conditions for many Mexicanos on the Westside were poor, suggesting structural factors as the cause for any unsanitary preparation of the food. Additionally, the article explains that seven chili vendors were shut down, suggesting that this was not a widespread issue. ("City Order 7 'Chili Queens' to Close," *San Antonio Light*, December 9, 1943).

29. SACS was not the first civic club to try to help the queens remain in the plazas by supervising their chili stands. A women's club in 1916 petitioned the city commissioners to allow the chili queens to continue to vend in the plazas. The article explains that the "picturesqueness of the chili stands appeals to the woman as an attraction" and explained that "the women promised to ensure that the chili stands are conducted in a clean and sanitary manner" ("Plea for Return of Chili Queens is Made by Santone Women," *Daily Advocate*, March 2, 1916).

30. In 1937, SACS also filed a petition with 130 signatures asking that the chili queens be allowed to vend once again in Haymarket Plaza and that the new market house be built quickly to include sanitary kitchens for the queens ("Chili Queens' Return Looms," *San Antonio Light*, December 6, 1937).

31. *San Antonio Express*, March 5, 1936.

32. *San Antonio Express*, May 27, 1928, D-7; *San Antonio Express*, September 23, 1928, 8D; *San Antonio Light*, January 25, 1928, 4B.

33. Gebhardt Chili 1923, inside cover. The images in the booklet include romanticized depictions of Mexican American culture that conflate Spanish and Mexican identity, such as a woman in Spanish flamenco attire on a balcony who is serenaded by a man in a Mariachi hat.

34. Gebhardt Chili 1923, inside cover.

35. Maverick's sterilization guidelines included a proposal for central receptacles with boiling water, the stipulation that the stands not operate until after dusk "when the pesky house flies have gone home to roost," and the use of sinks with hot water in the market house nearby. The total cost to the city estimated no more than $300 or $400 (*San Antonio Express*, July 5, 1939, 8A).

36. Night in Old Mexico Synopsis, 1936 and Fiesta La Villita Synopsis, 1943. Atlee B. Ayres Papers, MS 388, University of Texas at San Antonio Libraries Special Collections.

37. "Chili Queens to Pick Queen for Fair Trip," *San Antonio Express*, September 8, 1939, 11; "Selection of Chili Queens' Queen Due," *San Antonio Light*, September 7, 1939, 3-A.

38. "City Spends $800 to Re-Open Chili Stands Once Closed Up," *San Antonio Express*, July 6, 1939, 8.

39. "Miss Sybil Brown Wins the Contest," *San Antonio Express*, March 22, 1928. Quotes from *San Antonio Light*, April 22, 1928 and March 20, 1928; *San Antonio Light*, June 1, 1928.

40. Ayres had a company replicate lanterns for that year's event to mimic the Mexican lanterns he purchased in Mexico. Ayres's son, Robert Moss Ayres, also had a fondness for Mexican lanterns, as he owned a photo of "Chili Stands on the Northwest Corner of Alamo Plaza" (1908–1909). From the "Estate of Robert Moss Ayres, San Antonio, Texas," University of Texas at San Antonio Libraries Photo Collections.

41. "'Chili Queens' Announced for Harvest Festival," *San Antonio Light*, November 14, 1937, Part III: 7. Caption of photo reads, "From Left to Right: Mrs. Elizabeth O. Graham, Arthur Harris, Mrs. Edward Leighton and Mrs. Ethel Wilson Harris, seated, pictured in Spanish costume, which they will wear at the annual Harvest Fiesta, to be sponsored by the Conservation Society."

42. "'Chili Queens' Announced for Harvest Festival," *San Antonio Light*, November 14, 1937, Part III, 7.

43. "Events of the Day," *San Antonio Express News*, September 23, 1928, 8D.

44. "Texas History Day Program," *San Antonio Express*, March 5, 1933, D7; "Society," *San Antonio Express*, March 10, 1933, 6.

45. "Reporter Finds Vocation: She's Chili Queen for a Night," *San Antonio Light*, March 9, 1941, Part 1: 11.

46. SACS members and San Antonio society women who dressed up as "chili queens" continued well into the 1960s, and were featured in events referred to as "Return of the Chili Queens." The women who donned "chili queen" costumes at these events are most likely Anglo American, as evidenced by their surnames and accompanied photos. See *San Antonio Express*, May 15, 1962, Section C, 1-B; "Al-Ki-Anns to Entertain at "Chili Queens' Fiesta," *San Antonio Express*, May 3, 1963, Section C, 3-D; "Al-Ki-Ann Event in Home," *San Antonio Light*, April 28, 1963, 6-E; "Beta Sigma Phi Sets Benefit Public Supper," *San Antonio Light*, May 16, 1962; "Guild Is Sponsoring 'Return of the Chili Queens,'" *San Antonio Light*, March 6, 1964, 37.

47. The racialized and class distinctions between middle- and upper-class Anglos and working-class Mexicanas in San Antonio are evident in other fiesta events. In the Battles of Flowers parades of the 1930s, Anglo American women were queens and princesses, while African American and Mexican American women cooked, cleaned, and served the participants. In the months leading up to the Battle of Flowers parades, the most skilled Mexicana seamstresses of the West Side labored over the robes and gowns worn by Anglo American women (Blackwelder 1984, 6).

48. South Texas National Bank capitalizes on the chili queen phenomenon with a bank advertisement in the *San Antonio Express* on August 22, 1939, and in the *San Antonio Light* on August 23, 1939. The advertisement features a black-and-white sketch of a festive chili queen in a Mexican costume serving chili in Haymarket Plaza; Mexican pottery adorns the stand; the advertisement also includes images of men in mariachi hats. The advertisement reads: "The outdoor stands of the Chili Queens are as much a part of picturesque San Antonio as are the Missions and the plazas. In gaily decorated booths, women in native costumes sell Mexican dishes for a few centavos—attracting visitors and San Antonians alike. The South Texas National, too, attracts thousands of depositors and borrowers through the popularity of its complete banking facilities and friendly spirit."

49. "Delegates Invited to City by Alcalde," *San Antonio Express*, October 28, 1939.

50. "S.A. Will Fete Texas Mayors," *San Antonio Light*, November 10, 1939.

51. "City Hall Open House Slated," *San Antonio Light*, December 25, 1939, 10-A.

52. "Meat Inspection Status Changed," *San Antonio Light*, July 19, 1939.

53. Photo and caption from June 28, 1939, *San Antonio Light*, Section B.

54. Robb Walsh, author of *The Tex-Mex Cookbook*, suggests that a tent in a similar photo, also from Haymarket Plaza in the 1930s, was provided by chili fans from one of the local army posts (Scott Andrews, "Africa's Mark on San Antonio's Chili Queens," *SA Current*, October 26, 2011).

55. Series of photos from January 25, 1933. San Antonio Light Photograph collection, MS 359, University of Texas San Antonio Libraries Special Collections from the Institute of Texan Cultures.

56. A series of photos from September 1942 show SACS members posing in sightseeing boats on the San Antonio River. Photographs show Arneson River Theatre in the background. One photo shows "Miss Jean Champion, with guitar, and Miss Joan Brown, both in [Mexican] costume" who will take part in the Conservation society's "river fete and dance on the San Antonio river near La Villita" on October 3. San Antonio Light Photograph collection, MS 359, University of Texas San Antonio Libraries Special Collections from the Institute of Texan Cultures.

57. January 25, 1933; 1937; August 1939. San Antonio Light Photograph collection, MS 359, University of Texas San Antonio Libraries Special Collections from the Institute of Texan Cultures.

58. "Reporter Finds Vocation: She's Chili Queen for a Night," *San Antonio Light*, March 9, 1941, I: 11.

59. The exception includes the 1940s, when the food was cooked for the chili queen vendors in a central market kitchen due to sanitation regulations; many of the chili queens' family members, both men and women, worked in these kitchens ("Reporter Finds Vocation").

60. O. Henry, "The Enchanted Kiss," 1916.

61. E. Hough, *Forest and Stream* (1894): 270.

62. Stevens Point, *Daily Journal*, November 3, 1897.

63. "S.A. Queens Say Chili Is Sanitary," *San Antonio Light*, September 18, 1941, 16-A; "Reporter Finds Vocation."

64. "Reporter Finds Vocation."

65. "Reporter Finds Vocation."

66. "Reporter Finds Vocation."

67. "Former Chili Queen Could Lend Expertise, Spice to New Festival," *San Antonio Light*, May 22, 1987, B5.

68. Pete Cortez, the founder of *Mi Tierra* in 1941, was a supporter of the queens; before the city shut down the vendors' stands he delivered meat to them (Nelson and Silva 2005, 47).

69. "S.A. Queens Say Chili Is Sanitary."

70. "Chili Queens Order to Clean-Up," *San Antonio Light*, December 7, 1943, 4-A.

71. Two photos by Lee Russell from 1939 depict pecan shellers buying tortillas and fried beans from chili queen vendors. These photos illustrate the alimentary role that Mexicana vendors served to pecan shellers, serving to both male and female workers. See "Preparing plates of tortillas and fried beans to sell to pecan shellers, San Antonio, Texas," Call Number: LC-USF33-012075-M4, Repository: Library of Congress Prints and Photographs Division Washington, DC 20540 USA http://hdl.loc.gov/loc.pnp/pp.print; "Pecan sheller buying fried beans for her lunch, San Antonio, Texas," Call Number: LC-USF33-012075-M2, Library of Congress Prints and Photographs Division, Washington, DC 20540 USA http://hdl.loc.gov/loc.pnp/pp.print.

72. As a young girl in the 1920s, Emma Tenayuca frequented Haymarket Plaza with her parents, a space where unemployed workers and families would congregate, and social-ists and other political activists would give lectures on labor conditions confronted by Mexicanos in the city. In 1938, Tenayuca was elected by the city's more than 12,000 pecan shellers, the majority of whom were women, to lead their strike against poor working conditions at the pecan-shelling factories. Many consider the Pecan Shellers' Strike to be a major victory in the Mexican American struggle for economic and political equality in this nation (Ayala 2011). A historical marker dedicated to Tenayuca in Milam Plaza in San Antonio was unveiled in December 2011.

73. Due to their high numbers in low-skilled jobs, Mexican American and Mexican immigrant women were especially prominent in labor protests in Depression Era San Antonio, particularly in pecan-shelling industry strikes in the 1930s, and in garment industry strikes (Blackwelder 137, 141). One example of Mexicanas claiming cultural citi-zenship through labor activism in the public sphere in San Antonio includes the Fink Cigar Company Strike in August 1933, when 400 women walked off their jobs as part of the Fink Cigar Company strike; this strike was organized by Tenayuca

CHAPTER 2 — CLAIMING DOMESTIC SPACE IN THE US-MEXICO BORDERLANDS

1. Jovita González wrote *Caballero* with Eve Raleigh (pseudonym for Margaret Eimer) dur-ing the 1930s and 1940s. Based on correspondence between the two authors, María Cotera speculates that they began to write the novel, originally titled *All This Is Mine,* sometime between 1936 and 1938 (2008). The novel was not published during the authors' lifetimes, yet was discovered by José Limón with the assistance of María Cotera in the 1990s as part of a larger context of Mexican American literature recovery projects. The original manuscript of *Caballero* is in the E. E. Mireles and Jovita González de Mireles Papers in the Special Col-lections and Archives Department of the Mary and Jeff Bell Library, Texas A&M University–Corpus Christi (TAMU-CC). The Mireles Papers were donated to the TAMU-CC Library in 1992 by Isabel Cruz, who with the urging of local historian Ray J. García, a member of the Nueces County Historical Society, was advised to restore the papers. After Ray J. García advised Thomas H. Kreneck, special collections librarian and archivist at TAMU-CC about the Mireles Papers, they were made available to researchers. When editors Limón and Cotera confirmed the existence of the manuscript at TAMU-CC, they prepared it for publication under the title *Caballero: A Historical Romance Novel* (1996, ix); Garza-Falcón (1998, 79).

2. I use the term *Spanish Mexican* to refer to those men and women who trace their identities to Spanish-speaking communities in the Southwest border region and who lived under the Mexican flag after 1821. As Deena González notes, "even though these

communities referred to themselves as "españoles" or "Spaniards," the majority were not Spanish but mestizos, persons of mixed ancestry, specifically a person of Native indigenous and Spanish heritage" (1999, xix).

3. Initially a wartime emergency program, the Bracero Program spanned a twenty-two-year period, from 1942 to 1964, and led to the migration of approximately 4.5 million Mexican workers to the United States (García 1980, 28, 37–38).

4. For a further analysis of González's and Raleigh's co-authorship and a reading of the novel itself as a "collaborative novel about the gendered politics of collaboration," see Cotera (2007, 2008).

5. Nicole M. Guidotti-Hernández importantly argues that González's folklore writings enact imperialist nostalgia and "overt racism," contending that González relies on a "middle-class racist perspective that enacts its own violence, only discursively" (2011, 138, 30). Guidotti-Hernández closely reads González's folklore to reveal its "overt racism . . . in generic representations of Aztec Indians as stand-ins for disappeared Indian groups of Texas (the Comanche, Kiowa, and Lipan Apache, in particular) and African Americans" (2011, 138). This is a crucial and necessary argument. Yet Guidotti-Hernández's characterizations of the feminist scholarship on González, particularly her reading of María Cotera's—who she claims "firmly plac[es] González's work in a tradition of resistance" (2011, 138)—ultimately replicates a binary of racism/resistance itself. Instead, Cotera's scholarship carefully situates González's writings within their historical contexts and racial-class positionings.

6. My discussion of the central role of domesticity in González's and Jaramillo's claims to Spanishness and whiteness builds on the body of literature that analyzes the ways Spanish Mexicans in Texas, New Mexico, and California deployed Spanishness to distinguish themselves from Mexicans and Indians. See Garza-Falcón 1998; González 1999; Montgomery 2002; Nieto-Phillips 2004.

7. The separate spheres ideology was prevalent in feminist scholarship of the 1960s and 1970s and critiqued the male-defined American literary canon's neglect of women's history. These texts include Baym 1978; Douglas 1977; Tompkins 1985; Welter 1966.

8. Emphasis added. From "The Original Text of Articles IX and X of the Treaty of Guadalupe Hidalgo and the Protocol of Queretaro," Appendix I in Griswold Del Castillo (1990, 179).

9. Kate McCullough makes a similar argument about Mexican masculinity in her close reading of María Amparo Ruiz de Burton's *Squatter and the Don* (1999, 171).

10. While María Cotera argues that González and Raleigh wrote *Caballero* together as an extensive collaboration, previous scholars argued otherwise. Limón first argued that Eimer had a strong authorial role in shaping the romantic plot of *Caballero* but with the active participation of González (1996, xxviii–xxi); Garza-Falcón similarly explained— based on her interview with Austin historian Marta Cotera (the mother of scholar María Cotera) on March 8, 1993—that Eve Raleigh served as González's co-author mainly to get the manuscript published. Differently from Limón, Garza-Falcón recalled from her interview with Marta Cotera that Raleigh probably contributed to some editorial comments and suggestions on the content. (1998, 111–113).

11. For a further discussion of González's relationship to Dobie, see Cotera (2008). Diana Noreen Rivera also explores González's associations with Dobie, arguing that "González, acting with an oppositional consciousness, adapted Dobie's style for some of her folklore renderings, cleverly manipulating his ideology along with the Anglo American ethos of the 1930s, to speak to, confront, and revolt against the Anglo patriarchal academy in the forms of Dobie and the Texas Folklore Society" (2011, 81).

12. See also *The Apology Act for the 1930s Mexican Repatriation Program*, California Senate Bill 670 (2005).

13. The English translation of *marica* is "poof," which means a pampered darling; an effeminate man. The idiomatic use of *marica* is the same as the Spanish *maricon*, which is a derogatory term for a homosexual man (González 1996, 38).

14. This ethnographic perspective is evident in Jaramillo's other texts—a collection of short stories, *Cuentos del Hogar/Spanish Fairy Tales* (The Citizen Press, 1939); a cookbook, *Potajes Sabrosos/ The Genuine New Mexico Tasty Recipes* (1939; Repr., Santa Fe: Ancient City Press, 1981); and another autobiography, *Shadows of the Past/Sombras del Pasado* (1941; Repr., Santa Fe: Ancient City Press, 1972).

15. I am grateful to Nancy Armstrong for helping me see this reading of Juanita's transaction. Also see Nancy Armstrong, "Why Daughters Die: The Racial Logic of American Sentimentalism," *Yale Journal of Criticism* 7:2 (1994): 1–24.

CHAPTER 3 — DOMESTIC POWER ACROSS BORDERS

1. In this essay, Cabeza de Baca describes her home economics work in the third person. The use of the third person enables her to talk about her individual encounters as collective experiences. It also serves to rhetorically distance herself from such experiences, indicating her aim to add "objectivity" to her narrative.

2. While Cabeza de Baca had anticipated staying in Patzcuaro for only six months, she actually stayed eight. She explains that she did not want to leave until she was satisfied with the results of her work, which most likely included evidence of improved living conditions. After her work for UNESCO, she returned to New Mexico to continue her work for the NMAES (Reed 2005, 158).

3. Cabeza de Baca's writings include essays for the *Journal of Home Economics, The New Mexican,* the *New Mexico Extension News,* and her Spanish-language bulletins for the NMAES in the 1940s and 1950s, including *Los Alimentos y su Preparación* (1934) and *Boletín de Conserver* (1935), as well as her fictional text about a rural northern New Mexican family in *The Good Life: New Mexico Traditions and Food* (1949) and her cookbook *Historic Cookery* (1939; repr. 1958). Depending on the year and venue, Cabeza de Baca would pen her name as either Fabiola Cabeza de Baca or Fabiola Cabeza de Baca Gilbert, because from 1931 to 1941, she was married to Carlos Gilbert, a relationship she does not write about at length.

4. Her educational route toward a career was quite conventional for women of her social class. Cabeza de Baca attended high school and received a bachelor's degree in pedagogy with a minor in Romance languages from New Mexico Normal in 1921. She later received her bachelor's of science degree in home economics at New Mexico State University in Las Cruces in 1929. While attending college in 1916, Cabeza de Baca took her first teaching job in a one-room schoolhouse in the rural part of Guadalupe County in New Mexico—and spent more than ten years of her life there as a teacher.

5. Prior to the 1930s, most women of Mexican descent and native women in New Mexico used drying rather than canning as their primary method of food preservation because it was an inexpensive and efficient way to preserve food (Jensen 1982, 362). Yet with the devastation of the agricultural farms brought on by the drought, these women had a difficult time keeping up with food production. Home demonstration agents therefore introduced both canning and the pressure cooker into the rural households (Jensen 1982).

6. Her writings that did not focus on home economics include her autobiography *We Fed Them Cactus* (1954), as well as several articles for the magazine *Santa Fe Scene* and

newsletter *The New Mexico Extension News* in the 1940s and 1950s, which document her "Spanish" family and culture in New Mexico. Some of these articles include "Las Fiestas," published in *Santa Fe Scene*, August 9, 1958, 22; "La Merienda," published in *Santa Fe Scene*, August 23, 1958, 10; "Noche Buena for Doña Antonia: She Met Christmas with Arms Open," published in *New Mexico Extension News* 25.12 (December 1945): 2, 4. Cabeza de Baca was also an active member of Cleofas Jaramillo's La Sociedad Folklórica, an organization dedicated to preserving Spanish culture, folklore, and traditions (Reed 2005; Scharff 2003).

7. Even though Fabiola Cabeza de Baca's name connected her to Alvar Nuñez Cabeza de Baca, one of the first Spanish explorers to the Americas, Angélico Chávez's genealogy of Spanish Mexican families in *Origins of New Mexican Families* supports the claim that members of her family were not descendants of the explorer (Reed 2005).

8. Cabeza de Baca's autobiographical and cultural writings include long lists of her family's Spanish surnames and Spanish names for the New Mexican landscape. Rebolledo argues that such lists, "serve as a narrative response to a present marked by the loss of those names and places" (1994, xxiii).

9. Anne Goldman stresses how the dominant institutions Cabeza de Baca worked for greatly impacted her narratives about her race and culture (1996, 13). Maureen Reed, who has written one of the most extensive critical biographies of Cabeza de Baca, argues against those who read Cabeza de Baca as a colonizer and capitulator to dominant racialized narratives, and suggests instead that Cabeza de Baca's work for the NMAES advocated cultural progress while also affirming cultural traditions (2005). Merrihelen Ponce, another influential scholar, also reminds critics that Cabeza de Baca, as a member of a racially marginalized group in the US Southwest, was also a victim of neocolonialism (1995).

10. Cabeza de Baca was a member of the *Journal of Home Economics* editorial board, serving as an "unofficial advisor" in the capacity of "Reader Editor" in the 1940s, yet the power she had to shape the content of the journal is unclear.

11. The article's reference to Cabeza de Baca as Mrs. Gilbert contrasts with her rhetorical resistance to be referred to by her husband's last name after their divorce. For example, on a Red Cross Certificate dated November 1, 1946, Cabeza de Baca is listed as "Mrs. Carlos Gilbert." The document reveals that Cabeza de Baca crossed out "Mrs. Carlos Gilbert" with a pen and inserted her maiden name "Cabeza de Baca." Fabiola Cabeza de Baca Gilbert Papers, Center for Southwest Research, General Library, University of New Mexico, Albuquerque.

12. The second printing of the cookbook, the most well-known, added illustrations of food through the book and on the cover page, and the total production of the text in its various printings equaled over 100,000 copies (Reed 2005). The recipes were also later published in Cabeza de Baca's fictional text *The Good Life*.

13. Extension clubs were organized to provide farm women of various ethnic backgrounds a place to meet; women often met and received social support from each other in these clubs (Jensen 1986b, 48).

14. While a few sources cite Cabeza de Baca's ability to speak Tewa and Tiwa, relatives of Cabeza de Baca disagree on her abilities to speak the Pueblo languages (Reed 2005, 312).

15. Cabeza de Baca is also noted for starting a home economics column in the Spanish-language Santa Fe newspaper *El Nuevo Mexicano*. In this column, she featured New Mexican and native recipes. Several biographies of Cabeza de Baca also note, with little details on the specifics, how she hosted a weekly bilingual program on homemaking for the Santa Fe radio station KVSF (Reed 2005).

16. The Patzcuaro center was run as a co-operative effort by UNESCO, the Organization of American States, the UN Food and Agricultural Organization, the Labour Organization, the World Health Organization, the Government of Mexico, and the Center of Regional Cooperation for the Education of Adults in Latin America and the Caribbean (CREFAL).

17. As Jones explains, "If language had not yet been codified, its primitive nature prohibited its appropriateness for use in the modern world" (1988, 59). UNESCO's intent was to address illiteracy as a way to foster economic development, yet its aims toward Westernization had material consequences for native communities, specifically by furthering the loss of their native language in a modern context.

18. The scholarship and biographies on Cabeza de Baca only briefly mention Cabeza de Baca's work with UNESCO in either a short paragraph or few sentences, simply acknowledging that she did such work (Rebolledo 1994; Reed 2005, Scharff 2003).

19. In the post-1950s revival of domesticity, middle-class women also leverage gender norms in the public sphere, even though this period sought to ideologically and visually place women in the private sphere (May 1990; Nickerson 2003).

20. Fabiola Cabeza de Baca Gilbert Papers, Center for Southwest Research, General Library, University of New Mexico, Albuquerque.

21. Cabeza de Baca's visa and passport are included in the Fabiola Cabeza de Baca Gilbert Papers, Center for Southwest Research, General Library, University of New Mexico, Albuquerque.

22. General Lázaro Cárdenas (former president) donated his mansion, "La Erendira," named after the daughter of an ancient Tarascan chief, to UNESCO to run the center (Behrman 1951).

23. This distinction between the two articles could also suggest that Cabeza de Baca left certain information out of her speech to the Altrusa women's club, further indicating her performance to a mostly white home economics audience.

24. Interview by Paula Thaidigsman, August 29, 1975. Cassette Tape, Women in New Mexico Collection, Center for Southwest Research, General Library, University of New Mexico, Albuquerque.

25. Alice Bullock, "A Patrona of the Old Pattern," *The New Mexican*, May 19, 1968; Marie T. Walsh, "New Mexico's Famous Home Economist," *California Farmer*, October 16, 1954, 571.

26. Although Cabeza de Baca spent her career teaching other women how to cook, and published several cookbooks, she reportedly did not enjoy cooking. In a 1975 interview, for instance, she admits to hiring a housekeeper, and states: "Yes, I've always had help at home. I didn't do housework" (Reed 2005). Cabeza de Baca's niece further explains that Cabeza de Baca had hired help because of a leg injury from her childhood, but also because she did not like to cook. According to her niece, "She could always tell you how to do it but she never liked to cook" (Reed 2005). That Fabiola built a career in home economics but did not enjoy cooking herself, and even hired someone to cook for her, further emphasizes the various domestic performances she enacted throughout her life and career.

CHAPTER 4 — POSTNATIONALIST AND DOMESTICANA STRATEGIES

1. Arte Público Press published the novel from 1984 to 1986, followed by a slightly revised edition in 1989. At Arte Público Press, Cisneros's text was first placed on their "Young Readers" section of its catalog, but it failed to take off in this category because Arte Público was a small press with a limited audience. When Vintage Contemporaries

re-published the revised Arte Público Press edition in 1991, *The House on Mango Street* quickly became a popular text, as indicated by the abundance of critical and scholarly reviews of the work during this year (de Valdés 1993, 291). Alfred A. Knopf's reprint of *The House on Mango Street* in 1994 signaled its esteemed role within US literature. And in 1998, with multiculturalism already well-integrated into English department curricula nationwide, Cisneros was one of the first Chicana authors to be included in *The Norton Anthology of American Literature.* The twenty-fifth anniversary edition of *The House on Mango Street*, published by Vintage Contemporaries in 2009, further illustrates the text's esteemed status within US letters.

2. Ultimately, as Cisneros explains, "my house faded to work-shirt blue. The sun resolved the issue." Mark Jacob and Stephan Benzkofer, "10 Things you Might not Know about Chicago Authors," *Chicago Tribune Opinion*, May 29, 2011.

3. Proponents of Proposition 187 situated the bodies of Chicanas and Latinas, as well as the Latina/o domestic sphere, as perpetrating crimes against a white California citizenry, configuring Mexicanas as invading the nation through their fertility (Chávez 2007, 2001; Gutiérrez 2008;). Mexican immigrant women represented long-term settlement and signified the "dramatic growth of a 'minority group'" (Chávez 2007, 68; De Genova 2006; Gutiérrez 2008). Lisa Cacho suggests how Proposition 187 was a response to shifting racial demographics in California and a modern global economy that increasingly depends on the labor of immigrant women and children (2000, 392).

4. Cisneros is also the author of children's books, including *Hairs/Pelitos* published in 1997, a bilingual children's book based on the similarly titled vignette in *The House on Mango Street.* Cisneros also wrote the introduction to the fifteenth anniversary reprint edition of Garza's *Cuadros de Familia* in 2005.

5. In 1990, *Cuadros de Familia* received the American Library Association Notable Book Award; Best Books of the Year Selection, Library of Congress; Best Books of the Year Selection, *School Library Journal*; Pura Belpré Honor Award; and the BlueBonnet Award. In 1996 and 1997, *En Mi Familia* received the Américas Award for Children's and Young Adult Literature, Consortium of Latin American Studies Programs (CLASP); Children's Books of Distinction Award, *Hungry Mind Review*; International Reading Association Notable Books for a Global Society Choice; and was on the Texas Bluebonnet Award Master List.

6. Jamilah King, "LAUSD Names Echo Park School after Chicana Writer Sandra Cisneros," *ColorLines: News for Action*, July 5, 2011. http://colorlines.com/archives/2011/07/lausd_names_school_after_sandra_cisneros.html.

7. Las Hijas de Cuauhtémoc began in 1968 and published one of the first Chicana feminist newspapers in 1971, including *Encuentro Femenil*; from 1978 to 1981, Chicana activists at Long Beach State met as an informal group under such names as Las Mujeres de Longo and Las Chicanas de Aztlán; Chicanas in the greater Los Angeles area organized the first Chicana conference, held at California State Long Beach in 1971; Conferencia de Mujeres por La Raza took place in Houston in May 1971; Chicana feminist print communities included publications such as *Regeneración, Encuentro Femenil, Hijas de Cuauhtémoc, La Comadre, Fuego de Aztlán, Imagenes de la Chicana*, among others (Blackwell 2011, 7–8, 134).

8. See Anzaldúa, *Borderlands/La Frontera* (1987); *This Bridge Called My Back: Writings by Radical Women of Color*, ed. Anzaldúa and Moraga (1984); *Making Face. Making Soul: Haciendo Caras: Creative & Critical Perspectives by Feminists of Color*, ed. Anzaldúa; Moraga, *The Last Generation: Prose and Poetry* (1993); and Castillo, *Massacre of the Dreamers: Essays on Xicanisma* (1994).

9. Garza created *Curandera* (1977) and *Curandera II* (1979)—both included in her children's books (1990, 1996)—in the years after the Chicano/a Movement. Garza created the other illustrations that appear in her children's books in the 1980s and 1990s, either as stand-alone pieces or specifically for the books. The majority of Garza's illustrations in her children's books extend the thematic focus of the art she created during the Chicano/a Movement, which focus on cultural affirmation, family celebrations and rituals, and women's and men's roles in the domestic sphere.

10. During the Chicano/a Movement, Aztlán functioned as a "decolonizing imaginary to signify homeland and served as a mode of historical consciousness and a precolonial sense of place about the US Southwest" (Blackwell 2011, 102).

11. Garza states, "There was, of course, a lot of artwork that was heavily influenced by the muralists, Los Tres Grandes, so there was Chicano artists doing murals of *huelgas* and of *Los Rinches* beating up farm workers, and, you know, all kinds of scenes like that, dealing with protest, with injustices, in a mural format. . . . But there was very little that dealt with just ordinary everyday life of Mexican Americans. And I felt that . . . I formulated the concept that my position as an artist, my contribution would be to depict our lives as we know it, what we have grown up with, what we were made to feel ashamed of, put [it] in a fine-art form, the very best that I can do to make it available to our people so they can see themselves in the artwork and feel proud" (qtd. in Kalstrom 1997).

12. Cisneros's children's book *Bravo, Bruno*, published by La Nuova Frontiera publisher in Rome in 2012, indicates her goal to directly market her work for a global children's literature audience.

13. For the complete list of Garza's individual and group exhibits, see Garza's exhibition history in Cortez (2010, 108–115).

14. San Francisco–based Children's Book Press twice asked Garza to illustrate another writer's story before Garza said, "I don't want to illustrate someone else's story. Why don't I tell the stories behind my paintings?" Rachel Howard, "Culture on Campus," *SFSU Magazine Online* 6, no. 1 (spring 2006).

15. See Cortez (2010, 108–115).

16. The My Family/En Mi Familia exhibit traveled to the following locations: Austin Children's Museum, Austin, TX; Kalamazoo Valley Museum, Kalamazoo, MI; Pittsburgh Children's Museum, Pittsburgh, PA; Grand Rapids Children's Museum, Grand Rapids, MI; San Antonio Children's Museum, San Antonio, TX; Children's Discovery Museum, Brownsville, TX; and Minnesota Children's Museum, St. Paul, MN.

17. Anzaldúa's explanation for why she began to write children's literature echoes Rebolledo's assessment: "Here in California I met a lot of young Chicanos and Chicanas who didn't have a clue about their own Chicano culture. . . . [L]ater on when they were already twenty, twenty-five, or even thirty years old, they took classes in Chicano studies to learn more about their ancestors, their history and culture. But I want the kids to already have access to this information. That is why I started writing children's books" (qtd. in Ikas 2001, 9).

18. Historic examples of alternative kinship networks created by Mexicanas in the United States include support networks created among working-class women laboring in the factories and fields during the 1930s to the 1950s (Ruiz 1998) and many single female–headed households in the 1920s (Sánchez 1993).

19. For a further discussion of Garza's active involvement with the MAYO exhibit and Chicano/a Movement, see Cortez (2010, 15–20).

20. Examples of active Chicana feminist groups and conferences during the Chicano/a Movement in South Texas include: Mujeres por la Raza (MPLR) in Crystal City, TX,

founded by women active in La Raza Unida, the Chicano third party, in 1970; and the Conferencia de Mujeres por La Raza, which took place in Houston in May 1971 (Blackwell 2011).

21. During the Chicano/a Movement, women who critiqued patriarchal and nationalist structures were often deemed *malinchistas* or *vendidas.* Both Mexican and Chicano nationalist discourse configures *La Malinche* as both whore and traitor for "selling out" her people to the Spaniards (Paz 1961).

22. The history of artistic production, curatorial involvement, and art management by Chicana artists at the Galería de la Raza has not been adequately documented (Davalos 2001, 87–88). Graciela Carrillo, a founding member of Galería, is frequently overlooked as a founding member. Carmen Lomas Garza and María Pinedo, instead, are cited as the first Chicana staff members and artists to join the gallery. Historical accounts and chronologies of artist exhibitions at the Galería have elided the earliest exhibitions organized by and about Chicana/Latina artists, including the "Third World Women Art Exhibition" (1973), Graciela Carrillo's "Soñada Despierta" (1974), and Sue Martinez's solo exhibition (1977). The 1978 homage to Frida Kahlo curated by Carmen Lomas Garza and others has been included in historical accounts. Davalos argues that art histories have only cited three Chicana artists as exhibiting their work at the Galería prior to the 1990s, eliding many Chicana artists who did produce and curate art during this period (2001, 88).

23. See Anzaldúa (1987); Anzaldúa and Moraga (1984); Moraga (1993); and Castillo (1994). Anzaldúa's *Borderlands,* for instance, takes a postnationalist approach to Anglo American, masculine, and hetero-normative-dominated histories by accounting for and asserting feminist and queer histories (1987). Emma Pérez's work also exemplifies a postnationalist critique of nationalism with an approach to history that critiques linear narratives of Chicano/a male historiography, destabilizing national and colonial narratives (1999).

24. See Cisneros's *Woman Hollering Creek and Other Stories* (1991). For a further discussion of Cisneros's use of telenovelas as sites of gender socialization within Mexican and Chicano/a contexts in the collection's title story, "Woman Hollering Creek," see Saldívar-Hull (2000, 107–117).

25. In the first edition of *The House on Mango Street* published by Arte Público Press in 1984, the last line of the text reads "For the ones who cannot *get* out" (emphasis added). The line was changed to "For the ones who cannot out" in the 1988 Arte Público "Second Revised Edition" and was kept in both the 1991 Vintage Contemporaries edition and twenty-fifth anniversary reprint in 2009. The distinction between the line "For the ones who cannot *get* out" and "For the ones who cannot out" places different emphasis on the agency of those who live on Mango Street, as well as the agency of Esperanza and her ability to help the people of her community "get out." The myth of individualism would claim that it is the individual's sole responsibility and ability to "get out" of their socioeconomic circumstances, and that if they "cannot *get* out," it is due to poor personal choices and individual circumstances. By eliminating the verb "get" and thus the action of "getting" out of Mango Street, Cisneros's revised edition complicates agency and conveys the feeling that the people in Mango Street are indeed "trapped," and that they "cannot out" on their own.

26. In a *bildungsroman,* a protagonist moves through various stages of maturity, confronting obstacles that lead to a deeper understanding of the individual self within the larger social order; the protagonist also desires a physical removal from family and community, mostly in the form of departure, particularly through the completion of a formal education.

27. This focus on community locates *The House on Mango Street* in an "alternative Chicano tradition" of the *bildungsroman*, represented by texts such as Tomás Rivera's *. . . y no se lo trago la tierra/And the Earth Did Not Devour Him* (Poey 1996). Similar to other Chicana/o texts, *The House on Mango Street* illustrates a "decentering of individualism" through both content and experimentation (Calderón 1991).

28. Garza's illustrations function as modern-day documents of Chicana/o culture and life along the South Texas US–Mexico borderlands. In this sense, they function as contemporary Chicana/o *codices*, which visually document the presence of Chicana/os in the Americas. The concept of the Chicano *códice* was first explored in the traveling group exhibit "Chicano *Códices*: Encountering the Art of Americas," curated by Marcos Sánchez-Tranquilino, and which opened at the Mexican Museum in San Francisco in 1992. The exhibit was a response to "The Quincentenary," the 500-year anniversary of the European colonization with the Americas. The intent of the show was to both resurrect what was lost in the European and Spanish conquest of Mexico and to affirm Chicana/os as contemporary Aztecs in a conquered homeland (Gaspar de Alba 2001, 213). Thus, each artist, including Garza, was asked to use the codex format to depict their personal histories and experiences in the Americas (Leimer 2005). For the shows, Garza created two works: "Codex Lomas Garza: Pedacito de Mi Corazon" and "Homenaje a Tenochtitlan: An Installation for Day of the Dead" (Cortez 2010, 62, 67).

29. Both *Cuadros de Familia* and *En Mi Familia* are produced through collaboration: the paintings are by Garza, the stories are told by Garza, yet they are written, and thus mediated by, another writer, Harriet Rohmer. In *Cuadros de Familia*, the Spanish translations are written by Rosalma Zubizarreta, and in *En Mi Familia*, they are written by Francisco X. Alarcón. *En Mi Familia* formally lists David Schecter as the editor, while the back copy of *Cuadros de Familia* explains, "The text is the close collaboration between Carmen and editor Harriet Rohmer, who interviewed Carmen about each picture and prepared the final manuscript with the help of David Schecter" (*Cuadros de Familia* 32).

30. Garza's use of the *monito* (little pictures) aesthetic and materials, particularly gouache, have led many to claim her paintings to have a childlike and naïve quality. As *monitos*, Garza's paintings are quite small, on average one foot in length and two feet in width, with the smallest of her paintings eleven inches in length and seventeen inches in width. Garza also uses gouache rather than acrylics, a heavier, more opaque material that has greater reflective properties, which also gives her paintings a cartoonish quality. Garza recounts how she began to work in the style of the *monitos* when she found her mother's hand-made *lotería tablas*: "And so I decided I was going to paint my own set of *lotería tablas*, but I wanted to do a whole new version with new *monitos*, new figures that were relevant to contemporary Chicano life, Mexican American life" (Cortez 2010; Garza 1997; Mesa-Bains 1991). Garza continues, "It's taking from the past, adjusting it, and creating new. Making adjustments, adaptations. So I'm creating my new *monitos*" (1997).

31. In 2000, *Camas para Sueños* was also included in the major Smithsonian exhibit "Arte Latino: Treasures from the Smithsonian American Art Museum." *Cama para Sueños* was also chosen for the 2000 United States Census marketing campaign, along with thirteen other paintings by artists of diverse racial and ethnic backgrounds, to appeal to various ethnic and regional communities in the United States.

32. Ina Rampau, rev. of *Cuadros de Familia, Fifteenth Anniversary Edition*, by Carmen Lomas Garza, *Parents' Choice*. http://www.amazon.com

33. Qtd in Rachel Howard, "Culture on Campus," *SFSU Magazine Online* 6, no. 1 (Spring 2006).

34. See *Immigrant America: A Portrait, Third Edition*, ed. Alejandro Portes and Rubén G. Rumbaut (2006).

35. Susan Thomsen, "Family Togetherness," rev. of *Cuadros de Familia*, by Carmen Lomas Garza, May 1, 2006, http://www.amazon.com.

36. A Reader, "Teachers Must Have This Book!" rev. of *Cuadros de Familia*, by Carmen Lomas Garza, December 5, 2003, http://www.amazon.com

37. SB 1070 affirms the requirement that immigrants register with the US federal government and makes it a state misdemeanor to not have registration documents in one's possession at all times. It requires local law enforcement, during a lawful stop, detention, or arrest, to determine a person's immigration status if there is "reasonable suspicion" the person is an undocumented immigrant (Arizona State Senate, 2010). Arizona's House Bill 2281, also signed into law in 2010, banned ethnic studies programs in public schools, an effort led by state attorney general Tom Horne. Immediately, teachers, students, and administrators came together to challenge Horne's ruling, but on January 10, 2012, the Tucson Unified School District board voted to cease all ethnic studies programs, specifically Mexican American Studies curriculum and programs. In Texas, the State Board of Education approved controversial changes to the state's social studies curriculum, which amends and weakens the teaching of the civil rights movement, religious freedoms, and America's relationship with the United Nations, and hundreds of other items.

38. In response to the news that *The House on Mango Street* had been selected for Chicago's One Book Program in 2009, Cisneros explained that the selection of her book was "terribly appropriate" because of the loss of affordable housing in many neighborhoods due to gentrification. Qtd. in Patrick Reardon and Hal Dardick, "Sandra Cisneros's *The House on Mango Street* chosen for One Book, One Chicago," *Chicago Tribune*, March 12, 2009. Furthermore, *The House on Mango Street* was banned in Tucson, Arizona, public high schools when the Tucson Unified School District board voted to cease all ethnic studies programs, specifically Mexican American Studies curriculum and programs, on January 10, 2012; the text was included in the district's English/Latino literature curriculum.

39. Quoted in "Carmen Lomas Garza in the Artist Studio," *The Fine Arts Museum of San Francisco (FAMSF) Blog*, posted on April 21, 2011, http://deyoung.famsf.org/blog/carmen-lomas-garza-artist-studio-april-2011.

CHAPTER 5 — PATSSI VALDEZ'S "A ROOM OF ONE'S OWN"

1. The group claimed the name "Asco" at their first art show, "Asco, an Exhibition of Our Worst Work," held at Self Help Graphics in 1974. In doing so, they appropriated the negative term used by others to describe their work; "Asco" in Spanish means nausea or disgust. According to Willie Herrón, prior to 1974 "the word had never entered our vocabulary" (2000).

2. Gronk, Willie Herrón, Harry Gamboa Jr., and Patssi Valdez were the members of Asco in its classic period, often referred to as "Asco A," which stretched roughly from the early 1970s to the early 1980s. Even though Humberto Sandoval was a major participant in Asco A, he never considered himself a member of Asco, as he was not a visual artist. "Asco B" emerged after both Herrón and Valdez left to pursue solo careers in the early 1980s. It included artists Diane Gamboa, Marisela Norte, Max Benavidez, Linda Gamboa, Bibbi Hansen, Sean Carrillo, Barbara Carrasco, Jerry Dreva, and Teresa Covarrubias, among many others (Hernández 2007).

3. For a further discussion of pachuca/o and punk aesthetics in Asco's stylizations, see Habell-Pallán (2011). Valdez's face is painted white because *Instant Mural* took place after

The First Supper (After a Major Riot), in which each Asco member wore white face makeup in the style of *calavera* (skeleton) masks. Valdez's white face paint also emphasizes unnaturalness, an important visual element of punk.

4. *Instant Mural* was used as a backdrop at punk and art shows in East L.A. in the 1980s (Benavidez 2007, 35), further emphasizing the way Valdez's self-fashioning in the performance has been read as punk.

5. In addition to this book, Valdez's paintings appear on the covers of Pat Mora, *Adobe Odes* (Tucson: University of Arizona Press, 2006); Carla Trujillo, *What Night Brings* (Willimantic: Curbstone Press, 2003); John S. Christie and José B. Gonzalez, *Latino Boom: An Anthology of U.S. Latino Literature* (New York: Pearson, 2006); *Chicana Feminisms: A Critical Reader*, ed. Gabriela F. Arredondo, Aída Hurtado, Norma Klahn, Olga Nájera-Ramírez, and Patricia Zavella (Durham, NC: Duke University Press, 2003); and Jonathan Yorba, *Arte Latino: Treasures from the Smithsonian American Art Museums* (New York: Watson-Guptill Publications, 2001).

6. Noriko Gamblin, "Patssi Valdez." Flintridge Foundation Award Catalogue, 2001. http://flintridgefoundation.org/visualarts/catalog20012002_16-patssivaldez.pdf.

7. Valdez's solo exhibit "Distant Memories" took place at the Daniel Saxon Gallery in West Hollywood in 1992. It drew attention from art critics to her work as a painter of domestic interiors and still-lifes. This was not Valdez's first solo exhibit, but it was the first major solo showing of her paintings of domestic spaces.

8. Authors who do not subscribe to this view include Ramón García (1997), Tere Romo (1999), and Amalia Mesa-Bains (1999).

9. Susan Wiggins, "Patssi Valdez," *ArtWeek*, March 26, 1992, 15.

10. Gamboa Jr. took the photo of Valdez in *Instant Mural,* so it makes sense that the image was on the cover of *Urban Exile*, a text devoted to his life and work.

11. While the promotional materials for "Phantom Sightings" use Manuel Fernandez's *Self Portrait of My Father* (2006) and Margarita Cabrera's *Vocho* (2004), exhibition documents prominently feature Valdez's image. For instance, Valdez's taped body in *Instant Mural* graces the lower-right section of the exhibition brochure. Several newspaper reviews of the exhibit also include the image of *Instant Mural.* See Knight (2008).

12. On May 4, 2008, LACMA hosted a talk with artists Sandra de la Loza and Harry Gamboa Jr. They asked audience members to write questions anonymously on small notecards. On my card, I asked, "What do you think is the specific legacy of Patssi Valdez for contemporary Chicana/Chicano artists?" De la Loza's quote is in response to this question. Audio of this talk is available at the "Phantom Sightings" link on Harry Gamboa Jr.'s website, http://www.harrygamboajr.com/alist/phantom2.html.

13. In e-mail correspondence on July 28, 2010, Valdez explained that the shop in East Los Angeles was called "Hair Creations" and was owned by her mother; it was managed by her mother, her sister, and Valdez herself. They later opened another shop in Montebello, a few miles to the east, which was run by Valdez and her sister.

14. Valdez's statement comes from the four-part documentary *Chicano! History of the Mexican American Civil Rights Movement,* NLCC Educational Media, 1996.

15. Patssi Valdez, e-mail message to author, July 28, 2010.

16. Asco's ironic commentary on Hollywood's exclusion of Latina actors is best exemplified by their parody of the Academy Awards. In 1978, Valdez won a "No Oscar" for *A La Mode,* a plaster Woolworth's cobra spray-painted gold (Benavidez 2007, 46; James 1999, 24). In the photo-documentation of this event, which itself functions as a No Movie, Valdez proudly holds her "No Oscar" while wearing a low-cut, shimmery gold halter dress.

17. On West L.A. punk, see Spitz and Mullen (2001) and Spheeris (1981). On East L.A. punk, see Tompkins and Gunckel (2008); D. Gamboa (2005); Kun (2003, 2008); Habell-Pallán (2005, 2008); and Reyes and Waldman (1998). During the Asco B period, Teresa Covarrubias was also a collaborator in Asco. At a fashion show titled *Moda Chicana* at California State University, Los Angeles, in 1982, Chicana artists modeled paper fashions. In the show, Covarrubias pays homage to Patssi Valdez by appropriating the motif of the Virgen de Guadalupe, referencing Valdez's dress as La Virgen in Asco's *Walking Mural* (1972). *Moda Chicana* also included paper fashions by Diane Gamboa.

18. Patssi Valdez, e-mail message to author, July 28, 2010.

19. It is my hope that this essay will prompt further discussion and research into Valdez's clothing and dress as part of her self-fashioning, particularly research on Valdez's specific clothing styles and shopping. For instance, Valdez explains that the silver platform boots she wears in the Asco No Movie performance *The Gores* (1974) were bought in London by her sister. Valdez also describes how she shopped at "Zsa Zsa's" in downtown Los Angeles and that she was friends with the "Zsa Zsa sisters." Information from "Asco Artist-Led Walk Through: Gronk and Patssi Valdez" on October 27, 2011.

20. Patssi Valdez, e-mail message to author, July 28, 2010.

21. As scholars have recently noted, the period prior to the 1980s was characterized by fluidity between the West L.A. and East L.A. punk scenes (see Tompkins and Gunckel 2008). Scholars consider East Los Angeles punk to have officially taken root in 1980 in response to the exclusion of East L.A. bands from the West L.A. punk scene. The East Los Angeles punk scene included the bands Los Illegals, The Brat, Thee Undertakers, The Odd Squad, and The Plugz, among others who played at Vex in East L.A. The Chicano punk movement also took the form of backyard parties, which has been overlooked in histories of East L.A. punk; see Alvarado (2001).

22. On the juncture between East L.A. punk music and visual arts, see Tompkins and Gunckel (2008) and Kun (2003).

23. Gronk's references to punk can be found in his 1978 show at Los Angeles Contemporary Exhibitions (LACE) titled "Dreva-Gronk: Art Meets Punk." In an e-mail correspondence on August 12, 2010, Harry Gamboa Jr. describes The Vex as an "isolated situation that was embraced by Willie Herrón and attended by many," indicating that it would be incorrect to "assert that Vex influenced Asco."

24. *Hot Pink* (1984), a six-minute 8mm film directed by Valdez, captures 1980s L.A. punk youth culture. In the short, a group of young men and women are engaged in punk self-fashioning, hugging, touching, and kissing one another while gazing into the camera. They wear heavy makeup, spike collars, and black-and-white clothing and are shot in pink tones. *Hot Pink* had its public debut in "Phantom Sightings" at the Los Angeles County Museum of Art (LACMA) in April 2008; six months later it screened at the Austrian Film Museum in Vienna. Valdez's *Downtown Los Angeles* (1983), a hand-colored, three-panel photo-collage, features the same young men and women who appear in *Hot Pink* and was part of the traveling exhibit "Chicano Art: Resistance and Affirmation" (CARA) that began at the UCLA Wight Art Gallery in 1990.

25. For further discussion of Diane Gamboa's paper fashions, see Pérez (2007).

26. The exhibit displayed a series of mixed-media photo collages produced by Valdez in 1987, including *Self-Portrait, No! No! No!,* and *Man among the Ruins,* all of which exemplify a feminist punk aesthetic with the use of jagged and torn photographs.

27. Valdez's other solo works while in Asco function as commentaries on gendered oppression and femininity. These include mixed-media collages, *Jovita Zamora Photobooth*

Self-Portrait (1974–1975) and other photo-booth self-portraits and drawings that she created for *Regeneración* from 1974 to 1975. On these collages, Gunckel explains, "they conduct a complex and painful self-portrait that also function as an examination and deconstruction of femininity and self as performance" (2011, 163). For a further discussion and images of these multimedia works produced while Valdez was in Asco, see Gunckel (2011).

28. As a solo artist prior to working with the medium of painting in the 1980s, Valdez created many photos and multimedia collages, which incorporate elements of fashion and glamour, with some works drawing on punk aesthetics. Some of these include (all created circa 1980) *Bonne Nuit, Phyrah, Autumn, Homage to DeDe, Asco Paper Fashion Show, Billy Wearing Patssi Valdez Paper Fashion, Betti Salas in Web Green,* and *DeDe Diaz in Hot Pink.*

29. These exhibits include "Aqui y Alla," Los Angeles Municipal Art Gallery, Los Angeles, CA (1989); "Le Démon des Anges," Halle du Centre de Recherche pour le Developpement Culturel, Nantes, France (touring exhibition) (1989); and "Domestic Allegories," Galeria de la Raza, San Francisco, CA (1991).

30. See the *Chicano Art : Resistance and Affirmation, 1965–1985 (CARA)* exhibit catalogue; for a thorough discussion of CARA and its shortcomings in terms of gender representation, see Gaspar de Alba (1998).

31. Chicana/o artists who have exhibited and/or are represented at the Daniel Saxon Gallery include Carlos Almaraz, Stevel La Ponise, Leo Limón, James De La Torre, the late Gilbert "Magu" Lugán, Delilah Montoya, John Valadez, as well as other Asco member Harry Gamboa Jr.

32. Mesa-Bains also notes how Valdez used "party supplies; discarded movie-sets; the detritus from the edges of downtown Los Angeles; and bits and pieces from the bazaar and the Mercado" (2003, 40).

33. Méndez-Negrete's autobiographical *testimonio* of domestic violence and sexual abuse, *Las Hijas de Juan*, narrates the sexual violence and abuse that Méndez-Negrete and her sibling endured at the hands of her father (2006).

34. *Freedom from Want* appeared in the March 6, 1943 issue of the *Saturday Evening Post.*

35. Terms used in Mexican writer Rosario Castellano's short essay "'Leccion de Cocina/ The Cooking Lesson" (Ahern 1988, 207).

36. Valdez's focus on domestic interiors as spaces impacted by violence and abuse consistently shifted after her 1999 retrospective "Precarious Comfort." This exhibit did include a few paintings that represented Valdez's shift to a more utopian rendering of home, such as her 1997 painting *Saturday.* This painting depicts a brightly colored domestic interior with wide curtains that open to a view of an ocean with sailboats.

37. In her study of Rushdie's *Midnight's Children* (1981), Sarah Upstone suggests that magical realism "imbue[s] the home with an active presence that offers particular opportunit[ies] for subversion" and that magical realism opens up the home "as an explicitly political space by an acknowledgement of its trauma," and therefore the house becomes a space of resistance (2007, 264).

38. Valdez's painting *The Magic Room* toured in the "Arte Latino: Treasures from the Smithsonian American Art Museum" exhibit in 2000.

39. When Nava was seeking financing for the film, he saw an exhibit of Patssi's paintings at the Daniel Saxon Gallery, most likely works in her solo exhibition "Distant Memories" in 1992. Nava was intrigued by the "cartoonish" quality of her paintings, as well as their magical realist elements. While the film was in preproduction, Nava invited Valdez to work with art director Barry Robinson in shaping the look of *Mi Familia.*

40. As Jimmy Smits noted in an interview about his involvement in *Mi Familia*, "Most of the people on 'My Family' are working for less than they usually get paid because they feel it's important that movies like this get made" (McKenna 1995).

41. Valdez also worked as a design consultant for the theater production of *Luminarias* and for director José Luis Valenzuela's direction of the film version of *Luminarias*, another big(ger) budget Hollywood production like Gregory Nava's *Mi Familia*, although not as popular at the box office. *Luminarias* provides a female-centered narrative of Latina experiences in Los Angeles, following middle-class Latinas and the close networks they forge as they confront difficult personal relationships.

CHAPTER 6 — REDIRECTING CHICANA/LATINA REPRESENTATIONS

1. The Home and Garden Television network is distributed in 89 million US households, with headquarters in Knoxville, Tennessee, and offices in New York, Los Angeles, Detroit, Chicago, and Atlanta; HGTV is also distributed internationally. The website states, "HGTV owns 33 percent of HGTV Canada and provides much of the Canadian network's daily programming." HGTV branded programming can also be seen in 47 countries, including Japan, Australia, Thailand, the Philippines, Hungary, the Czech Republic, and the Slovak Republic. http://www.hgtv.com/about-us/about-us/index.html.

2. The episode (Episode HMH-S) aired December 1, 2003, 10 a.m. ET/PT. This is not the only time Rodríguez's home has been publicly depicted. The Chicano rock band Los Lobos used Rodríguez's home for the booklet of their CD *Good Morning Aztlán* (2002), which includes staged photos of various scenes in her home intended to represent a "Chicano aesthetic" (Diane Rodríguez, personal interview, June 21, 2004).

3. The segments are titled: "Mexican Holiday Décor" (Rodriguez's home), "Embossed Box," "Japanese Style-Wrapping," "Screen-Tree Topper," "African American Holiday," "Fruit Garland," "Stacked Centerpiece," "Aromatic Ornaments," "Barn Home Holiday Décor," "Modern Accents," "Wrap the House!," and "Copper Luminarias."

4. This quote was used on the website to promote the episode. Kitty Bartholomew states the following on the program, "Because she lives so close to the Mexican border she's able to find decorations that celebrate her Mexican American heritage." *Handmade Holiday with Kitty Bartholomew*, Home and Garden Television (HGTV). Episode HMH-S. Aired December 1, 2003.

5. *Handmade Holiday with Kitty Bartholomew*, Home and Garden Television (HGTV). Episode HMH-S. Aired December 1, 2003.

6. *Handmade Holiday with Kitty Bartholomew*, Home and Garden Television (HGTV). Episode HMH-S. Aired December 1, 2003.

7. Diane Rodríguez, personal interview, June 21, 2004.

8. The designated ethnic homes, specifically "Mexican Holiday Décor" and "Japanese Style-Wrapping," are integrated into the program only as cultural styles and not as ethnic and racial identities within the US nation. The exception is "African American Holiday," which invokes African American identity and culture with the phrase *African American*; despite this labeling, this segment also generalizes African American culture and identity.

9. Diane Rodríguez, personal interview, June 21, 2004.

10. Rodríguez further explains, "She [Patssi] brought in a lot of raw materials and then she brought the concept of the Christmas tree of various sizes, there were like seven of them and she had designed those, and she brought a nativity scene and she set up. I brought a lot of things I had gotten, all these saris that I had bought in Paris […] and I

had a lot of things that I supplemented [. . .] in the design." Diane Rodríguez, personal interview, June 21, 2004.

11. Diane Rodríguez, personal interview, June 21, 2004.

12. Diane Rodríguez, personal interview, June 21, 2004.

13. In this administrative role at the Mark Taper, Rodríguez actively supported new works by playwrights seeking to represent diverse images of Latina/os in US theater, producing scripts by now well-known Latina/o dramatists such as Nilo Cruz, Octavio Solis, Oliver Mayer, Ricardo Bracho, Ann García Romero, Marga Gomez, Evelina Fernandez, and Cherríe Moraga, to name a few.

14. The Latina playwrights Rodríguez has supported include Caridad Svich, Monica Palacios, and Carmelita Tropicana, among many others.

15. Rodríguez has directed Latina/o plays and performances by Dan Guerrero, Culture Clash, Migdalia Cruz, John Leguizamo, Luis Alfaro, and Luis Santeiro, among others.

16. Rodríguez has not only directed plays by Latina/o playwrights and stories focused on the Latina/o experience. She directed Erik Patterson's *Sick* (2010) for Playwrights Arena and Les Thomas's *Cave Quest* (2010) at East West Players, both in Los Angeles. She also directed Zina Camblin's *And Her Hair Went with Her* (2008) for the Fountain Theater in Los Angeles, Lynn Nottage's *Intimate Apparel* (2007) at City Theatre in Pittsburgh, and John Belluso's *Pryetown* (2006) for City Theatre and Playwrights Arena in Los Angeles. Among her many accolades, Rodríguez also received an Obie Award for Best Ensemble in 2007 for her performance in Heather Woodbury's two-part epic, *Tale of 2 Cities/An American Joyride on Multiple Tracks* at UCLA Live and at PS 122 in New York City.

17. Diane Rodríguez, personal interview, June 21, 2004.

18. Diane Rodríguez, personal interview, June 21, 2004.

19. Diane Rodríguez, personal interview, June 21, 2004.

20. The most recent exceptions to this racialized casting of Latinas with darker features in the marginal domestic role would include the major roles played by Jennifer Lopez, as maid Marisa Venturea, in *Maid in Manhattan* (2002) and Paz Vega, as maid and nanny Flor Moreno, in *Spanglish* (2004). Illustrating mobility within "the racialized poles of whiteness and blackness" (Ovalle 2011), actor Jennifer López—who after becoming successful in mainstream film and music, lightened and sometimes straightened her hair, thereby conforming to Hollywood beauty standards—went back to her natural hair color and lowered her hairline for her appearance of Marisa Ventura in *Maid in Manhattan*, suggesting how she conformed to dominant stereotypes of Latina maids.

21. For example, Morrison has played maids in both the crime drama *Columbo* (1993) and in the film *Troop Beverly Hills* (1989).

22. This anecdote is noted in many online biographies for Morrison.

23. Even though Morrison's character Rosario is horribly treated by her boss Karen on *Will & Grace*, Morrison credits the show's writers and producers for creating an atmosphere in which she could have flexibility to portray Rosario as "an older, Hispanic woman who is bright and smart and can hold her own," often resulting in comedic sparring between the two characters. For her role as Rosario, Morrison received three American Latino Media Arts (ALMA) awards for Supporting Actress (Biography www.shelley morrison.com).

24. Ontiveros's well-known domestic roles included Rosalita in *Goonies* (1985), Nora Manning in *As Good as It Gets* (1997), Louisa on *Veronica's Closet* (1997), Pilar on *Pasadena* (2001), and Lupe on *Leap of Faith* (2002).

25. The California courts quickly nullified Proposition 187 as unconstitutional. Congress later passed the Illegal Immigration Reform and Immigrant Responsibility Act in 1996, which, like Proposition 187, restricted access to healthcare for undocumented immigrants, except for emergency care. The act also increased the number of border patrol agents and technology, which further militarized the border zone (Segura and Zavella 2007, 10).

26. Two examples of Hollywood films that feature Latina maids in a narrative that strips Latinas of their own reproductive labor and configure the role of Latina laborers to service white domesticity include *Maid in Manhattan* (2002) and *Spanglish* (2004). Isabel Molina-Guzmán explains how these two films elide the exploitative conditions of Latina domestic workers within romanticized plots and function as mainstream media representations of Latina labor that are "cleansed of anti-immigration/imperialistic discourses and rearticulated through safer, historically familiar, and more comfortable representations of Latina domesticity and hyper-femininity" (2010, 20). This representation of Latina laborers as beholden to white women's reproductive capabilities shares similarities with the "mammy" stereotype that frames the depiction of African American maids in Hollywood film. K. Sue Jewell argues that mammies performed "tasks of domesticity and caring for the socialization and emotional needs of children and adult family members in her owner's or employer's family, while relegating the needs of her own family" (1993, 39).

27. Doerr's novel was published the same year as Chicano author Arturo Islas's *The Rain God*. Islas was a professor of English at Stanford from 1971 to 1991 during the same time and in the same program in which Doerr took creative writing classes. Islas's *The Rain God* narrates the lives of three generations of a binational Mexican American family, the Angels, living on the US-Mexican border. Islas's text is told from Islas's subject position as a gay Chicano professor, poet, and novelist who presents a transnational and queer perspective of Mexican American communities in the United States. The lack of attention to Islas's queer narrative of life on the border suggests that his text was not considered as "authentic" or as important as Doerr's. All the press, marketing, and praise went to Doerr's novel for presenting an "authentic" account of "Mexico." *The Rain God* did receive acclaim, but not from the mainstream media and press. Coincidently, *The Rain God*, like Doerr's text, received one of the other Bay Area Review Book Review Awards (Aldama 2004). Unlike Doerr, Islas had difficulty finding a publisher for his manuscript, and it took him over a decade to get his novel published. The popularity of Doerr's *Stones for Ibarra* over Islas's *The Rain God* suggests the power of whiteness and heteronormativity in the publishing industry in the 1980s (Barvosa-Carter 2000).

28. Doerr's awards for *Stones for Ibarra* include the Bay Area Book Reviewers Award, the Godal Medal of the Commonwealth Club of California, and the American Academy of Arts and Letters Harold D. Vursell Award.

29. Doerr spent a lot of time in Mexico, as her husband's family owned a mine in Mexico. Referring to her time in Mexico, Doerr says, "It is a mystical place" and "The Mexican spirit is very remarkable, but I'm still puzzling it out. It's not that they don't get sad, but they seem to take a long, long view or have a depth of perception that we lack." This quote is from an interview that took place at Doerr's home in Pasadena; the author begins the essay describing Doerr at her home "working out back with her Mexican gardener. The two finish their conversation in Spanish, taking exuberant delight in the wisteria that cascades from an expansive overhead arbor" (Daley 1997).

30. The fact that Doerr was 73 when she published this text, after going back to college in 1975 at Stanford and taking creative writing courses while earning a BA in history, seems to also be what made her novel so intriguing. Each review mentions with astonishment

that Doerr at 73 published *Stones for Ibarra,* almost seeming to praise her for this fact more than the novel itself (of course, this act is no small feat).

31. Hallmark Hall of Fame productions generally support a conservative notion of morality and propriety, so it is not surprising that the series chose to produce *Stones for Ibarra,* which fits well with other Hallmark Hall of Fame films focused on family values, particularly as the film is about a heterosexual Anglo American couple who seek to reconnect with their family history. The Hallmark Channel began as two separate religious cable channels and was renamed "The Faith and Values Channel" in 1993. The network began to eliminate religious programming in 1994 in favor of health and cooking shows, exercise shows, and family-friendly dramas and movies. The channel was officially renamed The Hallmark Channel on August 5, 2001, at which time the company eliminated religious programming, but maintained a focus on family and drama shows, classic sitcoms, and drama movies ("About Us," Crown Media Press, crownmediapress.com).

32. The character Tonto, played by Jay Silverheels, on the popular television show *The Lone Ranger* in the 1950s, is a strong example of the silent native "other" in Hollywood. Tonto speaks minimally and, when he does speak, he speaks in stereotypical broken English.

33. During World War II, many Mexican migrants came to San Francisco to fill worker shortages during the war. Prior to World War II, most Mexican immigrants and Mexican Americans lived in two neighborhoods, the South of Market (SOMA) zone and in an area surrounding Nuestra Señora de Guadalupe Church in North Beach. Due to wartime production needs, Latina/os from North Beach and SOMA were pushed south toward the Mission District (Sandoval 2002).

34. *Stones for Ibarra,* dir. Jack Gold. VCR cover, 1988.

35. INTAR was founded in 1966 and is the oldest Latino theater company in the United States producing work in English. Since its founding, INTAR has presented 65 world premieres of new plays by US Latino authors. The company's Hispanic Playwrights in Residence Laboratory, created and run by María Irene Fornes from 1981 until 1992, fostered and trained many of the most prominent Latino playwrights in the American theater, including Migdalia Cruz, Eduardo Machado, Carmelita Tropicana, and Nilo Cruz. http://www.intar.org.

36. Diane Rodríguez, personal interview, March 3, 2005.

37. Such critiques of Catholicism are not new to Latina theater and literature, and many Latina authors depict mothers internalizing and transmitting patriarchal views of gender to their children within feminist narratives. See Cherríe Moraga, *Heroes and Saints and Other Plays* (New York, West End Press, 1994) and Helena María Viramontes, *Under the Feet of Jesus* (New York: Plume, 1996).

38. Lilian's view that the hospital is not a safe place for her or her baby is not unfounded. In the 1970s, many Latinas, having no choice but to seek health care at county hospitals, were ill-treated and the target of medical procedures intended to stop their reproduction. The most extreme example is the forced sterilization of Chicanas at the Los Angeles County Medical Center during the 1970s. Scholar Virgina Espino points out how "Women came to the facility to give birth, and while they were 'under the duress of labor, drugged, and confined,' the doctors cut their fallopian tubes" (2000, 66). The Puerto Rican medical system also has a history of targeting Latinas' reproduction. In Puerto Rico, one-third of the female population was sterilized during the 1970s as a "population control policy" (Castillo 1997, 311). It is also worth noting that the US Department of Health, Education and Welfare played a major role in providing partial funding to Puerto Rico's sterilization program.

39. "Interview with Playwright Migdalia Cruz," Production Information from Lee Strasberg Website. http://www.strasberg.com, 2002.

40. Diane Rodríguez, personal interview, March 3, 2005.

41. Diane Rodríguez, personal interview, March 3, 2005.

42. Diane Rodríguez, personal interview, March 3, 2005.

43. Diane Rodríguez, personal interview, March 3, 2005.

44. Rodriguez did not indicate the reasons for Cruz's approval of the lighting change in my interview. My assumption is that the upbeat Michael Jackson music would have overwhelmingly shifted the tenor of the final scene, while the use of lighting might have worked appropriately with Cruz's configuration of Lilian as a Virgin Mary figure throughout the play.

45. Diane Rodríguez, personal interview, March 3, 2005.

46. The photographic still is included in Julio Martinez, "The Have-Little," rev. of *The Have-Little*, dir. Diane Rodríguez, *Variety.com*. http://beta.variety.com/review/VE1117917323.

47. Dave De Piño, "*The Have-Little*," rev. of *The Have-Little*, dir. Diane Rodríguez, *Showmag.com: An Online Entertainment Magazine*, www.showmag.com/theatre/theatre441 .html, 2/17/2005.

EPILOGUE

1. Following Arizona's lead, Georgia and Alabama have created similar legislation. In April 2011, Georgia enacted HB 87, or the Illegal Immigration Reform and Enforcement Act, an anti-immigration law like SB 1070, which empowers law enforcement to check the immigration status of those suspected to be in the country "illegally." In June 2011, Alabama's legislature signed into law HB 56, which is considered by many to be the nation's harshest anti-immigrant law, as it requires law enforcement to check the papers of anyone they suspect of being undocumented, makes it a crime to be without status, and directs and authorizes public schools to check the legal status of their students, among other anti–human rights regulations (Support Our Law Enforcement and Safe Neighbors Act, 2010; Beason-Hammon Alabama Taxpayer and Citizen Protection Act, 2011).

2. The controversial portions of SB 1070, including the requirement that police check the immigration status of those stopped or arrested, were blocked by federal judge Susan Bolton with a preliminary injunction in July 2010. In June 2012, the US Supreme Court upheld the portion of the bill that enables law enforcement to conduct immigration status checks, yet struck down the three other provisions, citing them as violations of the United States Constitution.

3. C. Alejandra Elenes, "Mujeres, Migration & Arizona's SB1070: Codifying Patriarchy and White Privilege," *MALCS Mujeres Talk* (blog), January 17, 2011, http://www.malcs .org/mujeres-talk/mujeres-migration-arizonas-sb1070-codifying-patriarchy-and-white -privilege/

4. Los Angeles–based artist Alma López is best known for her digital print *Our Lady* (1999), which ignited angry and impassioned protests in 2001 as part of the "Cyber Arte: Tradition Meets Technology" exhibit at the Museum of International Folk Art in Santa Fe, New Mexico. The print represents a computer-generated print of artist Raquel Salinas, adorned in roses, wearing a gown of pre-Columbian symbols while standing on a black crescent moon. She is accompanied by a bare-breasted female butterfly angel, depicted by performance artist Raquel Gutierrez, located in a supporting role underneath Salinas. Members of the local Latina/o religious community, fundamentalist Catholics, local and national religious activists, and "protestor pilgrims" with a colonial and nationalist

mindset attacked *Our Lady* for its challenge to patriarchal and heteronormative frameworks of gender and sexuality (Gaspar de Alba 2011, 213).

5. The California courts quickly nullified Proposition 187 as unconstitutional. Congress later passed the Illegal Immigration Reform and Immigrant Responsibility Act in 1996, which, like Proposition 187, restricted access to healthcare for undocumented immigrants, except for emergency care. The act also increased border patrol and technology, which further militarized the border zone (Segura and Zavella 2007, 10).

6. According to López, "I believe they are Mexican, probably 1930s. They were probably from one photo which I most likely cut out the areas I wanted to include. I don't believe I used the entire photo" (Alma López, E-mail message to author, January 14, 2001).

7. Maquiladoras have been a key site in the exploitation of Mexican and Central American women's labor (Gaspar de Alba and Guzmán 2010; Salzinger 2007; Wright 2007). Many women who work in the maquiladoras produce the digital technology that US residents and citizens use on a daily basis, including computer and television parts for major electronic corporations (Funari and De La Torre 2006). These women work in exploitative working conditions, in which their bodies succumb to not only health problems but also to the real threat of physical danger through sexual assault, as well as rape and murder. This has been the particular case of the massive numbers of women who have "disappeared" along the Juarez-El Paso border (Portillo 2001; Gaspar de Alba and Guzmán 2010).

8. This integration predates the passage of NAFTA, as the two countries became systematically linked in an economic and political restructuring that relied on the low-wage, flexible labor of immigrants outside the United States (Segura and Zavella 2007, 2, 5). The Border Industrialization Program (BIP), for example, drew women from Mexico and Latin America to the border region for work in the maquiladoras. NAFTA only served to formally increase the development of this industry (Segura and Zavella 2007, 12).

9. In Los Angeles, the majority of garment workers today are Latina/o immigrants from Mexico, El Salvador, and Guatemala, and approximately 58 percent are women (Bonacich and Appelbaum 2000). A 2000 census reported that 70 percent of garment workers were Latina/o, the majority of whom were Mexican immigrants, and 15 to 20 percent were Asian, particularly Chinese (Lu and Mak 2004).

10. Industrial homework transfers production by garment workers in their homes and as a result, shifts the operating costs, including workspace, electricity, and water, to the workers themselves, who already live in poor neighborhoods and homes (Miraftab 2007, 269).

11. The implementation of NAFTA, combined with the lifting of tariffs and quotas in order to increase trade of goods and services, resulted in the loss of thousands of textile and garment jobs in Los Angeles, which continues today. Despite these losses, however, the California apparel business continues to be a $24 billion industry with approximately 100,000 garment workers and 5,000 factories, and these figures do not include the informal economy. "Free Trade's Threat to California Garment Workers," Fact Sheet A, *Sweatshop Watch Report*, 2004.

12. Led by Rose Pesotta, a Russian Jewish immigrant dressmaker and ILGWU organizer from New York, the largely Mexican American female local union in Los Angeles began a Dressmakers' Strike in 1933 to protest their working conditions. The strike was the result of a strenuous organizing campaign that signed up workers using Spanish and English media, thereby countering a larger union discourse that believed that Latina workers were unorganizable. Many ILGWU organizers believed that, because of their social and racial position in society, Mexicanas would continue to work for low wages, and also perpetuated the gendered view that Mexican women were passive, thereby reinforcing prevalent domestic ideologies (Milkman 2006, 42). The Mexicana garment workers challenged

these beliefs because they were active leaders and participants in the Dressmaker's Strike, which lasted four weeks and affected 2,000 female workers in eighty factories (Sánchez 1995, 234).

13. The word invokes the Gold Rush of 1849, which generated over a quarter of a billion dollars in the first four years and led to a new generation of bankers who quickly turned to investing in financial ventures in the West (J. González 2000, 46). With the capitalized letters "GOLD," López also links the history of Mexican communities with those of Latina/os; it references the appropriation of gold during the Spanish conquest of the Americas (J. González 2000, 45–46).

14. With its depiction of Macrina López, the piece references Yolanda López's *Our Lady of Guadalupe: Margaret F. Stewart* (1978), part of *Guadalupe Triptych*. The other two images of Yolanda López's *Guadalupe Triptych* include *The Portrait of the Artist as the Virgen de Guadalupe*, which depicts López as a marathon runner, and *Victoria F. Franco: Our Lady of Guadalupe*, which portrays López's grandmother.

References

Ahern, Maureen, ed. 1988. *A Rosario Castellanos Reader: An Anthology of Her Poetry, Short Fiction, Essays, and Drama.* Austin: University of Texas Press.

Alarcón, Norma. 1989. "Traddutora, Traditora: A Paradigmatic Figure of Chicana Feminism." *Cultural Critique* 13: 57–87.

Aldama, Frederick Luis. 2004. *Dancing with Ghosts: A Critical Biography of Arturo Islas.* Berkeley: University of California Press.

Almaguer, Tomás. 1992. "Class and Racial Antimonies in Anglo-California: The Structural Integration of Mexicans." In *Chicano Social and Political History in the Nineteenth Century,* ed. Richard Griswold del Castillo and Manuel Hidalgo. Van Nuys: Floricanto Press.

Alonzo, Armando C. 1998. *Tejano Legacy: Rancheros and Settlers in South Texas, 1734–1900.* Albuquerque: University of New Mexico Press.

Alvarado, Jimmy. 2001. "Teenage Alcoholics: Punk Rock in East Los Angeles." *Razorcake* 3: 44–49.

Anzaldúa, Gloria. 1987. *Borderlands/La Frontera: The New Mestiza.* 3rd ed. San Francisco: Aunt Lute Books.

———. 1990. *Making Face. Making Soul: Haciendo Caras: Creative & Critical Perspectives by Feminists of Color.* San Francisco: Aunt Lute Books.

———. 2003–2004. "Speaking Across the Divide: an email interview." *SAIL: Studies in American Indian Literature* 15: 7–21.

Aranda, Pilar E. Rodríguez. 1990. "On the Solitary Fate of Being Mexican, Female, Wicked and Thirty-three: An Interview with Writer Sandra Cisneros." *The Americas Review* 18, no. 1: 65–75.

Armstrong, Nancy. 1987. *Desire and Domestic Fiction: A Political History of the Novel.* New York: Oxford University Press.

———. 1994. "Why Daughters Die: The Racial Logic of American Sentimentalism." *Yale Journal of Criticism* 7, no. 2: 1–24.

Arnold, Rebecca. 2001. *Fashion, Desire, and Anxiety: Image and Morality in the Twentieth Century.* New Brunswick, NJ: Rutgers University Press.

Arreola, Daniel. 2002. *Tejano South Texas: A Mexican American Cultural Province.* Austin: University of Texas Press.

Asencio, Marysol. 2009. *Latina/o Sexualities: Probing Powers, Passions, Practices, and Policies*. New Brunswick, NJ: Rutgers University Press.

Ayala, Elaine. 2011. "Marker to Honor Labor Leader: Celebration Is Today at Milam Park." *San Antonio Express-News* online edition, December 21.

Baca Zinn, Maxine. 1975. "Political Familism: Toward Sex Role Equality in Chicano Families." *Aztlán: International Journal of Chicano Research* 6, no. 1: 13–26.

Baird, David, ed. 2009. *Frommer's San Antonio and Austin*. New York: John Wiley & Sons.

Balderrama, Francisco E., and Raymond Rodríguez. 1995. *Decade of Betrayal: Mexican Repatriation in the 1930s*. Albuquerque: University of New Mexico Press.

Barvosa-Carter, Edwina. 2000. "Breaking the Silence: Developments in the Publication and Politics of Chicana Creative Writing, 1973–1998." In *Chicano Renaissance: Contemporary Cultural Trends*, ed. David R. Maciel, Isidro D. Ortiz, and María Herrera-Sobek, 261–284. Tucson: University of Arizona Press.

Baym, Nina. 1978. *Woman's Fiction: A Guide to Novels by and about Women in America, 1820–1870*. Ithaca, NY: Cornell University Press.

Bechtol, Ron. 1987. "Chili: A San Antonio Tradition." *San Antonio Monthly*, May, 31.

Behrman, Daniel. 1951. "Patzcauro: First H.Q. in the Fight against Ignorance." *UNESCO Courier* 5, no. 6: 7–12.

Benavidez, Max. 2007. *Gronk*. A Ver: Revisioning Art History, vol. 1. Los Angeles: UCLA Chicano Studies Research Center Press. Distributed by University of Minnesota Press.

Berg, Charles Ramírez. 2002. *Latino Images in Film: Stereotypes, Subversion, and Resistance*. Austin: University of Texas Press.

Blackwelder, Julia Kirk. 1984. *Women of the Depression: Caste and Culture in San Antonio, 1929–1939*. College Station: Texas A&M University Press.

Blackwell, Maylei. 2011. *¡Chicana Power!: Contested Histories of Feminism in the Chicano Movement*. Austin: University of Texas Press.

Bonacich, Edna, and Richard P. Appelbaum, eds. 2000. *Behind the Label: Inequality in the Los Angeles Apparel Industry*. Berkeley: University of California Press.

Bost, Suzanne. 2003. "Women and Chile at the Alamo: Feeding US Colonial Mythology." *Nepantla: Views from South* 4, no. 3: 493–522.

Broyard, Anatole. 1983. "Books of the Times," rev. of *Stones for Ibarra*, by Harriet Doerr. *New York Times*, December 7.

Broyles-González, Yolanda. 1994. *El Teatro Campesino: Theatre in the Chicano Movement*. Austin: University of Texas Press.

———. 2001. *Lydia Mendoza's Life in Music/La historia de Lydia Mendoza*. New York: Oxford University Press.

Bullock, Alice. 1968. "A Patrona of the Old Pattern." *The New Mexican*, May 19.

Bushick, Frank H. 1927. "The Chili Queens of San Antonio." *Frontier Times*. Austin: Western Publications.

Butler, Judith. 1990. *Gender Trouble: Feminism and the Subversion of Identity*. New York: Routledge.

Cabeza de Baca Gilbert, Fabiola. 1934. *Los Alimentos y su Preparación*. Circular no. 129. State College: New Mexico Agricultural Extension Service.

———. 1935. *Boletín de Conservar*. Circular no. 133. State College: New Mexico Agricultural Extension Service.

———. 1942. "New Mexican Diets." *Journal of Home Economics* 34.9: 668–669.

———. 1952. "UNESCO's Pilot Project." *New Mexico Extension News* 32.7: 4–5.

———. 1970. *Historic Cookery*. Santa Fe: Ancient City Press. Orig. pub. 1939.

———. 1975. Interview by Paula Thaidigsman, August 29. Cassette tape, Women in New Mexico Collection, Center for Southwest Research, Albuquerque, NM.

———. 1983. Interview by Ruleen Lazzell, Albuquerque, Good Shepherd Manor, February 9. Cassette Tape, Rio Grande Historical Collections, Oral History Collection, New Mexico State University, Las Cruces, NM.

———. 1994. *We Fed Them Cactus.* Albuquerque: University of New Mexico Press. Orig. pub. 1954.

———. 2005. *The Good Life: New Mexico Traditions and Food.* Santa Fe: Museum of New Mexico Press. Orig. pub. 1949.

Cacho, Lisa. 2000. "'The People of California Are Suffering': The Ideology of White Injury in Discourses of Immigration." *Cultural Values* 4, no. 4: 389–418.

Calderón, Héctor. 1991. "The Novel and the Community of Readers: Rereading Tomás Rivera's *Y no se lo tragó la tierra.*" In *Criticism in the Borderlands: Studies in Chicano Literature, Culture and Ideology,* ed. Héctor Calderón and José David Saldívar, 97–113. Durham, NC: Duke University Press.

Calvo, Luz. 2000. "Impassioned Icons: The Digital Art of Alma López." Paper presented to the American Studies Association Annual Meeting, Detroit, MI.

Candelario, Ginetta E. B. 2007. *Black behind the Ears: Dominican Racial Identity from Museums to Beauty Shops.* Durham, NC: Duke University Press.

Castillo, Ana. 1994. *Massacre of the Dreamers: Essays on Xicanisma.* New York: Plume Books.

———. 1997. "Massacre of Dreams: Essays on Xicanisma." In *Chicana Feminist Thought: The Basic Historical Writings,* ed. Alma M. García and Mario T. García, 310–312. New York: Routledge.

Chauncey, George. 1994. *Gay New York: Gender, Urban Culture, and the Making of the Gay World, 1890–1940.* New York: Basic Books.

Chang, Grace. 2000. Disposable Domestics: Immigrant Women Workers in the Global Economy. Cambridge: South End Press.

Chávez, Angélico. 1992. *Origins of New Mexico Families: A Genealogy of the Spanish Colonial Period.* Santa Fe: Museum of New Mexico Press.

Chávez, Leo R. 2007. "A Glass Half Empty: Latina Reproduction and Public Discourse." In *Women and Migration in the U.S.-Mexico Borderlands: A Reader,* ed. Denise A. Segura and Patricia Zavella, 67–91. Durham, NC: Duke University Press.

Chavoya, C. Ondine. 1998. "Pseudographic Cinema: Asco's No-Movies." *Performance Research* 3, no. 1: 1–14.

Chicano Liberation Youth Conference. 1972. "El Plan Espiritual de Aztlán." In *Aztlán: An Anthology of Mexican American Literature,* ed. Luis Valdez and Stan Steiner, 402–406. New York: Vintage.

Cisneros, Sandra. 1984. *The House on Mango Street.* Houston: Arte Público Press.

———. 1991a. *The House on Mango Street.* New York: Vintage Contemporaries.

———. 1991b. *Woman Hollering Creek and Other Stories.* New York: Vintage Contemporaries.

———. 1994a. *Hairs/Pelitos.* New York: Dragonfly Books.

———. 1994b. *The House on Mango Street.* New York: Alfred A. Knopf.

———. 2009a. *The House on Mango Street.* Twenty-fifth Anniversary Edition. New York: Vintage Contemporaries.

———. 2009b. Interview by Renee Montagne, April 9. Transcript, "'House on Mango Street' Celebrates 25 Years." National Public Radio (NPR).

———. 2011. Interview by *Talk of the Nation,* January 27. "New and Established Writers Redefine Chicano Literature." National Public Radio (NPR).

Coote, Robert James. 2001. *The Eclectic Odyssey of Atlee B. Ayres, Architect.* College Station: Texas A&M University Press.

Cortez, Constance. 2010. *Carmen Lomas Garza.* A Ver: Revisioning Art History, vol. 5. Los Angeles: UCLA Chicano Studies Research Center Press. Distributed by University of Minnesota Press.

Cotera, María Eugenia. 2007. "Recovering 'Our' History: *Caballero* and the Gendered Politics of Form." *Aztlán: A Journal of Chicano Studies* 32, no. 2: 157–171.

———. 2008. *Native Speakers: Ella Deloria, Zora Neale Hurston, Jovita González and the Poetics of Culture.* Austin: University of Texas Press.

Craik, Jennifer. 1994. *The Face of Fashion: Cultural Studies in Fashion.* New York: Routledge.

Cruz, Felicia J. 2001. "On the 'Simplicity' of Sandra Cisneros's *The House on Mango Street.*" *Modern Fiction Studies* 47, no. 4: 910–946.

Cruz, Migdalia. 1996. "The Have-Little." In *Contemporary Plays by Women of Color: An Anthology,* ed. Kathy A. Perkins and Roberta Uno, 106–126. New York: Routledge.

Daley, Yvonne. 1997. "Late Bloomer." *Stanford Magazine* online edition, November/ December.

Davalos, Karen Mary. 2001. *Exhibiting Mestizaje. Mexican (American) Museums in the Diaspora.* Albuquerque: University of New Mexico Press.

———. 2008. *Yolanda M. López.* A Ver: Revisioning Art History, vol. 2. Los Angeles: UCLA Chicano Studies Research Center Press. Distributed by University of Minnesota Press.

Dávila, Arlene. 2001. *Latinos, Inc.: The Marketing and Making of a People.* Berkeley: University of California Press.

Davis, Elmer. 1942. *Journal of Home Economics* 34, no. 9: 633–634.

De Genova, Nicholas. 2006. "The Legal Production of Mexican/Migrant 'Illegality.'" In *Latinos and Citizenship: The Dilemma of Belonging,* ed. Suzanne Oboler, 61–90. New York: Palgrave Macmillan.

Deutsch, Sarah. 1987. *No Separate Refuge: Culture, Class, and Gender on an Anglo-Hispanic Frontier in the American Southwest, 1880–1940.* New York: Oxford University Press.

Donkin, Ellen and Susan Clement, eds. 1993. *Upstaging Big Daddy: Directing Theater as if Gender and Race Matter.* Ann Arbor: University of Michigan Press.

Douglas, Ann. 1977. *The Feminization of American Culture.* New York: Anchor Books.

Dyer, Richard. 2008. *Stars.* 2nd ed. London: British Film Institute.

Ebert, Roger. 1995. "My Family." Review of *Mi Familia,* dir. Gregory Nava. *Chicago Sun-Times* online edition, May 3.

Enloe, Cynthia. 1989. *Bananas, Beaches, and Bases: Making Feminist Sense of International Politics.* Berkeley: University of California Press.

Espino, Virginia. 2000. "'Woman Sterilized as They Give Birth': Forced Sterilization and the Chicana Resistance in the 1970s." In *Las Obreras: Chicana Politics of Work and Family,* ed. Vicki L. Ruiz. Los Angeles: UCLA Chicano Studies Research Paper Publications.

Espinoza, Dionne. 2001. "'Revolutionary Sisters': Women's Solidarity and Collective Identification among Chicana Brown Berets in East Los Angeles, 1967–1970." *Aztlán: A Journal of Chicano Studies* 26, no. 1: 17–58.

Everett, Donald E. 1975. *San Antonio: The Flavor of Its Past, 1845–1898.* San Antonio: Trinity University Press.

Fanon, Frantz. 1963. *The Wretched of the Earth.* Trans. Constance Farrington. New York: Grove Press.

Fish, Peter. 2003. "Extraordinary Ibarra—Western Wanderings," rev. of *Stones for Ibarra*, by Harriet Doerr. *Sunset* online edition, March.

Fisher, Lewis F. 1996. *Saving San Antonio: The Precarious Preservation of a Heritage.* Lubbock: Texas Tech University Press.

Flores, Richard R. 2002. *Remembering the Alamo: Memory, Modernity, and the Master Symbol.* Austin: University of Texas Press.

Flores, William V., and Rina Benmayor, eds. 1997. *Latino Cultural Citizenship: Claiming Identity, Space, and Rights.* Boston: Beacon Press.

Foley, Kathleen. 2002. "Life's Diminishment in 'The Have-Little,'" rev. of *The Have-Little*, dir. Diane Rodríguez. *Los Angeles Times* online edition, March 21 (Home Edition), F40.

Foley, Neil. 2003. Review of *The Spanish Redemption: Heritage, Power, and Loss on New Mexico's Upper Rio Grande*, by Charles Montgomery, *American Historical Review* 108, no. 4: 1156.

Franco, Jean. 1988. "Beyond Ethnocentrism: Gender, Power, and the Third-World Intelligentsia." In *Marxism and the Interpretation of Culture*, ed. Cary Nelson and Lawrence Grossberg, 503–515. Champaign: University of Illinois Press.

Fránquiz, María, and Carol Brochin-Ceballos. 2006. "Cultural Citizenship and Latino English Language Learners." *California English: Journal of the California Association of Teachers in English.* Summer.

Fregoso, Rosa Linda. 1993. *Bronze Screen. Chicana and Chicano Film Culture.* Minneapolis: University of Minnesota Press.

———. 2003. *MeXicana Encounters: The Making of Social Identities on the Borderlands.* Berkeley: University of California Press.

Funari, Vicky, and Sergio De La Torre, dir. 2006. *Maquilapolis.* Documentary film. Produced by Vicky Funari and Sergio De La Torre.

Gamboa, Diane. 2005. "Unpopular Culture." Photo essay. KCET Departures, http://www .kcet.org/socal/departures/production-notes/unpopular-culture.html.

Gamboa, Harry Jr. 1991. "In the City of Angels, Chameleons, and Phantoms: Asco, a Case of Study of Chicano Art in Urban Tones (or, Asco Was a Four-Member Word)." In *Chicano Art: Resistance and Affirmation, 1965–1985*, ed. Richard Griswold del Castillo, Teresa McKenna, and Yvonne Yarbro-Bejarano, 121–130. Los Angeles: University of California, Wight Art Gallery.

———. 1999. Interview by Jeffrey Rangel, Los Angeles, April 1 and 16. Transcript, Smithsonian Archives of American Art, Washington, DC.

García, Juan Ramón. 1980. *Operation Wetback: The Mass Deportation of Mexican Undocumented Workers in 1954.* Westport, CT: Greenwood Press.

García, Ramón. 1997. "Patssi's Eyes." *Aztlán: A Journal of Chicano Studies* 22, no. 2: 169–180.

———. 2011. "We Love Patssi So Much: Patssi Valdez's Surrealist Looks." In *Asco Elite of the Obscure: A Retrospective*, ed. C. Ondine Chavoya and Rita Gonzalez, 326–334. Germany: Hatje Cantz.

García, Richard A. 1991. *Rise of the Mexican American Middle Class: San Antonio, 1929–1941.* College Station: Texas A & M University Press.

Garza, Carmen Lomas. 1990. *Family Pictures/Cuadros de Familia.* San Francisco: Children's Book Press.

———. 1996. *In My Family/En Mi Familia.* San Francisco: Children's Book Press.

———. 1997. Interview by Paul J. Karlstrom, San Francisco, April 10–May 27. Transcript, Smithsonian Archives of American Art, Washington, DC.

———. 2005. *Family Pictures/Cuadros de Familia.* Fifteenth Anniversary Edition. San Francisco: Children's Book Press.

Gaspar de Alba, Alicia. 1998. *Chicano Art Inside/Outside the Master's House: Cultural Politics and the CARA Exhibition.* Austin: University of Texas Press.

———. 2011. "Devil in a Rose Bikini: The Second Coming of Our Lady in Santa Fe." In *Our Lady of Controversy: Alma López's Irreverent Apparition*, ed. Alicia Gaspar de Alba and Alma López, 212–248. Austin: University of Texas Press.

Gaspar de Alba, Alicia, and Georgina Guzmán, eds. 2010. *Making a Killing: Femicide, Free Trade, and La Frontera.* Austin: University of Texas Press.

Gaspar de Alba, Alicia, and Alma López, eds. 2011. *Our Lady of Controversy: Alma López's Irreverent Apparition.* Austin: University of Texas Press.

Gere, Anne Ruggles. 1997. *Intimate Practices: Literacy and Cultural Work in U.S. Women's Clubs, 1880–1920.* Urbana: University of Illinois Press.

Gledhill, Christine, ed. 1987. *Home Is Where the Heart Is: Studies in Melodrama and the Woman's Film.* London: British Film Institute, 1987.

Goldman, Anne. 1996. *Take My Word: Autobiographical Innovations of Ethnic American Working Women.* Berkeley: University of California Press.

Gómez, Laura E. 2008. *Manifest Destinies: The Making of the Mexican American Race.* New York: New York University Press.

González, Deena J. 1999. *Refusing the Favor: The Spanish-Mexican Women of Santa Fe, 1820–1880.* New York: Oxford University Press.

González, Jennifer A. 1995. "Negotiated Frontiers: Contemporary Chicano Photography." In *From the West: Chicano Narrative Photography*, ed. Chon A. Noriega, 17–22. The Mexican Museum, San Francisco. Distributed by University of Washington Press.

———. 1999. "Archeological Devotion." In *With Other Eyes: Looking at Race and Gender in Visual Culture*, ed. Lisa Bloom, 184–212. Minneapolis: University of Minnesota Press.

———. 2003. "Invention as Critique: Neologisms in Chicana Art Theory." In *Chicana Feminisms: A Critical Reader*, ed. Gabriela F. Arredondo, Aída Hurtado, Norma Klahn, Olga Nájera-Ramírez, and Patricia Zavella, 316–323. Durham, NC: Duke University Press.

González, Jovita and Eve Raleigh [pseud. Margaret Eimer]. 1996. *Caballero: A Historical Novel.* Edited by José Limón and María Cotera. College Station: Texas A&M University Press.

González, Juan. 2000. *Harvest of Empire: A History of Latinos in America.* New York: Penguin Books.

González, Rita. 2000. "Patssi Valdez: Off the Wall and Out of the Box." *San Diego Latino Film Festival Catalogue.*

González, Rita, Howard N. Fox, and Chon A. Noriega, eds. 2008. *Phantom Sightings: Art after the Chicano Movement.* Los Angeles and Berkeley: Los Angeles County Museum of Art and University of California Press.

Griswold del Castillo, Richard. 1990. *The Treaty of Guadalupe Hidalgo: A Legacy of Conflict.* Norman: University of Oklahoma Press.

———. 1992. "The American Courts and the Treaty of Guadalupe-Hidalgo: A Century of Legal Interpretation." In *Chicano Social and Political History in the Nineteenth Century*, ed. Richard Griswold del Castillo and Manuel Hidalgo. Van Nuys, CA: Floricanto Press.

Gronk. 1997. Interview by Jeffrey Rangel, Los Angeles, January 20–23. Transcript, Smithsonian Archives of American Art, Washington, DC.

Guidotti-Hernández, Nicole M. 2011. *Unspeakable Violence: Remapping U.S. and Mexican National Imaginaries.* Durham, NC: Duke University Press.

Gunckel, Colin. 2011. "'We Were Drawing and Drawn into Each Other': Asco's Collaboration Through *Regneración.*" In *Asco Elite of the Obscure: A Retrospective*, ed. C. Ondine Chavoya and Rita Gonzalez, 151–165. Germany: Hatje Cantz.

Gutiérrez, Elena R. 2008. *Fertile Matters: The Politics of Mexican-Origin Women's Reproduction.* Austin: University of Texas Press.

Gutiérrez, Ramón A. 1991. *When Jesus Came, the Corn Mothers Went Away: Marriage, Sexuality, and Power in New Mexico, 1500–1846.* Stanford, CA: Stanford University Press.

Gutiérrez Spencer, Laura. 1994. "Mirrors and Masks: Female Subjectivity in Chicana Poetry." *Frontiers: A Journal of Women's Studies* 15, no. 2: 69–86.

Habell-Pallán, Michelle. 2005. *Loca Motion: The Travels of Chicana and Latina Popular Culture.* New York: New York University Press.

———. 2008. "Vexed on the Eastside: Chicana Roots and Routes of L.A. Punk." In Tompkins and Gunckel 2008, 25–29.

———. 2011. "The Style Council: Asco, Music, and 'Punk Chola' Aesthetics, 1980–84." In *Asco Elite of the Obscure: A Retrospective,* ed. C. Ondine Chavoya and Rita Gonzalez, 336–345. Germany: Hatje Cantz.

Hay, Calla, ed. 1951. "Cabeza de Baca Gilbert Describes Her Work on UN Project in Mexico at Altrusa Dinner." *The New Mexican,* December 11.

Hebdige, Dick. 1981. *Subculture: The Meaning of Style.* New York: Routledge.

Hernández, Daniel. 2007. "The Art Outlaws of East Los Angeles." *LA Weekly,* June 6.

Hernández, Ellie D. 2009. *Postnationalism in Chicana/o Literature and Culture.* Austin: University of Texas Press.

Hernández-Ehrisman, Laura. 2008. *Inventing the Fiesta City: Heritage and Carnival in San Antonio.* Albuquerque: University of New Mexico Press.

Herrón, Willie. 2000. Interview by Jeffrey Rangel, Los Angeles, February 5. Transcript, Archives of American Art, Smithsonian Institution.

Hondagneu-Sotelo, Pierrette, and Ernestine Avila. 2007. "'I'm Here, but I'm There': The Meanings of Latina Transnational Motherhood." In *Women and Migration in the U.S.-Mexico Borderlands: A Reader,* ed. Denise A. Segura and Patricia Zavella, 388–414. Durham, NC: Duke University Press.

Huaco-Nuzum, Carmen. 1998. "Mi Familia/My Family." *Aztlán: A Journal of Chicano Studies* 23, no. 1: 141–53.

Huacuja, Judith L. 2003. "Borderlands Critical Subjectivity in Recent Chicana Art." *Frontiers: A Journal of Women Studies* 24, nos. 2–3: 104–121.

Ikas, Karin Rosa. 2002. *Chicana Ways: Conversations with Ten Chicana Writers.* Reno: University of Nevada Press.

Jacobs, Elizabeth. 2000. "New Mexican Narratives and the Politics of Home." *Journal of American Studies of Turkey* 12: 39–49.

Jaehn, Tomas. 1994. "Concha Ortíz y Pino: Making History in Politics." *Women's Times,* October/November, 6.

James, David E. 1999. "Hollywood Extras: One Tradition of 'Avant-Garde' Film in Los Angeles." *October Magazine* 90, no. 3–24.

Jaramillo, Cleofas. 1939. *Cuentos del Hogar/Spanish Fairy Tales.* El Campo, TX: The Citizen Press.

———. 1972. *Shadows of the Past/Sombras del Pasado.* Santa Fe: Ancient City Press. Orig. pub. 1941.

———. 1981. *Potajes Sabrosos/ The Genuine New Mexico Tasty Recipes.* Santa Fe: Ancient City Press. Orig. pub. 1939.

———. 2000. *Romance of a Little Village Girl.* Albuquerque: University of New Mexico Press. Orig. pub. 1955.

Jennings, Frank W. 1996. "Women for All Seasons: San Antonio's Chili Queens." *Texas Highways,* January, 44.

Jensen, Joan M. 1982. "Canning Comes to New Mexico: Women and the Agricultural Extension Service, 1914–1919." *New Mexico Historical Review* 57: 361–386.

———. 1986a. "Crossing Ethnic Barriers in the Southwest: Women's Agricultural Extension Education, 1914–1940." *Agricultural History* 60: 169–181.

———. 1986b. "'I've Worked, I'm Not Afraid of Work': Farm Women in New Mexico, 1920–1940." *New Mexico Historical Review* 61: 27–52.

Jewell, K. Sue. 1993. *From Mammy to Miss America and Beyond: Cultural Images and the Shaping of US Social Policy.* New York: Routledge.

Jones, Phillip W. 1988. *International Policies for Third World Education: Unesco, Literacy and Development.* London: Routledge.

Kaplan, Amy. 2002. "Manifest Domesticity." In *No More Separate Spheres!: A Next Wave American Studies Reader*, ed. Cathy N. Davidson and Jessamyn Hatcher, 183–208. Durham, NC: Duke University Press.

Kaplan, Caren. 1987. "Deterritorializations: The Rewriting of Home and Exile in Western Feminist Discourse." *Cultural Critique* 6: 187–198.

Kaplan, E. Ann. 1992. *Motherhood and Representation: The Mother in Popular Culture and Melodrama.* New York: Routledge.

Kaup, Monika. 1997. "The Architecture of Ethnicity in Chicano Literature." *American Literature* 69, no. 2: 361–397.

Keating, AnaLouise, ed. 2009. *The Gloria Anzaldúa Reader.* Durham, NC: Duke University Press.

Kim, L. S. 1999. "Invisible and Undocumented: The Latina Maid on Network Television." *Aztlán: A Journal of Chicano Studies* 24, no. 1: 107–128.

Knight, Heather. 2001. "Joint Exhibit Illuminates Immigrants' Stories: Artists Hope Cupertino Show Alters Attitudes." *San Francisco Chronicle* online edition, March 30.

Krämer, Peter, and Alan Lovell. 1999. *ScreenActing.* New York: Routledge.

Kropp, Phoebe S. 2006. *California Vieja: Culture and Memory in a Modern American Place.* Berkeley: University of California Press.

Kun, Josh. 2003. "Vex Populi: At an Unprepossessing Eastside Punk Rock Landmark, Utopia Was in the Air. Until the Day It Wasn't." *Los Angeles Magazine*, March 1.

———. 2008. "A Space for the Possible." In Tompkins and Gunckel 2008, 21–23.

———. 2011. "The Personal Equator: Patssi Valdez at the Border." In *Asco Elite of the Obscure: A Retrospective*, ed. C. Ondine Chavoya and Rita Gonzalez, 356–360. Germany: Hatje Cantz.

Latorre, Guisela. 2008. *Walls of Empowerment: Chicana/o Indigenist Murals of California.* Austin: University of Texas Press.

Lefebvre, Henri. 1996. *Writings on Cities.* New York: Wiley-Blackwell Publishers.

Leimer, Ann Marie. 2005. "Performing the Sacred: The Concept of Journey in *Codex Delilah*." Ph.D. diss., University of Texas at Austin.

Lipsitz, George. 1986. "The Meaning of Memory: Family, Class, and Ethnicity in Early Network Television Programs." *Cultural Anthropology* 1, no. 4: 355–387.

Little, Walter. 2003. "Performing Tourism: Maya Women's Strategies." *Signs: Journal of Women in Culture and Society* 29, no. 2: 527–532.

López, Alma. 2002. "Tattoo, Santa Niña de Mochis, California Fashions Slaves, and Our Lady." *Frontiers: A Journal of Women's Studies* 23, no. 1: 90–95.

———. 2011. "It's not about the Santa in my *Fe*, but the Santa Fe in My *Santa*." In *Our Lady of Controversy: Alma López's Irreverent Apparition*, ed. Alicia Gaspar de Alba and Alma López, 249–292. Austin: University of Texas Press.

López, Tiffany Ana. 2000. "Violent Inscriptions: Writing the Body and Making Community in Four Plays by Migdalia Cruz." *Theatre Journal* 52, no. 1: 51–66.

Lorde, Audre. 1984. "The Master's Tools Will Never Dismantle the Master's House." In *This Bridge Called My Back: Writings by Radical Women of Color*, ed. Gloria Anzaldúa and Cherríe Moraga, 98–101. New York: Kitchen Table: Women of Color Press.

Lowe, Lisa. 1996. *Immigrant Acts: On Asian American Cultural Politics*. Durham, NC: Duke University Press.

Lu, Timmy, and Karin Mak. 2004. "Crisis or Opportunity? The Future of Los Angeles's Garment Workers, the Apparel Industry, and the Local Economy." *Sweatshop Watch and Garment Worker Center Report*, November.

Macaulay, Suzanne P. 2000. *Stitching Rites: Colcha Embroidery Along the Northern Rio Grande*. Tucson: University of Arizona Press.

May, Elaine Tyler. 1990. *Homeward Bound: American Families in the Cold War Era*. New York: Basic Books.

McClintock, Anne. 1997. "No Longer in a Future Heaven: Gender, Race, and Nationalism." In *Dangerous Liaisons: Gender, Nation, and Postcolonial Perspectives*, ed. Ann McClintock, Aamir Mufti, and Ella Shohat, 89–112. Minneapolis: University of Minnesota Press.

McCracken, Ellen. 1989. "Sandra Cisneros's *The House on Mango Street*: Community-Oriented Introspection and the Demystification of Patriarchal Violence." In *Breaking Boundaries: Latina Writing and Critical Readings*, ed. Asunción Horno-Delgado, Eliana Ortega, Nina M. Scott, and Nancy Saporta Sternbach, 62–71. Amherst: University of Massachusetts Press.

McCullough, Kate. 1999. *Regions of Identity: The Construction of America in Women's Fiction, 1885–1914*. Stanford, CA: Stanford University Press.

McHugh, Kathleen Anne. 1999. *American Domesticity: From How-to Manual to Hollywood Melodrama*. New York: Oxford University Press.

McKenna, Kristine. 1995. "Getting to the Heart of One Family's Life Movies: Director Gregory Nava Follows His 'El Norte' with a Colorful Epic Exploring Sixty Years in the Lives of a Struggling Latino Family." *Los Angeles Times Calendar Section* online, April 15, 1.

McLaren, Peter. 1994. "White Terror and Oppositional Agency: Towards a Critical Multiculturalism." In *Multiculturalism: A Critical Reader*, ed. David Theo Goldberg, 45–74. Oxford: Blackwell Publishers.

McMahon, Marci R. 2011. "Self-Fashioning through Glamour and Punk in East Los Angeles: Patssi Valdez in Asco's *Instant Mural* and *A La Mode*." *Aztlán: A Journal of Chicano Studies*. 36, no. 2: 21–50.

McRobbie, Angela. 1991. *Feminism and Youth Culture*. New York: Routledge.

———. 1994. *Postmodernism and Popular Culture*. New York: Routledge.

Menchaca, Martha. 2001. *Recovering History, Constructing Race: The Indian, Black, and White Roots of Mexican Americans*. Austin: University of Texas Press.

Méndez-Negrete, Josie. 2006. *Las Hijas de Juan: Daughters Betrayed*. Durham, NC: Duke University Press.

Mesa-Bains, Amalia. 1991. "Chicano Chronicle and Cosmology: The Works of Carmen Lomas Garza." In *A Piece of My Heart/Pedacito de mi Corazón: The Art of Carmen Lomas Garza*. Laguna Gloria Art Museum. New York: The New Press.

———. 1999. "Patssi Valdez: Glamour, Domestic Ruin, and Regeneration." In *Patssi Valdez: A Precarious Comfort/Una Comodidad Precaria*, ed. Tere Romo, 33–45. San Francisco: Mexican Museum.

———. 2003. "Domesticana: The Sensibility of Chicana Rasquachismo." In *Chicana Feminisms: A Critical Reader*, ed. Gabriela F. Arredondo, Aída Hurtado, Norma Klahn, Olga Nájera-Ramírez, and Patricia Zavella, 298–315. Durham, NC: Duke University Press. First published as "Domesticana: The Sensibility of Chicana Rasquache" in *Aztlán: A Journal of Chicano Studies,* 24, no. 2 (fall 1999).

Milkman, Ruth. 2006. *L.A. Story: Immigrant Workers and the Future of the U.S. Labor Movement.* New York: Russell Sage Foundation Publications.

Miraftab, Faranak. 2007. "Space, Gender, and Work: Home-Based Workers in Mexico." In *Women and Migration in the U.S.-Mexico Borderlands: A Reader,* ed. Denise A. Segura and Patricia Zavella, 269–285. Durham, NC: Duke University Press.

Miranda, Marie (Keta). 2003. *Homegirls in the Public Sphere.* Austin: University of Texas Press.

Mirandé, Alfred. 1977. "Chicano Family: A Re-Analysis of Conflicting Views." *Journal of Marriage and Family* 39: 747–756.

Molina-Guzmán, Isabel. 2010. *Dangerous Curves: Latina Bodies in the Media.* New York: New York University Press.

Monroe, Day. "Family Saving and Spending Plans." *Journal of Home Economics* 34, no. 9: 659–661.

Montejano, David. 1987. *Anglos and Mexicans in the Making of Texas, 1836–1986.* Austin: University of Texas Press.

Montgomery, Charles. 2002. *The Spanish Redemption: Heritage, Power, and Loss on New Mexico's Upper Rio Grande.* Berkeley: University of California Press.

Moraga, Cherríe. 1993. *The Last Generation: Prose and Poetry.* Cambridge, MA: South End Press.

Moraga, Cherríe, and Gloria Anzaldúa, eds. 1984. *This Bridge Called My Back: Writings by Radical Women of Color.* New York: Kitchen Table Press.

Morales, Alejandro. 1993. "The Deterritorialization of Esperanza Cordera: A Paraesthetic Inquiry." In *Gender, Self, and Society: Proceedings of the IV International Conference on the Hispanic Cultures of the United States,* ed. Renate Von Bardeleben, 227–235. Frankfurt: Peter Lang.

Mulvey, Laura. 1989. *Visual and Other Pleasures.* Bloomington: Indiana University Press.

Muñoz, José Esteban. 1999. *Disidentifications: Queers of Color and the Performance of Politics.* Minneapolis: University of Minnesota Press.

Muñoz, Lorenza. 1999. "A Painter's Great Escape." *Los Angeles Times* online edition, March.

Navarro, Mireya. 2002. "Trying to Get Behind the Role of the Maid: Hispanic Actors are Seen as Underrepresented with the Exception of One Part." *New York Times* online edition, May 16.

Nelson, Davia, and Nikki Silva, eds. 2005. *Hidden Kitchens: Stories, Recipes, and More from NPR's The Kitchen Sisters.* New York: Rodale Press.

Nestor, Sarah. 1978. *The Native Market of the Spanish New Mexican Craftsman, 1933–1940.* Santa Fe: Colonial New Mexico Historical Foundation.

Nickerson, Michelle. 2003. "Women, Domesticity, and Postwar Conservatism." *OAH Magazine of History* 17, no. 2: 17–21.

Nieto-Phillips, John M. 2004. *The Language of Blood: The Making of Spanish-American Identity in New Mexico, 1880s–1930s.* Albuquerque: University of New Mexico Press.

Noriega, Chon A. 1992. *Chicanos and Film: Representation and Resistance.* Minneapolis: University of Minnesota Press.

———. 1998. *Urban Exile: Collected Writings of Harry Gamboa Jr.* Minneapolis: University of Minnesota Press.

———. 2010. "Foreword." In *Carmen Lomas Garza*. Constance Cortez. A Ver: Revisioning Art History, vol. 5. Los Angeles: UCLA Chicano Studies Research Center Press. Distributed by University of Minnesota Press.

Nuñez, Lorena. 1993. "Women on the Streets: Vending and Public Space in Chile." *Economic and Political Weekly* 28, no. 44: 67–82.

Nyborg, Anne M. 2008. "Gentrified Barrio: Gentrification and the Latino Community in San Francisco's Mission District." Thesis, University of California, San Diego.

Obregón Pagán, Eduardo. 2003. *Murder at the Sleepy Lagoon: Zoot Suits, Race, and Riot in Wartime Los Angeles*. Chapel Hill: University of North Carolina Press.

O'Connor, John J. 1988. "TV Weekend; Glenn Close in 'Stones for Ibarra,'" rev. of *Stones for Ibarra*, dir. Jack Gold, *New York Times* online edition, January 29.

Olivares, Julián. 1988. Sandra Cisneros's *The House on Mango Street* and the Poetics of Space." In *Chicana Creativity and Criticism: Charting New Frontiers in American Literature*, ed. María Herrera Sobek and Helena María Viramontes, 160–170. Houston: Arte Público Press.

Ontiveros, Mario. 2008. "Christina Fernandez." In *Phantom Sightings: Art after the Chicano Movement*, ed. Rita González, Howard N. Fox, and Chon A. Noriega, 152–155. Los Angeles and Berkeley: Los Angeles County Museum of Art and University of California Press.

Orozco, Cynthia E. 2009. *No Mexicans, Women, or Dogs Allowed: The Rise of the Mexican American Civil Rights Movement*. Austin: University of Texas Press.

Ott, Katherine. 1996. *Fevered Lives: Tuberculosis in American Culture Since 1870*. Cambridge, MA: Harvard University Press.

Ovalle, Priscilla Peña. 2011. *Dance and the Hollywood Latina: Race, Sex, and Stardom*. New Brunswick, NJ: Rutgers University Press.

Padilla, Genaro M. 1993. *My History, Not Yours: The Formation of Mexican American Autobiography*. Madison: University of Wisconsin Press.

Palumbo-Liu, David. 1995. *The Ethnic Canon: Histories, Institutions, and Interventions*. Minneapolis: University of Minnesota Press.

Paredes, Raymund. 1982. "The Evolution of Chicano Literature." In *Three American Literatures*, ed. Houston A. Baker Jr., 33–79. New York: Modern Language Association.

Pasternak, Esther. 2002. "Curtain Calls Reviews: Dralion, The Blue Room, The Have-Little," rev. of *The Have-Little*, dir. Diane Rodríguez, *The Daily Bruin* online edition, April 2.

Paz, Octavio. 1961. *The Labyrinth of Solitude*. New York: Grove Press.

Pérez, Emma. 1999. *The Decolonial Imaginary: Writing Chicanas into History*. Bloomington: Indiana University Press.

Pérez, Laura. 2007. *Chicana Art: The Politics of Spiritual and Aesthetic Altarities*. Durham, NC: Duke University Press.

Permenter, Paris and John Bigley, eds. 2008. *Insider's Guide to San Antonio*. 3rd ed. Guilford, CT: Globe Pequot Press.

Pilcher, Jeffrey M. 2008. "Who Chased Out the 'Chili Queens'? Gender, Race, and Urban Reform in San Antonio, Texas, 1880–1943." *Food and Foodways* 16: 173–200.

Pilcher, Jeffrey M., and Donna R. Gabaccia. 2011. "'Chili Queens' and Checkered Tablecloths: Public Dining Cultures of Italians in New York City and Mexicans in San Antonio, Texas, 1870s–1940s." *Radical History Review* 110: 109–126.

Poey, Delia. 1996. "Coming of Age in the Curriculum: *The House on Mango Street* and *Bless Me, Ultima* as Representative Texts." *Americas Review* 24, no. 3–4: 910–946.

———. 2002. "Coming of Age in the Curriculum: *The House on Mango Street* and *Bless Me, Ultima* as Representative Texts." In *Latino American Literature in the Classroom: The Politics of Transformation*, chap. 5. Gainesville: University Press of Florida.

Ponce, Merrihelen. 1995. "The Life and Works of Fabiola Cabeza de Baca, New Mexican Hispanic Women Writer: A Contextual Biography." Ph.D. diss., University of New Mexico.

Portes, Alejandro and Rubén G. Rumbaut, eds. 2006. *Immigrant America: A Portrait.* 3rd ed. Berkeley: University of California Press.

Portillo, Lourdes, dir. 2001. *Señorita Extraviada, Missing Young Woman.* Documentary film. Produced by Lourdes Portillo.

Pratt, Mary Louise. 1992. *Imperial Eyes: Travel Writing and Transculturation.* New York: Routledge.

Quintana, Alvina. 1991. "Ana Castillo's *The Mixquiahuala Letters:* The Novelist as Ethnographer." In *Criticism in the Borderlands: Studies in Chicano Literature, Culture and Ideology,* ed. Héctor Calderón and Jose Davíd Saldívar, 72–83. Durham, NC: Duke University Press.

———. 1996. *Home Girls: Chicana Literary Voices.* Philadelphia: Temple University Press.

Ramírez, Catherine. 2009. *The Woman in the Zoot Suit: Gender, Nationalism, and the Cultural Politics of Memory.* Durham, NC: Duke University Press.

Rebolledo, Tey Diana. 1994. "Introduction." *We Fed Them Cactus.* 2nd ed. Albuquerque: University of New Mexico Press.

———. 1995. *Women Singing in the Snow: A Cultural Analysis of Chicana Literature.* Tucson: University of Arizona Press.

———. 1997. "Tradition and Mythology: Signatures of Landscape in Chicana Literature." In *The Desert Is No Lady: Southwestern Landscapes in Women's Writing and Art,* ed. Vera Norwood and Janice Monk. Tucson: University of Arizona Press.

———. 2006. "*Prietita y el Otro Lado:* Gloria Anzaldúa's Literature for Children." *PMLA* 121, no. 1: 279–284.

Reed, Maureen E. 2005. *A Woman's Place: Women Writing New Mexico.* Albuquerque: University of New Mexico Press.

———. 2007. "Performing Traditional Womanhood: Fabiola Cabeza de Baca and Hispanic Civil Rights in the 1950s. In *Rebels Without a Cause?: Renegotiating the American 1950s,* ed. Gerd Hurm and Ann Maria Fallon. New York: Peter Lang.

Reyes, David, and Tom Waldman. 1998. *Land of a Thousand Dances: Chicano Rock 'n' Roll from Southern California.* Albuquerque: University of New Mexico Press.

Rich, Charlotte J. 2009. *Transcending the New Woman: Multiethnic Narratives in the Progressive Era.* Columbia: University of Missouri Press.

Rivera, Díana Noreen. 2011. "Reconsidering Jovita González's Life, Letters, and Pre-1935 Folkloric Production: A Proto-Chicana's Conscious Revolt Against Anglo Academic Patriarchy via Linguistic Performance." *Chicana/Latina Studies: The Journal of MALCS* 10, no. 2: 46–91.

Rivera, John Michael. 2006. *The Emergence of Mexican America: Recovering Stories of Mexican Peoplehood in U.S. Culture.* New York: New York University Press.

Rodríguez, Chantal. 2011. *The Latino Theatre Initiative/Center Theatre Group Papers, 1980—2005.* Los Angeles: UCLA Chicano Studies Research Center.

Rodríguez, Juan. 1984. "*The House on Mango Street,* by Sandra Cisneros." *Austin Chronicle,* August 10.

Rodríguez, Richard T. 2009. *Next of Kin: The Family in Chicano/a Cultural Politics.* Durham, NC: Duke University Press.

Romero, Mary. 2003. "*Nanny Diaries* and Other Stories: Imagining Immigrant Women's Labor in the Social Reproduction of American Families." *DePaul Law Review* 52, no. 3: 809–847.

————. 2008. "'Go After the Women': 'Mothers against Illegal Aliens' Campaign against Mexican Immigrant Women and their Children." *Indiana Law Journal* 83: 1355–1388.

Romo, Tere. 1999. "Patssi Valdez: A Precarious Comfort." In *Patssi Valdez: A Precarious Comfort/Una Comodidad Precaria*, ed. Tere Romo, 9–32. San Francisco: Mexican Museum.

————. 2011. "Conceptually Divine: Patssi Valdez's Virgen de Guadalupe Walking the Mural." In *Asco Elite of the Obscure: A Retrospective*, ed. C. Ondine Chavoya and Rita Gonzalez, 276–282. Germany: Hatje Cantz.

Rose, Tricia. 1994. *Black Noise: Rap Music and Black Culture in Contemporary America.* Hanover, NH: Wesleyan University Press.

Ruiz, Vicki L. 1998. *From Out of the Shadows: Mexican Women in Twentieth-Century America.* New York: Oxford University Press.

Ruiz de Burton, María Amparo. 1995. [1872]. *Who Would Have Thought It?* Edited by Rosaura Sánchez and Beatrice Pita. Houston: Arte Público Press.

————. 1997. [1885]. *The Squatter and the Don.* Edited by Rosaura Sánchez and Beatrice Pita. Houston: Arte Público Press.

Saldívar, José David. 2012. "Transnationalism Contested: On Sandra Cisneros's *The House on Mango Street* and *Caramelo* or Puro Cuento." In *Trans-Americanity: Subaltern Modernities, Global Coloniality, and the Cultures of Greater Mexico*, chap 7. Durham, NC: Duke University Press.

Saldívar-Hull, Sonia. 2000. *Feminism on the Border: Chicana Gender Politics and Literature.* Berkeley: University of California Press.

Salzinger, Leslie. 2007. "Manufacturing Sexual Subjects: 'Harassment,' Desire, and Discipline on a Maquiladora Shopfloor." In *Women and Migration in the U.S.-Mexico Borderlands: A Reader*, ed. Denise A. Segura and Patricia Zavella, 161–183. Durham, NC: Duke University Press.

Sánchez, George J. 1993. *Becoming Mexican American: Ethnicity, Culture and Identity in Chicano Los Angeles, 1900–1945.* New York: Oxford University Press.

Sánchez, María Carla. 2001. "Whiteness Invisible: Early Mexican American Writing and the Color of Literary History." In *Passing: Identity and Interpretation in Sexuality, Race, and Religion*, ed. María Carla Sánchez and Linda Schlossberg, 64–91. New York: New York University Press.

Sandoval, Chela. 2000. *Methodology of the Oppressed.* Minneapolis: University of Minnesota Press.

Sandoval, T.F., Jr. 2002. "Mission Stories, Latino Lives: The Making of San Francisco's Latino Identity, 1945–1970." PhD diss., University of California, Berkeley.

Sandoval-Sánchez, Alberto. 1999. *José, Can You See? Latinos On and Off Broadway.* Madison: University of Wisconsin Press.

Santamaria, Francisco J. 1992. *Diccionario de Mejicanismos.* 5th ed. Mexico City: Editorial Porrúa.

Satz, Martha. 1997. "Returning to One's House: An Interview with Sandra Cisneros." *Southwest Review* 82, no. 2: 166–185.

Scharff, Virginia. 2003. *Twenty Thousand Roads: Women, Movement, and the West.* Berkeley: University of California Press.

Schmidt Camacho, Alicia. 2008. *Migrant Imaginaries: Latino Cultural Politics in the U.S.–Mexico Borderlands.* New York: New York University Press.

Segura, Denise A., and Patricia Zavella, eds. 2007. *Women and Migration in the U.S.-Mexico Borderlands: A Reader.* Durham, NC: Duke University Press.

Slocum, Rachel. 2011. "Race in the Study of Food." *Progress in Human Geography* 35, no. 3: 303–327.

Soldatenko, Maria. 2000. "Organizing Latina Garment Workers in Los Angeles." In *Las Obreras: Chicana Politics of Work and Family*, ed. Vicki L. Ruiz, 137–160. Los Angeles: UCLA Chicano Studies Research Center Publications.

Spheeris, Penelope, dir. 1981. *The Decline of Western Civilization.* Documentary film. Produced by Jeff Prettyman and Penelope Spheeris.

Spitz, Marc, and Brendan Mullen. 2001. *We Got the Neutron Bomb: The Untold Story of L.A. Punk.* New York: Three Rivers Press.

Stevens, Evelyn P. 1973. "Marianismo: The Other Face of Machismo in Latin America." In *Female and Male in Latin America*, ed. Ann Pescatello. Pittsburgh: University of Pittsburgh Press.

Telles, Edward E. and Vilma Ortiz, eds. 2008. *Generations of Exclusion: Mexican Americans, Assimilation, and Race.* New York: Russell Sage Foundation.

Tompkins, Jane. 1985. *Sensational Designs: the Cultural Work of American Fiction, 1790–1860.* New York: Oxford University Press.

Tompkins, Pilar, and Colin Gunckel, eds. 2008. *Vexing: Female Voices from East L.A. Punk.* Claremont, CA: Claremont Museum of Art.

Upstone, Sara. 2007. "Domesticity in Magical Realist Post-colonial Fiction: Reversals of Representation in Salman Rushdie's *Midnight's Children.*" *Frontiers: A Journal of Feminist Studies* 28, no. 1: 264.

Valdés, Maria Elena de. 1993. "The Critical Reception of Sandra Cisneros's *The House on Mango Street.*" In *Gender, Self, and Society: Proceedings of the IV International Conference on the Hispanic Cultures of the United States*, ed. Renate Von Bardeleben, 287–300. Frankfurt: Peter Lang.

Valdez, Patssi. 1999. Interview by Jeffrey Rangel, Los Angeles, May 26 and June 2. Transcript, Smithsonian Archives of American Art, Washington, DC.

Villa, Raúl Homero. 2000. *Barrio-Logos: Space and Place in Urban Chicano Literature and Culture.* Austin: University of Texas Press.

Walsh, Marie T. 1954. "New Mexico's Famous Home Economist." *California Farmer*, October 16: 571.

Weiner, Annette B. 1992. *Inalienable Possessions: The Paradox of Keeping-While-Giving.* Berkeley: University of California Press.

Welter, Barbara. 1966. "The Cult of True Womanhood: 1820–1860." *American Quarterly* 18: 151–174.

Wiggins, Susan. 1992. "Patssi Valdez." *ArtWeek*, March 26, 15.

Worth, Robert. 1999. "Guess Who Saved the South Bronx?: The Silent Partner in Community Development." *Washington Monthly* 31, no. 4 (April).

Wright, Melissa W. 2007. "The Dialectics of Still Life: Murder, Women, and Maquiladoras." In *Women and Migration in the U.S.-Mexico Borderlands: A Reader*, ed. Denise A. Segura and Patricia Zavella, 184–202. Durham, NC: Duke University Press.

Ybarra-Frausto, Tomás. 1980. *Carmen Lomas Garza/Prints and Gouaches, Margo Humphrey/Monotypes.* Exhibition Catalogue. San Francisco: San Francisco Museum of Modern Art.

Index

About the Author

Marci R. McMahon is an assistant professor in the English Department at the University of Texas, Pan American, where she teaches Chicana/o literature and cultural studies, gender studies, and theater and performance. She received her Ph.D. from the University of Southern California English Department, with affiliations in the Department of American Studies and Ethnicity.

CPSIA information can be obtained at www.ICGtesting.com
Printed in the USA
BVOW082312130513

320618BV00003B/4/P